CL16

Tel

Bradman's Invincibles

The Story of the
1948 Ashes Tour

Roland Perry

To Mary Newham

First published in Great Britain
2009 by Aurum Press Ltd
7 Greenland Street
London NW1 0ND
www.aurumpress.co.uk

First published in Australia and New Zealand in 2008 by Hachette Australia
(An imprint of Hachette Livre Australia Pty Limited)
Level 17, 207 Kent Street, Sydney NSW 2000

A catalogue record for this book is available from the British Library.

ISBN 978 1 84513 414 3

1 3 5 7 9 10 8 6 4 2
2009 2011 2013 2012 2010

Text design by Bookhouse, Sydney
Typeset in 11.2/13.95 pt Minion Pro
Printed by MPG Books Ltd, Bodmin, Cornwall

Contents

Acknowledgements

MY THANKS GO to Sir Donald Bradman, who was a prime source for this book. During our interviews for my biography, *The Don*, we talked for three weeks in May 1995 about the 1948 tour. I remember his keenness for me to comprehend his motives for making the tour, and the detail he recalled nearly half a century later was remarkable.

There is no doubt that the tour and its success gave him the most satisfaction of his entire cricket career. He would have had great thrills from say, his 1930 tour, but then he was a 21-year-old yet to experience the forces that will always attempt to bring down such a colossal talent. By 1948, he was nearly 40 years of age with several lifetimes of experience of what it means to be the best in a hugely competitive sporting environment. Bradman had sorted out what was important to him, and what was not. He had long ago pigeonholed or defeated his various enemies, and there was none left to conquer. Yet still there were goals and unfulfilled dreams, even for the highest achiever of any sport in history. This was apparent in our discussions. He responded with enthusiasm to questions about the tour, and why it was important to him, Australia and indeed, the UK at the time. Bradman did not believe in 1949, or in 1995 that his two old team-mates/adversaries Jack Fingleton and Bill O'Reilly, had done justice to the squad's achievements with their published works in 1949. (Bradman agreed, however, that they, or indeed even he, could not then have realised how this tour would stand the test of time for its unparalleled success.)

Fingleton's book, *Brightly Fades the Don*, was the first cricket book I ever read. He was not always flattering to Bradman, and it is widely known in cricket circles that they did not get on. But Fingleton's coverage intrigued me and made me hungry at age 13 to know more.

Since the late 1970s, I have interviewed many of the Invincibles (and several of the vanquished opposition England team) and touched on 1948 with them. In recent years when the opportunity to write this book arose, I had more in-depth discussions over the tour with Neil Harvey, Sam Loxton and Arthur Morris, who I thank for giving of their time when they must at times have been fatigued by quizzing about their grand achievements. They all maintained a keen memory and a sense of humour, which was a key characteristic in this amazing squad of sportsmen.

I have relied on interviews with many of the principals for dialogue and details of events; and also on a range of primary sources.

Others to contribute specifically on the topic with interviews, correspondence, files, information, photographs over about 30 years were Martin Ashenden, Alec Bedser, Eric Bedser, Denis Compton, Colin Cowdrey, Ian Craig, Alan Davidson, Godfrey Evans, Gus Glendinning, Basil Grapsis, Jack Grossman, Lindsay Hassett, Thos Hodgson, Ian Johnson, Bill Johnston, Ray Lindwall, Tony Maylam, the family of Keith Miller (notably Denis Miller, Bob Miller and Miller's niece Jan Beames), John Miles, Mary Newham, Lady O'Brien, John MacWhirter, Rod Mater, Alan Young, Peter Philpott, Doug Ring and Christina Robert.

My thanks to publisher Matthew Kelly and to Bev Friend.

The Tour

1
—

One More Campaign

Don BRADMAN HAD a dilemma early in 1948: should he tour England for one last Ashes competition? On the one hand, he was content with his position in sporting, business and private life. After thrashing an Indian team in the summer just past, he could retire after fine performances that had covered two decades as the greatest batsman of all time and outstanding leadership since he took the national captaincy in 1936. In business, he and his wife Jessie had taken over a broking firm in 1945, which he had to build and maintain as his own. After three years it was more or less stable and he had managed, just, to combine top cricket with a demanding job. Yet it bothered Bradman to leave it now for a tour that would last eight months with boat trips both ways. At home, he had the most supportive of wives and two young children, eight-year-old John, and six-year-old Shirley, whose mild cerebral palsy added to Bradman's concern about support for Jessie. On top of this, he was not confident about his own fitness. He had suffered from severe back problems, described as fibrositis, which like many such problems was not well defined or understood. It manifested as back spasms and persistent pain. Then there was a torn rib cartilage that caused him to retire hurt in the last Test against India in Melbourne when he was on 57 runs. It was the only time he had ever left the Test arena this way. It had to be serious. More than this, it was a reminder that Bradman was pushing 40 years. He knew what he was in for, having been on three previous Ashes tours. He would be called upon to be the star attraction at innumerable functions. There would be cricket six days a week. Every single opposition team up and down the country would demand that he played. Then there was the huge offer by a Fleet Street newspaper group – equivalent to around $800,000 today – to report the tour, as long as he did not play.

The other horn of Bradman's dilemma was a final challenge to one of the most competitive sportsmen ever. Where many Australian males of the era were gamblers, who would bet on the outcome of two flies climbing up a wall, Bradman, it was said, would prefer to race them. Whether it was beating Wimbledon stars at tennis, challenging Walter Lindrum at billiards, fighting out the South Australian squash championship, foot-races in the army (which did his back harm) or winning matches for Australia, South Australia or his local club Kensington Park, no one responded to competition like Donald George Bradman.

The British establishment had appealed to him to lead a final Ashes tour in the northern summer of 1948. He was really being asked to do it for the Empire and British morale. After the hysteria of victory in World War II, the realities of its toll had sunk into the collective spirit of the United Kingdom, which was in the economic doldrums after post-war years of austerity and rationing.

The sight of a bunch of fit Aussies, led by the legendary Bradman, touring the nation would be, it was expected, a special tonic when it was in need of inspirational diversions. That was all fine, and Bradman would always respond to his nation and the then closely connected 'mother country'. Yet he would have to have a goal beyond anything else ever achieved in Test cricket. Every cricket batting record worth noting had been his. Bradman had a Test average then well clear of 100 runs an innings, which ranked him as near enough to twice as important in winning any game than any other batsman in history. Given that the best of the rest weighed in with averages between 40 to 60 runs, his record was more or less unassailable. Bradman had led his team to Ashes victories at home twice in 1936–37 and a decade later after the war in 1946–47. He had held the Ashes on a tour of England with a weak Australian team in 1938, and he had been on two other tours in 1930 and 1934 when Australia had achieved Ashes victories. So winning at home or abroad had been achieved even to the satisfaction of this supreme sporting competitor, who psychologists would have to define as 'type A-plus'.

The challenge had to be greater than batting averages and winning the Ashes. And the only goal that superseded these was going through an entire tour without losing one game. It had never been done by any international team taking on the gruelling venture since an Australian Aboriginal team had criss-crossed the UK 80 years earlier.

Not losing one of the 34 scheduled games over six months of intense rivalry was the ultimate challenge to one of nature's perfectionists. This was the teaser that caused him to make a decision to lead on one final tour.

•

Judging from the telephone numbers being scored by England batsmen in the 1947 summer, and also some wonderful bowling efforts, Bradman and his fellow selectors would have to pick an outstanding squad, just to compete. The core batting group consisted of Bradman (39), Lindsay Hassett vice-captain (34), Arthur Morris (26), Sid Barnes (31), Bill Brown (35), Neil Harvey (19) and all-rounder Keith Miller (28). The core bowlers would be speedsters Ray Lindwall (26), Miller and left-armer Bill Johnston (26). The keeper would be Don Tallon (32), and Ian Johnson (30) would be in contention as the spinner. He had some pretensions as a batsman. Those battling to make an impression and grab a Test place would be all-rounder Sam Loxton (27), leg-spinner Doug Ring (29), batsman Ron Hamence (32), lively left-arm medium-pacer Ernie Toshack (33) and all-rounder (leg-spin and batsman) Colin McCool (31). Ron Saggers (30) would be the talented backup keeper.

Just five of the squad had experience in the UK: Bradman, Hassett, Brown, Barnes and Miller, who played plenty of top cricket while based as a pilot in England, 1943–45. With only one player under 26, it was the oldest team ever to tour, yet no one was game to call it 'Dad's Army'.

The squad had few, if any weaknesses. There were three outstanding batsmen fighting for two opening spots – (left-hander) Morris, Barnes and Brown. The next batsmen (assuming the third opener was retained) were top drawer – Bradman, Hassett and Miller, with the brilliant teenage left-hander Harvey expected to challenge. Bradman here provided the added dimension of being worth two batsmen. In effect, if he chose six specialist batsmen, he was always assured, in statistical reality, of seven.

Tallon was regarded then as the world's best keeper and Bradman ranked him forever as the best stumpsman he had ever seen.

This left four spots for bowlers, apart from Miller, who was expected to take one of the top six batting spots. His special all-round skills then, gave Bradman five bowlers instead of four. Lindwall would be the No. 1 bowling choice. Bill Johnston took another position, with his left-arm adding further variety. Nine positions went to outstanding players, who provided many useful combinations for a thinking leader. The other two positions would be fought over by the rest of the squad. Or at least that was the general thinking when the squad was announced. Yet the starting XI would be fluid with Bradman conscious of his core players and how the others fitted in around them.

Bradman had been there before exactly a decade earlier in 1938, when his dream of going through undefeated had been dashed in the Fifth Test at the Oval. Bradman was injured with a broken ankle before he could bat and his team could tackle the near-impossible task of overhauling England's silly season score of a massive 7 declared for 903. The then England captain Wally Hammond had let Hutton go on to the longest innings ever played in scoring 364, which eclipsed Bradman's world record of 334 made in 1930. Hammond was more than happy about being in a position to engineer this, even if he did not take Bradman's record himself. The England skipper had suffered by the brutal comparison with the Australian for almost a decade and it hurt. It had had a vast impact on his personality, character and mental state. The 1938 Oval massacre took a little bit back for the finest England batsman between the wars.

When asked to speculate on what he may have done had he not been injured, Bradman refused to be drawn. Could he have scored a double hundred or even a triple and thus staved off an England win? He made no comment in public at the time or after the event. It was his way.

What mattered to him deep inside was the defeat. Australia had drawn the series, and therefore retained the Ashes. His 1938 dream of overcoming the record of Warwick Armstrong had evaporated. Armstrong's 1921 team lost just one match outside the Tests, when an England XI at Eastbourne, under the leadership of veteran Archie MacLaren, beat the tourists by 28 runs.

But it became worse for Bradman in 1938. With him absent, the England selectors cunningly selected a post-Ashes Test-strength team for the Leveson–Gower XI festival match at Scarborough. Australia under Stan McCabe lost by 10 wickets. If McCabe was angered, Bradman was furious. It meant two losses for the 1938 season and the team was back behind Armstrong's team. The 1921 team did better. It won 3:0 in the Tests, as opposed to Australia and England ending the 1938 series with one win each and three draws. A more subtle, less obvious incentive for the captain was Armstrong's well-publicised criticism of him when he was first selected for Australia in 1928, before he toured England in 1930, for his method of handling Bodyline in 1932–33, and when he was first made leader in 1936. During all this Bradman remained mute and refused to respond. His method during his two-decade career was to let his performances provide the answers. Eclipsing Armstrong's leadership record would be Bradman's way of getting even.

The less-than-satisfying 1938 experience overall was another reason, not a minor one either, for Bradman's decision to tour again.

He had unfinished business.

2

—

Cruising

FREMANTLE WHARFIES LINED up to greet Bradman when he
arrived at the *Strathaird* on Friday 19 March. As he reached
the top of the gangway, the word swept the ship that he was
on board, and several hours before the 6 p.m. departure in
order to beat the posse of reporters and photographers. Bradman
felt they had taken enough pictures in the Perth three-day
match – Australia versus a Keith Carmody-led Western Australia
– that finished three days earlier. He appreciated that his visits
west had been scarce, and that the press was hungry. Bradman
had given a batting exhibition, making 115 in Australia's score
of 7 declared for 442. He had allowed photographers to snap
him, Morris (also 115) and Harvey (79), and had even stood
still for a photo portrait in his pinstriped suit when he arrived
at the team hotel. But that was enough. He had remained hidden
away, only appearing at meals or to sign a range of bats for
charity.

The touring party was under the management of 52-year-
old Keith Johnson, who had the same job with the Australian
services team in 1945. A stalwart of Sydney's Mosman club,
Johnson had the confidence of the skipper and every player.

This would go a long way to keeping the squad united on the gruelling, long tour, where harmony would be challenged by tight travel arrangements, the occasional poor food and accommodation offerings, and the usual press scrutiny. A factor that would help was the background of the players: 16 of the 17 were ex-servicemen.

'We were used to living together, cooperating, and working together,' Loxton noted.

'I think it [the ex-servicemen background] was important to how we would go on such an arduous tour,' Ring said, 'and we didn't expect much [in terms of luxuries].'

'We all had a chance to get to know each other,' Morris said, 'especially those players from other States. It built real camaraderie. After all, we faced a very long tour and it was better that everyone was comfortable with everyone else.'

Morris said present-day players didn't get that chance. Planes took them to a destination in a day, and a few days later they were playing. By contrast in 1948, the boat trip was to be followed by a useful build-up to the Tests.

Everyone except the skipper, vice-captain (Hassett) and manager had to share cabins, which was acceptable because all players were travelling first-class. By the time of the departure – after two weeks travelling to Fremantle via Perth and Tasmania (for matches) – cabin arrangements had been sorted. Some of the pairings were Lindwall and Miller, Johnson and McCool, and Hamence and Toshack. The most important of all was Loxton with young Harvey, which was to make sure he was not overawed by any occasion.

'The first thing I had to do was buy a dinner suit,' Harvey recalled. 'I didn't know what it was. There was a black-tie dinner on board six nights a week, and a cocktail party before hand.'

Bradman used the six-week voyage to work on speeches. Like any good general, he wished to be prepared. He never regarded himself as a gifted orator, and had been intimidated in the past by the verbal skills of the best British speakers, and the need for him to respond. Bradman rehearsed until he felt comfortable and confident. A saving grace was his humour. This, added to his native intelligence, pertinence, and grand vision for cricket, meant that he never made a dull or unimportant address.

There was also time for tactics. He met with Lindwall to discuss a potential problem regarding the no-ball rule that had badly upset Australia in 1938. On that tour, quick Ernie McCormick was no-balled 35 times in the first match at Worcester for overstepping the crease with his trailing leg.

McCormick showed his character at lunch by saying he would not be called again after the break.

'It's okay,' he quipped, 'the umpire's hoarse.'

Even Bradman laughed then, but the demoralising incident would not be repeated. Lindwall's problem on delivery was a long drag (as opposed to McCormick's overstepping) of his trailing right leg, which could often take him a boot length and more beyond the stumps before he let the ball go. Bradman knew that two of the best umpires in the land would stand in the opening tour game. They would be watching for Lindwall's well-known drag.

Bradman told Lindwall to make sure he did not offend in the early matches.

'Even if you don't take a wicket beforehand,' Bradman told Lindwall, 'your Test place is assured. The important thing is to concentrate on making sure the umpires don't "call" you. Taking wickets must be a secondary consideration for the time being.'

Lindwall was the one player singled out. He was a key to the captain's grand plan to win the Ashes, and Bradman did not wish him negated by any avoidable issue. The rest of the players were called to only one team meeting for the boat trip.

'Braddles kept it simple,' Loxton said. 'First and foremost he said, "We are going to win." He told us that there would be no curfews and no hard rules. We were just expected to turn up fit to play each time we were selected. He told us not to forget that happiness and team spirit "comes from within". That was the main theme of the meeting.'

•

Lindsay Hassett and Sid Barnes were the tour group's jokers, along with jolly Bill Johnston and the droll Doug Ring. With four humourists and 13 others with a strong sense of fun in the squad, it was always likely to be, at the very least, an enjoyable trip. Hassett and Barnes were given to practical, 'belly-laugh' jokes. Poker-faced Hassett, for instance, had left a goat in a team-mate's room at night on the 1938 tour. He was always the character with the sharp wit, ready with the ripping riposte, the timing for a laugh, and spontaneous, funny observation. Barnes' humour was always at hand too, but was more heavy-handed. He was the eccentric character. While Hassett was the team's court jester, Sid 'Bagga' Barnes was its commercial trader, always with some kind of transaction on the go. He had half a tonne of food and drink with him on the ship, and not all of it was parcelled for the British. A bottle of cherry brandy broke in his luggage and dripped onto the cabin floor. At first, stewards thought it was blood and that Sid could even be an axe murderer, or something similar. He had to give away an unbroken cherry brandy bottle to placate the stewards.

Barnes ran Hassett close too, as the team's practical joker. No April Fool's Day ever escaped his attention. During the First Ashes Test in Brisbane in 1946, a storm hit the ground. Large hailstones machine-gunned the members' pavilion, which was next to the team dressing rooms. Barnes lifted a block of ice from a bath where the beer was kept cool, crept out in the middle of the storm, and pushed the block of ice over the fence into the members' area.

'The members' swore that the block came down with the hailstones,' Keith Miller remembered.

Barnes was a natural non-conformist. He was the one player able to circumvent the 'no wives or girlfriends on tour' rule, by having his wife stay in Scotland so that they could meet on the trip. After the experience of signing 5,000 bits of paper with the team list on it for the 1938 tour, he sidestepped that chore by having a stamp made of his name. He gave a boy passenger two bottles of ginger beer to do the simplified chore using the stamp. But the boy placed the stamp in odd places on the list of the team and not always next to Barnes' printed name. Barnes was rebuked by tour manager Johnson, and had to explain his actions to Bradman. Barnes had to give his little helper another bottle of ginger beer and tell him to place the stamp in the correct place this time.

Ernie Toshack too, baulked at the signing work. Noting Barnes' ingenuity, he paid a passenger to forge his signature. He was in trouble also with the manager. When asked if he were doing the slips himself, Toshack assured Johnson that he was.

'Well, I notice that you are spelling your name differently,' Johnson said. 'You're dropping the "c" these days.'

•

The skipper did not emerge from his cabin before lunch. He attended the formal dinner each night in the dining saloon as did the rest of the party, who were intrigued and pleased to find so many women attending. On day two, 20 March, most of the squad emerged to play quoits and deck tennis. On day three there was a cocktail party given by Captain Allan (known as 'High-brow' because of his prominent eyebrows). The *Strathaird* passed close to Cocos Island en route to Colombo, Ceylon (now Sri Lanka) an eight-day, 5,000 km idyllic cruise in the Indian Ocean. All the players kept fit. Harvey recalled playing Loxton at deck tennis every morning and afternoon. 'There was also cricket practice,' Harvey recalled, 'but all our gear was stowed below deck so we used a makeshift bat, and a ball, which was fashioned by the crew from rope. The ball was dipped in a bucket of water at the bowler's end to make sure it skidded through.'

It was innovative and may not have helped their techniques. Yet it did keep their eyes in. Several players were destined to arrive in England with their fitness levels high and their reflexes sharp. Others took a more disdainful view of frenetic activity on board beyond dancing.

'The only thing to get "in" your eyes up on deck was smoke and soot,' Morris quipped. 'I preferred to enjoy the first-class travel.'

Miller, a naturally fit, naturally lazy character off the pitch, saved himself for the big contests. He paid more attention to the bevy of women on board.

The most important advantage of such a trip above all else was a bonding of the entire team, which augured well for the coming adventures on land. Even if different players would never be close, they would at least respect their team-mates and understand their characters and foibles, and how to handle them. They were unified by Hassett, the team comic, who organised and starred in the fancy-dress night. His Arab impersonation, indeed capacity to mimic everyone, including the revered leader, kept the squad amused.

Harvey and Loxton were taken into the hold below deck to look where all their gear was stored. Barnes happened to be there, checking some of his stock of goods from the trip. They got chatting. Harvey and Loxton were interested in the story behind Barnes being dismissed in the Sydney Test of the 1946–47 Ashes on 234, the same score Bradman was out for earlier after a big partnership between the two.

'Put it this way,' Barnes said, 'if I'd got out for 233, no one would have remembered my innings. If I'd made 235, no one would have forgiven me for topping Don. If I got 234 I'd be remembered. And that's what has happened.'

(This was similar to Mark Taylor scoring 334 not out against Peshawar in the Second Test against Pakistan in 1998. Taylor declared his team's innings closed with him on that score overnight. He could easily have taken Bradman's Australian Test batting record of 334, scored against England at Leeds in the 1930 Ashes. He could even have gone on to a world-record Test score. But Taylor considered Australia had enough runs after two days' batting, and he declared. Taylor will be forever honoured and remembered for this unselfish act. The difference between him and Barnes was that Taylor didn't realise how his declaration would be perceived. He was just being consistent as a man of character; whereas Barnes was looking for glory by being paired forever with Bradman.)

•

The players also had a chance to chat with some of the journalists who would cover the tour. Loxton and Harvey came across Jack Fingleton, a former Test opener for Australia while walking on the deck. He and Bradman had always niggled each other. They could never be friends.

Loxton and Harvey recalled how they exchanged pleasantries.

'You're going to find out about Bradman on the trip,' Fingleton said.

'Oh,' Loxton said, 'and what's that?'

'He only thinks about himself. He won't worry about you.'

'What do you mean?

'I'll give you an example: In the final Melbourne Test of 1936–37 [Ashes], I was fielding in the leg trap; O'Reilly was bowling. He delivered a half-tracker. The batsman smashed it straight at me and it hit me in the head. I heard a squeaky voice in the covers [Bradman] call "catch it!" That's how much he cared about his players. He thinks only about winning.'

Later Harvey and Loxton bumped into Bradman on the deck. Loxton asked him about the Fingleton incident.

'Sammy,' Bradman replied, 'one day you might be captain of your church team, and when you are you will have responsibilities to your players and your team.'

Bradman remembered the moment Fingleton was hit.

'I had to make a decision,' Bradman said. 'The ball [had rebounded off Fingleton and] was in the air. There was no hope for Fingleton, but there was a chance the ball could be caught.'

•

The Australians were allowed to find their land legs briefly in a game at the Colombo Cricket Ground played before 25,000 spectators in fierce heat, which took its toll. Bradman batted in the one-day match and appeared in a pith helmet, much to the delight of the crowd. Miller thrilled the fans in the white stands and under the bamboo in the 'outer' with some typical big hitting despite Ian Johnson's suspicions about the pitch's length.

When Australia fielded, Loxton came on to bowl. He delivered six full-tosses in his first over.

'You'd better bowl better than that if you want to do well in England,' Bradman said to him.

'The pitch seems to be short, Braddles,' Loxton said.

Bradman had the pitch measured. It was found to be 20 yards (18 metres) in length, two yards (1.8 metres) short. Barnes, oblivious of the shortened wicket and hot sun, made a sparkling 48 before suffering sunstroke and vomiting at the wicket. Bradman had a similar reaction back on board and was confined to bed until the ship reached Bombay (Mumbai). Once there, he got up to attend an official function on board the ship, but did not go ashore. He and most of the party had heeded the warnings about the remote chance of picking up various diseases because they had not been vaccinated.

Those who did venture ashore took in the sights: the racecourse, the zoo, Marine Drive, the congested bazaars, the hanging gardens of Malabar Hill and the stark Temple of Silence, where the bodies of Parsee Indians are laid out for vultures to feast on.

The Bradman aura had long ago swept India, even though he would never make an appearance there as a cricketer, or now as a tourist. Perhaps this enhanced the legend and the deification. University students who bellowed for him from the wharf seemed likely to go unrewarded. But after the reception, he did come to the ship's railing and wave to them. There was something special and enduring about the appreciation of him by Indians. Apart from his genius as a cricketer and artistry as a batsman, it seemed to revolve around his apparent lack of bellicosity, dapper style and generally undemonstrative, dignified yet genial demeanour. In many ways this was typical Indian, the nearest incarnation as a character and young man in the modern era being the brilliant Sachin Tendulkar.

After a further leg of the voyage along the Suez Canal, some of the Australians fell victim to other forms of prey at Port Said, the chief port for Cairo. One player boasted about the price he paid for a pair of shoes. When he showed them off to team-mates they noticed that one shoe seemed larger than the other. When measured they were found to be different sizes.

The *Strathaird* made its way through the Mediterranean without any further stops before its destination. The players were distracted from their role as happy tourists when an English film crew that had come on board at Port Said took footage of them playing various sports. The film was whisked by launch to Gibraltar and then flown on to London for showing long before the squad would reach England. Yet it did not stop the revelry, with Hassett conducting community singing in the Veranda Café, which he had done much of the voyage, and leading crocodile marches around the ship.

Most members of the squad partied all night and few had slept much when the ship docked at London's Tilbury at 6 a.m. on Friday 16 April, a cool and overcast morning. Bradman had retired early. He wished to be prepared for the double marathon, on and off the field, that he would have to face if his team were to make sporting history.

His first engagement was to greet the universally popular Marylebone Cricket Club president, the Earl of Gowrie, who came on board. His second was to introduce the team to England via a BBC broadcast to the nation. It heralded the resumption, on British soil, of the longest running international sporting competition (between just two teams) in modern history, which had been interrupted by war for the second time in 71 years.

A horde of press men, TV cameras, and photographers were there to record the event. Bradman concluded by saying:

'We are very glad indeed to be back in England again, and we're very anxious to get on shore and get on with the business.'

3

Plenty of Speeches, Not Much Cricket

WHEN BRITISH AUTHOR George Orwell in 1948 was writing a fictional classic about a future society run by a brutal totalitarian regime, he decided on a title by switching the last two numbers of the year and came up with '1984'. Orwell's nightmare was inspired by the Communist regime running the Soviet Union, but his setting was what he could see in London. The writer's overall vision was what the Australian tourists experienced at the docks themselves, which had been bombed, and when travelling by train or car up to London. The blitz by the Germans was evident in outer London, where complete terraces of homes had been flattened. There were gaps in the landscape. Dense residential areas had been the target for the Luftwaffe, which had been under orders from Hitler to bomb the British into submission. It had failed, but the scenery it left was desolate and for many of the tourists, bleak and sad.

'I can still see St Paul's standing erect and proud,' Harvey said six decades later, 'with all the buildings surrounding it, flattened.'

Bradman aimed to blend with the natives as much as possible. He decreed that wherever practicable the players would eat the same as the locals.

'It was a case of half a piece of toast [at the team Hotel, the Piccadilly] and one mushroom for breakfast,' Doug Ring recalled in an ABC documentary.

'There was no real meat,' Harvey said, 'just chicken and fish – "kippers" – and the sausages were not what we [Australians] would call appetising. Occasionally you'd get other fish, such as halibut and turbot. We all had food coupons and you need them for luxuries such as chocolate. Otherwise sweets were restricted pretty much to boiled lollies.'

'We were playing golf one Sunday,' Bill Brown remembered with amusement, 'and there was tremendous excitement around the club. I asked [one of the golf club members] what the excitement was about. "Oh, haven't you heard," the member replied, "we're having ham tonight."'

The tourists became conscious of their food parcels, which were sweet offerings and good public relations, but mere tokens for the British, who would suffer much longer in the brutal aftermath of the war.

Yet some in the touring party – Miller, Hassett and manager Keith Johnson – were aware that appearances could be deceptive. The landscape had been damaged but the spirit of the locals was intact, despite bruising. Cricket had played its part in the resistance to the enemy assault from the skies and in keeping morale high. The game's ruling body, MCC, with government approval, kept cricket going throughout the bombing, despite continual Luftwaffe attempts to stop it. Keith Miller, in particular, knew what this meant. In July 1944, he was batting at Lord's for the RAAF against British Civil Defence Services. Miller performed with skill in wet conditions and reached 96. An air-raid warning sounded. It was followed by the fearful low engine buzz of a German guided missile, or 'flying bomb'. The players remained on the field waiting to see if the missile passed overhead. If its whine were to stop, the players would duck for cover, knowing that the missile would go into a terminal dive and explode. This one detonated south of them. A leg-spinner was delivered to Miller just as another missile was heard coming in. He danced down the wicket and drove through mid-off to the boundary for his first century at Lord's. The second missile detonated much closer to the ground just as Miller acknowledged the applause.

It was a striking instance of the enemy being unable to break the spirit of the British. Now in a time of restoration, the Australians could do their bit to lift morale further by playing inspired cricket, and by being cheerful, which was their style anyway. The touring party could aim at helping to revive the spirit of a nation by example, or simply being there with Bradman, whose return was in itself a restoration to some sort of normality. After all, he had set cricket fields alight approaching a generation ago. His performances in five Ashes series in England and Australia in the 1930s were fresh in British minds. They recognised and acknowledged greatness in Bradman, and in him saw more than just sport. He and his squad presented, in a symbolic sense at least, that the Empire might not be lost and that Britain would be great once more, especially if it could win back the Ashes. What a boost that would be to morale. Economists predicted a huge boost in spending if England were to win.

The initial depressing image for most of the tourists was soon eclipsed by contact with the locals, especially on the public transport in the underground, on the buses, in the trains, and in the theatres and cafes. They had survived and were stoic, cheerful and welcoming. Soon all the squad were writing home of first impressions. Even the weather received favourable mentions. The mornings were brisk but the sun filtered through the mist and haze, and occasionally interrupted the rain.

Regardless of the weather, it was terrific to be in England during the spring of 1948.

•

Perhaps only Bradman was not really enjoying it. There was too much responsibility to relax. He looked forward to golf. It was a respite from the ramifications of his fame, which was at its zenith. He said he loved being 'an ordinary mortal' on the golf course. He wallowed in 'being envious' of those who could hit a golf ball with more precision than he. Before such escapes, the first of which was scheduled for day three, Sunday, he had to endure the incessant rounds of receptions. They began on day two, Saturday 17 April, when the squad gathered at Australia House to meet the high commissioner, the Right Hon. J. A. Beasley. Despite his reserve about these events, Bradman was happy enough at this one as he, the squad, and the commissioner greeted many old adversaries including Herb Sutcliffe, Jack Hobbs, Arthur Gilligan, Wally Hammond, Patsy Hendren, George Duckworth, Bob Wyatt, Maurice Leyland and Percy Chapman. Current players, such as Alec Bedser, and twin Eric, Len Hutton, and Denis Compton, had all declined invitations. They were busy tuning up in warm-up matches around the country, getting, they hoped, a running start before the Australians had their land legs.

The reception room fell silent when an official announced the arrival of Douglas Jardine. He shook hands perfunctorily with the greeting party, including Bradman, and wandered among the throng, which found its collective voice again. There had never been any love lost between these two since Jardine, as England skipper in the 1932–33 Ashes introduced Bodyline as a tactic to stop Bradman and defeat Australia. Yet there had been very few occasions when they were forced to acknowledge each other. Both remained diplomatic in public, but their meetings were always strained. Most members of the touring party were happy to engage Jardine, one reason being that none of the 1948 players, except for Bradman, had experienced Bodyline. Jardine, for his part, was a proud and convivial individual, who despite his upper-class manner, had been a top competitive sportsman who enjoyed the company of old team-mates and adversaries. His actions with Bodyline had been inside the laws but outside the spirit of cricket. But the instigation of those controversial methods to win back the Ashes had not altogether been his fault. He had been under the MCC's directive to stop Bradman, and was made the scapegoat for the bad feeling that Bodyline engendered. Yet such was the bedrock rivalry between England and Australia, Jardine had plenty of sympathisers in England for a job they considered 'well done'.

One of the touring Australian journalists, Andy Flanagan, in a radio broadcast back to Australia related an anecdote about Jardine at the reception. He joined the knot of guests that included the journalist. Up came another Englishman with an up-market accent, who was apparently a friend of Jardine. He asked Jardine if Bradman had ever given him an autographed copy of his book.

'No he didn't,' Jardine said, 'and what's more, I've never read it.'

'Arh, that proves it must have been a forgery.'

'What must have been a forgery?' Jardine asked.

'An acquaintance of mine was in a secondhand bookshop the other day and noticed a copy of Bradman's book, which on the fly-leaf bore the inscription, "To Douglas with the compliments of the author, Don Bradman."'

The book, first published in England in 1935, was called *How to Play Cricket*.

•

On Saturday afternoon the Australians trundled from the Piccadilly Hotel, their base for the next six months in the West End, the few kilometres to Lord's in St John's Wood, North London for their first net practice at the 'nursery' or far end of the ground. The skies were grey and overcast. It was cold. Several hundred overcoat-clad spectators, including many small boys, paid to watch this little cricket ritual of the first net at Lord's for the Australian tourists. For the cricket lover, or tragic, there was something 'important', even romantic, about this event. A dozen of the players were new to the British. They would be commented on by all the experts around the nets. Miller was an attraction, having been so brilliant with bat and ball in 1945 in the Victory Tests. There was also something enigmatic about Lindwall. Where Miller was all flamboyance and style, Lindwall was laconic and undemonstrative. His rhythmic run to the wicket was mesmeric and poetry in motion. Many would comment (now and in the future) on the similarity to the great Harold Larwood, Bodyline's most lethal exponent, and not surprisingly. Lindwall was just 11 years old when he first saw 'Lol's' smooth, near-perfect run to the wicket. He copied it there and then, and never looked back.

At this net, Lindwall merely rolled his arm over in the cold conditions, never removing his sweater. But every now and again he swung the ball either way, which impressed onlookers. Where Miller was known and appreciated, Lindwall was the unknown quantity. Yes, he had shown pace on Australian wickets. How would he fare in English conditions, where swing was often more effective than sheer pace? Doug Ring thought he knew. Batting against the speedster, he had his off-stump uprooted. He tapped it back in with his bat, only to see Lindwall send it cartwheeling to the back of the net again. This time, Ring drew laughter from the onlookers by leaving the stump where it lay and facing up again with just two stumps on offer for the bowler.

Photographers tried to position themselves to take shots of Lindwall's much publicised drag. But Bradman told them not to do it. No snapper dared take on the flint-eyed stare from 'the boss'. Bradman knew just about every press trick in the book, and he was not about to let them raise the temperature of the issue with back or even front-page shots of his main weapon's right boot well over the line and the ball still in his hand.

Leg-spinner Ring was amazed and disappointed at the slowness of the pitches. In one hard lesson, he was enlightened as to why there were so few outstanding wrist-spinners in England. Ring resolved to push the ball through faster, more in the style of Bill O'Reilly. Off-spinner Ian Johnson was also surprised by the lack of pitch response to his lobbed off-breaks. He would have to adjust too, or be belted.

Most of the batsmen looked in need of practice. Miller hit the ball well, and late in proceedings Bradman padded up. Most of the spectators had come to see him. His remarkable eye was quickly 'in', although even he had his stumps tilted back. He wasted no time in taking some of the batsmen aside to remark on the way they played on the slower English wickets. One such 'pupil' was Colin McCool. A few observers saw this as some sort of rebuke for him, especially in front of the crowd and plenty of journalists and photographers, who snapped the moment. Bradman showed the attacking stroke-maker that he was playing through the line of the ball too early on the slower wickets. If he persisted, he would be in danger of lobbing or edging catches. Bradman suggested he delay his strokes and that he should watch the ball onto the bat.

Bradman's tutelage of McCool was a clue to his thinking. He didn't spend his precious time with young Harvey or Loxton or Hamence. They were not in immediate contention for a Test spot. McCool was.

The players enjoyed themselves, but there was no larking about. Bradman was not a hard taskmaster, but he wanted every player to take their practice seriously. One reason was that the weather was forecast to be inclement for some time (it rained almost every day before their first game), which meant there would be very few hours for practice.

'We would not have had two decent hours in the nets in those first 10 days,' Loxton recalled.

•

On day three, Bradman and most of the players were able to immerse themselves in golf at Burnham Beeches club, thanks to his best mate in England, Walter Robins, who was the Australian Board of Control's liaison officer.

On day four, Monday, some of the local press began attacking Bradman. Ever since Australia emerged as a threat to England at cricket in the late 19th Century, the tourists had been put under scrutiny that was often thinly disguised psychological warfare, intent on lowering the visitors' morale. (It was the same when England toured Australia, where the local press picked up on any real or perceived weaknesses or problems of the visitors.)

The attacks were flimsy and non-specific, with vague remarks about the 1946–47 Ashes series in Australia. The main criticism, when boiled down, seemed to be that Bradman had played to win.

Typical of the 'assault' was an article by Peter Wilson in the London *Sunday Pictorial*.

'During the last series,' Wilson wrote, 'it was said that England went out primarily on a goodwill mission to Australia, while Australia under Bradman's captaincy, went out to win, and did so.'

It was hardly going to cause Bradman sleepless nights. Wilson also quoted from a book – *Cricket Controversy* – recently published by cricket writer Cliff Cary, which criticised Bradman's style of leadership and approach to the Ashes.

A London *Daily Mirror* reporter asked Bradman about the book.

'I have not read it,' Bradman said.

'Will you?' the reporter asked.

'No,' was the succinct response.

Another reporter asked Bradman what he was going to do about the 'Lindwall problem', meaning his drag.

'What problem?' Bradman said, expressionless, and before the reporter could reply he added: 'There is no problem.'

•

Bradman by this time early on the tour was receiving up to 600 letters a day of personal mail, which he felt the obligation to respond to. He did not get to bed before 1 a.m.

•

The lead-up to the first game against Worcester was dominated by luncheons, dinners, and other functions. They included the Silver Jubilee Service for the King and Queen, and the theatre (*Annie Get Your Gun*), where Bradman was accompanied by Lord McGowan, High Commissioner Beasley, the Mayor of Westminster, and legendary former England cricketer C. B. Fry.

On Tuesday the Sportsmen's Club entertained the team at lunch at the Savoy. Bradman made his first major speech of the tour. Using his dry, chipping wit, he noted that the King (George VI) said he intended to turn up at Lord's. Bradman feared this because he recalled Bill Ponsford getting himself out when he was on top of the bowling on the last occasion a reigning monarch (George V) watched them at the home of cricket (in 1934).

Bradman also remarked that Alec Bedser had delivered – at Adelaide in the 1946–47 series – the best ball that ever dismissed him. It was Bedser who had been the first person to telegram his congratulations when Bradman decided to tour in 1948. Bradman's tone left open Bedser's motive for being so eager to renew his acquaintance.

The players voted the dinner on Thursday night at the Cricket Writers' Club (held at the Public Schools' Club) in Piccadilly as the best. Grand speeches were delivered first by the Chairman, Jim Swanton, followed by H. S. Altham (who co-authored with Swanton, *History of Cricket*), Bradman, Canon Gillingham and finally Mr Justice Norman Birkett. Bradman was in such good touch that, just as in one of his big innings, he ploughed on well beyond his allotted time.

'He spoke brilliantly, matching it with the best,' Harvey said. As ever, Bradman had prepared to perfection, within his limitations. The BBC broadcast every word live. Because the speech was so good and witty, it even held up the nine o'clock news until he had finished. This was akin to stopping Big Ben.

Bradman chided Bill O'Reilly (on tour as a journalist and in the audience) for criticising Australia's excessive appealing after 'teaching our boys' how to do it. Bradman also suggested the Duke of Edinburgh (in the audience) was welcome to bowl to the Australians in the nets. On the evidence of photographs, his right hand (waving to the crowd) was well suited to off-spinning.

On a roll, Bradman defined the meaning of 'geriatric' (remembering that 'Jerry' was the slang for German):

'A German who takes a hat-trick.'

Then he told the audience that the meaning of 'germinate' changed after the war:

'By 1945 it was "humble pie".'

Jokes about the vanquished were rife three years after the war.

In between the jokes, Bradman appealed to English journalists not to spoil the Australian team's tour by 'subordinating cricket to sensations'.

'We do not think the game should be used as a vehicle for distortion or exaggeration of events,' he said. 'I think there are other legitimate events for stirring up a sensation.' Bradman paused for humorous effect and added, 'Even though capital punishment has been abolished.'

The Australian captain knew that his appeal would fall on deaf press ears. Bad news would always prevail over good. But he was taking the opportunity to put the opposition (press) on the defensive to stave off initial attacks if possible. It was Bradman's way on or off the field.

In this speech too, he announced that he would never again tour England as a player, and indeed, would never play first-class cricket again after this year.

Canon Gillingham, in his speech, produced a copy of a London paper, published the day the tourists arrived, and read the front page headlines:

'Australian Cricketers Arrive', and 'Murderers Reprieved'.

Sir Norman Birkett, once a famous lawyer, who had presided over the Nuremberg war criminal trials, was another accomplished after-dinner performer in the UK. He was also at his scintillating best on his feet that evening. Part of his gift was his mellifluous voice, which gave his oratory an unmatched flow and cadence. Perhaps because he spoke late, he began by saying:

'Gentlemen, I do not belong to that order of speakers who object when people look at their watches, but I do object when they begin to shake them.'

This caused raucous laughter. Cigar and cigarette smoke grew thicker.

He added:

'Recently I was called upon to address a convention of medical men, and I considered there is a great affinity between law and medicine. In Law, when we finish a case we generally sit down and wonder whether we have left anything out. In Medicine, I understand, they sit down and wonder whether they have left anything in.'

He touched on hospitality and recalled that when he was in America his hosts were boasting about it. A man from Oklahoma said:

'In my State we give 'em drinks between drinks.'

A man from Arizona capped that by saying:

'In the State from which I come, we know no such interval.'

Sir Norman observed what a wonderful thing it was to have Bradman there. Many people would find it such an experience to meet him that it reminded him of poet Robert Browning exclaiming in his memorabilia:

'*Ah, did you once see Shelley plain?*
And did he stop and speak to you?
And did you speak to him again?

How strange it seems, and new!'

Sir Norman closed by saying that one of the saddest things he had ever heard was Bradman remarking, so lightly (in the earlier address that night), that after the 1948 tour he would not be playing first-class cricket again.

'Life always gives opportunities for repentance,' Sir Norman noted to supportive smiles and loud applause.

•

Bradman never told his players that his main aim was to go through the 1948 season undefeated.

'But we all knew: we could sense it,' Sid Barnes remarked in his book, *It Isn't Cricket*. Confirmation of what everyone felt came with the selection of the Australian team for the first game – against Worcestershire. It was Bradman's blueprint for the First Test. In batting order, the team was: Barnes, Morris, Bradman, Hassett, Brown, Miller, Lindwall, McCool, Tallon, Johnson, Toshack.

This did not mean that the team was set in concrete. Bradman's mind was fluid and creative. After all, to win he had to attack, and the form players would take the initiative. If a fringe player demonstrated he had stepped up, he would be given a chance.

4

—

Hitting Worcester Running

THE TEAM LEFT Paddington early afternoon on 27 April in fine, cool weather and sped through Slough, Reading and Oxford on a three-hour, 225 km journey north-west to the Shrub Hill station at Worcester. Bradman took the time to answer a bulging suitcase of mail, which had been boosted since his BBC broadcast speech at the Cricket Writers' Club. The city's mayor and a big crowd greeted them, as they would on every scheduled stop. A fleet of new Austin cars formed a procession that took them to the Star Hotel.

On the way, Bradman's car was stopped. A girl from a florist's shop handed him through the window a cricket bat made of marigolds and leaves. Bradman smiled and shook the girl's hand. The procession moved on. He looked more closely at the bat and noticed that the word 'Don' had been woven into the handle.

'It touched me,' Bradman said, 'as did countless other thoughtful people with their letters, messages and gifts.'

While most of the other members of the party did some sightseeing, Bradman retired to his room to work on his mail before and after dinner for another three hours.

'That was just to open and read the letters,' he said, 'not answer them.'

•

The fair weather remained but was colder on the morning of 28 April, the first day of the Worcester game. These conditions were said by the locals to be satisfactory. The ground was on the banks of the River Severn. It was not unusual for it to be *under* the Severn. Flooding was common, and for this reason the pavilion was built on stilts, and, the unlikely story went, the heavy roller had to be anchored. Three extra stands were built for the game; many shops in the city closed for the afternoon and school children were given a half-holiday. A queue began forming at around 6 a.m. and the place was packed with more than 15,000 spectators long before play began. The Australians turned up, not with snorkel and flippers, but several sweaters each.

The photographic perspective that has made the ground famous is from the pavilion. Towering above trees beyond the far (eastern) side of the oval is the grand Cathedral. It was built circa 1084 and houses the tomb of King John, the last of the Angevin kings, who, under the threat of civil war, signed the Magna Carta, the original charter of English liberties.

Spectators were hoping that few liberties would be taken with the county, but they were aware that Bradman had selected a powerful side. It created, rather than hindered a carnival atmosphere, especially under a red and white striped marquee, where the buzz among spectators was all about Bradman, the legend. The papers had speculated about him scoring a double century in the game and the paying customers chatted about it over their thermos tea and biscuits. Bradman had hit 236 not out against Worcester in his first game on English soil in 1930. He began a second tour in 1934 with an energy-sapping illness, but his captain, Bill Woodfull, requested that he turn up and play at Worcester for the purposes of team morale and psychology. Bradman obliged his skipper, hit 206 and threw his wicket away. In 1938 on his third tour, he saw the value in the psychology of opening the season and the Ashes campaign with yet another double hundred – this time 258. Could any other player in the history of cricket perform with such will, skill and determination over such a long interval?

The groundsman, George Platt, said:

'There is nothing wrong with the wicket so he should have the best possible chance of doing it again.'

Now the question being asked around the ground was whether Bradman could make his fourth successive double at Worcester 18 years after the first. But it was the wrong question. Bradman could do it at will. The right query was, whether he would. Only the team doctor knew the answer was 'no'. Bradman was very conscious of not exhausting himself with huge scores. He could make them but run the risk of injury. If he were out of the team for any extended period during the season, he could kiss the unbeaten tour record goodbye.

•

The crowd would have to wait to see Bradman bat. Worcester won the toss and batted. Lindwall set a mood that the Australians hoped would last for the entire summer when he had opener Don Kenyon lbw with just the second ball of the match. Yet there was more interest in his right leg than whether he was troubling the batsmen. Several journalists, photographers and spectators positioned themselves square of the wicket at the bowler's end to observe him, some with binoculars.

The umpires too became more prominent than usual. Would they call Lindwall? Umpire Fred Root was at the bowler's end, Dai Davies at square leg. Root was a former bowler himself, always a useful thing for an umpire. He was also a 1920s exponent of the ignominious 'leg theory,' where balls would be delivered wide enough outside leg-stump for the batsman to find scoring difficult. Root had already expressed a vague sympathy for fast bowlers with the no-ball rule, and Lindwall would have to offend obviously to be 'called'. From another perspective, Root was expressing sympathy for all umpires. It was very difficult for him to look down at a fast bowler's foot at the wicket, and then jerk the head up to see the ball's release. First, the umpire had to watch the bowler's arm to see if it were a legitimate 'bowl' rather than a 'throw', and second, to see what happened when the ball reached the batsman. All this in a fraction of a second. Umpires had to be as good as any batsman at concentrating and reacting.

There was another factor involved. Root and Davies had been summoned to Lord's to see the MCC secretary, Colonel R. S. Rait Kerr. He informed them they had been chosen especially to have first sight of Lindwall's delivery.

The colonel told them their verdict would be important. He hoped they would not be influenced by any press comment. The umpires left the meeting with the distinct impression that Lord's wished to avoid any sensations at Worcester. In other words, unless Lindwall flouted the law, he was not to be called.

Bradman had drilled into the bowler that he should keep his back foot a long way behind the bowling crease. He should not try to bowl too quickly. Lindwall was under instruction to build his pace through the opening games, at least until he had passed the scrutiny of the umpires, and especially Frank Chester. Bradman regarded Chester as the best umpire in the world, a man who would call it as he saw it.

This early caution from both Lord's and Bradman defused the issue. Neither Root nor Davies called Lindwall or anyone else. Once this was settled within the first hour of the game, attention turned to batsman Charles Palmer, a bespectacled, diminutive schoolteacher, who looked more suited to the classroom than cricket. But his size was deceptive. He had strong wrists and excellent footwork. Palmer used these assets intelligently and to advantage in a fine knock of 85. Would England selectors take notice? Or would there be so many good performances that this first-up effort would be swamped from the collective memory of the home team's brains trust? Certainly no selector was there, which probably meant that form in the season opener, when the Australians were thought to be rusty, would be discounted.

The minds of spectators turned once more to Bradman on day two, in less favourable weather, as he joined Morris. Bradman came to the wicket at 1 for 79, and one local dreading his emergence from the pavilion was opening bowler, Reg Perks. He had been belted by him in 1930, 1934 and 1938 and had never taken his wicket.

Bradman had given his left-handed partner a big start. But with exquisite driving, he caught the elegant Morris in the nineties and vied with him for the first century of the tour. Morris just pipped him, causing his skipper to give him a mock angry wave of the fist. On 107, Bradman threw his wicket away by deliberately playing on. There was method in this apparent madness as he, not a bowler, broke his partnership with Morris, which was worth a healthy 186. Bradman was still niggled by that cartilage injury earlier in the year in the Fifth Test against India, and more importantly, he wished to give others some batting experience under English conditions.

The double hundred had been Bradman's special area of expertise. He had scored more of them – 37 – than anyone else in first-class cricket. (To this day he has made 12 trips into this special territory in Test cricket, which is far more than anyone else.) England's Wally Hammond had 36 first-class doubles, but in about four times as many innings. This scoring zone was now out of bounds to Bradman, and it was a surprise, if not a disappointment, to the capacity crowd to see him not bother about reaching it after a 152-minute knock, which included 15 fours.

Morris went on to a superb 138. This New South Welshman had an impressive temperament and discipline. He, like Bradman, wished to leave his imprint on the tour early. The rest of the batsmen struggled, except for Miller, who came in lower down the order than normal and played a lovely, big-hitting cameo of 50 not out, which included three towering sixes. McCool and Johnson took six wickets each for the match and did their chances of forcing a Test spot no harm, while the pacemen, under instruction, broke themselves in gently. Australia won comfortably by an innings and 17 runs. The gate for the game was double that of 1938, and both results were satisfactory for the tourists.

Rainy weather on day three, 30 April, necessitated sawdust being put down for the pace bowlers to avoid them slipping on delivery. As some of it was being sprinkled for Lindwall, a spectator called:

' 'Ere, go easy with yon sawdust! That's wasting a full month's ration of ruddy sausage meat!'

English sausages of 1948 were not too impressive.

•

On balance, Bradman didn't take much away from the Worcester experience apart from the win.

'The players were clearly short of practice,' he said. But the big plus in his eyes was Morris's form.

'He left no one in any doubt,' Bradman remarked, 'about his capacity to handle English wickets.'

It meant that two of his top order (he being the other one) had already found their feet.

•

A joy for Bradman, and the rest of the squad, was a dinner at the local guildhall. There were eight courses, each prepared by local farmers, and no speeches.

•

The schedule was tight. Soon after the Worcester game ended on 30 April, the squad was driven 170 km north-east through Stratford's delightful countryside and then Coventry, which had been bombed mercilessly by the Luftwaffe, past Birmingham and then on to Leicester. If nothing else, the tourists were getting a geography lesson concerning England's battering by the enemy in World War II.

They arrived at the Grand Hotel Leicester at 8 p.m. and were met by two former Sydney players, off-spinner Vic Jackson, and Jack Walsh, a left-arm, back of the hand (wrong 'un) bowler.

Oddly, this was the one night of the tour that people hardly recognised the Australians. Their hotel was filled with cloth-capped Rugby League fans from Yorkshire and Lancashire in town for a Challenge Cup Final at Wembley between Wigan and Bradford Northern.

The cricketers welcomed the relative anonymity, especially Bradman, who for two decades had been a superstar recognised and sought out by fans wherever the game was played. Any respite from incessant attention was a dream for him.

•

'Follow the crowd,' was the instruction to fans from outside the county in order to find the obscure Leicestershire ground at Grace Road. This was easy on the first day's play on 1 May. It had seating for 5,000 but a record 16,000 crowd turned up in the hope of seeing Bradman. Their wish seemed likely to be fulfilled. Australia won the toss and batted. A wicket – that of Brown – fell and there was a rush of men, women and children, armed with cameras towards the pavilion. Bradman had almost always come in at No. 3, but today he had put Miller in before him to 'run him into form' and because he had been batted down the order at Worcester.

There was initial disappointment as the dashing Miller stepped down the race.

'They had come from everywhere to watch Don,' Miller said. 'The crowd went crazy to get the first glimpse of Bradman walking down the race. You should have heard the hoots and groans when Muggins Miller walked out. Blimey! Do you reckon I was the most unpopular man in the land? I forced my way through the crowd, saying Bradman would be out in a minute . . .'

But Miller was intent on lasting a little longer than that. He and Barnes put on 111, when Barnes made way for the captain, who received a standing ovation. Bradman was in fine touch again, as he outscored Miller in a 159-run partnership before receiving a poor caught-behind decision when on 81. From that moment, Miller took control in a responsible 325 minutes of aggression mixed with defence on his way to 202 not out. One of his sixes hit a 16-year-old boy and sent him to hospital.

The innings was a reminder of Miller's exceptional ability with the bat. But the die was cast. He would be used – willingly – as a front-line bowler to partner Lindwall with the aim of blasting out England. At least, this was Bradman's plan. It would put paid to Miller's batting aspirations, as it had many batsmen who could bowl well at Test level. There was cold logic in Miller's fate. Australia had a surfeit of outstanding batsmen. Miller would be of far better use to the team as a bowler. If he made runs it would be a bonus. If he failed with the bat it would be of little consequence, at least in the Tests, or that was the theory. Evidence over 71 years of Test cricket was that it was tough, almost impossible for a player to sustain great form with bat and ball. The problem was more for the batting side of an all-rounder's skills. Once a bowler had put in a stint with the ball, he would find full concentration as a batsman a challenge. And with batting, especially at Test level, one tiny lapse led to downfall. On the other hand, if a bowler managed a long innings, he could still deliver with the ball, if fit. Little lapses when bowling were not survival threatening. An opposition batsman might slap a four off a poor delivery, but it would not spell the end for the bowler. He would live to fight next ball. Yet a batsman would be 'dismissed', as the term goes, from the field of play. The worst sentence a bowler received was a spell in the field before being given a second or third chance.

Miller had been compared favourably to the great Wally Hammond for his performances with the bat in the 1945 Victory Tests in England. After that, on return to Australia, Miller became a victim of his own wonderful skills as a bowler, and his own fierce competitiveness. On top of that, by opening the bowling he was doing the right thing by his country, which needed him.

Unfortunately for England, only the two ex-Sydneysiders, Jackson (who dismissed half the Australians) and Walsh (who impressed Bradman as a well-equipped bowler of the Fleetwood-Smith variety) troubled the Australian batsmen. These two professional foreign interlopers would never be chosen for England. No Leicester batsman scored more than 40 in either of the county's innings, and only two locals managed to reach double figures twice. This was despite a series of what the Australians thought were poor umpiring responses to their appealing, especially by umpire Alec Skelding. There was a bit of good-natured banter between him and Barnes, who reckoned he received a shocking lbw decision when on 78 on the first day. After about the 10th adjudication against the tourists, Barnes met Skelding at a reception after the second day's play and chided him, saying:

'That [ball] wouldn't have hit another set of stumps.'

'Nay, lad, you were out,' Skelding replied with a laugh. 'You'll see it's so if you check the papers this morning.'

'You know mate, you're a good bloke, but you need a dog.'

'Why a dog, lad?' Skelding asked. 'I'm not fond of them.'

'I mean a seeing eye dog. You were blind when you made those decisions.'

•

Miller's double hundred at Leicester was the stand-out performance in Australia's second successive victory by an innings. While it was appreciated by Bradman, he was more concerned with the bowlers.

Considering the cold and wet conditions, he was pleased with Ring and Johnson, who he thought did 'splendidly' in giving his team an easy victory.

Hamence, Harvey, Loxton, Saggers, Ring and Johnston played for Australia, which meant that everyone on the list had played a game. This wide selection indicated that Bradman was more concerned with giving everyone a chance rather than picking a near full-strength side to make sure he won or avoided a loss every game.

He thought events were 'swinging along quite smoothly' so he decided to rest himself for the third match – against Yorkshire at Bradford. Bradman was aware the schedule included another game against Yorkshire, which allowed him the excuse he needed to opt out the first time.

He needed to have an explanation for not turning up. No matter what the other Australians were doing or how well they were performing, the crowds would flock to see him. Every county was acutely aware that its gate receipts rocketed with him as a drawcard. His appearance would often mean the difference between a profit or a loss for the entire year for a host club. County officials pleaded with him to play. For them it was about money, for the crowds it was about Bradman and for Bradman it was about self-preservation. If he had his deepest wish, he would play a few tune-up matches and the Tests, just the way he did in an Australian season, and that would be it.

Bradman had to be content with just three days off. He and Barnes took off for London.

'We were on friendly terms,' Barnes wrote, 'and it is usually arranged in England that cobbers get identical matches off, if possible, so they can do things in common. We did some good business at the London Exhibition. I got myself the best movie equipment possible and Don enriched himself with a grand piano.'

•

While the 'cobbers' were shopping, Hassett led the tourists 200 km north for the clash with Yorkshire at the ground at Park Avenue, Bradford. It held only 20,000 maximum, and the intimate atmosphere was enjoyed by spectators and players. Did it all perhaps lead to a little complacency on the part of the tourists? If so, it was the wrong county to take lightly. A decade earlier in early July 1938, the weather had saved Australia from defeat in a game played in woeful conditions. Bradman played brilliantly in both innings, scoring 59 and 42, which were the equivalent of big hundreds under normal conditions. Yorkshire had only to make 150 to win at the commencement of the third and final day. It was three for 83 at lunch, with Herbert Sutcliffe 36 not out and confident he could lead Yorkshire to the first victory against the tourists for the 1938 season, and the first county to beat the Australians since Hampshire managed the rare feat in 1912.

Ten years on, tight terraces were packed for the start of play on 5 May, when Yorkshire's tough, long-term skipper Brian Sellers won the toss and batted on the type of wet wicket that held no terrors for his feisty club. Lindwall was not comfortable charging in under the conditions, so Hassett opened with Miller and Loxton.

Miller loved these slippery strips, which allowed him to revert to fast off-breaks. Fresh in his mind was his fine effort at Brisbane in the First Test of the 1946–47 series when, on a similar track, he was devastating.

The bitterly cold and wet weather didn't allow the game to commence until 2.30 p.m. The Aussies looked more like a football team as they entered the arena running and doing jump-ups, and sprints to warm up muscles while 'Waltzing Matilda' was played over the address system.

'It was freezing,' Neil Harvey recalled. 'We all had three sweaters on and had left the dressing room where there was a log fire.'

The Australians wanted to conquer Len Hutton, England's best bat, who opened for his county. His first run was cheered.

Loxton, given a chance to impress, learned why Lindwall had opted not to take the ball. Loxton tore a groin muscle and was out of the game after one over, leaving his team one short with bat and ball.

Johnston took over and showed his versatility bowling medium-pacers and his own left-arm spinners. Hutton's first run had become an event. He was intent on grim defence, searching for hand grenades in the deliveries. His next run took 58 minutes.

Miller had him caught by Harvey for 5. It was a blow for Yorkshire, and England, whose star bat would need to be in touch for the summer if England were to have a chance in the Ashes. His demise caused the county rot to set in. Miller (6 for 42) and Johnston (4 for 23) bowled almost unchanged and ran through proud Yorkshire for just 71.

Australia, just as proud, did not fare much better. It collapsed and brought Miller to the wicket at 4 for 38. Acting captain Hassett misjudged a pull shot off Frank Smailes – who also reverted from medium-pace to off-spin – and the ball went straight up. Five fielders hovered under it and Sellers caught it to send his opposite number to the pavilion. At 5 for 20, Australia was in danger of falling well short of Yorkshire's meagre tally. Historians and journalists searched the records. In 1902 Joe Darling's strong Australian side, including Victor Trumper, Clem Hill, Warwick Armstrong, Monty Noble and Hugh Trumble had been rolled for just 23. F. S. Jackson and George Hirst took five wickets each to clean up the visitors.

Miller would not have known this low record, but he put paid to it with the first ball he received by straight driving it to the metal sightscreen, which resounded with a 'clang'. The tourists were 5 for 24. The historians put away the record books for the moment, knowing that the next fact of interest would be whether the Australians lost to a county. Defeat had been a rare event. Essex had beaten them by just 19 runs in 1905. The result was even tighter in 1909, when Surrey won by a mere five runs. 1912 looked bad for the tourists when they were beaten five times: Lancashire did it twice, and Notts, Surrey and Hampshire once each. But in that year Australia was at half-strength after six of its stars fell into dispute with officials and opted not to tour.

Miller in 1948 would not countenance defeat. He was intent on driving hard at the bowlers, collecting two sixes and two fours in a face-saving cameo of 34 that lifted Australia to 101. It was still anyone's match when Yorkshire batted again. But the county collapsed a second time, Hutton this time falling for 11 to Johnston, who seized his opportunity, taking 6 for 18. This gave the long-limbed left-hander 10 wickets for the match, the first such haul by an Australian on the trip. Johnston would now be in contention for the First Test. Yorkshire's score of 89 left the tourists just 60 for victory. But no one was complacent now.

The damp wicket was near-unplayable. Australia fell apart again, losing 6 for 31, with Miller unable to repeat his first innings restoration. Young Harvey was partnered by Tallon and they scraped through until tea with the score at 6 for 47.

Bradman had been kept informed by Hassett of the match's progress, and the rollercoaster left him worried in his bunker at the team hotel.

'This is the last time you and I will be out of this team together,' Bradman told Barnes when the tea scores were relayed to them.

After the break, impetuous youth won through, after a stumping chance. With three runs to win, Harvey boldly hit a terrific drive over mid-on for six, to win the match by an uncomfortable four wickets.

Johnston observed:

'Harvey's six was a bit of a shock to the Yorkshire people. They didn't normally win (or lose) matches that way!'

Back in the dressing room, Hassett sat with his head in his hands saying: 'Why me? Why is it always me?' He then thanked Harvey and Tallon profusely.

Later he received a mischievous telegram with Bradman's name on it: 'You nearly lost our [unbeaten] record for me!'
It had been sent by Jack Fingleton.

5

—

Mixed Memories at the Oval

BRADMAN TOOK SEVERAL positives out of the Yorkshire threat to his grand plan. First, he believed that it was a good thing for the team to be hard pressed by a county so early in the tour. It put paid to slackness, which could occur if the opposition was weak. Second, Miller's performance with bat and ball had been encouraging. He was a match-winner by nature and had run into form early in both departments of the game. Third, Johnston had shown for the first time how effective he could be delivering big spinners when conditions suited. And fourth, the one big stroke for glory would do teenager Harvey's confidence no harm.

The only major negative out of the Yorkshire game was an evident weakness here and there against spin, especially with the ball moving away from the bat, and the inability or lack of desire to play back defensively.

Observing this match, Australia's former leg-spinner, Bill O'Reilly noted in his book, *Cricket Conquest*, that the Australians' Achilles' heel was turning wickets. From the bowler's point of view '. . . the batsman to fear was the one who could move back surely and watch the ball come off the pitch.'

•

Bradman was able to free himself from the pressures of fame for at least a night in his London sojourn when a friend invited him to dine with his family at the Savoy. His seat was close to that of pianist Carroll Gibbons, who was conducting his fellow players, the Savoy Orpheans. Unbeknown to Bradman, his friend had organised the seating and for Bradman to meet Gibbons backstage afterwards. Gibbons had been delighted. He was a big Bradman fan. And the admiration was mutual. Gibbons had been one of the cricketer's favourite pianists for years. Again, the superstar sportsman revelled in being just an ordinary 'fan' enthralled by one his heroes.

Backstage, Bradman enjoyed some duo-playing with Gibbons' fellow professionals.

'I loved those moments,' Bradman told me during our interviews in 1995. 'Those kinds of experiences – all too infrequent – away from cricket were precious [to me].'

After this reverie it was back to business and the public glare.

•

The Yorkshire match had taken less than two days, which gave the tourists a rare day off in London between matches before heading for the unprepossessing Oval in the urban Kennington district of south-east London's industrial belt. This Cockney playground was in the shadows of one huge and two smaller gasometers. They were being painted green, no doubt to give them an environmentally friendlier appearance in the sea of grey and grime of inner London. The surrounding tight, narrow streets were bustling and businesslike and a contrast to the soothing setting of most of the UK's beautiful cricket grounds. The game even spilt into the environs where blocks of flats were rebuilt after the war and named after famous cricketers: Stoddart, Lockwood, Lohmann, Surridge and Shrewsbury.

The Oval has a magnificent history, which most of the greats of the game would speak of with affection and enjoyment, and be proud to have done well there. Its Ashes record helped make it of historical significance. The First Test in England (or 'international', between England and Australia), was played there in 1880. Two years later, Australia won a Test by seven runs and this gave rise to the Ashes, when it was judged by one commentator that English cricket had 'died' at the Oval after the thrilling, tight game. The resultant Ashes from the 'cremation' became the trophy for which these two national teams would fight from then on.

•

More recent events there were on the mind of Bradman, who took charge of his team once more for the fourth tour encounter, this time against Surrey. He wanted no small measure of revenge against any opposition there after the Oval debacle in the Fifth Test of the 1938 Ashes. The loss by an innings and 579 runs remains the biggest in Test history.

A big crowd formed queues outside the ground on 8 May. More people kept pouring out of the nearby tube, the trams and buses, promising a full-house turnout of 30,000 Londoners wanting a glimpse of the Australians for the first time in the season.

Bradman would adopt a 'take-no-prisoners' attitude in this game. He arrived at the ground by chauffeur-driven car, a far cry from his first trip there by tube in 1930 when the 21-year-old wanted to save on expenses. Wearing a dark-blue suit, Bradman strode through the wrought-iron Hobbs Gates and looked up at the flats around the ground where people could be seen going about their home activities. Some of the tourists were never enamoured with this proximity to real life displayed around the Oval. It was a matter of perspective. While the flats seemed intrusive to some, to others, particularly observing journalists, the large size of the Oval itself pushed spectators too far from the action.

Bradman didn't bother about either perspective, being adept at blocking out the surrounds and concentrating wherever he played. On his walk to inspect the pitch, he noticed the results of direct hits by high-explosive and incendiary bombs, which were still evident. Only three years ago, the Oval was not expected ever to see cricket again. Then there had been barbed-wire barricades across the playing area. The outfield contained inset concrete bases for huts, searchlights and guns. Grass had grown long and coarse. Weeds studded the entire arena. Yet the will and tradition of the place, along with the determination of the Surrey committee, made it suitable for cricketers by the end of the 1945–46 winter; a remarkable feat by the head groundsman H. C. Lock, a former Surrey player.

Bradman found a changed wicket after this complete revamp and levelling of the turf. The differences were stark. Before the war, centuries were frequent. Swing bowlers could expect a lively wicket for an hour or so every now and again. Post-war, pace in the wicket was rare. Swing bowlers had to be patient between heavy morning and evening atmospheres. Bradman would have been surprised at the lack of 'green' in the pitch, which had been a feature at the Oval in his experience pre-war. It first looked to him more like a spinner's wicket, as it had been in the last two summers. It was even known to turn on the first morning of a match, which was never the case before the war.

Bradman's interest was just as much on the footmarks at one end as the state of the wicket on a good length. He was looking for the place where he twisted his foot in a dip and broke a bone when bowling in England's massive score in the 1938 Test. There was no hole after a decade, but Bradman's action demonstrated that his misfortune had been in the back of his mind, and not so much because he was injured. No doubt, with his perfectionist's view of every competition, he would have rued his bad luck. It robbed him of a chance of big score in one or two innings in 1938, which may have given his team a chance of saving the game. He once told me how he forever had nightmares about the way he was dismissed for 131 (bowled by a good wrong 'un from Walter Robins) in the second innings of his first ever Test in England in 1930. Bradman believed that he would have won the game for Australia if he had batted on. The fact that he made one fatal error after a big score rankled with him, especially when he had manoeuvred his team into a position where it might have won.

It's probable that he had similar regrets about what happened at the Oval on his previous visit there, and he would want to make amends. Yet this had been the ground for some of his triumphs too. The first was in this corresponding game against Surrey in 1930. The county's skipper, Percy Fender, had been one of Bradman's most vocal detractors. He had denigrated his performances in Australia in the 1928–29 series, and had said he was too 'unorthodox' to make it on England's wickets where there were green tops and wet pitches, on which the ball seamed around a lot more. Technique was vital, Fender wrote and told newspapers, and Bradman did not have the right methods for English conditions. This public criticism began during 1929 and continued right up until that Surrey match in 1930. The 21-year-old Bradman made 252 not out and his captain Bill Woodfull on the Saturday night had given him the nod to continue batting on the Monday after the rest day. Bradman, the super-fit, run-hungry young champion, was set to go to 400, a feat he had achieved already in 1930 playing for New South Wales against Queensland. But it rained and he didn't face another ball. The UK *Observer* called this innings 'a marvellous display of clever, stylish, and almost faultless batting'. It continued: 'The most ardent Surrey partisan could not grudge him any of his runs. Recollection of the innings will always be happy to those privileged to witness it.'

Fender did a lot of leather-chasing on that day, and journalists thought Bradman played his shots deliberately to make the Surrey skipper sweat – something Bradman denied. In the series-deciding Fifth Test at the Oval that year, he produced a great innings of 232 to win the series and snare the Ashes. In 1934 at the same ground in the corresponding Ashes game, he hit 244 off 272 deliveries in one of the finest Test innings ever played, and partnered Bill Ponsford (a magnificent 266) in a record link of 451 runs. This again won the match and the series, and once more took the Ashes back to Australia.

•

Bradman's careful pitch inspection on Saturday 8 May 1948 would have brought back more than memories of a snapped ankle bone. It would have reminded him that he had earned the right to regard this important venue as a happy hunting ground for him, perhaps more than any other Australian, and at the highest level of the game, up there with England's batting maestro from Surrey, Jack Hobbs.

Bradman's first useful step was to win the toss, and Australia batted and batted. Barnes, refreshed from his wheeler-dealing in the British capital, carved out a formidable 176, which all but sealed his First Test spot. His capacity to will himself a big score was impressive, and this day, he was a fluent mix of attack and defence. Morris scored another half century, and was fighting to the find the form with which he had begun.

Bradman was in a good mood after three days off, and it translated into a typical knock by the master when he came to the wicket just before lunch with the score at 1 for 136. One of the reasons he was so watchable was the professional manner he went about building an innings, as he did this day. He would begin by pushing for runs from the first ball he received and then move steadily from there. Bradman would watch the ball onto the bat, no matter who was bowling. He played straight for the first half hour and then he started to play his shots square of the wicket, becoming more adventurous as his innings progressed to 50 in 77 minutes. There was restraint in his strokes only in one way: he never lofted the ball. There was more carving than a master wood sculptor, more precision cuts than a master surgeon's exhibition, but nothing was hit skyward.

If the ball was pitched short, as it was by medium-pacer Stuart Surridge, who tried to bounce him, it received severe treatment but always with a stylish roll of the wrists so that Bradman was always hauling the ball down with his usual superb placement, making catching impossible. His 207 partnership with Barnes lasted only 138 minutes.

Bradman reached 146 in just 174 minutes with 15 fours before Bedser bowled a similar ball to the one that took his wicket for a duck in Adelaide in 1947. It pitched leg and took off-stump. Bedser proved it was not a fluke by dismissing Hassett, who had made a fine 110, the same way.

'That performance made it clear that Bedser would be our toughest hurdle in the Tests,' Bradman noted. 'We would have to have plans to curtail his effectiveness.'

Australia climbed to 4 for 479 at stumps. Bradman had a comfortable Sunday off playing golf knowing that his team could not lose against Surrey. But the shock of Bradford and the memory of 1938, along with the need for batting practice for Tallon and Johnson, caused him to bat on into the second morning on Monday. Australia reached a huge 632, which was as unassailable as it was unnecessary in a three-day game – but for the batting practice.

•

The round of dinners and engagements continued even on the nights during the games. On Saturday night after the first day, Surrey entertained the tourists at a dinner at the Armourers and Braziers Hall, with Lord Rosebery presiding, and this coincided with Surrey stalwart H. D. G. Leveson-Gower's 75th birthday. The short, slight and bubbly personality of English cricket remarked in his speech:

'I am most grateful to the Supreme Umpire for giving me the benefit of the doubt for 75 years.'

•

On Monday, the Australian bowlers then showed how futile such a big innings was from the point of view of a competitive game by dismissing Surrey for 141. All the bowlers contributed, with Johnson again impressing with a bag of five wickets. Only Surrey's attacking opener, left-hander Laurie Fishlock, batted impressively, hitting 81 not out and carrying his bat against a strong all-round bowling line-up of pace, swing and spin.

'It was a top performance displaying sound defence, aggression and always with adept footwork,' Bradman commented. 'Some of his off-drives were splendid.' At the time of the match, he was careful not to praise a batsman of such skill in the hope that the 41-year-old would be overlooked for the Tests. Worcester's Palmer was in the same category. England selectors knew that Bradman was as shrewd in his observations and judgements as he was honest. If he praised a player it would be noted by selectors.

The incident that drew most attention from the crowd had nothing to do with the cricket. A small dog bounded onto the field and no one could catch it. Finally Barnes trapped it and ran towards umpire Skelding who was adjudicating in an Australian game for a second time. Skelding, who Barnes had suggested needed a dog at Leicester, now recoiled as Barnes thrust it at him.

'Here,' Barnes said, 'all you need now is a white stick.'

Skelding's antipathy towards man's best friend was shown when he removed the bails and hurried towards the pavilion.

Barnes took the dog off the field.

'Strange how I suggested he find himself a canine companion at Leicester,' he said, 'and then one turned up at the Oval. Cricket's a funny game.'

•

No one, especially politicians, wished to miss the occasion to be with Bradman and his squad. On Monday night 10 May the team dined at the House of Commons at the invitation of its chairman, Sir J. Stanley Holmes. Labour prime minister Clement Attlee and most of his cabinet were present, along with notables from the opposition, including Anthony Eden. Attlee proposed the toast to the Australians and spoke of his love of cricket. He was a fervent Surrey supporter, who, for decades, walked from his Putney home to the Oval to watch his team.

A politician asked Hassett and Morris if they would like to meet Winston Churchill. The Australians suggested that the politician ask Churchill if he wished to meet them. The politician spoke to the great wartime leader on the other side of the room, and returned with Churchill's response: 'No.'

'At least he was honest,' Morris observed.

•

Most of the team, except for a few rebels such as Miller and Lindwall, were in bed before midnight. There was a game to be won against Surrey on Tuesday.

The highlight for Australia in the field was the athletic Harvey. He had failed with the bat making just 7, but he kept himself in the selection panel's collective thoughts by taking a stunning catch.

Late on day three, he was fielding under the shadows of the gasometer at wide mid-on. The last two were in for Surrey and Australia needed a final wicket before it became too dark. Surridge hit Johnson high and hard. Harvey ran 25 metres to his left. The ball was going for six.

'I knew if I didn't try something it would sail over the rope,' Harvey said. He sprinted and leapt high in the air, grasping the ball overhead with both hands, like an Aussie Rules high 'mark.'

'It was so dark,' Harvey recalled, 'that many of the fielders didn't know I had it, especially as I pocketed the ball on my trot back to the middle.'

•

Australia now had four successive victories, with three of them by an innings and plenty. There were still 30 matches to be played. After the shock at Bradford, Bradman was cautious.

In modern football parlance, he was taking it *one match at a time*.

6

—

Slaughter at Southend

B RADMAN PRESERVED HIMSELF for the second time and opted out of the fifth match – against Cambridge University. In the tradition of other skippers before him, he did not take the students too seriously, although he had always expressed admiration for the beautiful, peaceful venue near the centre of Cambridge, 100 km north of London. It had been opened in 1846 by F. P. Fenner, a tenant of Caius College, and from then on was known as 'Fenner's'. The large, smooth-as-velvet arena was memorable for the alternately patterned, seven-metre-wide, light and dark green stripes. The open pavilion was near the entrance gates and behind the bowler's arm. There were chestnut trees, with a marquee erected near them on the left bank, and to the right was another row of beech and copper-beech trees, with one *inside* the boundary line. Spectators, including many students wearing gowns, and on bikes, began arriving from across the open grass area of Parker's Piece early on the first day. They would normally laze about under the trees and the marquee, but with the Australians on view they found space hard to come by as 10,000 packed the ground on each of the first two days. A military band added a certain pomp to the occasion.

The setting was idyllic for the tourists as they took the field in filtered sunshine and a warmth that suggested spring had arrived, at least at Fenner's. Yet Miller and Lindwall warming up were not a pretty sight for the home side. Both bowlers were cranking up, notch by notch, as the First Test was just four weeks away. Twenty-one-year-old John Dewes was opening. The left-hander had been terrorised by Miller in the Victory Tests three years earlier when still a teenager. Miller had hit him three times in the body and the young man carried the welts for weeks and the memory forever. This time he puffed himself up with three towels as chest, hip and thigh guards, and looked like the Michelin Man as he strode to the wicket.

Miller and Lindwall tore in at him with lifting deliveries, which pushed him back. Then Miller speared in a yorker that sent Dewes' leg-stump cartwheeling. He was relieved to be over the torment, having made 6. The students stumbled to 167, and then opener Brown passed their score off his own bat, reaching 200 in Australia's 4 for 414 declared. Brown was relieved after a slow start to the tour with scores of 25, 26, 13 and 2.

The opener's fine technique seemed apt for the genteel occasion. There was nothing rustic about Bill's style and he looked every inch a top-class batsman as he stroked the ball with timing. Brown was well supported by the underrated Ron Hamence, who in contrast, was an attacking back-foot player. He showed form too, with 92. Hassett, another stylist, was happy with his 61 not out, giving him 281 without losing his wicket in two games against Cambridge over a decade apart. Among the bowlers, Miller's seven-wicket haul for the match augured well. McCool's 7 for 78 in Cambridge's second innings increased his chances of Test selection.

The only disappointment was for Harvey, who was run out for 16, on top of his scores of 12, 7, 18 not out, and 7. He was becoming concerned about his form.

•

Twenty-four-year-old Trevor Bailey, who played for Cambridge, had taken 0 for 43, and made 16 run out, and 66 not out. It was enough for selectors to pick him to play for Essex at Southend the next day. Bailey asked Australian manager Keith Johnson if he could hitch a lift in the Australian team bus for the three-hour drive, 120 km south. Bailey was astonished at the way the Australians enjoyed themselves. He wrote an article about the bus ride, saying he had just come back from the war, and had never experienced such behaviour. Australians were most 'peculiar' people.

'It amused us to read his reaction and the "war" comment,' Loxton said. 'Bailey may not have realised that a lot of us were ex-servicemen too. Perhaps he was shocked by the singing of Ron [Hamence] and Doug [Ring]. There was the odd risqué limerick.'

•

While the students were receiving cricket lessons from the tourists, Bradman back in London was fulfilling his role as Australia's uncrowned monarch in the endless round of functions he was asked to attend. Yet not all were tedious for him. Often forgotten was Bradman's job as an Adelaide stock broker. He was at home meeting big business (Imperial Chemical Industries was one host) and being greeted at the Stock Exchange. The latter's committee invited him onto the trading floor, where business stopped for him. The brokers had set up a mock pitch in the centre of the floor and he was asked to play a few strokes. One portly broker acting as W. G. Grace, replete with beard and trouser belt, bowled a red tennis ball to him. A comical game ensued and Bradman, being Bradman, hoisted the ball so high that it disappeared somewhere near the roof. He was offered a whisky and soda at the bowler's end, in the alleged tradition of Grace's era. Bradman took the drink to cheers from the crowd that gathered about him and looked out from many levels above the floor.

•

Refreshed, if not by the whisky, then the break, he returned for the sixth match – against Essex 60 km east of London, at the seaside resort of Southend. Four players chosen were unlikely to make the First Test: Hamence, Loxton, Saggers and Ring. The game began on Saturday 15 May in a carnival atmosphere in advance of the Whitsunday holiday. More than 16,000 spectators filled the ground and spilled onto the area under sunny skies. The predominant accent was Cockney in the buzz before the game began. Many East Londoners had headed for their nearest seaside resort in expectation of seeing the Australians at their peak and the local county faring better than Surrey. The players stayed at the Palace Hotel, which overlooked the long Southend pier, which had a train running along it and was advertised as 'a sea cruise without the discomforts'.

On Friday, all members of the tour group took advantage of the promenade along the sea front with its narrow strips of sand. Yachts and boats added to the picturesque setting being enjoyed by the thousands of holiday-makers, who had made their way to the resort by bike, bus, train and car. Southend was bedecked with flags, bunting, streamers and welcome signs. At night the big party atmosphere was enhanced by multi-coloured lights. The players found themselves caught in the flow of milling people in the carnival park or on the promenade. They took refuge in the fun parlours or one of the many bars, pubs and inns that festooned the foreshore. The tourists could not escape the seafood fare, and if you didn't like eels in jelly, oysters, cockles, mussels and fish, you might go hungry.

The next morning, Saturday, a most attractive start for the packed crowd was expected when Bradman won the toss and batted in lovely sunshine on an emerald field surrounded by a sparkling white picket fence. The tourists would be sure to go for their shots in keeping with the festive atmosphere surrounding them. Yet they were expected to have fair opposition from a good county bowling line-up, which a few days earlier had run through Derbyshire for just 32. Essex had four worthy bowlers: young Trevor Bailey, a fast-medium-pace swinger (who was on the verge of Test selection); Ray Smith, a containing (normally) in-swinger, who set a strong, almost leg-theory field; Peter Smith, a highly thought of leg-spinner, who had been one of *Wisden*'s Five Cricketers of the Year of 1946, and had been Doug Wright's understudy on the tour of Australia in the previous Ashes series; and Eric Price, a left-hand medium-pacer, who had transferred from Lancashire after heading its averages in 1946. The county's fifth choice was Frank Vigar, a slow-medium trundler, who had proved a useful wicket-taking change bowler.

'The intention was to give all our bats a go,' Bradman said, 'and for us to bat all day.'

Barnes, in particular, and Brown began at a terrific clip for openers, putting up the best opening stand so far of 145 in 98 minutes. Watching the ease with which the openers played, an Essex supporter said despondently to journalist Andy Flanagan:

'We'll never get Bradman out.'

'The way the openers are going,' Flanagan replied, 'you'll never get him in.'

But soon afterwards, Barnes, on 79, attempted a late cut. It was a fraction too late and when forced to hurry the shot, hit his wicket. This brought the festive crowd to their feet as they applauded Bradman. He smiled all the way to the wicket, 22 minutes before lunch.

'I remember when Bradman came in,' Brown said, 'there was a slow left-armer bowling [Vigar]. He [Bradman] danced down the wicket and made full-tosses out of each ball and hit them all for four. At the end of the over he came up to me and asked: "What does this fellow do, Bill? Does he turn them much?" None of the balls had hit the pitch.'

In the last over from Vigar before the interval he again hit four successive fours to the point boundary, and the ball hit the white picket fence in almost the same spot each time.

'Only got one shot sir?' said the keeper to Bradman, which was a fair sledge in 1948, especially to the Don.

Bradman, in his usual manner, ignored the comment. He smashed the next ball through mid-off for the fifth successive four. As he moved off for lunch, he turned to the keeper and said:

'That's another one.'

At lunch, Bradman was 42 not out off 18 deliveries.

•

After the long break, Bradman was in a destructive mood. He slammed another four fours in one over and raced to his century in 74 minutes. His easy access to the boundary made him consider he might this once break his rule about avoiding being at the wicket long enough to make a double hundred (outside the Tests, at least). At the other end, Brown maintained his touch from Cambridge and moved along steadily. With his score at 153, he had a 'hoick' at the ball and was out caught off Bailey.

Miller then came to the wicket looking apathetic after snoozing in the sun and enjoying his siesta more than the pulverising of Essex. The score was 2 for 364 after the Brown/Bradman partnership of 219 runs in 90 minutes had taken the game to just after half-way in the second session. Miller had no desire to take part in the Saturday afternoon matinee showing of *The Slaughter at Southend*. In a disappointment for the crowd, a shock for Bailey, and a surprise for Bradman up the other end, Miller walked across his wicket and let the ball hit it.

'Thank God that's over!' Miller exclaimed to the keeper, and stalked off. Lindwall, sitting in the pavilion as a spectator, thought he had simply missed the ball.

'I think it was just a case of not having his eye in,' he told Morris, who was not at the game. But Bailey, who would love to have claimed two legitimate Australian wickets in two balls, was convinced that Miller had deliberately thrown his wicket away. So was Bradman, who turned to the bowler and said: 'He'll learn.'

Miller later claimed that he surrendered his wicket on purpose. The irony of this act was that the wicket statistic went to Bailey, who would develop into an all-rounder rival for Miller. When they got to know each other's game, the Australian would never again give the Englishman (no sucker, and one of cricket's more intelligent, strong characters) such a break.

This lack of competition was not to Miller's liking. He preferred a contest and as cricket writer John Arlott observed, he looked for 'worlds to conquer, not for the already conquered lying open for exploitation.'

Miller reached the pavilion, head high, yet with an uninterested look. Perhaps he had simply disliked being disturbed from his sun-soaked reverie, or maybe there was the challenge of a pretty girl who took his fancy. Whatever the reason for his opting out, it was still an unusual act, which was never again repeated by him in first-class cricket.

Bradman's generosity was directed not to the bowlers, but the crowd, as he entertained with nothing short of a brilliant exhibition, moving to 187 in just 124 minutes of controlled, clinical destruction, hitting 32 fours in a wagon wheel of shots that had a wide spread of spokes. A two-hour spell at the wicket, with a 40-minute break, allowed him to pace himself without the fear of aggravating injuries. In his first ever game against Essex, Bradman would like to have gone on to his 38th double hundred in first-class cricket, but it wasn't to be as he missed a big cross-bat swing to leg and was bowled. Nevertheless, Essex became the 12th county against which he had scored at least a century, surpassing (Australian) Warren Bardsley's tally of hundreds against 11 counties.

Bradman's knock was up there with some of the fastest big hundreds ever played in England but still fell well short of Gilbert 'the Croucher' Jessop's 190 in just 90 minutes made in a county game in 1907. Yet this comparison should be seen in the context of their averages. Bradman's was five times that of Jessop's at Test level, and three times the Englishman's in first-class games. Bradman, pushing 40 years of age, would have been well satisfied with his capacity for the grand batting gesture. It would have given him the confidence to know that if it were necessary he would be fit enough still to deliver a massive Test score.

His effort was followed by a first tour century for Loxton, a furious big hitter (who kept up Bradman's pace with the extra attraction for the crowd of sixes), and another first-up hundred for the artistic Saggers. The latter's fine skills were in contrast to his bludgeoning partner. They added 166 in 62 minutes together at the staggering rate of three runs a minute, which was too quick for the scoreboard. The operators ran out of numbers and were often well behind the actual score.

The tail fell away in the last half hour and Australia, in 350 minutes, and 10 minutes short of scheduled stumps, reached an all-time, first-class record for a day of 721. This extraordinary tally was 58 runs more than the previous record in first-class cricket made in 1947 by Middlesex against Leicestershire.

Later the Essex skipper Tom Pearce would enter a club composed of people who had achieved a special act. His was to lead a county that dismissed the Australians in less than a day!

This merciless display sent shockwaves through the counties, and the potential England team to face Australia in a few weeks time. It was a clear indication that this was not a squad of individual champions but a team of players who could combine to achieve great deeds. The batting bonanza exhilarated Bradman himself more than anyone. He could see now the creative possibilities for this team and its capacity to achieve almost anything.

Even an entire season without a defeat.

•

Even more of the Australian team's mentality was seen on Monday when Essex batted. Miller, insouciant with the bat on Saturday, now tore in like a demon with the ball.

'Miller bowled faster and more grimly than he had done all tour,' John Arlott noted in his newspaper report of the game. 'The fielding was as a tight as in a Test Match. There was going to be no nonsense about "giving Essex a chance."'

Barnes fielded so close to the bat that he gave credence to the term 'silly' mid-on, and exemplified the pressure Bradman and his team were prepared to put on any opposition. Essex batsman Ray Smith belted Toshack for four. The ball whistled past Barnes' ear.

'That won't drive me away,' the Australian said defiantly.

In the next over from Toshack, Smith hammered a half volley straight into Barnes' foot. The ball rebounded to the boundary. Barnes, who must have been in agony, did not show it and said nothing.

The next ball, Smith smashed the ball straight at Barnes for a third time. He put up his hands. The ball burst through them into his chest, and bounced off him. Barnes stuck out a hand and grabbed the ball.

'I told you you wouldn't drive me away,' Barnes said to an incredulous Smith. Not all the Australians were as foolhardy. Barnes was later forced to have treatment for his foot and chest. But his determination, expressed perhaps in more discreet or different terms by others, was typical of the team's mentality.

Arlott was impressed by the Australians' dedication to winning for their country:

'There is no full-time professionalism [in Australia]. Many of the men making this tour are doing it at a financial loss. There are strict rules against players being accompanied by their wives, and against broadcasting and writing. They are here to play cricket and will not be diverted from that purpose.'

Arlott dubbed the difference in playing against Australia in comparison with all other nations as 'Australianism'. He dated this 'quality' as beginning at the Oval in 1882 when the tourists fought back twice after looking defeated. Arlott had been observing Australian teams since Armstrong's tour in 1921. He didn't rank the cricketers as any better than England's. The difference, he believed, was their singlemindedness as a team.

The 'unit' was never more focused than now. Miller's ferocity and Toshack's swing destroyed Essex, which stumbled to all out 83. Johnson, who was not required to bowl in Essex's first innings, took 6 for 37 in the second as the county – one short due to Bailey fielding a hot shot on Saturday and injuring a hand – was dismissed for 187. It was saved from a humiliation by captain Tom Pearce, who pushed forward at every single ball, and Peter Smith, who kept a straight bat no matter what came at him. They added 133 for the seventh wicket by applying themselves with good sense and courage.

The size of the win – by an innings and 451 – was becoming more the norm than the exception.

7

Swords Drawn at Lord's

Bradman stepped down for the third time in seven matches, and on 18 May let Hassett take the tourists the 185 kilometres west to Oxford University to play its XI at the Christ Church ground. On the road into Oxford, those in cars could see the most famous edifice in the town, the Tower of Magdalen College. Before the game, several players and journalists in the touring party were taken for a drive into High Street, where many of the colleges and their beautiful gardens were located. Choir music wafted from one of the many chapels. It was a long way from the crowded holiday at Southend, and had special charms that would make the short visit relaxing in a different way. At Oxford, the eternal village of youth, the tourists could sense the magnificence of this ancient university.

It was an inspiration, which was needed for the players to lift themselves for these games against the universities that were rarely competitive.

Hassett had the students' measure even before the game commenced. Oxford's skipper, the popular Tony Pawson, offered Hassett the choice of the heavy, medium or light rollers.

Hassett, the master of the straight face, asked:

'Haven't you got a spiked one?'

'I don't think so,' Pawson replied with the appearance of thoughtfulness. 'I'll ask our groundsman.'

This earned the Oxford captain the sobriquet 'Spike'.

The country setting in fine spring weather created an enchanting atmosphere, in which the Australians revelled. Many had country backgrounds and appreciated the break from the industrial city environs. There wasn't a block of flats or belching factory in sight. Instead there was a quaint pavilion and many spectators sitting on chairs.

Australia continued on its merry run-making way, not this time with a brute of a score as at Southend, but a big enough one – 431 – to shut the students out of any remote thoughts of an upset. Brown joined Morris in century hitting on tour with his third – 108 – and again demonstrated a technique straight out of the instruction book of Christopher Sly (*How to Score a Century*) and Bradman's *The Art of Cricket*. In fact, Brown, with his high elbow, straight bat and follow-through, could have written his own with photos that would stand up with the best of the manuals. Morris, calm and collected as ever, looked in his best form all summer until he was run out for 64. He still had not reached a peak, but two fifties and a century so far were reasonable for someone who felt that he had yet to approach his best. Loxton, with another attacking innings (of 79), was pressing his claim for a Test place, but his bowling was not strong enough to make him a threat to Miller, the leading all-rounder in the Australian ranks. The students struggled in much the same vein as their rivals at Cambridge, and were removed for 185 and 156 in yet another convincing outright win. Toshack's movement off the wicket was never mastered as he collected three wickets in each innings.

Australia's fielding, with Harvey and Loxton magnificent, was emerging as a huge asset as the tour warmed up. One incident would be remembered by cricket aficionados at the game. The students' Philip Whitcombe hit the ball to Loxton at mid-off. He moved a few yards down the wicket and stood outside his crease. Loxton shaped to throw down his wicket. Whitcombe didn't move. It was not that he was being cheeky or defiant. He had seen fielders at mid-off attempt to hit the wicket at the bowler's end. But no one, in his experience of first-class cricket, would bother hurling the ball 30 metres (from mid-off) at the batsman's wicket when he was a step and a bat stretch from safety. Loxton held back the throw and tossed the ball back to the bowler, Toshack. Toshack ran in to bowl again. Whitcombe drove the ball hard to Loxton once more, but this time, the fielder collected the ball and knocked down the stumps with Whitcombe unable to scramble back. The incredulous batsman turned to look at Loxton with a shake of the head.

It was a brilliant signal that these tourists meant business with every facet of the game at all times, against weak or powerful opposition.

•

Morris and Miller were invited to dinner by Douglas Jardine, who had watched his ancient alma mater do battle with his old enemy. The Australians enjoyed his company and found him 'charming and interesting'.

'I'd met him several times before,' Morris said, 'and we talked about everything except Bodyline. In fact, I never discussed it with him, nor, as far as I know did any of the others [Australian cricketers].'

•

Bradman, Hassett and Morris, the tourists' selection panel, sat down and chose their team for the first big 'international' of the summer, in the traditional game against Marylebone Cricket Club at Lord's.

'These meetings were harmonious and we all had a say,' Morris recalled, 'but if Bradman wanted something – a player in – or if he wished to override the roster we had for county games and, for instance, give a bowler more work, then he would. He was the captain.'

The trio came up with the likely First Test team: Barnes, Morris, Bradman, Hassett, Miller, Brown, Johnson, McCool, Tallon, Lindwall and Toshack. The top six in the order was a very strong line-up. The bowling, with leg-spin, off-spin, left-arm medium pace, and two speedsters, presented Bradman with a good range of options, which was what he always wanted. Before the war, he was never allowed such richness. He may have lost the great Bill O'Reilly with his unequalled standard of leg-spinning; but he had gained in the decade since his last visit to the UK two outstanding pacemen.

MCC presented the best opposition for the Australians so far on tour: Hutton, Robertson, Edrich, Compton, Donnelly, Yardley, Cranston, Griffith, Deighton, Laker and Young. Six, perhaps as many as eight of them, would be expected to be chosen for the First Test. The England selectors did not choose Bedser. He had loomed as the main threat to Australia with the ball and it was decided, wisely, to hold him back for the Tests. Yet they had offered up Hutton. Better, it was thought, to run him into form against the bowling he would have to conquer if England were to win.

Len Hutton was, in fact, the batsman Bradman and the Australians feared most. His iron-willed capacity for the big score was their main worry. The captain would do everything within his power and within the rules to prevent him from a repeat of his 13 hours-plus marathon innings in the Fifth Test of 1938.

It was clear that the gritty Yorkshireman (if that is not a tautology) was very much in Bradman's thoughts. One day travelling in a taxi across London, he said to Barnes:

'You know Sid, we can't afford to let Hutton get control of us. I've got an idea that if you can worry him by fielding up close, on top of his bat almost, we might rattle him. What do you think?'

Barnes, like all members of the squad, including the more rebellious Miller, would do just about anything the skipper wished.

'That's all right with me,' Barnes responded, which was both brave and foolhardy, given the thumps he had taken at silly mid-on at Southend.

'Do you mind how close you field to him?'

'Not a bit,' Barnes said, adding, 'I don't think he can knock my head off.'

Barnes was aware it was rare for Hutton to loft on the on-side, and he was not a compulsive or confident hooker, especially after a serious wartime arm injury.

'More often than not,' Barnes remarked in his book, *It Isn't Cricket*, 'he dropped to earth like a felled log when the ball was flying. He was no lover of fast bowling.'

This was more propaganda than fact, for has there ever been an opener who would relish Miller and Lindwall, or any of the lethal speed combinations coming at them? Only a fool or a liar would say he was not a little apprehensive about that leather missile soaring at the upper body at 150 km/h. Yet Barnes was just as emphatic about another factor concerning Hutton, which demonstrated how far the Australians concerned themselves with the 'mind games', or psychology in cricket.

'We knew that he very much helped our cause in the English dressing room,' Barnes remarked. 'He would paint a depressing picture of how hard it was in the middle against our fast bowlers. This, naturally, did not help the morale of those to follow.'

This may have been true. But the Australians may have been just as guilty of this. Bradman had made public his admiration for Bedser's capacity to deliver fine leg-cutters that started on leg and hit off. This would not have helped his fellow batsmen, knowing that if Bradman said he was unplayable, then what hope would they have against such brilliant bowling? Perhaps the only difference was in demeanour and timing. Bradman was never gloomy in the dressing room. Nor did he dwell on his dismissals with batsmen about to go in. He preferred to say: 'I got a good one', or 'fancy that', or even simply, 'I missed it.'

The Barnes 'in-your-face' fielding strategy was to be trialled at Lord's in the MCC game. He and Bradman judged that the dangers to a close fielder were minimal, although they would be higher if the man batting with Hutton decided that Barnes should be removed forcibly from his fielding spot.

•

Bradman loved Lord's and was invigorated whenever he entered the main gates. He had respect for the ancient ground, which was the MCC home and a leading British institution. He had played what he considered to be his finest ever Test innings of 254 there in 1930. He had also been in the last losing Australian Test side at Lord's when Hedley Verity took 15 wickets for 104 in one of the great spin bowling feats of Ashes cricket. Bradman loved the atmosphere and traditions at Lord's, with its pavilion and Long Room. The latter tested the nerve of every visitor going out to bat. Members, some perched on high chairs, would clap him politely as he clip-clopped his way on the specially designed wooden floor past the tables and through the doors to the pavilion steps. The test of character would come after making a duck and having to tiptoe back through the Long Room, often in pointed silence. Bradman dearly desired a century every time he played at Lord's on this last trip, and looked likely to achieve his aim first up when he won the toss and batted on Saturday 22 May.

The ground only held about 34,000 – the record (by 1948) was the 34,800 that were sardined into it for the 1938 Lord's Test, and it seemed nearly as tight for room in this game. The players who had not examined the arena at practice on their second day in the UK were astonished at how close the pitch seemed to the Tavern side of the ground. Many thought it was the shortest boundary they had seen in first-class cricket. It seemed to be drawn even closer by thousands of spectators being allowed to spill onto the grass near the rope. The slope on the ground was also bemusing. The common cry was, couldn't the powers-that-be level such an important showpiece of the game? The MCC could do this of course, but then the uniqueness of Lord's would be lessened. It would be like trying to establish a plausible explanation for, and then 'fixing' of the alleged 'ridge', which always seemed to affect the way the ball behaved off the deck at one end of the pitch. No self-respecting MCC president would ever countenance such sacrilege.

Lord's appeal was its eccentricity. No other cricket facility in the world harboured as much establishment stuffiness. The further ingredients of the old-father-time weather vane, members' pavilion, wrought-iron W. G. Grace Gates, and the more public 'Tavern' added to its character. Throw in the slope, lopsidedness, dip and ridge, not to forget the amazing cricketing deeds over 170 years, and this in part explains its individuality.

•

Morris fell lbw to Edrich for 5, and this brought Bradman to the wicket early to lusty applause. He and Barnes, who had a good understanding at the wicket, settled in for a long, strong partnership. Bradman looked set for his usual 100, but to everyone's shock, including his own, at 98 he edged one from John Deighton to Edrich in slips. The master batsman appeared to linger at the pitch in disbelief. It was very unlike him to miss such an opportunity. In fact, it was the closest to a hundred he had ever come in first-class cricket without going on with it, although he was not immune to dismissal in this nervous strip between 90 and 99. In 338 first-class innings for his entire career he had gone down in the nineties on five occasions including this last one at Lord's. On another 117 occasions (for his entire career) he had pushed through the century barrier. Bradman's momentary hesitation at the crease, after clearly being caught, would have been more surprise than disappointment. His capacity to will himself a score on such an occasion had rarely deserted him, especially if he managed to survive the first half hour when all his keen calibration of length, swing and pace off the wicket were not perfect. Perhaps this was an indicator that Bradman of 1948 was not the great Don of the 1930s. (It reminds me of him much later in life being depressed that his golf was not what it had once been after his stroke in late 1995. With such gifts at hitting a spherical object, he was most unhappy when the inevitable fall off of his game occurred in his last five years. Despite this, he still won his club's handicap event at age 88, and could regularly score under his age.)

Yet he was hardly out of touch. His run of scores so far in England was 107, 81, 146, 187 and 98. Since the beginning of the year, he could add 132, 127 not out, 201, 57 not out (all against India in Tests), and 115 for an Australian XI in Perth en route to England. This amounted to 10 successive scores over fifty, with six centuries and a double hundred. Of course, there was not the sparkle and adventure of youth. Bradman was loath to stay at the wicket for too long, but there were hardly any signs of decline in terms of his incredible run productivity. He had an older, wiser head now, and this compensated to a fair degree for the lost suppleness of youth.

His supreme self-confidence remained. He was buoyed by the reception he was having everywhere in England, and the fine form of, and prospects for, his team in this MCC contest, the eighth for the season.

The only sour note on day one at Lord's occurred when Lord Tennyson arrived at the Australian dressing room after Bradman was out and watching his team pile on the runs. An attendant told him Tennyson was at the door and wished to see him.

'I wouldn't oblige him, if I were you sir,' the attendant added, 'he has been drinking rather heavily, I would say.'

Bradman told the attendant to tell Tennyson he (Bradman) was indisposed. Tennyson took it as a snub, and later rang and complained to some of his press contacts in London and Sydney, without telling them that he was inebriated at the time. The next day, Sunday, several stories appeared speaking of Bradman's 'needless brusqueness and lack of tact.'

It was just the sort of item the press wanted. Journalists, news desks and editors had become sick of all the positive stories about the tourists – or 'Bradlines' – as they were called. Newspapers wanted controversy, something to shock and tarnish the Australians' image, and maybe upset their smooth path to the Ashes series.

A drunken Lord was as good a vehicle as any.

Bradman was more concerned with the touch of his players. Barnes, workmanlike and attacking, and Hassett, delicate in timing and precision stroke-making, also hit good half-centuries. These efforts, along with a power-laden century from Miller, allowed Bradman to instruct his team to let loose on Monday morning after a wet break day, Sunday. First Miller, and then Lindwall and Johnson, with even more gay abandon and heaving, cracked the England spinners to all parts of Lord's.

Miller was transported back to the Victory Tests and the England versus Dominions game of 1945 in which he let loose like a cannon in the 1812 Overture. Lord's had been his playground from 1943 until mid-1945, when not on war pilot duty for the RAF, he played for the RAAF and rose to be the best and most enterprising batsman in the UK. This 163 was a reminder that he could deliver at a high standard and would do so, if he were not called upon to bowl too much. These high-energy, sustained big innings required stamina and freshness of mind so that errors were minimised.

Twelve mighty sixes were smote in the morning session. Tavern spectators were forced to do more dodging of leather bullets than elbow raising as Miller, Johnson (80), and Lindwall (29 not out) wrought mayhem. Off-spinner Jim Laker, a likely Test candidate, was given horrific treatment. This would either be seared into his memory and destroy his career, or would be put down to experience and stored for later remedies, or reprisals. The Australian bats craved the ball turning in to them. It allowed them to hit with the spin. Traditionally, antipodean batsmen preferred this to the leg-spinner, who could move the ball away. The exception was the champion off-spinner. Laker was not one, yet.

Australia powered to another big score – 552 – and sapped England's spirit. Miller and Lindwall opened with hostility in the hope of securing a further advantage over Hutton, but he defended grimly. Instead, Miller removed Jack Robertson and Edrich cheaply. Yet it was the irritatingly vocal (to the England bats) Toshack who did the real damage. He ripped through the line-up with his leg-stump line to take 6 for 51 after bowling non-stop for 27 overs in just over three hours. His battle with the dashing Compton, the biggest danger batsman to Australia after Hutton, was worth the entrance fee alone. It ended with Toshack delivering an away-swinger that Compton was lured into chasing. Tallon dived to his right across the slips fielders and held a superb catch, which demonstrated that the keeper was running into form too.

It was clear that England's second and third star bats – Compton and Edrich – had been lulled into a false sense of superiority after plundering county attacks for record numbers of runs and centuries in the previous season. Up against class, they were found out for loose shot-making. Techniques needed tightening to face the Australian bowling line-up, brilliant fielding and astute captaincy. It all added up to a shock for the British press and public.

Barnes, as planned, fielded devilishly close to Hutton and the other batsmen. There was some controversy about whether he put a foot on the pitch itself.

'Hutton said nothing to me,' Barnes said, 'and he didn't look at me. But I could see his dislike in his face. He preferred his own hand in his pocket and not mine.'

Barnes was aware that umpire Frank Chester was watching him closely. Regarded as an umpire who liked to be recognised, even on occasions to be the showman at the centre of attention, Chester would love to have caught Barnes with his foot on the pitch. The umpire would have warned him and this would have created a sensational news item. Barnes, being Barnes, decided to have some fun with the umpire, by facing him and lifting a left toe as if he were about to place his foot on the pitch as the bowler came in.

'Chester began to stop the bowler,' Barnes noted, 'and I quickly turned back and placed my toe well clear of the pitch.'

Barnes reckoned that all the batsman were uncomfortable with him literally under their noses. Judging his reckless positioning as 'good nuisance value', he decided to field this way to all the opposition for the rest of series, if he could.

•

Hutton may have been concerned, but his dismissal had nothing to do with Barnes, and he acquitted himself very well, given the intensity of the opposition, with 52 and 64. He top-scored in both innings and looked on this occasion to be in a class of his own. Compton, Edrich and Robertson were themselves top-line batsmen, but they all struggled in both innings, especially against the pace attack. Hutton's performance, however defensive and unimaginative, gave him confidence, although the Tests still promised to be an ordeal for him. Miller and Lindwall were pacing themselves towards the First Test – now 16 days but still four matches away. They both aimed to peak in that game, especially Lindwall, who was a planner. Miller was more spontaneous and basic, even whimsical in his approach. He would simply decide to lift his rating on the actual day. These two intimidators were good mates, yet so different. Both had been shaped as characters by war, which at times had been achingly nerve-racking in different ways. They counted themselves lucky to survive. Miller was airborne for a lot of the time in Mosquito fighter planes, which were made of wood. He had so many hair-raisingly close shaves with death that a term arose during the war that everyone in the RAAF and RAF had heard of: *Miller's luck*. Those experiences left him with a nervous disposition that translated on the field to some of the most blistering moments with bat and ball in the history of the game. They were bursts – adrenaline rushes – in keeping with his war interlude. Lindwall was in New Guinea in Signals, and saw little action, although he was in Port Moresby when it was bombed by the Japanese. He had the unenviable job of night guard duty when the enemy was raiding Australian camps. It was still a tough war, and he made light of the dangers, saying that the 'nearest I came to serious injury' was from a wasp sting in the eye. He was also weakened by tropical dengue fever and malaria. Lindwall's war then had more of a dulling experience on his nervous system, and perhaps because of this, and his natural make-up, he was a more taciturn, laconic individual.

It followed that these two types of men were different propositions for Hutton to face. Miller would bowl steadily for a while and then would suddenly deliver a nasty bouncer, or quicker away-swinger that would leave a batsman floundering. Lindwall possessed another kind of menace. The batsman never quite knew what was coming. His armoury included the most lethal of short balls. It was delivered with a more round-arm action and would soar at the throat. Lindwall's trick, whether intentional or not, was to use it sparingly. Always in the back of the batsman's mind was that it could be coming any moment. He was also one of the finest ever exponents of the yorker. He clean-bowled a lot of his victims with it. It was used a little more than the short ball, but was still a surprise weapon. Hutton, therefore, had to deal with two contrasting types of temperaments, who allowed no respite. Even off the field they were contrasts in personality. Miller would happily engage Hutton at a reception, whereas Lindwall could be surly and uncommunicative. Once at a function, Hutton asked Miller to tell Lindwall he wanted to chat with him. Lindwall responded with a dismissive expletive. He didn't wish to make contact.

It was Lindwall who suggested the 'freeze' for a batsman coming to the wicket. He would not look at him or pass any comment or pleasantry. It was a psychological ploy to unhinge a batsman. This often worked for 'Atomic' Ray as he was known. His entry into international cricket coincided more or less with the era of atomic bomb development, and Lindwall was regarded as a lethal bowling weapon to batsmen worldwide.

Bradman favoured him too. He knew how to draw the best from him.

•

The MCC rolled over for just 189, and Bradman again enforced the follow-on. In another insipid display, the game was over before lunch on the third day when the MCC struggled to 205, giving Australia another big innings win. It allowed Bradman to make a considered assessment of where his team stood after eight matches of the arduous tour. He often spoke like a pessimist, acted like a pragmatist, and never considered a game or series won or lost until a whole choir of overweight women were singing. Yet he left Lord's confident his team could 'more than hold our own' against anything England could produce.

Translated, this was captain-speak for a strong feeling Australia could win the Ashes.

8

—

Run to the Ashes

BEFORE THE COMMENCEMENT of the series, the tourists still had to negotiate four counties en route to the First Test at Trent Bridge, Nottingham. The tour selectors had more or less settled on nine players – Bradman, Hassett, Morris, Barnes, Lindwall, Miller, Johnson, Tallon, Brown and Toshack. There would be a raffle for the last two spots, which would go to the players who managed to burst through in the run-up games.

Match nine was to be played 300 km north-west of London against strong Lancashire at Old Trafford, Manchester. There was much interest among the tourists in this venue, which would stage the Third Test. The Luftwaffe's penchant for bombing the city was evident in the damaged pavilion and some of the stands, which had yet to undergo renovation. One structure seemed to have been blasted out of existence.

Old Trafford was one of the few grounds where the pavilion ran parallel with the pitch. This allowed sightscreens to be used at both ends, which was sometimes a luxury in England, even at some Test match arenas. The light here was good too. The steady march of industry and business had not yet encircled the ground, although there were threats of this encroachment judging from the number of cranes on the skyline of Manchester's heart, which was 5.5 km away.

Five thousand hardy fans sat in the rain and cold as the Australians gathered around the wicket on the first day. It was agreed that it appeared like a shot-maker's playground. Cyril Washbrook, the Test opener, would attest to this. He had developed his hook and square cut here to profitability. But that was theory on 26 May, which was rained off. The loyal Lancastrians waited until the lunchtime announcement that there would be no play and then trooped off without complaint.

How the wicket would play on a sunny second morning was anyone's guess. Lancashire's Ken Cranston won the toss, put the Australians in on a pitch drying out in the sun, and set a defensive field, which seemed to defeat the purpose of bowling first. Yet while he was cautious, he showed some lateral thinking by bringing on a left-arm finger spinner of the Hedley Verity variety, Malcolm Hilton.

As Cranston was setting the field, a spectator yelled:

''Ere, Cranston, you've got the lad at the wrong end!'

Then someone else called:

'Leave Ken alone, he's a dentist, not a proctologist!'

The fair-haired, 19-year-old Hilton had barely made the side for the first time but managed to remove Barnes, Bradman and Johnson cheaply on a wicket that was conducive to his nicely floated turners from around the wicket. Bradman's wicket grabbed the headlines. It was his first dismissal under 50 in 1948. He played a cut, deflected the ball onto the stumps and was out for 11. The 'story' was irresistible: 'Teenager Debutant Snares Bradman'.

Hilton was made a superstar overnight, with every newspaper running the story, mostly on the front page. Australia crumbled for 204, despite a neat partnership between Loxton (39), still with groin trouble, and Harvey (36). This was Harvey's best knock and came after some very basic coaching advice from Bradman. Harvey had been worried about his form, and requested Loxton to ask Bradman what he (Harvey) was doing wrong. The teenager had been reluctant to approach the captain himself.

Loxton saw 'George', (Bradman's second Christian name), as he called the skipper, and came back to Harvey with an observation:

'George says to keep the ball on the ground.'

'What?' Harvey said. 'That's it?'

'Yep. George reckons your technique is fine. If you don't loft anything you minimise your chances of getting out.'

Harvey was bemused. But Bradman's words, as ever, were carefully chosen. He had a high regard for Harvey's skills and felt he had no weaknesses at all against spin or pace. Bradman believed little in coaching for players who had reached Test level, other than providing basics about how to use skills in certain environments, such as when he advised McCool how to play his strokes on slower English wickets. Bradman felt that it was futile for him to tamper with Harvey's style, especially when it was faultless. The directive to 'keep the ball along the ground' was calibrated to make Harvey concentrate on the basics. It had just about worked in the first innings.

Johnston made a late bid for Test selection by taking 5 for 49 in the county's modest 182. Bradman came to the wicket in the second innings after a double failure for Morris, and he moved swiftly to 43. Cranston brought Hilton on and stacked his off-side. Bradman tried to thrash him on the on-side, was beaten three times and finally stumped after a wild swing that left him in an undignified heap on the pitch. This was an anomaly for Bradman's behaviour at the wicket. No great batsman was as vanity-free. His self-restraint was unmatched, even if he had smashed two or three fours in succession, or even one of his 44 sixes in first-class cricket. He would not get carried away with a rush of blood. Instead, he would calibrate his response to the following deliveries purely on their merit; whether or not they were hittable. To see him having three successive swings and misses was a surprise. He would often have a go and throw his wicket away at the end of an innings, but never when he was constructing one. The only time Bradman had done this previously mid-innings was during Australia's second innings of the Adelaide (Third) Test of the Bodyline series when facing Hedley Verity, by coincidence or otherwise, the finest exponent ever of Hilton's bowling style. Bradman had been dismissed by Larwood in the first innings for just 8. Australia was chasing 532 for victory. Opener and captain Woodfull was in and prepared to put his body behind every Larwood delivery for as long as it took to win. Bradman came to the wicket at 2 for 12. He batted brilliantly and hit his nemesis Larwood out of the attack. Jardine brought on Verity. Bradman, 'pumped' after this personal victory over Larwood, pulled the spinner for two successive fours, then hoed into him with a heave for six over mid-on. This was his first ever six in 12 Ashes Tests. It took Australia to 100, still 432 short of victory. He had hit 66 at better than a run a ball in an 88-run stand with Woodfull. The adrenaline pump continued. Bradman stepped down the wicket to belt Verity again and hit the ball straight back to the bowler for a caught and bowled.

After that, Australia collapsed for 193 – 339 short of victory. Woodfull carried his bat to be 73 not out and never forgave Bradman for his impetuosity. He was the one player capable of scoring a big double or even triple hundred under the circumstances. Now, 15 years on, in far less demanding circumstances that were in no way critical, here was Bradman again looking like a batting profligate against a relative novice left-arm spinner. Back in the dressing room, he had a good laugh over his comical batting ballet, knowing he had erred. He was human, after all.

The roar from the crowd when he was stumped was matched by a feverish response from the press. There were immediate demands for Hilton's inclusion in the Test side. But this was unlikely. His five wickets for 135 for the match was not world shattering, although his raw talent was obvious. Cooler heads would prevail among Lancashire officials, who were not influenced by press overreaction. They did not even have plans for him to be a regular player, which partly mystified Bradman. In his private notes, he agreed it would be folly for England to choose such an inexperienced bowler for a pressure Test in good conditions. But he regarded Hilton as talented; a player to be supported and encouraged, and not treated as a week-to-week proposition, who would be made to feel insecure about his place in the county side.

Australia managed 4 for 259 in some useful batting practice in the second innings and the game ended in a tame draw. Harvey managed a sweet cameo of 76 not out on the still turning wicket and hardly lifted a delivery off the turf. Top form seemed close. (Harvey regarded this innings as the turning point for him in 1948. It was his first fifty for the season.) Loxton went after Hilton in a bright fifty. Ron Hamence, perhaps the unluckiest member of the tour group, played handsomely for his 49 not out. Yet the well-equipped batsman would have trouble breaking into the powerful Australian line-up.

Bradman came away from the game buoyant and pleased with the form of Harvey, and Johnston, who was offering another strong option with the ball. Morris's touch was the only concern. But he would have at least two more games of the three remaining before the Tests to lift his rating.

•

The captain wished to step down again from duties at Nottingham, 110 km south-east of Manchester, in the 10th match, but pleas from local officials caused him to change his mind. The Trent Bridge ground as a cricket venue was the brainchild of an enterprising bricklayer, William Clarke, who stepped up in the world by marrying the owner of the Trent Bridge Inn, Mary Chapman, in 1837. He created the ground on the flat land behind the Inn and next to the River Trent. The venue grew from there. In the next 130 years it became Nottinghamshire County's ground and developed a solid history.

Stands were built to encircle and capture the deeds of the game's giants.

Bradman had made two centuries in three Test appearances at Nottingham and hoped to make a third in the Test beginning in 11 days time. For now it was a useful hit-out, which would familiarise the players with the surrounds. A crowd of just under 27,000 – not far off capacity – filled the ground for day one on 29 May and made it close enough to a Test match atmosphere.

Lindwall bowled at top speed for the first time in England, taking six Notts wickets cheaply, three with spearing yorkers, in 15 overs of terror bowling. He conceded no runs in his last five overs, and only 14 overall. This sort of form put Lindwall into a class of his own. He was one of those select group of cricketers (including Trumper, Bradman, O'Reilly, Morris, Harvey, Greg Chappell, Lillee, Warne, McGrath, Gilchrist and Ponting for Australia; and Grace, S. F. Barnes, Hobbs, Hammond, Verity, Bedser, Hutton, Trueman, Statham, Knott and Botham for England), who, if transported forward or back 100 years in time, would still be dominant.

Lindwall's style and success had plenty of the tongues wagging in the terraces. Many of the locals remembered one of Nottingham's favourite sons, Harold Larwood, when watching the Australian.

When one spectator near the fence challenged Lindwall with the call:

'You've copied Larwood!'

Lindwall was unfazed when he called back:

'And why not? He was the master!'

At age 11, Lindwall first saw Larwood bowling at Sydney in the First Bodyline Test in late 1932. He went home after the game, lined up the rubbish tins in his street and charged at them copying the Notts champion's smooth run and delivery. He never changed and only refined his technique in Sydney club cricket less than a decade later.

Lindwall's verve at Nottingham brought a smile to his captain's lips.

'You could see his great rhythm building even in the nets,' Bradman recalled. 'He was working into good condition.'

Only Reg Simpson (74 runs), an Ashes prospect, and Joe Hardstaff Jr (48), an experienced Test player, showed timely resistance, as the home team collapsed to sheer pace for 179. The taller, younger Simpson had the same fluency and style as Hardstaff.

•

Hardstaff was a veteran, who Bradman and Hassett remembered only too well from the Oval Test of 1938 for his 215 partnership with Hutton, and his own effort of 169 unconquered. He was aged 27 then and could have expected a stellar career for another decade at least. Here he was a decade on, doing well against a testing international attack. Hardstaff demonstrated how hungry he was straight after the war at age 35 in the first Test of the first post-war Test series – against India at Lord's – scoring 205 not out in 315 minutes of top-class batting. This was as good as it could be for the upright, experienced right-handed attacker.

•

The Australians continued to receive red carpet treatment from the British establishment that couldn't get enough of them. Bradman had more invitations than he could cope with. In the Sunday break this time, he and his team were entertained by the Duke and Duchess of Portland at Welbeck Abbey. This was one invitation Bradman would not turn down. When recuperating after a life-threatening illness in 1934, he and his wife Jessie stayed at the Abbey as guests of the Duke's father. Bradman was surprised to hear the Duke say that when he died his son would not be able to pay for the upkeep of the Abbey. This was symptomatic of the landed gentry across the UK after the war. The last of feudal England had been brought undone by the prolonged and costly conflict and its political aftermath.

'If the [British] people as a whole are benefiting [from social and economic change],' Bradman wrote in his book *Farewell to Cricket*, 'one cannot complain, though I cannot escape the feeling that I had witnessed the passing of a traditional element of English life.'

Bradman missed the irony of the Duke taking him and his team for a bus drive through Sherwood Forest, the home of the legendary Robin Hood, who, myth has it, robbed the rich to give to the poor. This was rather like the philosophy of the ruling Labour Party, which was causing some of the dislocation of the social structure, and the redistribution of wealth in the Britain of 1948 by taxing the asset rich.

'He [Robin Hood] was a bit of a hoodlum who robbed,' the Duke remarked dryly to Bradman as they inspected the Forest, which had been largely sacrificed for the war effort. Much of the timber had been felled and regrowth was expected to take time.

As if to exemplify the Duke's financial plight, they came to a closed gate. The Duke got out and knocked on the nearby cottage. An old pensioner hobbled to the front door.

'What about opening the gate?' the Duke asked politely enough.

'And what about you puttin' in a pane of glass in my window like you promised,' came the hostile response.

'Terribly sorry,' the Duke replied. 'Will have it attended to straightaway.'

The disgruntled old fellow then opened the gate for the bus. The Duke slipped back on board.

The tourists had heard the exchange, and were amused.

'Bit of a pain, really,' the Duke mumbled, which drew a laugh.

•

Australia's response to Nottingham was 400, with Bill Brown collecting his fourth century, Bradman a brisk 86, and Miller a stylish 51. Morris's run of low scores continued, and opportunities were dwindling for him to run into form. In Notts' second innings, Hardstaff became the first player to score a century against the tourists. His partnership again with Simpson (70) allowed the county to stave off defeat at 8 for 299.

Bradman once more refrained from comment at the time, but in his diary of the tour noted that Simpson was 'definitely, in our minds, a future England batsman'.

But were the England selectors watching and of the same opinion?

•

There was one setback for the Australians. Bradman gave McCool plenty of work with the ball, believing he was still a likely selection for the First Test. Unfortunately, his spinning finger (third on the right hand) split open. This was a common problem for spinners of his 'leggie' type. The constant friction of ball on skin developed calluses, which would sometimes be torn off, exposing raw flesh and causing bleeding. Cricketers down the decades had this problem. There was no solution but to let the wound heal and another callus form. (A solution was discovered nine years later by leg-spinner Richie Benaud, who had the same problem. A pharmacist in Timaru, New Zealand, told him to rub oily calamine lotion into his wounds, and then to add boracic acid powder to make a waxy filling. It had worked on New Zealand servicemen from World War II and the Korean War, who had leg ulcers. This method worked for Benaud too.) The injury looked likely to rule poor McCool out of contention for the initial Test selection. This left the race wide open for another bowler, who had a chance to emerge in the remaining two games against Hampshire and Sussex.

•

Accordingly, the selectors chose Doug Ring and Bill Johnston in the team for the next match at Southampton, 300 km south of Nottingham, against Hampshire, yet another county rich in cricket history with its Broadhalfpenny Down, where games had been played for centuries. Most famously, the Down was the playground of 'Hambledon men', especially in the late 18th Century when Hambledon was the strongest club in the UK. Locals claimed the Down was the 'Cradle of Cricket', which was romantic but chronologically and geographically awry. The myth built and tradition remaining from those heady days was described by writer John Nyren:

'There was high feasting held on Broad-Halfpenny Down during the solemnity of one of our grand matches . . . How those brawn-faced fellows of farmers would drink to our success. And, then, what stuff they had to drink! Punch – that would make a cat speak . . . Ale that would flare like turpentine . . . then the quantity the fellows would eat. Two or three of them would strike dismay into a round of beef.'

There were many descendants of the 'brawn-faced' fellows in the modest mid-week house at the less romantic but far more comfortable Southampton on Wednesday 2 June. And plenty of their forebears would have been at the ground in 1934 when a full house of 15,000 on a Saturday watched the Australians. Fourteen years on, the locals so much wanted to see their beloved county team become the first to defeat the tourists.

Bradman, pacing himself (and perhaps thinking he had been there, done that at Hampshire, with scores of 191, 0 and 145 not out in his three previous tours) opted out of the match. Hassett inspected the wicket, which was wet but drying out fast, and decided to send the opposition in. He had played at Hampshire in 1938 when the pitch was slow. It would break up as the match progressed. Since the war, it had been grassy, with a tendency to improve for the batsmen by the final day. Aware that recent history suggested it was safe to bat last, Hassett took that option.

Johnston seized his chance. He bowled his left-arm medium-pacers with pinpoint accuracy for all but four overs from one end, taking 6 for 74. He delivered 38.4 overs with 14 maidens, while his main rival for a Test spot – fellow Victorian Ring – only had seven overs and took 1 for 19. Barring miracles, in the selectors' collective mind, Johnston was in the Test line-up. Hampshire's 40-year-old opener, John Arnold, resisted well and as he approached 50 (runs, not years) looked likely to repeat his fine feat of 1934, when he hit 109 not out against Woodfull's Australians. But Loxton came on for just three overs and bowled him for 48, which led to the county crumbling for 195.

Australia was 2 for 54 at stumps with Brown (0) and Barnes (20) dismissed. Hassett was in with Miller and there seemed to be no alarms. But the bells began ringing the next morning when the team fell apart like an old Buck Rogers pocket-knife (fashionable in 1948) against the off-spin of Charlie Knott and left-arm orthodox finger spin of James Bailey.

The farmers enjoyed the show. Some of them were already well primed for a lunchtime visit to the local pub to cause some dismay for a round of beef, and ale. Eight tourists went down for an additional 63 in just 85 minutes. It would have been a lot less but for Miller, who was often an inspiration in these panic moments. He had one of his war-derived adrenaline rushes, and went into overdrive with three thumping sixes off Knott, who curled the ball into him nicely for his swings to leg. In one smash, Miller let go of the bat with his right hand and ended up with his torso twisted, corkscrew fashion. To the uninitiated this would have looked like an agricultural shot. But he always had control and often ended in this pose. The farmers loved it. His 39 saved face for the tourists before Knott had his revenge and bowled Miller when he was going for one too many lusty blows.

Australia was all out for 117 – 78 short and enough for those alarm bells to be heard all the way to London and the Piccadilly Hotel where Bradman was 'relaxing'. The news was about as soothing as the big dipper at Luna Park for the captain. He regretted stepping down for a fourth time in 11 games. Bradman sent an urgent telegram to Hassett:

'Bradford was bad enough but this is unbearable, heads up and chins down.'

Hassett was tempted to send back a reply:

'Your orders carried out, but many jaws and necks broken.'

Bradman observed that the last part of his telegram may have presented a problem, but his attitude was understood. Hassett conveyed the Orwellian orders from Number One to the troops. Miller revelled in this tight situation and turned it on with the ball. He tore in from one end and proved the perfect partner for the steady Johnston. They both took five wickets, giving Johnston 11 for 117 for the match. He could do no more than that, and without knowing it, had cemented his place in the Test team. Arnold was the rock for Hampshire once more, scoring 43 out of the paltry return for the county of 103.

Australia was left with a target of 182 for victory. It had to bat again just before lunch on day three. The spinners opened with the new ball on a turning wicket. Knott removed Barnes lbw for a duck. Australia was 1 for 3 at the long break. Bradman heard the score and feared the worst. Hassett promoted fellow Victorian Johnson for the next session. Brown, who was having a productive tour that already bordered on the prolific, remained steady at one end while Johnson opened up with the blade. He pulled out a range of attacking strokes to take the game away from hopeful Hampshire with a dashing cameo of 74. Brown remained 81 not out as he and Hassett steered the Australians home to an eight-wicket win.

Bradman, back in his London bunker, breathed easily again.

After 11 games and a third of the tour gone, his dream of an unbeaten tour was still alive but decidedly uncertain.

9
—

Battle for the Last Spot

W HILE THE AUSTRALIANS struggled for a while at Southampton, England played 'The Rest,' virtually a Second XI, at wet and cold Birmingham from 2–4 June. England fielded close to a full-strength side, in batting order: Washbrook, Robertson, Edrich, Yardley, Compton, Hardstaff, C. J. Barnett, Godfrey Evans, Bedser, Wright and J. A. Young. The Rest was: Fishlock, A. E. Fagg, Simpson, Palmer, G. M. Emmett, Cranston, V. Broderick, S. C. Griffith, Robins, H. J. Butler and W. H. Copson.

This composition of The Rest partly reflected performances against the Australians, especially those of Laurie Fishlock, who 'carried his bat' for Surrey; Reg Simpson, who batted well in both innings for Notts, and Charles Palmer, who so impressed in the first game at Worcester. Bradman's mate Robins was a strange choice, although at one point he was being touted and rumoured to captain England, especially as Yardley's lumbago was playing up.

Sadly for England, and especially the challengers among The Rest, the weather didn't allow a stand-out performance that would have impressed the selectors enough to force selection in the First XI. Fishlock was a case in point. He opened and had his innings interrupted five times by rain in scoring a creditable 35 but in the slow time of 150 minutes. Only Griffith with 38 not out did better for The Rest. Simpson and Palmer made low scores, as did Robins, which solved nothing for the national selectors.

Bedser and Wright, in the conditions, did well for England, taking four wickets each. Robertson needed a century but managed 41 to make a bid for a step-up, while Edrich's 72 (top score) only confirmed his fine season so far. The one positive for England in the wash up (an appropriate cliché here with rain playing such a part), was Yardley's fine 46. It meant he was fit for the Test. Robins would have needed a century, and to have taken some wickets, if he were to force himself over Yardley for a tilt at Bradman.

Robins was bowled for 5, and he didn't roll his arm over at all. The selectors didn't discover much they didn't know, except that Palmer could bowl. He had Edrich caught for 72. Bill Copson of Derbyshire seemed an odd selection. He was a veteran, but could still bowl fast-medium. He proved awkward for England, dismissing Washbrook (4), Yardley and Compton (0) for 39 runs and not much meaning. He had little hope of opening the bowling for his country at age 40.

John Arlott bemoaned the exclusion of Worcester's slow left-armer Dick Howorth, who had not done anything exceptional in his chance against Australia in April when he dismissed Barnes and Brown for 109 runs off 38 overs. Howorth won himself a Test spot in the Oval Test in the previous season against South Africa, when he took three wickets in each innings.

'He had suffered on the West Indies tour [completed in April 1948] from being fit,' Arlott observed in his book *Gone to the Test Match*. 'With many other players unfit he had bowled too many overs in the heat, and returned tired to the damp English spring.'

This suggested that Howorth's Test career would have been extended by being unfit.

The only conclusion to draw from the game was that the selectors had chosen the strongest XI to represent England except for the exclusion of Bedser, and Hutton, who was making heaps of runs for Yorkshire. One hit-out before the Test on 29 and 31 May against Sussex saw him score an unbeaten 176 not out. Prior to that he had notched 72, 100 not out, 100 and 20. Against the Australians were those two gallant half centuries for the MCC, and his two failures – 5 and 11 – for Yorkshire. Hutton was in formidable touch. He could not have been better prepared for the Nottingham Test.

•

Bradman was driven down to Brighton for the match at adjoining Hove beginning 5 June versus Sussex, the last game for his team before the Tests. The ground was a short walk from the grand Regency buildings and the sea front, with its rock and pebble beach, which bemused the Australians, who were used to golden sands. Those who did venture into the water so early in June were surprised at how cold it was.

Brighton's cricket zenith had occurred in the early 19th Century, with first-class games beginning in W. G. Grace's peak years from 1872, a year after they moved to the present Hove site, a former barley field on the Sandford Estate.

One of Sussex's most famous 'sons' was Indian Ranjitsinhji, a descendant from Rajput stock, who brought Eastern magic to Sussex, Cambridge University, England and wherever he played. Ranji's name adorns one of the scoreboards, and with good reason. He once scored two centuries in one day against Yorkshire.

Comparable feats had been frequent. More often than not Hove presented a wicket where the ball came through at a good pace and height. Ranji's nephew Duleepsinhji hit 333 in a day at Hove against Northamptonshire in 1930. Locals told the Australians about the amazing performance by a chap called Alletson from Notts in the 1920s. He hammered 189 in 90 minutes, with the last 89 coming in 15 minutes after lunch. Old-timers put this rapid rate of scoring down to the marvellous food and drink provided by the Hove caterers. In 1948 they were still an attraction for Bradman's team and its swelling entourage of journalists and followers. The caterers worked overtime at the north, or 'aristocratic' end – away from the sea – where there were marquees used by the Brighton Social Club and local dignitaries, the deckchair enclosure and parked cars, which included a few Rolls-Royces. This was the 'posh' end also because it gave the spectator a sense of superiority looking down a slope that dipped an extraordinary 6 metres end to end.

The Australians, coming 150 km east from Southampton, found the Hove ground's west-side pavilion like a maze with hidden corners and stairways. They managed to find their way to the middle in the fine weather for the beginning of the county's innings. And no sooner had they begun it, than it was in danger of being over, thanks to Lindwall. With the breeze at his back, he steamed in with that smooth, Larwoodian run. Without reaching top pace, he knocked back the off-stumps of five batsmen in his haul of 6 for 34. The Sussex bats appeared mesmerised by Lindwall's length and varied pace.

There were high hopes for Hugh Bartlett, who hit a century in 57 minutes against Bradman's 1938 team. But there was no Lindwall to trouble him then. It was clear from the way the bowler pawed the ground as Bartlett took block that the Australians were waiting for him. The batsman scratched around for 8 runs before Lindwall sent his off-stump cartwheeling with his only super-fast ball of the match.

Loxton rushed in with his usual aggressive look from the other end but was more steady than menacing in picking up three useful wickets in the county's submissive score of 86. He was another player now with an outside chance of Test selection.

After the Hampshire horrors, normal service was resumed with the Australians piling up a massive first innings score of 5 declared for 549. Bradman was happy with his own form as he delivered a typically masterful hundred at a run a minute with 12 fours. He was thrilled with the terrific innings by the two left-handers, Morris and Harvey. Morris batted as if he were unaware of his recent slump in composing 184 and a wonderful wagon-wheel full of 26 fours.

After disembarking in England and hitting the ground running at Worcester with 138, Morris had been less than satisfied with scores of 17, 3, 65, 26, 64, 5, 22 and 5. Some in the Australian journalists' camp were quick to carp about his technique. Jack Fingleton, a former Test opener, wrote of Morris's 'double shuffle' to the ball. But Bradman supported Morris, saying his methods had brought him this far, and he should continue with them. Even Bradman had a slump – once on the 1934 Ashes tour when he was retarded by a mystery illness. Then his average fell back to 57 for the first half of the tour, when it would normally have sat around 100. He hit his way out of it with a big score in much the same way Morris did at Sussex.

At this point, Hassett was helpful to Morris, advising him to go for his shots.

'It meant me moving my feet,' Morris reflected, 'and it more or less did the trick.'

Harvey too emerged from his shell with what Bradman saw as a 'brilliant' unbeaten 100. The skipper noted that he would be 'knocking very hard at the door for Test selection'.

This was Harvey's best performance so far. (He later judged it as his best innings for the tour outside the Tests.)

Lindwall, with another haul of five wickets, destroyed Sussex again. Only opener Henry Parks with 61 held back another complete collapse, yet still the seaside team was sent off early to the beach for just 138. The result was another lopsided victory by an innings and so many runs that Sussex could probably have been put back in for another three innings without passing Australia's first-innings tally.

Lindwall had been nursed perfectly by Bradman, who choose him for just two-thirds of the pre-Test games, giving him only light work in the first six of them, and not urging him to bowl flat-out. In Lindwall's last two games against Nottingham and Sussex he cranked up to full pace, especially in the last game when he sent down 34.4 overs. The returns of 11 wickets for 59 spoke for themselves.

The tourists had played 12 matches for 10 wins and two draws. They had two scares at Bradford and Southampton on wet, difficult tracks. But that apart, this 1948 Australian squad was at least extraordinarily good, and at best, something else.

•

Bill Johnston's consistent top form saw him selected in the last remaining slot in the Australian line-up for the First Test, but not until the selectors took the weather into account on the evening of the game. Leg-spinner Ring had been in the team for the sake of balance, but in the end, Johnston's capacity to deliver both pace and spin (which for the orthodox left-armer, or finger-spinner, turned away from the right-handed batsman, similar to right-arm leg-spin), if the wicket was slippery, was taken into account favourably for him.

Australia had liked the idea of a leg-spinner in its side since 1911–12, beginning with Dr Herbert ('Ranji') Hordern, who in that season took 32 wickets at 24.37 in a losing team. Clarrie Grimmett broke into the side in the mid-1920s and was magnificent in England in 1930 with 29 wickets at 31.90, and dominance of Wally Hammond, England's leading batsman. This was followed through the first half of the 1930s with the outstanding Grimmett–O'Reilly combination, then O'Reilly on his own in the last half of the 1930s.

Ring and McCool were the post-war leg-spinners, but neither was in the class of those who had represented Australia before them. Ring was proving accurate, but his flight of the ball was ineffective. McCool had taken wickets, yet he was not causing accomplished batsmen too many concerns because of an inconsistent length and failure to push the ball through fast enough. County players seemed to have time to dance to him.

His finger injury left the way open for Ring, but in the end he had not done enough in the face of Johnston's surge.

The First Test line-up in batting order read: Morris, Barnes, Bradman, Hassett, Miller, Brown, Johnson, Tallon, Lindwall, Johnston and Toshack.

Loxton looked at the scorecard with those names with a mixture of awe, pride and depression.

'I said to Harvey,' Loxton recalled, '"Have a look at this line-up! There's no way we'll ever get a game in a Test match. We're here to make up the numbers." Seven of the first nine had scored Test hundreds, and the other two were pretty handy with the bat. Tallon had a 92 to his name [in a Test] and was a very good bat when he put his mind to it. Ian Johnson [the other non-centurion] was no slouch either.'

No matter how good the player, he would always be frustrated looking on at team-mates when not selected. But Loxton's assessment was not quite right. Harvey was made 12th man, making good Bradman's prediction that he would be 'knocking on the door' of the team. He even seemed a chance to play because Barnes had food poisoning all week. But like all Australians, Barnes would do everything to recover for the opener to an Ashes series, and he did.

Harvey had made his run for selection too late. His scores of 7, 7, 18 not out, 7, 16 (run out), 23, 36, 76 not out, 1 and 100 not out in eight of the 12 games prior to the First Test, were not quite enough. The problem for the Victorian teenager was that unless those in the team lost form, he would find it tough to force his way in. He had to keep making big scores and the chances were that a spot would open up for him before the series was over. There would be no denying his class and talent, which had been on show at Manchester and Hove, not to forget his pluck at Bradford, and his brilliant fielding skills.

The selectors had opted for a varied pace attack – speed-men Lindwall and Miller, and left-arm medium-pacers Toshack and Johnston. Johnson would provide the spin, but with the new ball due every 55 overs, Bradman's thinking was clear.

•

England dumped the idea of Robins as captain and chose Yorkshire's unflappable Norman Yardley to lead. Yardley was an all-rounder, not expected to dominate with either bat or ball. Six specialist batsmen were selected – Hutton (Yorkshire), Washbrook (Lancashire), Edrich (Middlesex), Compton (Middlesex), Hardstaff (Nottinghamshire) and Charles Barnett (Gloucestershire). Barnett, once an opener, had excelled himself against Australia at Adelaide in 1936–37, and 126 at Trent Bridge in 1938, an innings in which he just fell short of a century in the first session of the match.

The bowlers were Bedser (Yorkshire), John Young (Middlesex), a left-arm orthodox spinner, and Laker (Surrey). Bill Edrich's short bursts of fast bowling would be called on to complement Bedser's swing. Yardley and Barnett would be the support.

Right up until late on the night before the Test, England had dithered over whether to play leg-spinner Wright (Kent) and/or George Pope (Derbyshire). Both were called to the ground believing they had a chance to play. But Wright, like Yardley, had been troubled with the ubiquitous lumbago, and did not feel ready to play. Pope had played in three of the Victory Tests in 1945. Just before those matches he met Keith Miller in an exhibition match, and had shown him how to bowl a leg-cutter.

Experienced observers regarded Pope as the best leg-cutter since S. F. Barnes captured countless wickets with it. Pope could bat too, and would have been an imaginative choice at Nottingham. But he was overlooked. At 37 years, his age was against him in comparison with the final choice of the 25-year-old Laker. Reg Simpson (Nottinghamshire) was made 12th man.

When Bradman sat down with his co-selectors at the Victoria Hotel to consider England's team he was unperturbed. Apart from Bedser, the bowling line-up seemed to hold few terrors for Australia's batsmen. He was confident that his speed quartet could blast through England's finest. But Bradman was never over-confident. The unpredictability of weather, injury and form had taught him over two decades to be flexible and ready for anything in cricket.

•

He had a good look at the pitch on the evening before the Test at Trent Bridge and pronounced the hard surface and darker shade of brown as right for batting. Trent Bridge had been an excellent strip but hell for bowlers, apart from in the first hour when it had some movement. It was covered at night too, which lessened the chance of it deteriorating over the six days (Sunday was always the rest day) of the match.

Bradman felt that he had prepared his team as well as possible for the first Ashes in England in a decade. Both teams were ready.

So was the cricket world.

10

—

Patience at the Bridge

THE FIRST DAY of the First Test at Nottingham was symbolic in a similar way to the First Victory Test between servicemen at Lord's days after the end of the war. The oldest running international competition was on again in England after a 10-year break. There was a terrific atmosphere at the arena on Thursday 10 June 1948 that can only be generated by the anticipation of the first ball of the first match of an Ashes series. This was made more nerve-racking by the damp and cold at Nottingham. Murky clouds hung overhead and made the winning of the toss an uncertain thing.

It rained a little overnight and neither captain had changed into his cricket gear as they inspected the pitch at 11.25 a.m. with enough photographers for a Royal wedding following them, and a full house watching on in surprising silence. There wasn't even a polite clap for the leaders, but when they returned in their cricket clothes for a second inspection just before midday, there was a ripple of applause. Even from the stands, the wicket seemed to have transformed into something more like a green top, depending on the eye of the beholder, or their colour-blindness. No one could agree if it were green or dark brown.

But the forecast rain would affect its bounce, no matter what the hue. Too much water would kill it; a sprinkling might just freshen it up for the quick bowlers. Bradman would have batted had he won the toss, but he lost it and Yardley had no hesitation in going in first.

Bradman remarked to the team when he entered the dressing room:

'That might be the luckiest toss I've ever lost.'

Lindwall warmed up in the dressing room, bouncing up and down, doing press-ups and running hard on the spot. He believed in preparing his body, whereas Miller strolled out to the pitch as if he were never going to be thrown the ball.

Hutton and Washbrook walked out to recommence the Ashes to ringing applause from an appreciative crowd. Washbrook, cap at a rakish angle, shoulders square and back ramrod straight, looked taller than his medium height. The extra inches were in his confident gait and determined jut of the chin. Hutton, with his nose like the metal plate of a Roman helmet, seemed nervous. He would like to have had a quiet word of greeting with Miller. Hutton knew Lindwall, all hostility and silent menace, would not even look at him. But Miller was a friendly chap, who loved to fraternise with England players, especially his mate Compton. Yet even he, on this grey morning, did not meet Hutton's eyes. Nor was he remotely near muttering a 'good luck'.

Hutton examined the wicket, did some jittery gardening, flipped his bat in his hand, touched his cap, plucked at his shirt and tapped his crease. Even Lindwall's concern about the slippery run-up, which needed much application of sawdust, was looked on with an air of suspicion.

•

Lindwall would not bowl flat-out to start with. In contrast, Miller didn't even seem to measure his run-up, although he had paced it out in recent years. He swept back his mane of hair, and steamed in at top pace for the first over.

It was no fun for Hutton or Washbrook. No finer pair of quicks had ever opened an attack, and the pitch was very much in the bowlers' favour to begin with. Both batsmen would be on the lookout for the shorter ball from Lindwall, which was telegraphed sometimes by a more round-arm action, causing the ball to skid from the pitch from such a low angle that it left the receiver in two minds about jumping up on the toes to defend, or ducking. It was the most dangerous ball in cricket. No one wore protective headgear, and as the delivery shot up at chest, throat and head level for the average-sized man, there was an understandable fear about facing such a bowler.

Miller was a different, just as tough customer to face. His run-up to the wicket was loping and loose, and he had a high, more classic action, bringing the ball down from a greater height than the shorter Lindwall. Miller could generate serious bounce, and had the capacity to move the ball away to slips for the right-hander. This variety of speed from both ends meant there was nowhere the batsman could go for respite, except by rotating the strike and scampering down to the bowler's end.

This morning, Miller looked more penetrative. Washbrook had bad memories of facing him in the Victory Tests, and being struck painful body blows. He was in trouble in Miller's first over. But with the opening ball of his second over, he clean-bowled Hutton (3) middle stump with a ball that did not seem to deviate as it slipped between bat and pad. One of the finest batting technicians of all time had transgressed by showing daylight between bat and pad when playing forward.

The crowd gasped then went silent at the painful sight of the disturbed wicket, and the even more disturbed batsman as he sauntered back to the dressing room.

England went to lunch on 1 for 13, and there was a downpour. With Hutton licking his wounds, there was more gloom in the England dressing room than outside. After lunch Lindwall induced a snick from Washbrook to Johnson at slips, but he grassed it. Soon after Washbrook hooked Lindwall high to fine-leg. The ball looked to be going for six, but Brown took a good running catch. England was 2 for 15, and the advantage of winning the toss had all but evaporated. The purists in the press box and around the ground shook their heads at this injudicious shot for an opener. Most of the best openers in the first half of the 20th Century had put their hook-shots in the locker, only to be taken out for club, county and State games, just occasionally. But Washbrook loved the shot. This day he was an unhappy hooker, but he remained unrepentant.

Compton came to the wicket. The scoring colossus of 1947 had been sharpened up after his poor experience in the MCC game against the tourists. In one match, he had seen the standard he had to reach and the champion sportsman set himself for it. The way he moved his feet between balls, like a soccer star (which he had been) warming up, suggested he was far better prepared mentally for this game. Compton began by square cutting Miller to the fence. No one hated this treatment more than this bowler. He clapped the shot, and many observers took this at face value – a great sportsman acknowledging another – but it was more like a clap of thunder. He called for the ball to come back to him quickly. Back went his thatch of hair and in went Miller. He hurled a scorching bumper at Compton, testing their friendship. The crowd reacted in protest. Miller repeated the treatment to more howls from the terraces.

But he had to bend his back to get some life from the softer pitch. It was now tougher for the pacemen to get the ball through above wicket height. Miller and Lindwall seemed to hold fewer terrors for Compton and partner Edrich. Sensing this, Bradman was not slow to make a double change. It was a rare one in Test cricket with two left-armers – Toshack and Johnston – into the attack.

How Bradman enjoyed his power compared to his last visit to England a decade earlier! Then he had McCormick, a down-on-confidence speedster, McCabe, a fraud of a fill-in medium-pacer to partner him (similar in many ways to Edrich masquerading as an opening bowler for England), and then the spinners – O'Reilly and Fleetwood-Smith. By the Fifth Test of 1938, with McCormick dropped, Bradman was down to the weakest Australian attack in the history of Ashes Tests with the overworked O'Reilly the only top ranked bowler in the line-up. Australia paid the price and saw England reach 7 for 903. Now Bradman had four genuine top-line pacemen, with a variety of strengths. Johnson would come on for some spin variation if needed, plus the further luxury of being able to take the new ball after only 55 overs.

But just as his leadership creative juices were running with thoughts of the permutations and combinations at his disposal, Lindwall – his number-one striker – reported groin strain. Bradman rested him without giving any hints to the opposition or the crowd that there was a problem. It didn't matter initially as Toshack attacked the leg-stump, running the hand over the ball so that it would dart away to leg or come in from the off. Johnston, for variety, could swing it both ways. He was the happiest man in the squad before receiving his chance and the same after it. He bowled Edrich, a very nice wicket first up in an Ashes contest in England.

England was 3 for 48. Joe Hardstaff marched to the wicket. This was his reward for being the first, and, so far, only batsman to hit a century against the Australians. He stroked the first ball well enough and brought a big cheer from his home-town Trent Bridge crowd to stir the long-resting ghosts of William Clarke and Mary Chapman. But next ball, he was Hardstaff the adventurer, cutting wildly. It sailed to the agile Miller at slips. He snaffled it with a stunning somersault-with-pike dive. England was 4 for 48.

Miller was now bubbling. Bradman, again using instinct, threw him the ball and said quietly to him:

'Great catch, Nugget. Now see if you can clean up your mate.'

Miller streaked in with extra puff. He obliged his captain by bowling Compton behind his legs after he moved too far across.

England was 5 for 48.

Yardley and Barnett were together. Bradman took some time setting his field to them, chatting with the bowlers and calibrating fielding positions as he did so. The batsmen appeared in good touch with some lovely cover-drives, a couple of cuts, and several on-drives. But none of them penetrated the field setting. This built frustration and not the score. Bradman had Johnston and Toshack back in the attack together. Johnston bowled Barnett when he pushed forward and played on. Bouncy keeper Godfrey Evans came to the wicket and played attacking strokes. He was dropped by Bradman in the covers, but moved the score up to 6 for 74. Toshack straightened a delivery and trapped Yardley lbw. Then Morris held a fine catch at forward short-leg to a solid stroke from Evans.

England went to tea at 8 for 74. It was a pathetic effort, with well-equipped batsmen pushing forward and getting out. Back-foot play, such a feature of the Australian method, was neglected. Credit had to go to the bowlers, and Bradman, who used his three key men judiciously.

Lindwall would not return after tea. He was replaced by the brilliant Harvey in the field. The despondent buzz of discussion at the break in the crowd and on the radio, which was broadcast direct for the first time to Australia, was whether England would reach 100, or set a new low record for the home team at Trent Bridge. The figure was 112 in 1921 against Armstrong's team.

Laker decided he had nothing to lose by playing his strokes, and not always off the front foot. He had scores to settle too. Fresh in his mind was the humiliation of the belting he received on a spring morning just 17 days earlier at Lord's in the MCC match. He lost count of the sixes sailing over his head. Laker had yet to convince anyone he would develop into a world-class bowler, but this young Surrey man had character. He showed it with the blade, reaching 50 in an hour in the last session, and in a face-saving partnership of 89 with Bedser. Miller belatedly had him caught by Tallon for 63. Johnston had Bedser caught by Brown for 22.

England reached 165. It was still woeful, but Laker had kept England in the game. Smiling, easy-going Johnston had a dream beginning to his Ashes experience in England, taking the bowling honours with 5 for 36 off 25 overs.

'This opportunity,' Johnston said, 'established me as a Test player. It gave me confidence and I went on from there . . .'

Miller took 3 for 38, and had done his job removing England's two best bats and the troublesome Laker.

When Australia batted, Barnes showed he was over his food poisoning, although he appeared gaunt. He was confident but playing with the restraint an opener should show, in line with the conventional thinking that the job was to take the brunt of the speed attack, take the shine off the ball and set the foundations for an innings. Barnes had morphed into an opener to make sure he played for Australia, when there were no guarantees about spots 4, 5 and 6. Bradman would always take No. 3 in any batting order ever devised. That left three positions and with the plethora of talent, Barnes had made a shrewd post-war move. It meant sacrificing his accomplished all-round attacking approach to batting for a place in the Australian team, which he chose. Yet the decision did not to change his character. He treated umpires with brusque humour and ran the risk of upsetting them with appeals against the light.

Morris was steady and in no hurry. Australia reached 0 for 17 at stumps.

Sunshine threatened on day two, Friday, and there was not as much cloud cover. Australia was in a strong position and still had at least two days to bat if it could or it wished. Morris was unlucky the next morning to have a ball from Laker clip his right pad and curl onto the stumps. He had battled hard for his 31.

It was 12.50 p.m. and the score 1 for 73 when Bradman strode to the wicket to thunderous applause and cheering. Yet most of the crowd would be hoping he was dismissed early. For two decades this one player stood between England and victory. If he got a start, it often meant England would lose or have no chance of winning. In 1948, the window of opportunity for removing him was just a little longer and wider. He had to gather all his batting faculties over more time. The important thing was that they were all still there, no matter how scattered in the first 20 minutes at the wicket.

Yardley brought on Bedser, who Bradman regarded as the best medium-pacer he had faced in 20 years as a Test player, even ranking him above England's Maurice Tate, which was the highest praise. The field was set differently, with three players coming in close on the leg-side.

Bradman defended rather dourly for him but picked up 19 before lunch. After the break, Barnes (62) pushed at Laker and edged it behind. Evans' response would have made a high-board diver proud, as he leapt backwards and held a catch in his right glove. The score was 2 for 121. It remained on 121 as Laker induced a forward-push and snick from Miller (0) to Edrich in slips.

Bradman, ever adaptable, had put Miller in before Hassett and Brown to boost the scoring rate. That didn't work, but it didn't inhibit the captain's flexibility. He promoted Brown, in heart, mind and performance an opener, to take the new ball before Hassett. Brown's defence caused Bradman to attack more. He began dancing to the spinners, hitting Young and Laker through the off-side. Apart from his thinning hair, the Bradman of 1948 at these occasional moments was almost indiscernible from the Bradman of the 1930s. He always said that the greatest of all battles was the skilled batsman against the skilled spinner. The classic cricket combat of the 20th Century was Bradman versus O'Reilly. In the 21st Century it has been Warne versus Tendulkar or Lara or Pietersen, or in domestic cricket in Australia, Warne versus Mark Waugh or Ponting. Bradman was thinking of the spectator as much as the contest when he put this one-on-one competition on a pedestal. A spinner delivering

6 balls in less than two minutes to a batsman with the capacity to dance to the ball, or use the crease on the back foot, is arguably the highest form of the game. This is the same for the combatants, and for spectators, from the connoisseur to the fan not so concerned with the technical. Encounters such as these certainly quicken the game too, and heighten it as a spectacle.

With Bradman moving into his element, Yardley, no less a shrewd skipper, brought himself on and broke the partnership by conning Brown (17) into pad play, which led to an lbw.

Australia was 4 for 185. The lead was 20 and England had manoeuvred itself into the game. Yardley used leg theory by asking all bowlers to deliver down leg-side to a stacked leg-side field. It was unconventional cricket to the point of being a different game, which could be called 'on-side attrition'. Unless the batsman took big risks by trying to break through the field or by attempting to play reverse shots (that is, a right-hander, switching to play left-handed or vice versa) and hoicking the ball into the vacant off-side – this led to boring cricket. Bradman hated this style and had never employed it. He was not against using the rules to his advantage, but he had contempt for anyone not relying on a strong contest between bat and ball. It was Bradman that initiated the change in the lbw rule to make it tougher for the batsman who used his pads outside the off-stump to avoid hitting the ball. In fact, he went further than the rule eventually instated, where a batsman would be deemed 'out' if he did not play a stroke at a ball hitting him outside the line of the off, and with, in the umpire's mind, the ball going on to hit the wicket. Bradman would have had a rule where the batsman was out this way, whether or not he was deemed to be playing a stroke. In other words, he wanted that bat versus ball contest to be mandatory. Now, in a different instance, Yardley and his bowlers were delivering rubbish that avoided the basic contest.

Bradman and Hassett decided not to hit the ball. They just let the deliveries slip through harmlessly and tediously. Yardley's tactic was to reduce Australia's scoring through day two, and limit its lead. Bradman was gambling that he could step up the scoring at some point, with the aim of building such a tally that it would be England batting last and not Australia. He was not often called upon to show such patience, but he kept his main objective intact, which, as ever, was to win. He had more than three days to do it. He and Hassett occasionally showed their displeasure. Bradman did not play a shot during two complete overs. At the end of the second over, he shook his head ever so slightly, while standing cross-legged. Hassett once marked his block well outside his leg-stump as if he would face-up there. The Australians (or was it the bowlers?) were booed and slow-clapped, a first for both batsmen.

Bradman reached 50 in 100 minutes and was bogged down on 78 for the last 20 minutes before tea. After the break he began to play his strokes again, but he was still forced to go slowly. As usual, he did not dawdle in the 90s, moving to his 28th century in Tests and his 18th against England. It took him 211 minutes, which made it his slowest. Bradman remained 130 not out at stumps, with Hassett 46 not out and Australia on 4 for 293 – 128 runs ahead with three days to go.

That night, Bedser had a few drinks with Bill O'Reilly. The Australian sat him down with pen and paper to advise Bedser how he should set his field to Bradman, with the aim of forcing him to give a catch close in on the leg-side. Bedser had been setting these kinds of fields to Bradman during several contests, but he listened to O'Reilly. There was one difference he suggested. Instead of three fielders close in on the leg, one of them should be placed at fine-leg, 10 metres from the bat. Bradman loved the leg-glance and if he was fed it, he would nibble, O'Reilly said.

Saturday morning, day three, was blessed with the sun and a packed crowd filled Trent Bridge, hoping for a breakthrough but expecting Bradman to go on to his 13th double hundred in Tests. He scored two to mid-wicket, then two through the covers. The crowd clapped politely. Bradman turned to Evans.

'What's that for?'

'You're first to a thousand for the season, Don,' Evans said. 'Congratulations.'

(Bradman would later learn he beat Middlesex's Jack Robertson by 13 minutes.)

Bradman celebrated with the best shot of the match: a superlative cover-drive for 4. Next delivery, Bedser swung the ball across the stumps. Bradman leg-glanced it hastily and dead straight to Hutton, who snaffled it and held the ball above his head in delight. The crowd roared as much in surprise as pleasure. Bradman was on his way for 138.

O'Reilly and Fingleton, both perennial Bradman detractors in private, cheered in the press box. O'Reilly had snared Bradman once more. Bedser, in O'Reilly's eyes, was merely the conduit. It was and still is accepted that players pass on tips to each other, but it may be the only case in history where a retired player, not involved in the game at all, sat down in the middle of a competition to coach – with diagrams – the player from an opposing team the way to dismiss the opposition's best batsman. Evidently O'Reilly would rather see Bradman out than Australia win.

The spectators recovered, and gave Bradman a prolonged appreciative applause, which was partly from relief and partly a farewell. Australia was 5 for 305.

Hassett then took over the prime defensive role, losing Johnson and Tallon cheaply before Lindwall came in without a runner. This raised eyebrows after Yardley had allowed a substitute (Harvey) to field for him.

Lindwall started well and with a slight limp. He was discomforted.

'Only a very bad injury would have influenced me to ask for a runner,' he wrote in his autobiography, *Flying Stumps*. 'I can't settle down to my normal game if I have to think of a runner with me.'

The comment demonstrated Lindwall's commitment. He wanted no distractions from an innings for his country. It was a more than useful one of 42 in 120 minutes, lifting the score with Hassett to 8 for 472. Hassett's century took him 305 minutes, and it was his first in a Test in England. Australia was now 307 ahead. Hassett was out soon after for 137, and then the tail – Toshack and Johnston – wagged the total up to all out 509. The lead was 344.

Australia was in command, but a bowler short. Unless someone stepped up, with a little over two days to go, the First Test was heading for a draw.

11

—

Compton the Gallant

AUSTRALIA ENTERED THE field for the final session on
Saturday with Bradman wondering how he was going to
conjure 10 English wickets without his key striker. The only
answer was tight, accurate bowling and pressure from the fielders.
Harvey, substituting for Lindwall, was ready to provide youthful
inspiration in the field. The vocal Tallon would back up his
skipper with growls, urges and appeals, which at times seemed
to demoralise the batsman rather than fire up the fielders. But
his deeds, rather than his vowel-crushing accent, meant more
when he took a good catch off a sorry Washbrook down the
leg-side for 1. Miller had struck again early, knowing he would
be in for more bowling than he liked now that Lindwall was
incapacitated.

Harvey was a revelation in the covers. Hard shots were
played. All eyes and cameras swung towards the boundary. Then
they returned to see this nifty fielder hurling the ball in baseball
style over the stumps. He was one of the best fielders ever for
Australia. (Bradman was the best as a youth in the 1920s and
first half of the 1930s. Harvey was one out of the box in the
1940s and was joined by Norm O'Neill in the 1950s. They

often prowled the covers together and very little squeezed past them. Paul Sheahan was a fielding panther in the 1960s. In the 21st Century, Australia has had Ponting, Symonds and Michael Clarke.)

Bradman brought on Johnson and he dismissed the struggling Edrich (13) caught behind. Soon afterwards he looked to have Compton out lbw, caught back on his stumps and hit well below the knee roll. But umpire Chester turned down the appeal from the bowler and keeper. Compton seemed ready to leave the wicket. But as few, if any, batsmen have ever 'walked' on an lbw, he stayed.

He and Hutton fought on and moved the scoreboard along to 50 in 65 minutes, which was good going under the conditions. It wasn't long before Hutton had 50 himself. He was in sparkling form with a cover-drive and back-cut off Miller to match Bradman's cover-drive in the first overs of the day. Three fours from the one Miller over of off-spin had the bowler switching back to speed, his dander up because of the spanking from Hutton. The first ball was a throat-high bumper to Compton, who had to go up on his toes like a ballet dancer. It wasn't a pose that the crowd appreciated, unless it was a Notts bowler being the aggressor, such as Larwood or Voce in the previous decade. They were incensed that Larwood had been the scapegoat for Bodyline and that Voce had been restricted in its use when he returned to England after the 1932–33 series in Australia. They would hoot any opposition bowler, especially an Australian, who seemed to get away with similar tactics. But as hostile as Miller could be, he never delivered anything remotely like Bodyline where everything was pitched short on or about the leg-stump. The aim with that special bowling style was to cause the ball to rear up into the batsman's chest, with five or six players positioned for the catch from the ball that was fended off by the batsman.

Miller was riled by the crowd. He delivered a searing bouncer that Compton evaded. Off the field they were the best of mates and had been since the war years. But the spectators would not have believed it.

Miller's next over was the last of the day. He decided he would throw everything into it and have an extra beer later. He put two fielders close in on the leg-side, which suggested he would lift the ball into Hutton's rib-cage in the hope of forcing a catch. He shortened his run and delivered two more bumpers. The fourth ball of the over cannoned into Hutton's right arm up near the shoulder. The batsman pulled away from the wicket in pain. Hutton had badly injured this arm during a combat training accident in the war. He had been operated on twice to graft bones from his legs on to it. The arm had a long scar and was noticeably shorter. When it was struck by a thunderbolt like this, it hurt and brought back psychological scars from the injury, the operations and the fear that it could be damaged again. Miller had done the same thing during the 1945 Victory Tests when he had battered Hutton and Washbrook in his first real display of menace with the ball. He was at it again, this time with more control and accuracy.

Miller showed some sympathy by deciding not to deliver another bouncer that night. Until now only a group of louts had been catcalling and booing him. Now many, including a section in the members' stand, joined in for a loud howl of protest.

There were cries of 'You wouldn't bloody do that if we had Larwood!' and, 'Get off, you Aussie bastard!'

When Hutton recovered, he faced up again. Miller began his run. The booing increased. He stopped half-way and sauntered back to the top of his mark. There he waited hands on hips for the booing to stop, which it did. He bowled again. Hutton defended a straight one. He leg-glanced the last ball of the day for four to end the day with a small victory.

Miller took his sweater and straggled off the field behind his team-mates. A horde of demonstrators, allegedly including colliers from Larwood's former mining district, fired by more than one too many drinks, ran onto the arena and remonstrated with Miller as he neared the members' pavilion. Police cut them off and Miller climbed the steps, pullover slung over his shoulder, unperturbed. He had been in plenty of stoushes with tougher men than the inebriated members of this unruly mob. Besides, he knew that if there were a scuffle, a dozen Australian team-mates would have been in the action in support of him. Loxton and Johnson, both useful with their fists, stood at the dressing room door, watching to see if the mob hurled anything more than abuse.

It was an unpleasant end to the day's play that had produced sterling Test cricket. England had reached 2 for 121 with Hutton on 63 not out and Compton 36 not out. There was still a deficit of 223 runs. Australia had not had things all its way. The game was destined to go another day, and perhaps into the final sessions of day five.

The press reports condemned the crowd rather than Miller. Former England captain Arthur Gilligan on the BBC was critical of the Notts members.

'It's ridiculous to start this nonsense,' he said on radio. 'It makes me furious.'

•

On Monday morning, before play commenced on an overcast day four, the Notts secretary, Captain H. A. Brown, appealed to the crowd over the loudspeakers to leave the conduct of the game to the umpires.

He said:

'Let us keep Nottingham a place where Test matches can continue to be played. On Saturday the Australian, Miller, was booed and there was much subsequent publicity in the press. These Australians are great sportsmen. They stood by the Empire in the war and we should be pleased to greet them. Let us show them how really pleased we are and give them a warm-hearted greeting this morning.'

Brown's remarks were quaint but unnecessary. For a start, Saturday in the late afternoon sun was a long way from a cool, sober Monday morning. Second, the crowd composition would have been different. Saturday's hooligans would not have been there, although no doubt many of the members who lost their composure were in attendance. The more committed fans turned up for day four and they applauded the Australians when they came onto the field. Yet still the undercurrent of attitude, especially towards Miller, remained. He was the 'bad boy'. The crowd hurled plenty of abuse, especially when he bowled Hutton for 74. He may have lost what appeared to be Miller's slower arm-ball (an off-break that went straight on) in the gloom of the pavilion, on a ground without sightscreens, but his top-class innings was over, and about half of what was required. Hardstaff was in, and now more the billionaire than the millionaire, slashing outside the off-stump. He was missed in slips. Morris lost the ball in the dark. A few moments later, the umpires stopped play for bad light and the players were off the field for an hour. They resumed in better conditions and under orders from Yardley to go for their shots. He thought it better to have runs on the board before getting caught on a 'sticky'. And more profitable too to have Australia on that wicket. Hardstaff thought Yardley's directive suited his attitude anyway. He went for his strokes, outscoring Compton. At lunch England was 3 for 191, Compton 63 and Hardstaff 31.

Compton had survived a stumping, two dropped catches behind and one in slips, and that lbw decision he seemed prepared to 'walk' for. But being a champion, he put all that behind him and was in fine touch after lunch. He proceeded to mix defence and caution with his fine array of shots, which made him the most exciting batsman in England. His century was a classic. Those who had seen most of them in Tests agreed that it was his best, mainly because of the opposition, the conditions, with bad light and interruptions, and the state of the game.

Fielder Harvey was enthralled. It was the first time he had seen Compton at close quarters in full flight.

'I thought, "Boy, this bloke can bat!"' Harvey said. 'It was a pleasure to field to him and witness such a performance close up.'

Hardstaff advanced to a creditable 43 before Toshack had him caught. Barnett again failed with 6, and there were none of the fireworks of yesteryear. At 37 years and against the most powerful attack he would ever face, he was found wanting.

Bradman's skills as captain and tactician came to the fore in tough circumstances. He had to place his field to contain but not go totally defensive. He also had to juggle his tiring attack. Miller was valiant, but struggling. Johnson and Johnston were asked to deliver accurately and on a good length.

Compton kept rising to the occasion and was unconquered on 154 at stumps, with Evans on 10 not out. The score was 6 for 345. England had performed gallantly to lead by one run, with still four wickets in hand.

•

The gloom and drizzle returned on day five. Australia had the luxury of letting Miller loose again with the new ball not too long into the morning. Compton had settled in again. He needed to forget his wonderful achievement on the day before and start as if it were another knock, and he did. When Compton reached 184, Miller let go a brutal bumper, which Tallon believed was the fastest delivery of the summer. Compton was never going to shirk a challenge from his mate; he shaped to hook, changed his mind and turned his head. His evasive action caused him to overbalance and fall on his wicket. Compton stood up, dusted himself and looked up the wicket at Miller, who was laughing.

'You bastard!' Compton called.

Miller pushed back his hair and laughed again.

It was a sad end to a brave performance. His 410-minute innings had pushed his country to 61 ahead, giving it a small measure of hope.

Miller had taken on the burden left by the absence of Lindwall. He lifted his rating by bowling Laker for 4 after lunch. Evans carried on with his confident strokes mixed with streaky ones. He reached 50 before Johnston had him caught behind. England reached 441, a thin lead of 97.

Johnston took 4 for 147 off a marathon 59 overs, giving him 9 in a match he would never forget. Miller took 4 for 125 off 44 overs, in an effort he would prefer to forget. Without Lindwall, he was forced to lead the attack and bowl more 'stock' overs than he would care to. Miller over-extended himself and aggravated a back injury sustained in late 1943 during the war. He had been in a wrestling match at Ouston, near Newcastle in England's north. After that, whenever he bowled for long periods, his back would give way. On top of that, his fatigue and injury restricted his batting. This was disappointing for a player who began his Test career as a batsman who could achieve the heights. Moments like these, when he did his job as an all-rounder, meant he was restricting his chances of great achievements with the bat. Bradman had nursed him on tour and he had not been over-bowled. But the captain had no option at Nottingham.

•

Australia had three hours on the final afternoon to reach 98. Barnes decided to finish the game as quickly as possible and was mainly responsible for Australia being 0 for 24 after four overs. At 38, Bedser bowled Morris (9) with an in-swinger to the left-hander. Bradman came in, again, to substantial applause. Bedser moved an in-swinger across him. Bradman played an identical shot to the one that removed him in the first innings. It flew once more straight to Hutton, placed a little wider at short square leg. Bradman was on his way for his first duck ever in a Test in England. Australia was 2 for 48, but in no danger except from the weather, which closed in quickly with Bradman's departure. This hastened Barnes along again and he stroked his way beautifully to 60, playing as he said, 'like a German band'.

The score was 93, with Hassett on 20 not out.

'How many to win?' Barnes asked an umpire.

'Four,' the umpire misinformed him.

Barnes hammered Young for four, grabbed a stump and charged for the pavilion, only to be summoned back. Australia still had one to make for victory. Hassett hit the winning single, and the souvenir stumps were snaffled by keeper Evans and other England players before Barnes could complete the winning run. He slammed his bat down near the wicket in disgust.

Certain that he would receive a strong press for his hard-hitting cameo in bad light, Barnes told the hotel front desk to provide him with a copy of every newspaper for the next morning. He was stunned and dismayed to see that every paper concentrated on Bradman's duck with analysis of his other ducks.

'What's the use?' Barnes thought. 'Whether Don gets a hundred or a duck he still gets the publicity. The rest of us are only there to make up the team.'

This would have annoyed his captain too. Yet all the Australians were more concerned with what the scorecard said in the papers:

Australia had won the First Test by eight wickets.

It was now on to Lord's.

12

—

Ray of Hope

R AY LINDWALL WAS Bradman's only concern in the nine-day break before the Second Test at Lord's. The captain would give him the two county games off in the hope that he could get himself fully fit. Lindwall was his number-one strike weapon, but Bradman did not wish to be caught one bowler short, as he was for most of England's batting at Nottingham.

Bradman stepped down for the 14th game of the tour, against Northamptonshire at Northampton, a day after the Test on 16 June. But there was no rest from the wicket for five players: Barnes, Morris, Hassett, Johnson and Johnston. They had to make their journey *tout de suite* 100 km south from Nottingham. In came Hamence, Loxton, Harvey, McCool, Saggers and Ring. Despite the determination to not lose a contest, every player was receiving chances to press his claims for Test selection, especially against the weaker counties.

The poor weather continued. Despite this wicket usually being a good one to bat on, even in wet conditions, it was probably a useful toss to lose in front of a full house in the small-capacity stadium (about 13,000). Johnston and Johnson, with three wickets each, and Loxton, over his groin injury (two wickets) made short shrift of the county. At one point it was 7 for 61. Ramesh Divecha, a young Indian studying at Oxford, and in his first county game, managed a top score of 33, which pushed the Northants tally up to 119.

Bert Nutter ran rampant when Australia batted, taking 5 for 57 with his steady, accurate medium-pacers. Hassett steadied his team with a stylish 127 (including 17 fours), and demonstrated how clever he could be with the blade when little was at stake. In the Test, his century had been responsible, restrained and solid. Defence was the order of the game. In similar weather circumstances against the county, but without nullifying leg-side bowling, he was allowed to give full flourish to his wide array of strokes. Morris drove his way to a fine 60, enough to suggest his form was holding and building. McCool notched an unbeaten 50, but the batsmen who most needed to shine – Barnes, Hamence, Loxton and Harvey – couldn't manage good scores.

Barnes was out to Nutter early in the innings, and disappeared from the ground for the next few hours while Australia struggled. He was aware from his 1938 trip that Northants was known for its boot and shoe manufacturers, and he stocked up on them.

'The factories are exceptionally kind to us,' Barnes noted, 'and they are quite close to the ground . . . even the 12th man could have a try on and still be on call for emergencies.'

Barnes, it seemed, never wasted a moment on tour.

•

Australia was all out for 352, which was modest by its standards. Northants offered little resistance in its second innings, reaching 169. Johnston maintained his excellent season with another four wickets, while Ring, with 4 for 31 off 19 overs kept himself in front of the selectors.

•

Bradman returned for the second bout against tough Yorkshire, this time at Bramall Lane, Sheffield, and joined the squad coming north 170 km from Northampton. The tour selectors put a strong side in the field with the still vivid memory of getting out of jail at Bradford in early May.

First impressions of this ground were not enchanting. As the players arrived, they were struck by the sense of enclosure by industry. They could hear the screeching from a saw mill, and the hammering from a factory. They could see a brewery chimney belching soot and black smoke, which the workers would stoke harder when the opposition was batting. But this most competitive squad under the most successful competitor in the history of the sport soon began to warm to the atmosphere that pervaded this ground. On the surface it seemed hard and uninviting – not Lord's, or Cambridge or Oxford. But at heart it reflected the huge comprehension and character of the Yorkshire crowd that appreciated cricket more than any other in the UK. Bradman spoke of this to his players and they sensed they were in a bullring when they practised before the game. Long before they were due to start, the stands were packed. Lengthy queues of overcoat-clad spectators wearing hats snaked around the streets. At one point, those who had tickets were accidentally shut out when the gates were closed before play started. It seemed that hundreds would storm the ramparts unless let in, which they eventually were.

The sight of thousands outside the ground made the Australians feel as if they were about to compete in the nearest thing to a Test. The Yorkies wanted a home win, but they knew this would not happen unless a real dog-fight ensued. The spectators were on the edge of their seats, willing something sensational from the first ball. They were disappointed. But the second delivery gave them the start they wanted. Ron Aspinall uprooted Barnes' middle stump.

'I have never heard such a roar,' Barnes said. 'This was a good ball. It swung late and yorked me . . . I don't mind unfastening my pads to such a ball. I gave Aspinall full marks for it.'

Bradman felt like a gladiator entering the Coliseum, with the mob waiting to give him the thumbs down for execution if he made one single error. He joined Brown. Aspinall started to bounce Bradman on instruction from Yardley, who was smarting after the attack by Miller at the Nottingham Test. But Aspinall was not Miller or Lindwall. He was quick for a few overs, but Bradman thrived on the challenge, swivelling into position for the hook. He was in touch and moved swiftly to 50 in 75 minutes off 60 deliveries, while Brown got his head down for just 19 in the same time.

Yardley, as aggressive now as he had been defensive in the First Test, brought on Johnny Wardle, who was billed as the successor to the late Hedley Verity, whom Bradman later chose as the left-arm spinner in his best ever England XI. Wardle could bowl orthodox spinners as well as the Chinaman (the left-hander's leg-break) and the wrong 'un. Bradman was impressed. Wardle delivered perfect length, spun the ball well, and achieved deceptive flight. He was off here and there in his direction, which could be expected from a bowler with the lot – finger and wrist spin. He induced a premature drive from Bradman to a ball that dropped in flight and he was caught driving on the up for 54, the top score for the innings. Australia was boosted by determined knocks from Harvey (49), who was in scintillating form, and Hamence (48), who fell to Alec Coxon also. The tall, lean Yorkshire paceman's form was increasing his chances of Test selection with an inspired 4 for 66, which did most to reduce Australia to all out 249. He was adept at swinging the ball away from the bat, a skill which had been left to atrophy in England because of the lbw law that limited its capacity to take a wicket. (England bowlers were frustrated by the apparent uselessness of bowling a delivery outside the line of the leg-stump, and see it swing across or into the pads for no result. But the out-swinger's beauty was its effectiveness in moving away from the swing of the bat and inducing an edge to slips.)

Wardle walked away with good figures too: 3 for 37. A selector was watching. Such was the obsession with Bradman by the England selectors, the team, the media and the fans, that anyone who troubled him, or dismissed him, would be considered for the Tests. The fact that he could not be the player he was in the 1930s seemed irrelevant.

Rain fell on the Sunday, and made it tougher for batting on the Monday, but Yorkshire did well, scoring 206. Eight of the top nine batsmen managed starts, including Hutton (39, caught off Toshack). But the left-arm swing of Toshack (7 for 81), supported by Johnston was the county's undoing, despite some anomalous fielding in which the Australians grassed several chances. Toshack and Johnston sent down nearly 82 overs between them. Miller bounced Hutton and his opening partner Harry Halliday, and was booed and abused.

Cries of 'Just like bloody Larwood!' and worse came from the incensed crowd similar to the way spectators had bayed at Nottingham. Miller, once the crowd pleaser, who would even oblige during the war by responding to the mob, was now defying it with a nonchalance that riled them even further. Yet his fire didn't last long. After four overs, he broke down. His long stint at Nottingham had fatigued him and strained his 'dodgy' back. Certainly Bradman was aware of his effort, and did not call on him at all in Yorkshire's second innings.

Australia batted again and Barnes in the middle of a 'trot' – a run of low scores – went for 6. Brown (113) and Bradman (86) then put on 154 for the second wicket, and pushed the game out of Yorkshire's reach. This was Brown's fifth century, drawing him level with Bradman. It was painstaking stuff from Brown, and he was out of sync with the aggression of the rest of the batsmen. Oddly Bradman, after another masterful exhibition, turned a leg-glance straight to Hutton off Aspinall to be out the way he had at Nottingham courtesy of Bedser, as instructed so enthusiastically by O'Reilly. Bill would claim this one as well.

With Miller unfit to bowl, and Toshack and Johnston fatigued after their marathons in Yorkshire's first innings, Bradman delayed his closure to 5 for 285, allowing Harvey a second cameo (56) and Yorkshire no chance of winning. In the last half hour, even Hutton and opening bat Halliday, who rarely bowled other than in the nets, sent down a few overs, perhaps in mild protest against Bradman's belated declaration, which had been barracked by the vocal crowd. They had wanted him to make a game of it, but Bradman had in mind another agenda, preserving his bowlers, and practice for the Tests. Yardley responded by sending in his tail-enders for the 70 minutes that Bradman left Yorkshire to bat. Bradman, in turn, gave Hamence and the spinners all the overs. Hamence gave himself something to dine out on for eternity by bowling Hutton for 10.

The game finished two hours earlier than normal because the Australians had a train to catch back to London. Yorkshire was 4 for 85 at stumps in a disappointing draw for them, but not the Australians. Bradman had set his team to defy Yorkshire, one of the few teams with any chance of causing an upset. They had their two chances and were unlucky. Yet they had not managed to topple the tourists.

•

England's defeatist (or 'drawist') policy of selecting a team top-heavy in batting and hoping to contain Australia was abandoned in favour of a more balanced squad. They gave marching orders to Young; Barnett, who was more a batsman for 1938 than 1948; Hardstaff, who was too profligate for the economical style needed in Test innings constructions; and Simpson, who had made no transgressions but was simply unlucky. Pope departed like the ghost of a Pontiff – believed in by many but seen by few. He had been a passing thought at Nottingham and passed over at Lord's.

Now in favour were Coxon after his Bramall Lane efforts, Doug Wright, who was fit again, and Warwickshire's skipper 'Tom' (Horace) Dollery, a batsman expected to stand up to Lindwall and Miller. The addition of two bowlers, it was hoped by critics, would relieve England of the need to call on Edrich, who delivered 22 overs for returns of 0 for 92 at Trent Bridge. He was at best a change bowler, who ran in, all puff and wind, but was ineffective against the Australian line-up.

On paper, Wright seemed the most inspired and attacking bowling inclusion, especially as his run-up had been made less manic. It once varied from a parody of a jerky skier on a steep slope to John Arlott's description of him 'skipping along as though hobbled like a fractious horse'.

His perambulation to the bowling crease caused mirth from onlookers in Australia in 1946–47, but he had his moments on that trip, especially at the MCG against Victoria, where no one laughed when he bamboozled the batsmen.

•

The main worry concerning the Lord's Test for Bradman and his co-selectors was the fitness of their two main strikers Lindwall and Miller. Lindwall claimed his groin was 'progressing' after missing the two county games and he expected to be 'right' for the Test, beginning Thursday 24 June, two days after the drawn Yorkshire game. Miller had complained about his back but was available for selection.

In the end, Lindwall was the only player under a cloud. On Wednesday afternoon, the team gathered at Lord's for practice. The hardest worker was Barnes, who had asked the ground staff to bowl to him for an hour before his team-mates arrived. Bradman directed Lindwall to bowl a long stint in the nets. The bowler went through his paces, watched by the captain. At the end of it, Bradman asked him how he felt.

'Fine,' Lindwall said, his laconic self intact.

'You know, I don't like it,' Bradman said. 'We can't afford to run risks of losing a bowler early in the match. I can't get out of my head that you damaged a muscle badly only a few days ago. Muscles don't heal as quickly as that. We'll wait until the morning and see how you are then.'

Lindwall shrugged. The leg had stood up so well during the practice that he was confident he would be fit in the morning.

In the dressing room at Lord's, shortly before Bradman went out to toss, he queried Lindwall again.

'How is it, Ray?'

'It's okay, Don.'

'I've thought about it again. I'm still doubtful whether we should take a chance with you.'

Lindwall was upset at the prospect of missing his first Test at Lord's. He played his 'last card'.

'Look, Don,' he blurted out, 'I'm absolutely sure I shall be all right. Leave me out on form if you want to; but not on fitness.'

Bradman considered him.

'All right,' the captain said with a smile, 'keep your hair on; you've talked me into it. We'll take the gamble.'

13

Lindwall's Lord's Bluff

IN A COMMENDABLE bid for immortality, a well-dressed 60-year-old gentleman, Bill Davies, was pictured in many of the papers as the first man in the line on St John's Wood Road waiting for the gates to open for the Lord's Test. Mr Davies had plonked his box down at the admission point at 10.30 a.m. on Wednesday 23 June – 25 hours before the scheduled commencement of play.

When asked about his fortitude, staying power and keenness, he said he had seen Bradman make 254 at Lord's in 1930, which was the finest batting display he had witnessed in half a century of watching the game. He wished to see him score another hundred at Lord's, but with England winning and 'something special from Compton and Hutton'.

Mr Davies had just missed the previous season's Test at Lord's and this time he was taking no chances. By 6 p.m. his family had delivered him a hot meal, thermos tea, and a multi-pack of cigarettes that would see him through the night. Snuggled up under a blanket, he was set.

'I don't care if it rains,' he said. 'I'm here to stay.'

By midnight another 200 people had joined him in the line, which gradually grew through the night to around 1,000 by dawn. Early Thursday, Mr Davies was the head of an unending snake fed by people pouring out of the nearby underground station, buses, cars and taxis. By 8 a.m. there were huge crowds milling and queuing right back to Wellington Road, a block north. At 9 a.m. Mr Davies paid his 40 pence (including tax) and was followed into the stands by 20,000 other fans. The gates were shut at 11.20 a.m., 10 minutes before play was due to commence. Another 20,000 people, not quite as well prepared and inspired as Mr Davies, were left out in the cold. Not that it was any warmer inside the ground, where people wore overcoats and hats. Storms had struck other parts of London, yet Lord's so far had been spared, although the sky was threatening.

The Australians were bussed to the ground. At the Grace Gates, Ian Johnson asked the driver to stop. Out of respect to the traditions of Lord's and W. G. Grace, he insisted on getting out and walking through the Gates.

'That act by Ian reflected how we all felt about playing there,' Morris said.

•

When Bradman (baggy green on and no blazer) and Yardley (wearing his blazer and no cap) walked out to the middle for the toss, they drew polite applause, which was always the way at this holy place for cricket worshippers. Fans had spilled onto the arena behind the ropes ringing the arena, making the hallowed turf seem smaller than ever. The captains were followed by the usual group of photographers looking like a flock of geese.

Bradman was unsure about the greenness and it concerned him that it could be lively, but he put aside his second thoughts, and went for the percentage option when he won the toss. He tapped a shin and smiled in a signal to Barnes and Morris to put on their pads. Australia was batting.

The night before the game at a dinner in the Lord's Tavern, Barnes told Ring:

'I'll make a hundred at this ground. I won't be coming back.'

Barnes had three incentives to do well at Lord's. A year earlier when in England he had asked officials if he could have a net there, but had been refused. He took it as an unkind act of pomposity and snobbery and vowed to make a century in a retaliatory gesture to the cricket establishment HQ. A further incentive was that Barnes put an £8 bet on himself to reach three figures, receiving odds of 15 to 1. He would walk away with a nice collect of £120, a hefty payout in 1948. (After the match-fixing revelations of the late 1990s, this sort of bet would not have been allowed. But it wasn't the same as the bets put on Australia *losing* a Test in the 1981 Ashes by Australians Rod Marsh and Dennis Lillee, who were both playing. They received odds of 500 to 1 and fat payouts. Their thoughtless action was not corrupt, but it could have been construed that way and would have seen them thrown out of the game in the 1990s when match-fixing was revived as an issue in cricket.)

The third incentive was a special dispensation from the draconian Australian Cricket Board to have his wife at the game. Yet she was not allowed to stay at the Piccadilly Hotel with him.

Revenge, money, love and fame. Barnes had all the emotional inspiration he needed for a big performance. He was cautious from the first delivery and determined not to take chances until the ball was 'as big as a pumpkin'.

Coxon hurled an innocuous wide ball down leg-side. Normally Barnes would have dealt such a gift a fearful blow to leg. Because of the self-imposed pressures, he nudged at it and sent an easy catch to Hutton at fine leg-slip. Barnes was on his way for a duck, his pay-back, bet and fame dashed for the moment but on hold if Australia was to bat again.

Australia was 1 for 3. Bradman was in. Knowing that this was probably the second-last time he would ever bat in a Test at Lord's, the crowd gave him a loud and long reception. He claimed never to have nerves at the wicket, which may well have been true. His scratchy beginnings were partly because he needed that extra time at nearly 40 years to calibrate his skills, and partly because the ball was coming through at varying lengths, and also swinging on a damp, green wicket under a heavy atmosphere. He was virtually opening and this was often tough for a No. 3, who traditionally liked to start playing his strokes early, if not immediately.

The scoring was slow, and didn't pick up until Wright came on. He seemed to have a mandatory no ball in his first over each match this season. Morris, hearing the umpire's call early, had plenty of time to smack a six over mid-on.

Bedser was relieved after bowling for more than half the first session and no doubt Bradman believed he had won a small battle. After Bedser dismissed him twice in the leg trap at Trent Bridge, Bradman had been reticent with his glances. This batsman's nature was to respond with aggression and never let the bowler dictate. But the folly in pushing too hard at the glance had him in two minds. After Nottingham, there was a sense that the Surrey swinger had if not his measure, then some answers to his dominance. There was a real sense of David versus Goliath when compact, lean Bradman, all 5 ft 7 in (173 cm) of him, faced the broad-shouldered Surrey giant. But who was Goliath? Over the past 20 years, Bradman had been that colossus. Now Bedser, the thinking person's big man, was striving for dominance.

No bowler of pace or medium pace had ever had Bradman's measure. Nor had anyone prevailed over him for a complete series. Larwood, despite the myths concerning Bodyline, got him out four times in eight innings in that fateful 1932–33 Ashes. Yet only on two occasions did Bradman 'fail' with a low score against Larwood – at Adelaide when Bradman hit 8 in the first innings, and at Brisbane, when he managed just 24 in the second innings. The hysteria about Bodyline aside, by the end of the series, Bradman learnt, however anxiously, not to tame Larwood as before, but to handle him. The problem for Bradman in that series was as much Larwood's brilliance and ferocity, as remaining vigilant once he was seen off. Twice in the 1932–33 series, Verity had quickly taken Bradman's wicket after he had won a battle with Larwood. The one–two punching combination of Larwood's pace followed by Verity's spin, was a big factor in England winning the series.

On balance through all their combat in three seasons in 1928–29, in Australia, in 1930 in England and in 1932–33 in Australia, Bradman had by far the better of Larwood, the Nottingham Express, who was derailed more times than not. Only Hedley Verity could claim to be nearly on equal terms with Bradman over three seasons of encounters. In Australia, O'Reilly was mostly mastered by him, but not until after a real battle.

Big Alec Bedser now was making a claim, and he added to it by dismissing him soon after lunch, and for the third time, in that leg trap – caught Hutton – for just 38. This had been a mixed innings and by Bradman's standards, a failure. He had batted 115 minutes, and after a period of control, had again lapsed with his timing on the leg glance. Bradman, inside, still refused to believe that he had a problem with the ball swinging across his pads, at which he continued to flick. This stroke had been a steady run producer for him over two decades of first-class cricket, and he would never acknowledge defeat over its use. Was this stubbornness, or the 1930s Bradman inside the 1948 version pushing to emerge?

The cautious Hassett came to the wicket at 2 for 87. England at this moment could claim to be on top with two of the world's great bats back on the Lord's balcony. Morris proceeded steadily and just to remind everyone there was an aggressor inside the dutiful No. 1 in the batting order, he would open up with a punishing shot. One full-blooded pull bounced over the rope at mid-wicket full of running. Later he cut a ball from Yardley so late that it was posthumous. He too was set on a century in his first Test at Lord's. But with unassuming, undemonstrative Arthur, there was no self-boosting bet with a bookie at good odds; no firing up over a spat with an official; no particular female companion in the crowd to impress, and no special desire to steal the limelight from anybody. Apart from his artistry with the blade, Morris had the most coveted sportsman's gift of all – the will to reach a particular goal. Morris set his mind for centuries in the first innings in a new country on a tour, which he had achieved at Worcester; now he was brightly flowing towards a century on debut at Lord's. This kind of quiet determination was an asset of few in the history of cricket. It was one thing to wish for something, and another to set about doing it.

While Hassett held up an end, Morris drove handsomely through the covers, and pushed with typical grace through mid-on. He reached a century with two successive drives off Coxon with Australia on 160, a big share for an opener.

'It was one of the great feelings, and moments, of my cricket life,' Arthur said.

'He was absolutely superb,' Harvey recalled. 'As a young kid like I was, it was just magic to watch him play. Not only at Lord's but match after match.'

On 105 and the score on 166, he was caught in the gully by Hutton, off Coxon. Hutton had changed his position at fine leg-slip by moving a few metres to gully for the left-hander.

Morris's innings was the kind that stays in the memory. It was a neat classic. A bigger innings would perhaps have needed him building slowly again to say 150, bringing an interrupted memory of his flow, before he pushed further. Instead he had delivered what he wished at Lord's and was on his way.

Yet his dismissal caused the tourists to stumble. Miller came, was hobbled by balls hitting his legs, and then left after falling lbw to that brawny, brainy hulk Bedser. After tea, Hassett, curtailing his own natural stream of strokes, was yorked by Yardley after a charmed life for a sluggish 47. Brown, uncomfortable down the order instead of opening, again fell lbw to Yardley, this time for 24. Johnson proved patient for a while, but then had a slash at that imposter Edrich, brought on as a change bowler, and was caught by a grateful Evans.

Tallon, often underrated as a batsman, sauntered to the wicket for a 35-minute stay and struck a sweet 25 not out.

Having lost the advantage of batting first, Australia stumbled to 7 for 258 at stumps.

•

Mr Davies was there again early on Friday, along with another full house, in expectation of a quick Australian collapse as would befit yesterday's show. But cricket is not theatre that meets expectations. Nor is one performance like another night after night. Yes, Tallon, as anticipated, moved to a well-compiled fifty, and Lindwall made a blustering 15, before that bull Bedser did what was expected of him and chased them out of the arena. But then two batting clowns entered the bullring to torment the England beast. Australia's many matadors had been seen off. Now these foolish bladesmen, Johnston and Toshack, caused heartache for the spectators by hanging around, playing shots that would embarrass up-country tail-enders. Balls flew over slips and flopped over covers. The bulls looked confused and deflated. The last wicket jesters added 30, and Australia reached 350, when most of the crowd thought the visitors had no right to be anything like that. 270 would have been no psychological barrier for the home team. But 350 was ominously like those healthy tallies Australia had mounted in 10 of the 13 games played in England before this one.

The Australians added 92 in 70 minutes in the morning. The momentum was with them.

•

Bradman tossed Lindwall the ball and wished him a quiet 'good luck' as Hutton took block on leg-stump. The crowd hushed.

Lindwall swept in from the pavilion end to bowl his first delivery at just three-quarter pace. Just as he let go of the ball he felt a stabbing pain in his groin.

'After all my bombast in the dressing room,' Lindwall said, 'that was a frightening moment.'

Lindwall straightened up after the follow-through and glanced nervously at mid-on where Bradman was stationed. The captain's eyes were on Tallon as he tossed the ball back to him. Lindwall, in real pain, was relieved. He now would do everything to hide the recurrence of his groin strain.

In fact, Bradman had noticed Lindwall's contorted face when the injury flared. But shrewdly the skipper pretended he did not notice. His reason was that Lindwall would do everything to fake his fitness and bowl as well as possible. It would be another matter if he broke down completely. But Bradman knew of Lindwall's background as a top Rugby League footballer. Most players at the top in that sport were used to carrying injuries and adjusting to them. On a slow walk back to his mark, Lindwall kept a blank façade. Yet he struggled to make it through his first over, a maiden.

Bradman tossed the ball to Miller. He shook his head and tossed it back. Bradman walked up to him.

'How do you feel, Nugget?'

'No good, Don. My back still hurts.'

Miller claimed he told Bradman earlier in the dressing room that his back was playing up and he wouldn't be able to bowl. The captain had told him to see how he felt on the field. His back had not improved. Bradman turned and tossed the ball to Johnston, who was delighted at the opportunity to open the bowling for Australia in his first game at Lord's.

Bradman was now concerned. Miller presumably would not bowl at all in the match. Lindwall, his other striker, was hurt, and trying to conceal it. How long would he last? Would Australia be two top bowlers short when they needed to remove 20 England wickets to win? At this moment, the Lord's Test was in jeopardy, as was the aim to pass through the UK undefeated in 1948.

Bradman's capacities as a leader were strategic and tactical. They were bolstered by an unmatched comprehension of cricket history, law and precedence, not to mention his batting achievements. But he left a lot of room in his leadership for instinct. His antennae told him to let Lindwall stay on and support his toughness as a bowler and quiet desperation to do well in his first effort ever at Lord's. After all, Lindwall had fought stubbornly to be selected when Bradman's instincts were telling him that his number-one striker could not possibly have recovered from a groin problem in a week. The skipper's senses were right. Now he went with them again. Instead of giving Toshack a chance at the other end, the ball was thrown to Lindwall again.

Every one of his first 18 deliveries left him with a knife in the upper leg, yet his body was warming up and he was daring to lift his pace, ball by ball. There would be no extra surge of bumpers today, although Hutton and Washbrook were not to know it. Part of Lindwall's menace was the concern about when, and how often, he would unleash his potentially deadly bouncer. The batsmen had some relief knowing that Miller, the intimidator at Trent Bridge, would only be a threat in slips in this match; but the quieter, brooding Lindwall was always a worry.

He began his fourth over. The second delivery was at top speed. He moved a ball away from Washbrook, who edged it to Tallon. There was more than the normal exuberant reaction from Lindwall and Bradman at the departure of this batsman.

Fifteen minutes after lunch, Bradman brought on Johnson, which was a huge weight off Hutton's shoulders. He had seen off Lindwall. Facing an off-spinner, who gave the ball more inviting air than Laker, was such a lovely sight for the batsmen. Bradman would have had in mind his own sense of relief when seeing off Larwood in the Bodyline series. It caused a rush of blood when seeing harmless spin twirling down the wicket from

Verity, who he tried to hit out of the park once too often and was dismissed. Hutton didn't even have time to become excited by Johnson. He pushed forward to a slow, well-pitched-up ball and was bowled.

Hutton had been at the wicket 65 minutes for 20. Bradman's sweat over a possible loss in that moment between the first over and the second, when he thought his two top bowlers were injured, had now evaporated. The sight of Hutton's back as he wandered despondently to the pavilion and the silent opprobrium of the unforgiving Long Room confirmed that the game had swung Australia's way.

Bradman, the most consultative captain Australia ever had, chatted with Lindwall. It was brief.

'You right for another spell, Ray?'

'Yep, Don.'

Lindwall proceeded to clean-bowl Edrich and Dollery in three balls. England was 4 for 46 and in disarray. Compton and Yardley were brought together and forced to defend their way out of trouble. Yet Compton's feisty, confident style could not be subdued for long, especially on this good second-day wicket. He began to use his favourite stroke, the sweep, which Miller called the finest sight in England next to the hills of Derbyshire, and the eyes of Princess Margaret. *Down on one knee, body forward and head over the ball.* Compton's sweep was textbook perfection and it exhibited what the illustrations and texts never tell the student: confidence, courage and timing. Yardley played within his limitations. He waited for the right ball to hit to the on and pushed forward to Lindwall, aware that after two bowling spells, 'Atomic Ray', this day, was not inclined to blast out anyone with bouncers. Yardley delivered a captain's knock. These two added 85 runs in 118 minutes.

England was 4 for 133.

Fifty-five overs were up and Bradman took the new ball. Compton (53) succumbed to Johnston's swing and was caught by Miller in slips. One run later, Lindwall bowled Yardley (44), leaving England on the ropes at 6 for 134.

The tail made some sort of defiant movement without wagging enough to give its owner and fans joy. There was little gaiety and some relief as England reached 9 for 207, and avoided the follow-on (150 short).

●

Lindwall bowled Bedser before noon on day three in front of the packed Saturday crowd, giving him 5 for 70 off 27.4 overs. Four of his victims were bowled. Fast bowling against quality opposition on a near-perfect wicket rarely matched this. Add to this the sheer determination of Lindwall carrying an injury to which lesser characters would submit, and his effort at Lord's would stand the overworked description, 'great'.

14

—

Barnes' Storming

BARNES NOW HAD his second chance to secure his bet, please his wife and thumb his nose at the Lord's administrator who had shown him so little respect a year earlier. He played himself in, eschewed any aggression, and examined each new bowler like an entomologist dissecting an insect. Morris was sound and more confident. The wheel of self-belief had turned full circle and he was enjoying his strokes, even the defensive ones. At lunch, with Australia on 0 for 73 and Barnes on 25, Morris had reached an untroubled 40, and he was thinking about a relaxing lunch, then an assault on a second century in a Test. He had done this once before in an Ashes Test, in Adelaide in 1946–47.

Any thoughts of another hundred were dashed by Wright, who bowled him for 62. The time was 2.52 p.m. and approaching the middle of the second session. Australia was 1 for 122, and in a strong position with a lead of 267 that effectively meant England could not win.

This was reassuring for Bradman as he came down the stairs from the balcony, through the door to the Long Room for the last time in a Test. He passed the members on their high chairs waiting for a further feast of wickets, through the door, down the pavilion steps to the gate, and finally onto the arena.

The pavilion, then the rest of the crowd rose to him. Aware of Bradman's early hesitancy, Yardley crowded him against Laker, who was circling for a kill. The batsman started uncertainly but settled quicker than in his previous three Test innings. Bedser kept feeding him the ball that swung away down legside, but Bradman checked himself from the usual punch at it. Barnes took up the cudgels against Laker and was lucky to survive a second missed stumping by Evans, who was having a bad day. It was made worse by Barnes, who thumped the bowler through covers for four, and then bowed to the sardonic cheers from the crowd. Barnes may have put himself under pressure to perform, but his luck and good form were telling him that he would probably reach a century. Players in his class did not fret over being dropped or missed behind the stumps. They knew that in most innings of three hours there would be one or two opportunities for the opposition to dismiss them. Survival only indicated that a hundred was there for the taking.

They took the score to 1 for 222, and a partnership of 100. Bradman had his 50 (in 98 minutes), and Barnes was on 96. He dithered on that score for 10 minutes before off-driving Coxon for four. His century had taken 255 minutes. He received applause from the crowd, a grin and handshake from his captain. He waved to his wife. All he needed now was his bookie to open his wallet and Barnes' day would be complete.

'Sid Barnes was the best batsman of coping with the new ball I ever saw,' Morris remarked. 'And I think but for six years of war, Sid would have been second only to Bradman as the greatest batsman I ever saw. He was a brilliant player.'

It was 5 p.m. Australia now had a lead of 361, with almost a full complement of batsmen intact. The bowlers and fielders were tiring, and there were more than two days left to play.

Barnes celebrated by swinging Laker for two sixes over long on, and driving him either side of the wicket for four. He took a single to keep the strike, taking the tally for the over to 21. Laker would have had a nasty sense of déjà vu after his last pasting of sixes in the MCC match at Lord's. But he was proving a hardy character intent on retribution, if not now, then in another Test, or even another series. Barnes continued with the slaughter against all the bowlers, but inevitably skied a hit and Washbrook took a catch right on the boundary. Barnes was on his way for 141, which was nearly a pound a run when he accounted for his bet.

Australia was 2 for 296.

In the dressing room, puckish Hassett got up from chair in front of the TV. He had been watching Australia's John Bromwich playing at Wimbledon.

'Aw damn! I've got to go out and bat,' Hassett said. 'I'm going to miss it.'

He trotted along the Long Room's linoleum with the applause for Barnes still going and then strode to the wicket, his walk, either intentionally or not, looking like a Groucho Marx impersonation.

He played Yardley on to his wicket for a first ball duck and off he went, on what was now the longest walk of all, back through the Long Room to the sounds of diffident coughs and little else. Hassett returned to his chair in front of the TV saying:

'Well, at least I didn't miss much of the tennis,' he said. 'Is it the same game [of the set]?'

'It's the same point,' one of the Australians said. The rest of the players convulsed in laughter.

'You bastards!' Hassett muttered.

Out in the middle, Yardley rapped Miller on the pads. England and the crowd went up as one.

'Not out!' said the umpire. Miller shook his head and gestured humorously to the crowd, who laughed at their own impetuous appealing. Miller then heaved a mighty six over square leg into the grandstand.

To everyone's surprise, Bradman edged a ball from Bedser to Edrich at slips and was on his way 11 short of a century. He had avoided the leg trap, after three successive dismissals there, but he had fallen to Bedser for the fifth time in the season – four times in four starts in the Tests. Bradman, it seemed, had fulfilled his own implied prophecy about Bedser's skills, aired in the first week of the tour at the Sportsman's Club lunch at the Savoy.

This was the 14th successive Test match versus England (in which Bradman batted) that he had made at least 50 in one innings or the other, a remarkable feat of consistency unmatched in Ashes cricket or Tests against or for England.

Bradman left Lord's in a Test for the last time. The crowd gave him a strong ovation. He knew he had a few more chances for a farewell innings at Lord's, in games against Middlesex before the Fourth Test, and the Gentlemen of England after the Fifth Test. For now, he would settle into contentment soon enough, given Australia's position in the Test.

At stumps on Saturday night it was 4 for 343, a lead now of 478.

•

Despite rain interruptions, Bradman had no intention of declaring until well into the afternoon of day four, Monday, after letting Miller loose in his element in an atmosphere without pressure. He was dancing between the showers, cutting, driving and hooking in a manner which reminded most of the Lord's spectators of his fabulous performances in 1945. Brown (32), still a fish out of water batting at No. 6, was precise; a neat technician, who would not be flustered by fans, bowlers or batting fury from his partner.

The declaration came at 7 for 460. The lead was 595, and this was overkill. Yet Bradman was still going for a win. He felt he had enough time in four and a half sessions to dismiss England. The timing of the declaration and the mammoth score it had been set simply meant England had no chance to win the game.

•

The home team began its hoped-for marathon at 3.20 p.m. on a wicket that had been livened up just enough to allow Lindwall and Johnston to extract some response from it. Johnston had Hutton dropped by Lindwall in slips when he was on naught. After that, the batsman seemed intent on grim defence, with the odd heart-stopping wave at balls he should have left. He took 72 minutes (which included a 38-minute rain delay) to score a run, and he was not having fun. Washbrook, bouncier, and more energetic, seemed to be up for the challenge, however futile any emotion would be in facing Lindwall, in particular, under the conditions.

Hutton (13) edged to Johnson in slips off Lindwall with the score at 42. The England champion was out of his misery, and in turn, somewhat out-of-form when facing this Australian attack. But he was not alone. Edrich did not relish Lindwall's shorter deliveries, and he kept dropping under them, unprepared to chance the hook, or any shot. Bradman took Lindwall off. It was a relief for Washbrook and Edrich, to see him slipping on his short- and long-sleeved sweaters. Gone, for the moment, was the danger of this less (for England) than lovable Aussie, who seemed to have distaste for opposition batsmen, with whom he refused to fraternise. He would be rested at backward point.

Most observers thought Bradman had erred in taking his gun bowler off too early, but there was, as ever, thought behind the move. Toshack held no fears for the batsmen with his nagging leg-stump accuracy. Their adrenaline rush would have subsided with the sight of an amiable fellow removing his sweater and preparing to bowl.

Edrich had not scored for 20 minutes. As soon as Toshack appeared he went to drive him and edged another catch to Johnson in slips. The change down at the bowling crease had worked again in this innings. With England at 65, Toshack delivered an unintentional swinging full-toss, which Washbrook (37) tried to cut. He was late in the stroke and edged the ball.

Tallon squeezed his glove under it, which reached him as a yorker.

Harvey, Loxton, Miller and Bradman judged it as one of the most remarkable catches ever made behind the wicket. To them, Tallon was a flawed genius.

The ever-jaunty Compton was joined by burly Dollery. Bradman had Lindwall removing his sweaters for a dash at the new man, but these two looked in no trouble for the last half hour of the day.

England was 3 for 106, still 489 behind with one day to play. The odds were now with an Australian victory, weather and Compton permitting.

Bradman was in good spirits. He looked forward to Sunday off, with victory on Monday very much on his mind.

•

The team spent Sunday afternoon at Windsor Castle at the invitation of the Earl of Gowrie, VC, Lieutenant Governor of Windsor and a former Governor-General of Australia. Tour members wandered the rooms looking at treasures, documents and other relics from British history. Some were taken with the suits of armour worn by kings in medieval Britain. It reminded the Victorians in the group of bushranger Ned Kelly, and the older members thought it could be useful, though a bit ponderous, against Bodyline.

Queen Mary, the Queen Mother and the widow of King George V, received the team in the grounds of Frogmore House, which dated back to the 1680s and had been bought for Queen Charlotte in 1792. It was set amidst the extensive Home Park of Windsor Castle and surrounded by scenic gardens.

'She was an extremely regal person,' Johnson said, 'last of the straightbacks, and she was wearing a sort of turban-type hat.'

The only three with cameras on the day – Brown, Ring and Loxton – were hovering, wondering if they could photograph her.

Ring asked if he could take a shot of her.

'That's what I'm here for young man,' she replied.

That prompted Brown and Loxton to take photographs too. Brown finished his snaps quickly, but Loxton wanted Bradman in the shot with Queen Mary. Both the captain and the Queen obliged and stood close to each other looking a fraction uncomfortable. Loxton took his time with his Box Brownie, and in the tradition of all amateurs, couldn't quite get his camera to work. Bradman and the other players became fidgety as the Queen Mother waited and looked less and less amused as the seconds ticked by. Finally Loxton was ready and had his camera operating.

'Arh, got it!' Loxton said. 'Now, Your Majesty, a nice big smile for the dickie bird please.'

'To her everlasting credit,' Johnson recalled, 'she gave a bit of a half-laugh.'

When they got back in the bus, a bemused Bradman said to Loxton:

'Sam, you can't talk like that to royalty.'

'George,' Loxton said, 'she cracked it for a grin, didn't she?'

Bradman shook his head and had to smile himself.

•

The captain was learning a little about well-placed irreverence. Later in the afternoon, the Earl of Gowrie had the group for an up-market 'tea' that would put the Ritz in the shade. Among the guests were Lord and Lady Tedder. Air Marshal Tedder, the former deputy to General Eisenhower in World War II, and the man in charge of all air operations in Western Europe, fooled around with the group. He put a towel across his arm and pretended to be a waiter.

With a full tray in his hand, he approached Miller, whom he befriended during the Victory Tests in the summer of 1945.

'Excuse me, sir,' Tedder said. 'Your tea, sir.'

'Thank you very much, boy,' Miller, who had been an RAAF Flying Officer on secondment to the RAF, replied in an exaggerated pompous English voice as he accepted the tea. He then handed Tedder a coin, saying, 'Here you are, boy.'

'Thank you very much, sir,' Tedder replied, with a mock tug of his forelock.

•

On day five, Johnston delivered a match-winning away-swinger off a good length, which was a tough delivery to negotiate even for a set batsman. Compton, his eye not yet in, edged it to slips. Miller dived, and added circus juggling to his fielding repertoire as he snaffled a stunning catch on his back at the second attempt. It was the 'something special' from bowler and fielder to remove England's No. 1 batsman, given Hutton's sudden form decline. Despite his incapacity to bowl, Miller was worth his place in the team for fielding alone.

Dollery added the defiance expected of him, but made one error that sealed the game, and perhaps even his fate in this series. Lindwall had been delivering the odd bouncer after none in the first innings. Dollery was ready to duck or hook every ball. Perhaps he noticed Lindwall's round-arm slinging action, which often signalled the throat ball. He ducked. The ball came through on a good length, missed him and knocked over the stumps. It was an ignominious end to a battling innings, in which Dollery (37) had appeared the best of England's bats on the day.

The indefatigable Evans produced an unbeaten 24, but the rest of the tail, as was their right, under the hopeless circumstances, collapsed.

In the field, there was an ungainly scramble for a stump souvenir when Miller fought and tumbled on the pitch with Hassett. Miller's strength won the struggle.

England was rolled for 186. Toshack had taken 5 for 61, yet Lindwall was the difference taking another three wickets and 8 for 131 for the match.

How precarious a game is cricket? Had his groin played up as it did in the Nottingham Test, and had he been less determined, England would have had a far better chance of victory. Luck was with Bradman and his men and Australia was the winner by 409 runs.

The captain was smiling more. Australia had to draw at least one of the last three games to retain the Ashes, which was the primary aim. It had all but achieved this with Australia leading the series 2:0.

•

Not all the Australians celebrated. Johnson, who had bowled well in the first innings, was let off his duties at the crease in England's second, because of a near tragedy at home. His tiny son had fallen headfirst down stairs at the family home in Melbourne. The toddler was concussed and in serious danger. Mrs Johnson had phoned her husband. They had an urgent discussion. Johnson was ready to go home, knowing that a boat trip would take several weeks, and that a plane trip would be difficult to arrange quickly.

'The most dangerous period will be in the next 24 hours,' his wife informed him. 'You wouldn't be able to return in time. I think you should stay until we see how he goes.'

This misfortune put the game, no matter how grand, in perspective. Johnson was to spend an anxious time waiting to hear more news. The boy recovered over the next few anxious weeks, and Johnson did not have to leave the squad.

15
—
Morris's Minor Classic

AUSTRALIA REACHED THE mid-way part of the tour, and a day after the Lord's Test was across London at the Oval doing battle with Surrey, in the 17th game of the arduous tour. This was the danger period for most tour squads, including this particularly focused and dedicated group. The players had nine days and two county games before the Third Test at Manchester. There were distractions. The tennis at Wimbledon took precedence in the public mind for the next week or so. The summer was in full swing, with the lads receiving invitations, both official and unofficial, to attend enough parties and functions to satisfy even Miller.

Bradman and manager Keith Johnson had to create a fine balance between fun, functions and the fixture. The captain wanted to keep an edge on his players' keenness without them becoming bored, homesick, worn-out and rusty. With these things in mind, he decided to lead against Surrey, give those battling for a place another chance, and to rest his pacemen. He wished also to see the men's singles final at Wimbledon, especially with Australian John Bromwich a big chance to make it. In came Hamence, Harvey, Loxton, McCool, Saggers and

Ring. Out went Morris, Johnson, Lindwall, Tallon, Barnes and Johnston.

•

On the night the Lord's Test finished, Keith Miller, an inveterate concert-goer who loved his classical music, slipped into a tuxedo for a show at the Albert Hall, and then a party afterwards. He didn't straggle back to the Piccadilly until breakfast time. He bumped into Bradman coming out of his room.

'Good morning, Keith,' Bradman said.

Miller knew he was in some sort of trouble. Bradman would normally address him as 'Nugget'. The formal 'Keith' was ominous. At the Oval that morning, Wednesday 30 June, Bradman won the toss and put the county in – minus its star Alec Bedser (who had made way for his brother Eric). Bradman's aim was to win the game as soon as possible in the hope of everyone heading for Wimbledon on Friday afternoon, 2 July.

Miller was in no state to bowl, but he could hide behind his alleged back problem, which the skipper now doubted was as bad as the champion all-rounder was making out. Bradman placed Miller at fine-leg and opened the bowling with Loxton and Toshack. At the end of each over, Miller had to trudge from fine-leg at one end to fine-leg at the other. Miller, still high from partying, chatted to spectators, who were amused by his plight, which was Bradman's minor, unstated punishment for disobeying his only tour rule that each player had to turn up fit to play when selected.

'I can lend you my bike,' one Cockney called from close to the boundary.

'That's a good idea,' Miller replied.

A few minutes later, the bike was handed over the fence to Miller at the end of an over. He cycled to the opposite fine-leg position, much to the amusement of the crowd and the cricketers. Bradman could not help laughing, and soon brought Miller to a position closer to the wicket. Later, Miller was tossed the ball. He delivered one maiden, which was a fraction wayward, and signalled to the captain that his back wouldn't take any more.

Surrey's Jack Parker, batting lustily at No. 5, curtailed for three hours Australia's steady mowing down of the Surrey order. Parker hit 10 fours in his 76 before Ring trapped him lbw. The leg-spinner was steady, taking 3 for 51. Three others, Loxton, Hamence and Toshack (2 wickets each), shared the spoils with Ring.

The county made 221.

Bradman asked Hassett and Hamence to open the Australian batting, but with the latter out for a duck, the captain was soon at the wicket with the score at 1 for 6. Showing remarkable fitness, and no signs of the rib injury, or the fibrositis that had long plagued him, Bradman gave a standard display of his unmatched style of innings architecture. His first 50 took 54 minutes and he was 84 not out at stumps in 91 minutes. Thursday morning, he and Hassett, playing a support role with beautiful strokes that matched his skipper's, carried on where they had left off in a partnership of 231. Bradman reached his hundred in 110 minutes at a run a ball, and then had some fun hitting at everything with the aim of throwing his wicket away. He eventually skied one to mid-on and was on his way for 128 in 140 minutes with 15 fours. It was his sixth century of the tour.

Hassett a half hour later completed his century and also went on the rampage to be out at 139. Harvey was run out for 43, but did enough for Bradman to believe he was ready for an advance to Test level at the next appropriate moment.

Australia was all out 389.

Surrey went in again and Laurie Fishlock (61, with some special driving), Parker (81 in three hours, giving him a fine double) and Errol Holmes (54) held up the tourists' plans to sample the strawberries and cream and champagne at Wimbledon. The county reached 289. McCool seemed the most eager to depart for the tennis, as he bagged 6 for 113 in a long spell of nearly 46 overs, which demonstrated that his injured finger was at least standing up.

This left Australia 122 to make.

Harvey, now in beautiful form with the bat and brimming with confidence in the field with his acrobatic catching skills, wanted to open the batting and go for the runs. So did Loxton. He approached Bradman as they walked off the ground.

'What must you do to get a knock in this side?' Loxton asked.

'I'll tell you what you've got to do,' Bradman said. 'You and your little mate [Harvey] can put on the pads and open.'

Harvey (73 not out, including two sixes and eight fours) and Loxton (47 not out), who had proved themselves power-hitting partners before, knocked off the runs in 57 minutes by early Friday afternoon.

When they returned to the dressing room only Hamence, the next man in, was still in his cricket gear. The rest of the squad were in their lounge suits ready to make a dash for Wimbledon.

'We had to make our own way to the tennis by train,' Loxton recalled.

Bradman could be excused for deserting his batsmen. He had been invited into the Royal Box. When he arrived, TV cameras swung to him and spontaneous applause broke out. Bradman smiled, shook hands with the Duchess of Kent, who was sitting in front of him, and then sat down in front of Sir Norman Brookes, himself a former tennis champion. In the fifth set, Bromwich had three match points. He was leading 5:2 and 40:15. Sir Norman leaned forward and whispered:

'He must win! He can't lose all three.'

'I agree,' Bradman said.

But Bromwich ended losing *five* match points, and the title to American Robert Falkenburg.

Bradman had sympathy for the loser, who was in despair after coming so close and failing. He wanted to commiserate with the tennis champion directly but when Bromwich was in the nearby radio broadcast box, the cricketer gave him a sympathetic wave. Bromwich gestured with his hands in a manner that suggested he had come to terms with his loss. Later Bradman, who had played and beaten plenty of Wimbledon participants in friendly tennis matches in 1930, pointed out that many players would have given up a lot to be a runner-up at Wimbledon. Lindwall was most upset for his good mate Bromwich, with whom he played tennis at a local club in Sydney. Lindwall knew how good the Australian was, and how hard he had trained for the event.

The American winner later complained that the crowd was biased against him, and he was right. Any Australian competing against anyone other than a British player in 1948 would have been supported.

But after the Australian cricket team's run of 17 matches, with 14 wins and three draws over two and a half months, the British public yearned for them to be defeated, if only by a county. With this in mind, Bradman reluctantly turned over the reins to Hassett for the match against Gloucestershire at Bristol, beginning the day after the Wimbledon final. Bradman went off to the country to stay with his mate Walter Robins, aware that, in terms of tour matches, the tourists were half-way, and therefore at the beginning of the run home. Bradman, and the rest of the squad, were now more conscious of the captain's third aim for the tour to go through undefeated. (The other aims were to retain the Ashes, which was most likely, and then to win the series outright.)

•

The players loved the hilly town of Bristol, 200 km west of London on the south west coast, with its cluster of 16th-Century churches in the old city, ancient bridges, maritime heritage and position on the rivers Frome and Avon. The city's cricket history was rich too, with the ground at Ashley Down first used in 1888. Dr W. G. Grace, then 40 years, and with a decade of top cricket still in him, was one of its more famous performers when playing for the county. New additions after the war had been a covered stand for the members, and an uncovered mound stand on the public side of the ground that seated 3,000 people.

Approaching 18,000 turned up to watch the Australians on 3 July, and restricted the normal joy at Bristol of being able to roam around and admire the flower beds and trellises of rambler roses. The most prominent building seen from the ground was the grey edifice of Mullers Orphanage, which had let all its children watch this special Saturday encounter. The Bristol Aircraft factory was a kilometre away. The sky was filled with planes taking a look at the crowded arena.

The wicket here had never been perfect, but since cricket resumed in 1946 after the war it had been good for batsmen, if they played straight. The strip tended to keep low. If a player wanted to stay at the wicket for a big score, he had to eschew cuts off the off-stump or cross-bat slashes that would often see the batsman lbw or bowled. In 1947 it was transformed back to the spinner's paradise it had been pre-war, but the turf specialists seemed to have gone too far. Games at Bristol now only lasted two days. Gloucestershire had two star tweakers: Tom Goddard, an off-spinner, and Cecil ('Sam') Cook, who was left-arm orthodox. Together, they were already half-way to snaring more than 300 wickets for the season.

Hassett and Co were conscious of these spin twins. When Australia won the toss and batted, the instruction was to go after them, especially the 48-year-old, lean and statuesque Goddard, with his bucket hands. He was a crowd favourite, who would receive enormous support. Goddard had played once against Australia in the Old Trafford Fourth Test of 1930, when he was a mere lad of 30, taking 2 (Fairfax and Hornibrook) for 49. Eighteen years on, he was being touted by the press as a replacement for Laker, whose returns at Lord's of 2 for 138 had not pleased England's selectors.

The Australian selectors kept Harvey, Loxton and McCool in the line-up, which was a fair indication that they were in the running for possible Third Test call ups.

Barnes (44), after some electric square cutting, became another notch on Cook's hefty 1948 belt when caught by Jack Crapp, but not until he had been in a 102-run stand with the rampant Morris, who was in magnificent touch. Any real or imagined weaknesses had been ironed out in his century at Lord's. Now he was as free as the pilots in the planes buzzing over the ground. The 'shuffle' across the crease before playing at a delivery, the armchair critics were saying, was now gone. Morris sailed to a hundred before lunch, displaying all the strokes, from drives to cuts, pulls and hooks.

(Morris achieved the pre-lunch century on two other occasions – once for New South Wales in Sydney, and once for Australia in South Africa.)

Bradman heard the scores on the radio, along with all the other county match scores, and marvelled at the speed of accumulation of his players, who had pushed towards 200. This allowed him to relax and enjoy himself in the company of Robins. The situation at Bristol was not Bradford or Southampton. After just one session, it was near impossible for the Australians to lose.

'After we [Barnes and Morris] were through the new ball,' Morris recalled, 'on came Tom [Goddard]. And I went after him. When he bowled [round the wicket] to an off-side field, I hit him to the on. When he bowled to a leg field, I hit him through the off field, or lofted him. I was on a high and really did have the bowling by the scruff of the neck.'

It did not matter if Goddard, Cook, or any of the five other bowlers were in front of him; the left-hander was in total control, not giving a chance as he powered on to a second hundred before tea. His other partnerships were 136 with Miller (51) and 162 with Harvey (95).

'On reaching 290,' Morris said, 'I thought, "Wouldn't it be nice to get 300," and then promptly hit a full-toss back to the bowler [Colin Scott]. I just lost concentration.'

This terrible lapse came after five hours. Morris had hit 290 out of 4 for 466, at a strike rate of well over a hundred. Had he reached that 300, he would have joined a select group of Australian bladesmen – Victor Trumper, Charlie Macartney (against counties), and Bradman (twice in Tests) who had smashed triple hundreds in first-class matches in England. (Later Bob Simpson in a Test, and the remarkable Michael Hussey, with three triples against counties, along with Justin Langer and Darren Lehmann hitting one triple each, would be added to this illustrious list.)

Australia reached 5 for 560 at stumps on day one.

'Neil Harvey and Sam Loxton further ripped Goddard apart,' Morris said and added, dryly, 'that was the last we read of his taking over from Jim [Laker].'

Goddard's figures were 32 overs, 0 for 186. Not once was he heard to utter his West Country burring, drawl of, 'How were it?' Somehow he managed three maidens. His biggest problem was the Australians' nasty habit of dancing down the wicket at him. Goddard had been used to county batsmen playing him from the crease, and allowing him to take control. The tourists belted him off a length and were like a pack of jackals who would not let up. It was the end of any further Test aspirations.

Cook did better with 3 for 146, but three other bowlers reached their centuries. This blitz put the success of two capable county spinners, with their huge wicket-taking tandem sprees in 1948, in perspective.

Harvey continued on his steady, run-making way, being careful, but not fastidious about Bradman's early instruction not to hit the ball in the air. He did not always obey this directive, especially when hooking or gliding beautifully to the spinners to loft them into empty outfields. His reselection in the Test side was now a matter of when and not maybe.

Loxton, too, boosted his chances with a forceful, whirlwind 159. His hitting method, in the tradition of the outstanding bludgeoning batsman, was to let technique well and truly become the servant of aggression. It was practical too. Loxton would often come to the wicket after the early crease-dwellers such as Barnes, Hassett, Bradman, Morris, Brown and Miller had eaten up most of the batting time. If he were to be noticed, Loxton had to strike out from the first over he faced, more in the manner of a one-day player of the 21st Century than a Test middle-order batsman of the first half of the 20th Century.

McCool hit a commanding 76, and if he were to follow this up with another bag of wickets, he too would be presenting strong credentials for a Test spot.

Hassett declared at 7 for 774 on the second morning, Australia's second 700-plus score and the highest for the summer so far.

Gloucester, a strong county this year, had some notable batsmen, including Charlie Barnett, already discarded from the Tests, and Crapp, who now had his chance to impress. The short, slight opener George Emmett had no idea that he was under scrutiny in this match. Moves being contemplated by England selectors meant he was on trial without knowing it.

Emmett opened well and made 43. More importantly, he seemed to have little trouble with Lindwall or Loxton. Such was the mindset of the England selectors that it could well have been enough. Crapp lasted 210 minutes in making an unconquered 100, which had to be noticed. He was only the second player outside the Tests to reach this mark against the tourists.

During this innings, Barnes fielded at third man, or fine-leg, seemingly uninterested in proceedings in the middle. What was on his mind? A bet at the nearest race track? A deal to send a car or two to Australia? Certainly it would have little to do with the cricket. Hassett, normally a disciplinarian despite his court jestering, let him do his thing, and did not make an effort to direct him anywhere. Barnes just sauntered the length of the field at the end of each over to take up his position. When Ring came on to bowl his leg-spinners, he set his field and was perplexed about Barnes' grazing a long way from the middle on the big ground.

'Have you noticed Barnes wandering around at third man?' he asked Hassett.

'What makes you think you're any different from the rest of us?' Hassett replied, deepening the mystery of the dreamy fielder.

Barnes later, in his own time, meandered to somewhere near covers, where he remained, still without orders or reaction from Hassett. Many players wondered what Bradman would have made of it all. Then again, Barnes would never have behaved this way with his 'cobber' running the show.

Gloucestershire reached 279. Johnson, in better spirits after news that his son was off the critical list and on the mend, celebrated by capturing 6 for 68.

Hassett, poker-faced, pretended to be unsure about enforcing the follow-on with the opposition 495 behind. Gloucestershire *was* asked to bat again, and it mustered only 132. Johnson took another bag of 5, giving him 11 for the match.

There was irony in his form as opposed to that of Goddard. Before the game, Bradman had told Johnson to observe Goddard.

'It's a chance to be educated by the methods of a really outstanding off-spinner,' Bradman told him, 'He can delivery leg and off theory, and has, flight, and variations in length, and spin.'

Later, Johnson had a laugh with the captain over the advice.

'I learned how *not* to bowl to Morris, Harvey, Loxton and McCool,' Johnson said.

•

The Australians left Bristol with a renewed confidence at a critical moment of the tour in preparation for the middle Test of the series. There was healthy rivalry for one or two possible spots in the line-up. Even Ring, discarded since before the First Test, was back in contention. Now every single member of the touring squad was in good-to-excellent form, giving the selectors an embarrassment of riches from which to choose the Third Test squad.

•

Loxton's fine touch with the bat, exceptional fielding and steadiness with the ball got him the nod from the selectors in place of Brown, who was dropped for Manchester, where the pitch was helpful for pace bowlers. Had Miller been well enough to bowl, Brown may have retained his spot. But with Australia now a bowler short from the full contingent it expected to put on the field, a stock bowler was required, and preferably someone who could bat. McCool's injury was troubling him again, and Ring had not done quite enough to force his way in.

•

Deeper problems in the England camp emerged with the news over BBC radio that Len Hutton had been dropped from the England side. It was a huge shock, even for the Australians, and one of the most controversial omissions in cricket history. In Australia in 1928–29, Bradman had been dumped after one match, in which he scored 18 and 1. Yet he didn't have a Test record to defend. Hutton had been England's best batsman since 1938 and the decline of Wally Hammond. Hutton's form at Nottingham had been good, despite being hit and troubled by Miller, and his early difficulties with Lindwall. It was true that he had struggled against Lindwall at Lord's in both innings, and this was without the threat of Miller. Should they both be back in harness at Manchester, it was thought that he would be humiliated and perhaps then dumped for the series. Better, it was suggested, that he recover some form in county games before coming back confident at his home ground of Leeds for the Fourth Test. (On 3 July, Hutton made just 15 for Yorkshire against Surrey at Sheffield, which would not have helped the perception of his form. In the same game, Wardle took 6 for 17 in Surrey's second innings, which added to his status.)

That was the gist of the England selectors' logic. No thought seemed to be given to the humiliation for such a champion cricketer, still in his prime, in the middle of the hottest contest of his life. Not much consideration too, had been set aside for placing him down the order. From one perspective this was understandable. To slip him in at 3 or even 4, or 5, with another, lesser light (and there was no better opener in the UK than Hutton) taking his position at the top of the order, would perhaps have been a bigger blow to his dignity than dropping him altogether. There was no real glee in the Australian camp. The captain and his bowlers believed they had his measure in 1948. In eight starts against Australia, Hutton had failed five times, and had yet to score 75 in one innings. His aggregate against the tourists in 8 innings was 242 for an average of 30.25, about half what was expected. Yet the Australians were lifted by the omission. It was a clear message that the England selectors were rattled and had no answers at the top of the order to the pace attack. Bradman would not rest easy. He anticipated Hutton's return for Leeds, and the Oval, the scene of his 1938 triumph. Still, the Australian captain was comforted in knowing that his grand plans to upset Hutton, with pressure from dangerous pace and Barnes fielding so close, had worked so well.

Left-hander Jack Crapp's century at Bristol, as foreseen by several critics, secured him an England cap at age 35. George Emmett was selected after his modest showing in the same game, which was not a move to inspire. Only Compton had demonstrated the capacity to take on the Australians and he had done it with dash, courage and skill.

The further disarray and uncertainty in the England camp was exposed by the dumping of Alec Coxon after the only Test of his career. But at least it was at Lord's and he took three fine wickets – Barnes, Morris and Brown. Coxon's form for

Yorkshire afterwards was strong too, when he took 6 for 17 in Surrey's first innings of the Sheffield game. But it was too late.

Laker and Wright were omitted for Lancashire paceman Dick Pollard, who could swing the ball both ways, and spinner Young, who had played at Nottingham. Pollard, also aged 36, would be on his home track, where he had success against India in 1946, taking 7 for 87 for the match. Wardle was made 12th man, which was no doubt in part a reward for dismissing Bradman at Bramall Lane. The fixation of the media with the Australian captain had to be seen in the light of the fact that he would bat more than 20 times before the end of the Test series, and the England selectors could not reward every player that dismissed him. He would often be asked for his opinion in public or private about a player, who may have bowled against him, even dismissed him. Bradman's every word would be absorbed and passed on like a permanent breeze of comment around the cricket world. He would try to be diplomatic and fair, and despite the opportunities for mischief, he would never have been misleading. During the Lancashire match in late May Bradman had told England selector Robins that Pollard had always troubled him and he feared him more than Bedser, despite his praise for him earlier in the season. Robins, who trusted his great Australian friend, made a mental note on Pollard's behalf. Now he was in.

In 1946–47 in Australia, when Bradman complimented Doug Wright, whose figures rarely looked exceptional (for instance, in that series he took 23 wickets – the most in the Ashes series – but at 43.04), he (Bradman) was accused of playing mind games with England's selectors. Yet good judges agreed with Bradman. Wright was an outstanding bowler, who peaked in 1947 with 177 wickets at 21.12. But his 2 for 123 at Lord's was not enough.

Laker's 2 for 128 at Lord's belied his misfortune with several dropped catches and missed stumpings. But there was high regard for him in England's cricket hierarchy. As with Hutton, you could bet he would be back sooner rather than later.

England had finally, sensibly jettisoned the concept of one medium-pacer backed up by stop-gap alleged merchants of swing. More of an 'attack' in the true sense had been chosen, with some spin and still opportunities for the overrated Edrich, and the underrated Yardley.

Four changes – Hutton, Coxon, Laker and Wright out, for Emmett, Crapp, Pollard and Young – meant there would be a different atmosphere in the England dressing room, especially in the bowling corner. Yet no one, especially Bradman, expected an easy run at Manchester.

•

Sam Loxton recounted the tale of how Crapp and Bedser had been playing in a county game, Surrey versus Gloucestershire at the Oval, after which they travelled up from London by train. When they arrived at England's hotel, Bedser was detained by an autograph hunter in the foyer. Crapp approached the reception desk alone. He was conscious of not being as recognisable as his travelling colleague, so when he spoke to the female receptionist he perhaps overreacted.

She looked up from the register and said:

'Bed sir?'

He replied, defensively:

'No, Crapp!'

Without batting an eyelid, the receptionist pointed towards the corridor on the left and said:

'Second door on the right, sir.'

16

Manchester: The Battle of Mid-Way

MANCHESTER LOOKED IN fine shape. It may have been cold and cloudy but the ground was a lush green, and even the Luftwaffe kisses evident in the stands in late May had been given a makeover by 8 July, the first day of the Third Test. Bradman's poor run with the coin toss continued. Yardley decided to bat in front of the huge crowd, which was still being directed in by loudhailer as the first ball was sent down by Lindwall to Washbrook. The batsman looked confident on his home turf, as did diminutive Emmett, unruffled in his first Test. They mustered 22 in half an hour, before Johnston bowled a special delivery. It began outside leg-stump but deviated to pitch on that stump's line. Washbrook (11) played for an on-drive, missed it, and looked back to see his middle and off-stumps tilted back.

Washbrook wandered off, head bowed in front of Lancashire fans, who were so disappointed or shocked that they remained silent. Not even the slightest ripple of applause undulated over the stands. Bradman said he had not experienced such a reaction since he pulled the first ball he received in the Bodyline series (at Melbourne) onto his stumps and was on his way for a duck.

Edrich joined Emmett (10) and soon Emmett joined Washbrook in the pavilion after pushing at a short, leg-stump line of delivery from Lindwall. Barnes, positioned precariously close as usual, took the catch. The fielder was making this under-the-nose position his specialty, and it was not just bluff. He wanted the ball to come to him, within reason.

England, at 2 for 28, was no closer to solving its opening problem. Hutton, at home in Yorkshire and watching on TV, would have mixed feelings: comfort from knowing he had not been upstaged, discomfort from the continued Lindwall/Johnston dominance of England, and helplessness from being an impotent couch potato.

Near-disaster followed when Compton, a gutsy but not always competent hooker, attacked a short no ball from Lindwall, which seemed to scream, 'Hit me!' Compton took his eye off the ball, hooked too early, and managed to edge the ball into his face. He staggered from the wicket, blood coming from a cut above the eye. Compton was concussed and had to retire hurt.

England was effectively 3 for 32 for the moment, but no one was counting Compton out. If ever a cricketer could come back and bat after such an injury, it was the dasher from Middlesex. His soccer days had seen his knees twisted and his back battered, and he kept coming. The red leather missile, streaking off his own bat at 160 km/h and splitting his forehead open, was just another distraction from his job, however painful and momentarily mind-numbing.

Out walked Crapp. There was no swinging of the blade, or running on the spot, or squinting at the sky. He seemed almost apologetic for being in such company. He began with a push to backward point for a single, and appeared as if he might say 'sorry' to Lindwall, who would not have accepted his apology anyway. A few overs later, Lindwall bounced Edrich, who took a nasty blow on the hand. The batsman was not happy. Lindwall didn't even shrug. He moved back to his mark, did some jumps, and then rocked in to deliver another bumper. Edrich was disturbed by this treatment.

Crapp and Edrich, always a battler at the wicket, remained reticent after this minor roughing up except for a six by Crapp off Johnson in the final over off the session. It was such a surprise that those who missed it were not sure if it had been hit or thrown over the fence. Crapp's body language after the smash straight over the sightscreen was the same as it had been when he pushed forward. He gave no clues of his transgression to dozing spectators who woke up to the burst of applause.

The score at lunch was 2 for 57.

The England camp let it be known that Compton intended to bat again, but without saying when. Crapp showed another side after the break and hit some handsome drives. Both batsmen were untroubled and Bradman was counting down the overs to the new ball. The scorers were meant to assist by putting out coloured discs. When none appeared, Bradman informed the umpires and the discs were pushed out rapidly, but still inaccurately. Bradman was the only one counting, and he told the umpires when 55 were up and he could claim the new ball. They checked with the scorers. The Australian captain was correct, numeracy being one of his many assets. He tossed the ball to Lindwall.

After some Crapp punishment, Lindwall delivered a spearing swinging yorker. The batsman, believing it would pass well outside off-stump, did the 'leave', the bat held high. The ball crashed into his heel, dead in front. Crapp was on his way for a well-compiled 37. Johnston removed Dollery (1), bowling him with an in-swinger. Lindwall soon after had Edrich caught behind for a typically gritty 32.

England was 5 for 119. Compton reappeared with a plaster over his forehead. The crowd applauded long and hard. On the way to the wicket, he passed Miller, who said with a laugh:

'You're plastered.'

'You will be, if you bowl,' Compton retorted.

Yardley fell to Toshack for 22. England was 6 for 141 and in trouble again.

Compton was dropped early by Tallon, and he took full advantage of the lapse. He and Evans pushed the scoring along at a run-a-minute for 75 until Evans (34) had a go at Lindwall and was caught. Compton was dropped again by Tallon on the final ball of the day.

England reached 7 for 231 at stumps with Compton 64 not out and Bedser on 4 not out. It was still a mediocre return, but a lot better than expected when half the side was out at 119.

•

Compton took headache powder and reported a fair night's sleep. He came out on Friday to a huge roar from the more than 30,000 present. Spectators were quick to notice he was sporting a real black eye, not for the first or last time. He continued a charmed life being dropped again by Tallon. In between these chances he played a superb innings, ably supported by the defending Bedser, who used his height to stretch forward, bat straight. Compton reached his century with a tidy, confident on-drive off Toshack for four. It had taken him 235 minutes with nine fours. Soon after this achievement, Lindwall regularly beat Compton, but these deliveries would have tested any batsman. He may have had a concentration lapse, not helped by the sideshow of a dog on the ground, a not uncommon occurrence in 1948. The rampant animal held up play as it baulked past fielders, some of whom were footballers in other lives. Sam Loxton, a former Australian Rules footballer for St Kilda, tried a low tackle. The dog sidestepped him with ease, much to the mirth of Miller, who had played in the same team with Loxton.

Despite the distractions of this and Lindwall, Compton made it to lunch on day two with 113 not out; Bedser was on 37 not out. England was 7 for 323, and now in a strong position.

After lunch, Compton moved on at a pace. He pushed a ball into the covers. Bradman and Loxton charged at it, sidestepped each other and let the ball through. Compton called Bedser. Loxton, always brilliant and giving it everything in the field, pounced on the ball and speared it into Tallon, who lifted the bails, with Bedser (still on 37) well short.

Strongly built Pollard, with a ruddy face and red hair to match, came onto the arena with his sleeves rolled to the biceps.

England was at 8 for 337.

Barnes was fielding at mid-wicket. He overheard Compton meeting Pollard.

'Now Dick,' Compton said, 'leave it all to me. Don't you try to score at all. I want you to keep your end up, and I will go for the bowling.'

Barnes thought there would no risk to him. On his own volition, he moved into a position close to Pollard on the on-side. Johnson delivered a tempting lob. Pollard's eyes lit up. Compton's firm directive was forgotten. Pollard swiped at the ball, hitting it in the meat of the bat. It collected Barnes a fearful blow over the ribs on his left side. His knees buckled and he collapsed. Some morons in the crowd cheered as fielders rushed to him. Barnes couldn't see out of his left eye. He was paralysed down the left side. He was carried off the ground by four policemen with an anxious Bradman in tow. Bill Brown was delegated to take him to hospital. It seemed that Australia was left one man short for the rest of the game.

After this drama, Bradman kept the field out to Compton, content to let him have singles so that the Australian quicks could strike at Pollard and Young.

England wriggled up to 363, with Compton remaining not out 145. He had played better innings, but none as courageous. In a poor Ashes for England so far, Compton, with two big hundreds, was England's one true hero.

Lindwall, with 4 for 99, had the best bowling figures.

•

Australia opened with Morris and Ian Johnson, and both received blunt sledges as they strolled out to bat.

'Hope you get a duck,' and 'You won't last long,' were some of the more gentle comments shouted at them.

'And that was from the members!' a surprised Johnson remarked.

The remarks were no kinder when Bedser put paid to this opening experiment by having the makeshift No. 2 caught at the wicket for 1. Australia was 1 for 3. The loss of Barnes was made to look much bigger when Pollard trapped Bradman (7) lbw, beating him off the pitch. The crowd loved the sight of umpire Dai Davies' finger going up. A prolonged celebration followed as Bradman looked over at Pollard and said, 'Well bowled.' He then sauntered off, perhaps thinking of his words about Pollard to his mate Robins. The fans' own Lancashire 'laard' had done it!

With Barnes disabled and unlikely to bat, Australia was effectively 3 for 15, and in deep trouble for the first time in the series.

Morris, dependable now, it seemed, in every innings, set about with Hassett rebuilding the Australian position. They struggled for runs against top-class bowling from Bedser as usual, and Pollard, another workhorse, off a very long run. They were seen off. Yardley brought on Young. Hassett seemed determined to hit him out of the attack. Once more the change down to spin, or something less problematic than the two big pacemen, led to a batsman's downfall. Hassett (38) tried to drive the spinner over the in-field, like a golf drive, but the ball sailed straight to Washbrook in the covers.

Australia was 3 for 83. Miller (23 not out) and Morris (48 not out) made it through to stumps with the score at 3 for 126.

•

Saturday morning, a further massive crowd were settled into their seats long before the Australians marched out to bat. Back in the dressing room, the team had been surprised to see Barnes turn up. He showed everyone his massive rib bruising. He assured Bradman that he was fit to bat and then went to the nets behind the pavilion, out of sight from his skipper. He had trouble standing and more than once went down on one knee from pain.

'Sid will bat,' Bradman told Loxton in the dressing room, 'but you go in before him at the fall of the next wicket.'

Loxton sat on the balcony, padded up. Barnes came up to him, also wearing his pads.

'What are you doing?'

'I'm in next,' Loxton said.

'Who said so?'

'Braddles.'

'Well, forget it. I'm in next.'

Moments later, Miller was beaten by Pollard and found lbw in much the same manner as Bradman. Loxton got up. Barnes pushed him back in his seat and hurried out to bat. Moments later, Bradman appeared.

'It was farcical,' Loxton said. 'Bradman asked why Sid was in, and not me.'

Out in the middle, Barnes went up to Pollard and shook his hand, but he didn't have much strength for many other gestures. A few runs later, Morris's vigil ended with his score on 51 caught by Compton off Bedser.

Australia was 5 for 139, with Barnes, still very much disabled from the way he moved, and Loxton. Loxton pushed for an easy run, but Barnes (1), with no legs, and heaving rather than puffing, refused. Minutes later, Loxton called for another run. Barnes responded, but collapsed at the other end. Bradman ran onto the field and helped carry Barnes off. He went to hospital for the night.

Loxton, in his first Ashes Test, batted as if it were in his 20th, and managed an effervescent 36 before Pollard bowled him. Edrich came on and surprised everyone by delivering bouncers at Lindwall. This was payback for the hell the

Australian had given him, most recently in the first innings. The third one hit Lindwall on the hand, and he was uncomfortable being given some of his own medicine. One reason was the fact that he had never faced short-pitched bowling, especially not in the nets from Australians. In domestic and Test matches, no one dared to pepper him with bouncers because he was the most dangerous bowler in the world. Besides that, there was an unwritten code in all forms of cricket that fast bowlers did not deliver bumpers to tail-enders. However, any player with pretensions to batting skills was a legitimate target for the fast rising ball.

Edrich made the case that Lindwall could bat, and the Australian would agree with that. In his youth, Lindwall had wanted to be a batsman rather than a bowler. Edrich knew too, he would receive bouncers whether or not he hurled them at Lindwall. He had nothing to lose if he attempted to brutalise the Australian.

Lindwall kept wringing the hand that had been struck. At the end of Edrich's hostile first over, Lindwall gave the thumbs-up to Miller in the Australian dressing room. Edrich's brave action was certain to cause retaliation.

Bedser later claimed Lindwall caught in the covers for 23 valuable runs. He and Tallon kicked the score along to 221 – 142 in arrears.

England was back in the series, and looking for a win, if the weather held.

17

—

Miller's Back

IN THE BREAK between innings, Miller told Bradman he would like to try out his injury, and open the bowling. If Barnes was quirky, Miller was unpredictable, a man of whims and emotions. He had not wanted to bowl in the England's first innings, and there could not have been a problem with his back a day earlier if he was ready to fire today. Yesterday he had even told some of his team-mates that he did not intend to bowl even spinners again on tour. Some players, including Loxton (and several in Miller's family) reckoned he was a lazy individual, which may have been, in part, his reason for opting out of bowling. Another just as likely explanation was that Miller was taking the opportunity provided by his injury to concentrate on his batting, which many had urged him to do because of his exceptional talent. Whatever his motivation, or lack of it for refusing to bowl, he now wanted the red cherry in his hand. The most likely reason was the fact that his good mate Lindwall had been bounced by Edrich. Miller wanted to join Lindwall in payback and bullying of the England bats for daring to retaliate.

England lost Emmett for a duck in the first over when he hung his bat out to Lindwall's third ball, an away-swinger, and was caught magnificently low to his right by the diving Tallon.

Edrich marched out. The crowd, aware of the personal battle between him and Lindwall, were on the edge of their seats. The tension went up another notch when Bradman tossed the ball to Miller. A buzz ran through the crowd. Were Washbrook and Edrich about to receive a battering from both ends? More experienced observers expected Miller to sacrifice pace for accuracy in deference to his back. But no, he tore in and bowled faster than Lindwall.

Lindwall was a cooler customer. He warmed up first, getting that groin and other muscles warm before he thought about Edrich's upper body as a target.

Miller let go a soaring bouncer at Washbrook in his second over. The crowd was irate, but this kind of delivery, effectively a 'wide' (it was not called by the umpire), was no threat. The electricity in the middle, with looks, glares and the odd verbal comment, was palpable.

Lindwall was warmed up by his third over. He let go two short ones at Edrich. Umpire Davies no-balled the second one. Lindwall stopped on his walk back to query the call.

'It was your drag,' Davies informed him. The umpire made a mark with his foot, 30 cm behind the white line. This was an odd piece of refereeing at an odd time. Lindwall had complied all summer with the accepted ruling, and this was the first time he had been no-balled. Bradman, at mid-on, stood watching and listening. Had Davies been caught up in the tension? Umpires were human, and it was probable. Lindwall bowled again, but began arguing with Davies and mumbled something about 'letting us get on with the game'.

At the end of the over, Davies threw Lindwall's sweater at him, instead of passing it to him. It fell on the ground. Lindwall remonstrated. The umpire flicked an I-couldn't-care-less hand at the bowler. Now bowlers, batsmen and the crowd were all involved.

Bradman moved across to Lindwall and spoke to him as he walked to the top of his mark.

'Settle down Ray,' he said, 'and forget about the umpire.'

Lindwall, still riled by the jumper throwing episode, shook his head, not in disagreement, but in disappointment at the umpire. Washbrook, no doubt over-excited by events around him, swung Lindwall high to long on. Hassett circled under the ball, settled, watched it into his hands, and spilled it. The crowd laughed with relief, and the pressure cooker atmosphere at the ground was released. The only person not ready for their mirth was the individual with most humour: Hassett.

The Lancashire supporters' worry was that their local hero would forget himself and sky another one. But their fears were allayed in the next few overs as Washbrook drove three fours off Lindwall and one off Miller. Bradman replaced Lindwall with Loxton, signalling for the moment that England's batsmen had won a small battle within the war. Washbrook (50 at tea) and an inspired Edrich thrilled the fans in a dash for 70 minutes before tea.

After the short break, Bradman brought Lindwall back for another spell and he parted Washbrook's hair with the fastest ball of the match. The batsman lost sight of it and all but moved into it. Another skirmish had begun. Edrich's confidence reached a series high. He on-drove Miller for four. The bowler's unpredictability as a character was only predictable in these moments. A shrewder bowler such as Lindwall might attempt a yorker after being belted for a boundary. Miller did the obvious thing. He bent his back (no pain apparent any more) and sent down a bouncer. Edrich ducked it neatly. He made the mistake of grinning at Miller, who, eager to charge at the batsman again, turned off a shorter run and hurled another short ball at Edrich. It crashed into his elbow as he fended at it. Miller grinned. The crowd booed. The bowling was not Bodyline, but it was hostile enough in an atmosphere akin to the 1932–33 season. Miller delivered two more bouncers to antagonise the batsman and the crowd even more. At the end of the over, Bradman moved across to Edrich and gave him words of sympathy, assuring him that there would be no more bouncers. Bradman then trotted over to Miller and told him desist from delivering any more short balls. Lindwall was given the same directive.

Aware that he would not receive any more rough treatment, Edrich looked as if he would cut loose and build England's lead, especially when Bradman further eased the tension by bringing on Johnson and Toshack. Yet again in the series, the change of pace produced a wicket. Washbrook and Edrich began to score freely, looking for runs off every ball. Then Washbrook drove one to the on. Morris moved quickly to it. The batsman's call was 'Yes! . . . No!' followed by hesitation in the middle of the pitch. Edrich was committed and ran through. Morris whipped the ball in for a direct hit. Edrich was on his way for 53 when there would have been plenty more in him.

The partnership was 124 in 122 minutes. With the score at 2 for 125, England was sitting pretty with a lead of 267.

Compton came in to the sounds of wild cheering. He was now a national hero, and looked in charge even before he had received a ball. But cricket is a cruel leveller. A few minutes later he edged a delivery from Toshack to Miller in slips, and was on his way to the pavilion for a duck. His timing, as ever, was good. He had failed to score at the exact moment he could afford to fail. Every other time he had succeeded. Washbrook, enjoying his charmed existence, weighed into Lindwall again. Hassett circled as before.

'Catch this one!' Lindwall called, which was an unhelpful sledge.

Hassett dropped his second for the afternoon. This time the elfin vice-captain saw the humour in his out-of-character ineptitude in the field. He trotted over to a policeman, borrowed his helmet, and ran onto the field with it.

Bradman grinned. It had been one of those days.

England ended a most satisfactory Saturday, having outplayed Australia. The score was 3 for 174. The lead was 316 with seven wickets in hand. The Test was all but in the bag for the home team.

•

The rest day – Sunday – was gloomy. Monday, day four of the game, was wet. The players were forced to amuse themselves in the dressing room. 10,000 fans sat in the rain, waiting in hope and prayer but not reality. The only minor spark of encouragement and interest for England was the second day across at Bradford in the Yorkshire versus Middlesex game where Hutton was batting. It rained less there, and he was able to top-score for his county with 87. Given Emmett's two failures, there was every chance Hutton would return to the Ashes contest for the Fourth Test, at Leeds.

In the Australian dressing room, Loxton kept repeating:

'You needn't worry boys, she's coming up from Burnley. It's pouring out there.'

He was right. No play was possible all day.

•

Yardley had no choice but to declare at 3 for 174 on the final day, Tuesday 13 July. More rain delayed play until 2.15 p.m. The wicket was soft when the experiment of Johnson opening with Morris was tried again.

'Bedser moved the ball both ways in the air and off the pitch,' Ian Johnson recalled, 'but Arthur hit every ball in the middle.'

At the end of the over Morris came down the pitch and said to Johnson:

'It's doing a bit. We'd better stick around or Alec will run through us.'

Johnson was happy to let Morris face Bedser.

'It was tremendous to watch a master batsman handling a master bowler. Arthur took everything Bedser could deliver from an extensive repertoire.'

Yardley had Young on early, and he was successful, snaring Johnson for 6. In came Bradman at 2.49 p.m. to join Morris with the score at 1 for 10. The captain was vigilant, aware that the aim was not to lose wickets. He took nearly half an hour to open his account, which would have been some sort of record for him anywhere in the 600 or so innings of cricket he would play in his entire career, school matches included.

He and Morris had to negotiate a tough period on the sodden pitch. English journalists, such as Archie Ledbrooke, who had covered Bradman's four tours, were reminded of stories, exaggerated and some mythical, of his mixed performances on poor wickets.

'His [Bradman's] reputation for throwing his wicket away on bad pitches,' Ledbrooke wrote, 'the memory of Verity at Lord's in 1934 [when Bradman on 36 hit a return catch to Verity]; his recent display against Hilton on the same stretch; his reckless – but how brilliant! – stroke-play on the wet Oval pitch of 1930 [when he made 232 against Larwood and Co.]; – all these things came back to the mind of one who has seen much of Bradman in four tours . . . Here was the occasion for a great innings . . . or one to leave forever a blot on his reputation.'

Bradman, anchored at the Stretford end, took much of Bedser. Morris stayed put at the Manchester end. Both batsmen watched every ball onto the bat and hit everything, literally but for one ball, in the middle. They displayed excellent footwork in combating the spinners Young and Compton.

'When the ball was dropped short,' Ledbrooke said, 'Bradman hooked the two slow left-handers with a vigour, an intensity, and a boyish enthusiasm . . .'

Morris, who started the series 'dependable', and then developed to a higher level of batting than anyone else, could add 'adaptable' to the descriptions of his skills. He would not have encountered many tracks like this in his cricket career, but here he was pushing forward or back, watching the ball like a hawk eyeing a rodent, and missing nothing.

'I've read a lot of rubbish about the state of that wicket,' Morris said, 'but I was out there, and it was hard work. It was even difficult to just keep your feet. Some critics wanted to dismiss our efforts, simply because they were trying to make out that Don couldn't play on difficult pitches.'

For 70 minutes and 27 overs, they stayed put at their respective ends, hitting the occasional four and running safe twos.

Yardley threw Edrich into the attack for some hostility but Bradman turned on him with a hook for four through the allegedly intimidating leg trap, and then an on-drive for the same result off a slower ball. Yardley immediately retired Edrich.

Rain came lightly and livened up the pitch enough for Bedser to receive lift, but later it poured and drove the players off the field for tea. Bradman and Morris had finessed and battled their way through to a point where Australia could not lose. Another 45 minutes play was allowed in the final session of the Test before it ended in a draw.

Morris remained unconquered on 54, his second fifty of the match. Bradman, in his 50th Test, had batted two hours for 30 not out. Australia was 1 for 92.

The game had fizzled to a tame finish, the rain being ruinous and unfair to England, which most likely would have otherwise won the game. Instead it was down 0:2, and the Ashes contest was over. Australia would retain the trophy, which it had now held for 14 years since 1934, even if it lost the last two games of this five-match series.

Bradman left Old Trafford satisfied that he and his team had reached their first goal. But he would not be happy if England came back and won the final two Tests. There was much prestige now in winning the competition outright, especially after the 1938 result of one win to each side and three draws.

18

—

Hangovers and Royals at Middlesex

AFTER ITS showing at Manchester, England was buoyed further by the excellent continuing form of Len Hutton, who scored 59 and a scintillating 132 not out in his two innings for the ancient Players versus Gentlemen fixture at Lord's from 14 to 16 July. He helped himself to 18 fours, in the third strong performance in succession since his dumping from the Test team. He also captained the players and out-generalled Yardley, who led the Gentlemen, which was a pointer for the future. Hutton would have to be chosen for the Leeds Test. If he wasn't there would be a lynching of England's selectors on Ilkley Moor.

•

While England's players set themselves for better performances after Manchester, some of the tourists, particularly Miller and Lindwall, were at their celebratory best for the next four nights before the next fixture against the County Champions Middlesex at Lord's. At 8 a.m. on the morning of the match, they were on their way back from a very late night of drinking and carousing when they decided to avoid the lift at the Piccadilly just in case they met Bradman in the foyer. They took the stairs to the floor but had the misfortune to bump into him coming down for breakfast.

'Morning Nugget; morning Ray,' Bradman said, without even a frown of disapproval. He would not have been concerned about Miller this time because he wasn't playing. But how would he handle Lindwall?

Middlesex won the toss and decided to bat, which meant Lindwall would be expected to open the bowling. When the Australians were in their dressing room, Lindwall, who was hung-over and without sleep, approached the captain.

'Don, I'm not feeling all that well,' Lindwall said, 'could I be excused from bowling duties this morning?'

'I don't want Middlesex getting off to a good start,' Bradman replied. 'Open up and we'll see how you go.'

Lindwall inwardly groaned, but he expected only an over or two.

•

Lindwall straggled onto the field behind his team-mates in front of a Saturday sell-out crowd at Lord's. Harvey and Loxton warmed up by throwing the ball to Tallon.

Lindwall opened the bowling but was ineffectual. At the other end Johnston removed Jack Robertson (2) early, bringing Edrich to the wicket. He and Compton would have been sick of the sight of the tourists so soon after the Manchester Test, but for one thing: England had been on top and they wished to gain a psychological advantage with thumping big scores, especially as King George VI and Queen Elizabeth would meet both teams on the second day. This hoped-for dominance would set matters up nicely for England in the Fourth Test, starting just two days after the scheduled finish of the Middlesex encounter.

Bradman was displeased with Lindwall but, as usual, he handled the situation with his own style of discipline, as he had with Miller at the Oval against Surrey. He didn't want any of his players, especially his key strike bowler, off-side and moody with two vital Tests to play. Yet he still had to make a point about 'turning up fit to play', which was his only dictate when he addressed the tour group on the boat over.

It was a particularly warm July day. Bradman knew he would not extract much bowling penetration out of Lindwall in his state. The captain still had to make a point without losing sight of the desire to win, or not lose, against a strong Middlesex line-up, which boasted four Test batsmen – Robertson, Edrich, Compton and Dewes – in its top six. Lindwall delivered a steady, accurate spell of five overs, which was a remarkable effort given his condition. Bradman juggled his bowlers at the other end; first Loxton replaced Johnston, then Ring replaced Johnston. All the time, Bradman kept throwing the ball to Lindwall, who was nearly out on his feet. At a break between wickets at the end of an over in the pre-lunch session, Lindwall lay on the grass. Bradman came up to him, dropped the ball at his feet and said:

'Have a nice time last night, Ray?'

Lindwall kept bowling for the two-hour session, delivering 14 overs on the trot in the heat. Fortunately for his later friendship with Bradman, Australia was doing well at the other end. Johnston had Edrich (27) beautifully caught behind by Tallon, and so denied him the chance to carry on from his form at Manchester. Compton came in, and after looking as if he may have been out the night before with Miller and Lindwall, settled down with good touch, which was a continuation of his form all season against the tourists.

At lunch, an exhausted Lindwall showered and sat quietly in the dressing room without bothering to eat. In the middle session, Loxton bowled Compton (62 in 135 minutes) just as he appeared set to take the attack apart. Middlesex folded steadily after that to be all out 203. Lindwall bowled 16 overs, with three maidens and even managed 1 for 28. Johnston and Loxton took three each.

Australia stumbled late on the Saturday afternoon, losing 3 – Brown (8), Bradman (6) and Harvey (10) – for 53. The Sunday rest day meant that Lindwall could recover from his hangover. He reported fit for duty on day two, Monday, vowing to himself never to transgress on tour with Bradman again. Both were delighted to put their feet up and watch Morris and Loxton in a blistering 172-run partnership in 115 minutes. While some players were feeling the pressure of the long tour, Morris kept on building with his superlative, sustained performances, and was in the form of his life. He notched his fourth century of the tour (109), while Loxton, his confidence also on a career high, thrashed 123, his third hundred. He was proving himself with bat and ball, and determined to keep his Test spot. Morris had completed an amazing week, collecting 504 runs.

The Royals had watched the afternoon session with Loxton hitting sixes and Morris stroking drives. The teams were lined up for them at the tea break. Bradman introduced them to each of his players. Barnes, still sore and not a starter in the upcoming Fourth Test, was first one onto the field, wielding his movie camera and taking footage of the Royals. He had been given permission, although the press would falsely make an incident out of the event, saying that he didn't have permission (which would have later repercussions with the Australian Board of Control).

Lindwall came out blasting on Monday afternoon. After Johnston had bowled opener Syd Brown (3), Lindwall delighted in trapping Edrich lbw for 1. The bowler showed rare emotion by clapping his hands together – just once – but enough to register that he enjoyed this wicket more than most. On fire, he then bumped unlucky Robertson, who was hit on the jaw when attempting a hook.

The Australians rushed to him. There was booing and some angry comments from the crowd.

'Don't take any notice of those fools,' courageous Robertson said as he was steadied by Bradman and Loxton. 'It was entirely my fault.'

The batsman was forced to retire hurt with a fractured jaw, another victim of Australia's hostile opening attack. Left-hander John Dewes, who had been roughed up by Miller on several previous occasions, showed courage in getting behind or under Lindwall's thunderbolts. He managed an excellent 51 before McCool was brought on to remove him. Denis Compton's brother Leslie also demonstrated exceptional intestinal fortitude in a 73-run stand with Dewes, which forced the game into a third day after Middlesex collapsed for 135. Australia polished off the 22 runs required without loss, giving it a 10-wicket victory.

It was the tourists' 16th win from 20 starts with four draws.

•

Bradman had no particular fears, except for an expected staleness in his team, as he sat down with Morris and Hassett to pick the Fourth Test team for Leeds. Tallon had a finger injury and had to be replaced by Ron Saggers, a fine keeper. Australia lost a little in batting from this change, but not enough to be of concern. Tallon's touch of genius was shown in taking near-impossible catches and stumpings, but these could not be frequent, perhaps once or twice a series. Genius recognises genius and Bradman would always pick Tallon in his best ever World XI. But Saggers would do. One more distinct factor lost would be Tallon's aggressive appealing, and support for all the bowlers. Where he was deafening, Saggers was mute. Saggers hardly ever went up in support of his bowlers for lbw. Umpires in Australia often looked for the Saggers barometer in an appeal. If Ron went up for a catch behind or even an lbw, then the umpire might be more inclined to follow. This lack of devil in the field would be accentuated without the injured Barnes. His forceful style and fearlessness close to the wicket would be a serious loss. All this would be advantageous to England. Less predictable was the impact of Harvey in his first Ashes Test instead of Brown (in replacing Barnes). Brown was an opener, and most critics believed he would be the automatic choice. But the Australian selectors thought a different way. Bradman wanted the luxury of an extra bowler, especially at Leeds where runs would often be plentiful. This meant Loxton would stay. Harvey was primed up for return to Test cricket, so he had to come in. Hassett, who had experience as an opener, was promoted or demoted, depending on the perspective, to join Morris at the top of the order.

So Saggers and Harvey replaced Tallon and Barnes, with Brown being unlucky to miss out. The two new men were told on the morning of the match that they were playing. It was the first Ashes match for Saggers and Harvey.

'They [the selectors] told me at breakfast,' Harvey remembered with a laugh. 'I was having kippers as usual. I pushed them aside. I was too nervous to eat after that.'

England continued cricket's version of musical chairs, bringing back Hutton as everyone had predicted, and Laker, and picking Lancashire captain all-rounder Ken Cranston, for Young (who could be nicknamed 'Yo-yo' in this series), Emmett and Dollery. The merits of including an all-rounder were debated, but Yardley liked the idea of a sixth option with the ball. Cranston gave him that and some padding for the batting department. England's response was in part an answer to Australia's inclusion and relative success so far with Loxton. Some critics – including O'Reilly from Australia and Arlott from England – were scathing about the use of all-rounders. They both believed that the all-rounder was a phantom. Either choose a specialist batsman or bowler, they cried. There was much sense in their attitude, especially if the conditions called for a specialist, such as a spinner on a sticky wicket. In support of this thinking, there had been some debate within the England camp about the inclusion of another spinner, particularly Young, who spun the ball the opposite way to Laker. Leeds could be spinner friendly, especially on the final day in good weather, which was expected for the Test's duration. But in the end Cranston was given a chance.

•

The Headingley ground at Leeds was chosen for Tests ahead of Bramall Lane and Bradford because it could accommodate more fans, with 30,000 seats that had the luxury of a backrest. There was plenty of room for thousands more on the grass. This was always a consideration playing Australia and especially in 1948, when officials could count on one hand when they *didn't* play to full houses. Leeds happened to be a convenient city for a cricket venue too. All roads in Yorkshire led to it, and within Leeds itself Headingley was accessible. In 1948 it was in a residential setting, with no factory in sight. It also served as an athletics and cycling facility, with a track separating the spectators from the cricket boundary; and a Rugby League football ground. The latter's dimensions meant that the cricket arena was on the small side. There was a distinct drop running north to south, and a real sense of running up or down a slope to bowl. Fielders at the southern end were often surprised by the ball picking up speed as it approached the boundary. One weakness, already often encountered by the Australians on tour, was the lack of a sightscreen at both ends. It seemed bizarre, even careless for officials not to install them, especially as this would be in England's interests more than Australia's. Balls would often be lost in a kaleidoscopic sea of coloured and white shirts at the pavilion end. Every batsman would complain about it, and some would complain louder when they claimed their wickets had been lost this way. Added to this was the irritation of people moving as the bowler was coming in, which upset a batsman's concentration. Against this, Headingley usually provided an easy paced wicket that would make pacemen grumble and batsmen smile knowing that bad luck, no sightscreens and moving spectators not withstanding, there were runs aplenty in it for them.

Headingley was 'young' by British standards, with the first Test being played there in 1905. Strangely, England had never won at this ground, which has been a happier hunting place for Australians. Charlie Macartney made 151, including a century before lunch, in 1926. Bradman enjoyed this ground as much as any Yorkshire cricketer, and with good reason. In the three Leeds Tests of 1930, 1934 and 1938, he made 334 (also a century before lunch), 304 and 103. The respect for him at Headingley reached beyond legend to the celestial. The cricket supporters in Yorkshire above all admired the way he played the game, as it reflected the image it had of the best of themselves – hard, but fair and with outstanding spirit. They did not mind being spiflicated by the likes of Bradman. They took it as an honour that he performed at his very best at their ground. The Yorkies wanted to see the back of him like the rest of England. He had caused heartache to the national side's aspirations for too long. But if he were to perform again with something special in 1948, then the locals would not begrudge it. They would appreciate for the last time the skills of the type of cricketer that might come along once a century. Spectators who saw him in 1930, 1934 and 1938 would say innumerable times over the rest of their lives: 'I saw Bradman at Leeds,' not quite with the awe of the young girls who claimed to see the Virgin Mary at Lourdes, but with a similar measure of satisfaction, and perhaps a touch more credibility.

Such was the character of the Yorkshire cricket fans, if they had to murmur it again, or for the first time after 1948, they would set aside county and national feelings and say it with pride.

19

England's Leeds Lunge

CELESTIAL OR OTHERWISE, Bradman was as irritated as the next skipper to keep losing the toss. He called incorrectly for the seventh time in eight flips of the coin as captain in Tests in England. The wicket looked perfect for batting and the sun was out for the 35,000 fans that crammed into Leeds for the first day, Thursday 22 July, of the Fourth Test. There was still much to play for, and nothing would please England and its fans more than to upset Australia with a win here and then another at the Oval. This would leave the series all square, with England holding sway in the draw at Manchester and therefore a moral victory in the series, despite the Ashes being retained by the tourists.

Although there was little benefit in winning the toss in the first three Tests, there was a distinct advantage in the prevailing conditions at Headingley when Hutton and Washbrook strode out to do battle. Washbrook was in touch, although his risky performances at Manchester could easily have ended in disaster. Hutton, with three good innings in succession during his enforced lay-off, was as ready as he could ever be for the toughest encounter in world cricket. He received a wonderful home-town cheer, which would have been in sympathy, admiration and encouragement in about equal measure.

A spell seemed cast over the arena. The crowd hushed as Lindwall flowed in with his majestic, smooth run to the wicket. Spectators were mindful that England's openers were yet to survive the initial overs in six starts in the series. The spell was broken when Hutton drove Miller for four in the third over of the day.

There was no penetration from the bowlers on a lovely batting strip. Bradman, not content to concede or die wondering, rang the changes in the first 50 minutes, but to no avail. England climbed nicely yet slowly to 50 in 75 minutes. Washbrook was more sober with the serious, dedicated Hutton up the other end, and he concentrated on defence early. No cuts and pulls, so far; just nudges and singles in the main.

Hutton's determination not to attack reminded some players of the Englishman batting against O'Reilly in 1938 at the Oval. After a long period where he did no more than nudge the ball close to the wicket for singles, Hutton pushed one past the bowler.

'Well done, Len,' O'Reilly said. 'I didn't know you had the strength.'

Circumstances were becoming different at Leeds. As Hutton and Washbrook gained the measure of the bowlers and the wicket's pace, they began to play strokes. Hutton gave a chance to Hassett standing in a more discreet short-leg than Barnes, but he dropped his third for the series.

England went to lunch at 0 for 88. The batsmen continued on after the break very much where they had left off.

In the middle of the second session, Loxton, who had exhausted himself with scores of long sprints at third man and fine-leg, heard a spectator in the crowd near him say:

'Son, skipper wants thee.'

Loxton looked up to see Bradman signalling to him. He was on. Hutton mistimed a drive that flew to Hassett, who dropped another one. Loxton hustled on, but could not further penetrate the openers' defences.

The score mounted to 165 before Bradman was able to take the new ball. He tossed it to Lindwall. Hutton seemed unperturbed. He soon drove the speedster for a stylish four through extra cover. Lindwall came back and bowled a much quicker ball. Hutton (81) played forward when he could just as easily have played back, and was bowled neck and crop. It was sudden and unpredictable, when spectators were praying for a century from him. Yet he had returned to something like his best. Now with four successive solid innings in first-class games and a Test, Hutton's confidence had been restored.

England score line read 1 for 168. Up and down the length and breadth of the UK, people tuned in to radio and TV, or picked up the early newspaper editions. The score made them blink. What was happening at Leeds? Another well-fought-for 100 runs were added before Washbrook (143) edged Johnston to Lindwall at slips in the last over of the day. This was his second Ashes century against Australia – the other had been made in Melbourne early in 1947.

England was 2 for 268 at stumps on day one. It had been a struggle, even a grim one at times, but compared to all other opening days in the series so far, this was the best start by either side.

Edrich was 41 not out. Night watchman Bedser was on 0.

•

Even more fans – approaching 40,000 – turned up under dull, overcast skies for day two, and not surprisingly. England was expected to push on to around 600 by stumps. The wicket was so tame that Bedser batted with ease, using his size to push forward or back. Lindwall, busting himself, could not break through. Edrich, who had mastered himself and the opposition in the second innings at Manchester, was performing similarly here, and barring mishaps was on his way to a century. These

Sam Loxton with the 'baby' of the tour, Neil Harvey, on the RMS *Strathaird* as it prepares to sail for the United Kingdom in 1948. Loxton acted as the teenager's 'guardian' on tour.

Bill Brown plays a typically defensive stroke in the first practice session of the tour, at Lord's. The crowd paid for a glimpse of the tourists. Brown's copybook technique and concentration helped the team through the difficult periods between Tests, and played a part in keeping the tour defeat-free.

Bradman gives Colin McCool instruction during the first net practice at Lord's. The 'lesson' was instructive for another reason. The fact that the captain bothered to do this publicly at the very first 'net' was an indicator that McCool had been pencilled in for the First Test.

The Australians take the field for the opening match against Worcestershire. Bradman is accompanied by Lindsay Hassett, Ernie Toshack and Colin McCool (in the background).

Bradman practises at Lord's. He loved and revered the place,
and always wanted to win there.

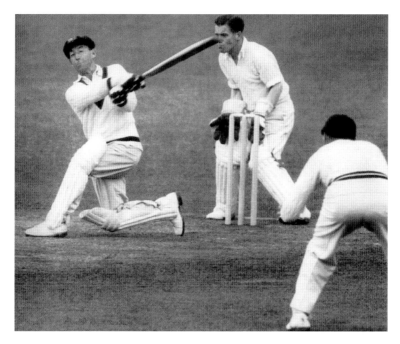

Lindsay Hassett hits to 'cow corner' in the opening game against Worcestershire.
He was a brilliant deputy, keeping the humour running in the team, while
leading astutely in Bradman's absence.

Keith Miller delivers a classic drive in his masterly innings against Leicester. Miller preferred to be known as a batsman, but his bowling was so good, especially in tandem with Lindwall, that he was forced into an all-rounder's role for the team's sake.

Keith Miller seems to lose his head while taking a catch from Joe Hardstaff in the First Test.

Keith Miller appears to be doing his press-ups when stumped by Evans off Eric Hollies for 5 in the Fifth Test.

Sam Loxton lashes out. He was a reliable medium-pace bowler and tireless fielder; and Bradman loved his bulldog spirit and endeavour.

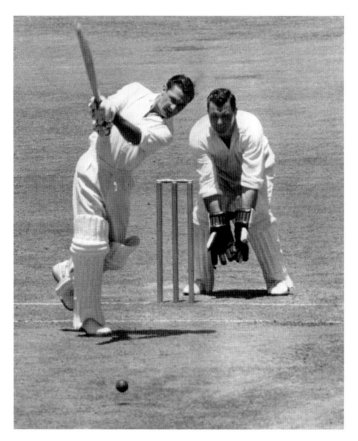

Neil Harvey played baseball in the off-season. It improved his eye and fielding skills, and there was no better cover fielder in Australian cricket. He had few peers in footwork against the spinners.

Left-arm paceman Ernie Toshack at Lord's during the first 'net' of the tour.
He was a more than useful back-up to Lindwall, Johnston and Miller,
taking 11 wickets in the Ashes.

Bill Johnston took 27 wickets for the Ashes – but was just beaten
in the averages by Lindwall (who also took 27 wickets).

Sid Barnes vowed to get a century at Lord's – for a bet, his wife, and revenge against officials who refused to let him practise there. He was dismissed for a duck in the first innings but hit 141 in the second, achieving his goal.

Sid Barnes, the wag, attracts attention by parading like a butler in a first-class match in Australia – one of several incidents that upset the authoritarian Australian Cricket Board.

two were watchful enough to negotiate the second new ball for the innings. Once through this ordeal, it was Bedser who opened up against the change down bowlers, belting first Toshack then Johnston for 14 each. Bedser reached his 50 in just under two hours at the crease, and had done much more than his guard duty overnight in protecting the big guns to follow.

At lunch England was 2 for 360, Edrich on 76 and Bedser 52. This brought back nightmares of England at the Oval in 1938 for Bradman. After lunch he even tried Morris with his slow-turning Chinamen. The move helped Edrich along to his century. That target of 600 seemed easy, but as is often the case after a long partnership and a milestone, a wicket fell. Bedser (79), chancing his arm once too often, was caught and bowled by Johnson. The partnership had been 155. That brought Compton striding to the wicket to join a set Edrich with the score at 3 for 423. England had rarely been so well set up in more than 70 years of Ashes cricket.

Edrich reached 111. In deference to Lord Nelson (one eye, one leg, one arm), some in the crowd balanced on one leg to avoid a mishap on this number of superstition. The fatigued batsman gave it credence when he hooked and was caught by Morris at square leg.

Compton quite naturally arrived in a belligerent mood. He began to play his shots like the cavalier he was, but earlier than he would normally attempt. Crapp (5), perhaps in a more relaxed frame of mind than normal, played all over a Toshack delivery and was bowled. Untroubled, Compton caressed a delightful leg glance of Lindwall with the third new ball, which Saggers, emulating Tallon, dived to his left and snaffled. Compton was on his way, again when in a less than vital moment, for just 25.

England was 5 for 447. Australia was not yet back in the game. But it was a brave or foolish commentator who would write them off; not with the mentality of Bradman, and the skill of his batting line-up.

Then Loxton came on and ran through the tail excitedly, for he had been unlucky the day before, and these were his first wickets in Ashes cricket.

When Pollard arrived at the wicket, Hassett caused an amusing stir when he positioned himself close to him, but then ran away in mock fear.

Loxton took 3 for 55 off 26 overs, which were the best returns. England was all out 496. English fans and reporters were unhappy with both the collapse of the last eight wickets for 73 and the final score, such was the respect for the opposition. But in any cricket nation's language and experience, near enough to 500 runs in the first innings would mean a draw at least and a win at best, with no chance for the side batting second to win.

•

Australia began its chase with a shock when Morris (6), played a very uncharacteristic lofted shot off Bedser and was nicely caught by Cranston on the run at mid-wicket. The score was 13. All eyes turned to the pavilion. Several thousand fans rushed to form a human tunnel honour guard from the pavilion to 30 metres from the wicket. Bradman, the twice triple Test centurion in this stadium, walked out, if anything distracted and slightly embarrassed, but still mightily honoured by the unprecedented reception. A huge roar was followed by cheering and clapping. Bradman doffed his cap once, then a second time. When this was not enough to quell the crowd, he waved his bat, something he would never have done before when *arriving* at the wicket.

The tunnel dissolved. Bradman was touched emotionally as he took block to Bedser.

The crowd went dead silent, as it had with the first ball to Hutton the day before. Bradman used his wrists to flick the ball towards the boundary and only a dash by Compton saved a four. He stopped the ball, soccer-style with his foot, as he had done often enough for Arsenal and England. Edrich came on to deliver bouncers and Bradman smashed him for three fours. Those who had observed him at Leeds in 1930 and 1934 sensed he had set himself for something special in his last, or second-last appearance in Test cricket in Yorkshire. This was perhaps his best start in the Test series so far. At stumps, he had scored 31 runs of calculated belligerence and luminescence, with Hassett, in his solid role again in this series, on 13.

Australia was 1 for 63, some 433 in arrears. It did not appear enough to those with long memories of Bradman's triple centuries. If he were to achieve half one of those scores, Australia would probably overtake England.

•

A Test that had all the hallmarks of a classic, or an upset, or something special, twisted again in the first half hour on day three Saturday, in front of a third massive crowd. It had rained overnight, making the uncovered wicket greasy. This encouraged Bedser and Pollard, who knew they had to burst themselves going for wickets early or else chase a lot of leather all day on this wicket. Bedser brought a brute of a delivery back hard from the off and it cannoned into Bradman's box causing much pain, hobbling and frowning. He was tough, but not used to being struck anywhere, such were his reflexes and reactions of body, feet and hands. Pollard at the other end brought the fans to their feet when he had Hassett caught by Crapp in slips.

At this moment, Harvey wandered into the dressing room to pad up.

Miller came in, drove for three and let Bradman face an antagonistic Pollard. Still discomforted by the Bedser hit, Bradman was caught at the crease neither forward nor back to a quicker delivery that pitched on leg-stump, kept low and hit off. If the fans were on their feet for Hassett's dismissal, they were airborne with 10,000 cloth caps thrown high for this one. Bradman (33) left, his frown more studious now as to what had gone wrong. Australia was 3 for 68, still well over 400 behind, and in deep trouble. Harvey remembered the roar, which is unique to cricket when a champion's wicket falls early or unexpectedly. It is shorter and sharper than say, a response to a powerfully hit hook for six. The noise now signalled something else. He looked out the window to see Bradman's off-stump knocked back. Harvey had just put his right pad on, the front leg protection for a left-hander, and which gave him a sense of comfort. Harvey then had to rush to attach his left pad. *This was it:* his first walk to the wicket in an Ashes Test.

Though with 'butterflies' aplenty in his stomach, he arrived in the middle looking composed. Miller recalled Harvey saying to him (although the teenager himself could not recall saying it):

'What's going on here, Nugget? C'mon, let's get stuck into 'em!'

Harvey played out Pollard's last two balls with aplomb. This began one of the finest partnerships – with both players in superlative form – ever witnessed in Ashes or any cricket. Normally one player shades the other, or one plays a secondary role in such a pregnant moment with so much at stake. But here was Harvey playing surely an unmatched first-up Ashes innings, with Miller in an inventive mood, which for him meant controlled attack with eye and mind in complete harmony over and above even the extraordinary. Miller lifted Laker's first ball, a long hop, over the square leg fence. Harvey faced him, and had trouble calibrating the ball turning away from him. Miller decided to take the strike to Laker, keeping Harvey away from him for a little while. Then, acting on instinct, Miller went after the off-spinner in much the same manner he had in the MCC game two months earlier. He struck an off-drive, one that he had not produced as much this summer, mainly because of his bowling, which fatigued him. This caused him to bat falling away to the on, and to favour strokes on that side of the wicket. Two balls later he launched into a low, skimming Exocet of a straight six that sent spectators diving for cover.

Miller strolled to Harvey at the end of the over.

'Feel better?' Miller asked with a grin.

Those two shots helped Harvey over nerves. He too went after the hapless Laker with two successive drives either side of the wicket for four.

Miller continued his violence. He launched into a stupendous drive, which went further up than he would have liked, seemingly at first short of the long-off boundary. The ball swirled high. Hutton hovered with intent a long way under it very close to the boundary but the ball floated well into the crowd for six, and struck a blonde girl in a green dress. Someone in the dressing room joked that he always went after blondes and was a hit with them, but this was no laughing matter. An ambulance officer arrived and led away the distressed and limping victim of Miller's unintended assault. She was the second casualty (the other being a young man at Leicester) from his spectator-monstering for the summer . . . so far.

He next hurled his blade at a Yardley delivery. This sailed high over long-on for another six. Miller reached 58. When a batsman of this striking calibre is in a zone such as this (think of Kevin Pietersen or Adam Gilchrist in the 21st Century) there will always be a chance or two, and the opposition must take them or suffer badly on the scoreboard and in the psyche. Yardley fed him a good delivery. Miller lunged, connected with the edge of the bat for the only time in the innings, and was caught stunningly by Edrich at short fine-leg after the ball had ricocheted off Evans' skull. It took something spectacular to get rid of this public menace in such unbelievable touch.

This was Test cricket at its best, from the best in the world, and individuals that would rank with any in their field over the entire history of the game – all in 93 minutes of cricket.

The partnership was 121. Australia was 4 for 189. Despite the hypnotic efforts of Miller and Harvey, Australia was still a staggering 307 behind. Surely this was it, many fans thought. England would take back control of the game. No team could keep this up; not even Bradman's impressive unit. Few knew of Harvey's determination. He was not for a moment disturbed by Miller's departure. He had now been joined by his very good mate and tour mentor Loxton, himself every inch the athletic aggressor right up to his pugilist's proboscis.

At lunch Harvey had skipped to 70; Australia was 4 for 204, and still nowhere near even avoiding the follow-on. But if spirit and attitude counted for anything, the tourists were still in the Test match.

•

After the break, Harvey continued on as if he had lunched on the run at the wicket without missing a beat. Loxton, by contrast, could not settle before he ate, or after it. Yardley called for the new ball. There was a confidence in the English step that said a breakthrough was imminent. But Loxton, inspired by what he had seen in the morning, and by the need to complete or carry on the job, lifted his rating against the swinging red missile. He just missed a six of Pollard on the on-side. Two overs later, he punched this bowler for three hard hit fours to off, leg and straight. The crowd drew breath. Here was another equally forceful foil for the stylish young Harvey that threatened England even more as the lead began to unravel. Harvey was smiling, relaxed, even cheeky in his execution of shots against the new ball. He drove the ball through a wide arc on the off from backward point to straight, showing that, with various calibrations of the open-faced blade and perfect footwork, he could play every stroke against every bowler.

This link too passed a hundred. Australia streaked through 250 with such ease that the fans forgot for a moment that Australia was playing catch-up faster than they would have liked. Harvey reached 90, and was most cautious for the next 45 minutes, inching towards an important moment. It added to the pressure on him, but he came through and reached his century. Boisterous Loxton bounded to him and pumped his hand, seeming even more enthusiastic that the centurion himself.

'That was the proudest moment on the whole tour for me,' Loxton said.

Leeds rose to a new champion. They would have wondered if they were seeing the changing of the guard, the passing of the Australian batting baton from one ageing right-hand champion – Bradman – to a left-hander half his age.

Laker bowled Harvey for 112, in an innings of just under three hours. He hit 17 fours, an outstanding feature being his elegant square cutting. Just as Morris's gem at Lord's had been decapitated cleanly before he could spoil it with a build to a second hundred, Harvey's was nipped at a point where it was more than cameo, and less than a big innings.

Bradman was full of praise for the young left-hander's effort, ranking it as a great innings no matter what the age of the player. Bradman had been Archie Jackson's partner when he first played a Test at Adelaide in the 1928–29 Ashes series and was the youngest player ever to score a century on debut. Jackson, who scored 164, was also 19 years old and a few months younger than Harvey. (Bradman himself was 20 years at the time of the Jackson debut.)

In comparing them, Bradman said:

'They were very different in many respects. Jackson was a right-hander. He was tall, thin and relied on grace and finesse not force, to play his shots. He preferred the delicate late cut and fine-leg glance, but rarely pulled the ball, or gave it a full-blooded drive. He liked the cut and cover-drive. All this reflected his mind. Harvey by contrast was a left-hander, and compact, while deceptively strong for his size. Shorter players never look as graceful as taller, leaner types. [But] Harvey had all the shots, and relished the powerful hook or pull. Jackson needed a fast, hard wicket that would allow him to create his strokes, whereas Harvey could still use his strength on different, slower turning pitches.'

Bradman did not go as far as saying it, but he implied that Harvey's debut innings was even better than Jackson's, and up there with the best ever played.

•

Harvey's departure at Leeds put the focus on Loxton. Like a trouper on the vaudeville boards, he strutted his stuff as if he was meant to, and was being given time and space to do it. This rugged six-footer didn't so much hit the ball; he attempted to belt it out of shape. Laker again was the target. Loxton sent four of his deliveries into orbit for six each time, two over mid-on and two over mid-off. Umpire Frank Chester several times visited the boundary where people were sitting and made histrionic play of making out he had found the exact spot where the ball had landed, just to verify Loxton had actually hit a six.

One of the sixes was the best Bradman ever saw hit. Decades later he could still remember the arc of Loxton's bat as he swung up and under it. The ball went straight and 20 rows back into the stand. Neville Cardus wrote that he got a crick in the neck watching it go up. Robins was standing next to Bradman on the balcony when the ball was struck. He was stunned that a batsman would play this way when chasing a massive score. (It was reminiscent of Adam Gilchrist in the 21st Century.) Loxton, it seemed, was squaring off for Harvey's dismissal. Spectators who had spent the morning alert to Miller's assault were forced now to take evasive action to avoid being battered by Loxton. He streaked into the 90s, deserving a century for his sheer vitality.

'Sam's batting was the very essence of belligerence,' Bradman noted. 'His whole attitude suggested defiance. When he hit the ball, it was the music of a sledge hammer, not a dinner gong.'

Yardley came on. Loxton made such a brutal attempt at a strike you would think he was trying for something more than a six, if it were possible, to bring up his hundred.

'There was a rugby ground right behind the Headingley Oval,' Loxton said, 'and I was trying to hit Yardley there. I reckoned that if I did that, they'd give me 7!'

But he was bowled by Yardley and on his way for 93 in 135 blistering minutes. In included five sixes and eight fours.

Politician Robert Menzies (past and future Australian prime minister) was in the dressing room. Loxton entered. Menzies said to him:

'Rather a rash shot, Loxton.'

'Well Boss,' Loxton said, 'I suppose you've made a few bloody mistakes in your own time too!'

It was a day for Australia's heavy hitters. First, Miller, then Harvey, followed by Loxton. Now it was Lindwall's turn. It was past 4 p.m. England's bowlers and fielders were struggling. He batted with flourish and on this excellent wicket looked every centimetre the batsman he once aspired to be.

Bradman had instructed Johnston and Toshack to use their reach to play forward unless the ball was very short. They were instructed to use the drive as the basis for all their shots. Through the season this had begun to work well, and Australia's tail wagged more often than not. In this instance, it was vital that the tail stuck with Lindwall. Johnston was out for 13, caught by Edrich off Bedser, the ninth wicket falling at 403.

Johnston was to stay at the wicket and act as injured Toshack's runner. Not knowing this, the crowd and some journalists were confused. Why didn't Johnston leave the field? Johnston decided to have some fun by pretending that he disputed the obvious catch by Edrich. He looked upset as he waved his hands and his bat, going from the umpires to the fieldsman as if he were refusing to decamp the scene. Some fans even booed and catcalled Johnston. The ruse was not cleared up until Toshack reached the pitch and took block, with Johnston moving quietly now to square leg as the runner.

Lindwall led the way in a 55-run partnership, which brought Australia more and more into the contest. He was 76 not out at stumps, with the limping Toshack on 12 not out, and Australia at 9 for 457.

Australia had lost 8 for 394 in one of the most frenetic days in Ashes history. The tourists had stroked, belted and hustled back into the game after being out of it for the first two days.

20

—

Emperor with Pads

SUMMER HAD ARRIVED, at least in Leeds. Sunday was pleasant and Monday was even better for the fourth successive sell-out crowd with people spilling onto the area beyond the ropes. Bedser snapped up Lindwall (caught ankle high at slips by Crapp) after he had added just one to leave Australia all out 458 – 38 behind.

Hutton and Washbrook started England's second innings watchfully, as they did on the first day, but accelerated earlier once settled and reached 72 without loss at lunch. The lead was 110. With 10 wickets in hand, this professional, splendid batting by the openers had restored England's control of the contest.

Johnston was driven for six by both batsmen and Bradman withdrew him. The Australians could not afford to let matters get out of hand. Too many runs too quickly would give England more time to dismiss Australia. Hutton and Washbrook brought up their fifties with ease, while Bradman went for containment, hoping to cause a rash shot. Washbrook provided it, hooking Johnston once more. Harvey had demonstrated his importance purely as a batsman. Now he showed his fielding skills and athleticism again in a burst around the boundary to catch the ball low down. It was all done in the action of running and he didn't stop, delivering a drop-kick (he was a talented Australian Rules player) to Saggers, and a grin for his team-mates.

England was 1 for 129. The openers had provided their second century link for the match, proving that the same feat performed at Adelaide in the 1946–47 Ashes was no fluke. Without addition to the score, Hutton tried to hit Johnson again, but only succeeded in lifting the ball to mid-on where Bradman took a good running catch.

The situation was tailor-made for Edrich and Compton to take the game beyond Australia's reach. They both knuckled down to the job and pushed England to 2 for 209 at tea, Compton on 42, and Edrich 33. England was approaching 250 ahead with one session left on day four. The bookies were now taking bets on an England win or a draw.

No one except a reckless gambler would bet on an Australian win from here.

•

The onus was now on England to move the score along quickly if it wished to have a chance of winning. Bradman was juggling an attack without Toshack, who was the best bowler to tie up the batsmen. The burden fell on Lindwall and Johnston.

Runs and time now entered the equation. Edrich obliged by stepping into Johnson (who was England's favourite bowler to hoe into, as Laker was Australia's), for three fours and a six. England raced to 252 before Lindwall came into the attack with the new ball and trapped Edrich (54), who was looking dangerous, lbw. The lead was 290.

Crapp did as his captain ordered in a quick 'burn' at the wicket for 18 before playing a ball from Lindwall onto his stumps. Yardley (7) then hooked Johnston. Harvey ran to take another catch, this time over his head. Johnston struck again, having Cranston caught behind for a duck. England was 6 for

278. Fifteen runs later, Compton (66) had a wild slash off Johnston and was caught by Miller in the covers.

England was 331 ahead with three wickets left.

Bedser joined Evans at 5.45 p.m. and in the last 45 minutes of play, the game appeared to slip away from Australia. First Bedser slammed four fours in his crisp stay for 17 runs before Miller had him caught by Hassett, who was grateful to accept a chance. England was 8 for 330. Then Evans, accompanied by Laker eager to take some of his own back from the Australians, thumped the score up to 362 – a lead of exactly 400.

If Yardley declared, Australia would need to score at nearly 70 runs an hour, or in round figures, four runs an over. No team had remotely approached this rate of scoring for so many runs to win in the fourth innings of a Test.

Bradman gave nothing away to his team-mates. But he did in confidence say to the team scorer, Bill Ferguson, that he thought a win was beyond Australia, especially on a last-day turning wicket, when it was presumed that Laker would be assisted by Compton bowling his left-arm leg-spin. But Bradman did not convey this pessimism (or realism) to his team. While he could not bring himself to say, *We'll win this*, he did tell them: 'We can win this,' with the characteristic certitude that had marked his demeanour in competition all his life.

Morris was optimistic.

'I thought we had a fair chance,' he said. 'Of course, events had to run our way. But I was irritated the next morning to see all the papers saying we were finished. Some even expected the game to be all over by lunchtime! We were told that the wicket would turn so much that we would be found wanting. This wrote off our outstanding batting line-up, all of whom were more than competent against spin. The press reaction persuaded me to prove them wrong.'

Morris also factored in Yardley's need to go for a win with not the best spin line-up England could put in the field. Laker was a worthy opponent, but he had been severely dealt with by the Australians all summer. No matter how much the wicket spun, all the batsmen would feel confident about belting him out of the attack, if the circumstances were right. Compton would be trickier because of his left-arm turn. But he was not a regular Test bowler. How would he go if Morris went after him and smashed him off his length? It was one thing to be an occasional county spinner, and a more-than-useful net bowler. It was another to take on the best batting line-up in recent times, if not in history, in the pressure-cooker conditions of a vital Test match.

•

Yardley batted on for two overs the next morning, wasting six minutes – and another 10 for the change of teams batting, and declared at 8 for 365, with Evans 47 not out, and Laker on 15 not out. Johnston with 4 for 95 had the bowling figures in adverse conditions.

This left Australia's target at 404 for victory, which looked out of the question. Yardley had used the rules to his advantage. He asked for the heavy roller before England faced its two overs, with the aim of breaking up the pitch and therefore making it more conducive to turn on this fifth (sixth, with the rest day) and final day. Yardley had to gamble on the balance between offering the Australians a slim chance to win, while still giving England the opportunity to bowl them out. Most observers at that moment (and not with the benefit of hindsight) felt Yardley should have declared overnight or even 40 minutes before stumps on day four, to give England the opportunity to attack the tired batsmen, who had been chasing leather all day.

Yet still, the challenge to Australia was the biggest in Test cricket history. The previous highest fourth innings score in England had been 263. No side had been set a challenge after a declaration and won. Australia would have to score at the fastest rate of the match to win.

•

This was so far the Test with everything – amazing theatre for four days, and with the prospect of an England win the gates were shut before Hassett and Morris arrived at the wicket. Bradman neither gave a directive to attempt to force a draw; nor did he say make a suicide bid for runs. In typical style, he had suggested the openers settle in and then play their natural game. As Morris's native state this summer was an attacking one, the approach was keenly awaited by the big crowd.

The openers were most cautious to begin with on a crumbling, dusty, turning wicket. This approach had reporters writing that Australia had no intention of chasing victory. Six overs from Pollard and Bedser produced as many runs, which at that rate meant Australia would be 0 for 100 by the close of the day. One way or another, this was sure *not* to be the scorecard.

Yardley did not achieve a breakthrough with pace and swing. So he made the obvious move of bringing on Laker early. He had to weigh no wickets and few runs against an opportunity to see if the spinner could snare a wicket. Both the Australians were most adept at using their feet and the crease to play spin. Morris was prepared to hammer them hard from their very first overs. His 'killer' approach had been seen to most devastating effect against Tom Goddard at Gloucester. The spinner had taken such a pasting that he could not be considered for the Tests. Now Morris turned on Laker. Thirteen runs were plundered from his first over. This threw the pressure back on Yardley. He could not afford to let that happen too often. He had a word to Laker, who tightened up, and bowled often to Hassett. Australia had scored six runs in the first 28 minutes. In the next 32 minutes they added 38 to be 0 for 44, with one sixth of the day gone. At the first hour's rate, Australia would get nowhere near the target. But Yardley had Compton now in the attack partnering Laker. Morris, intent on more damage, took 10 runs from Compton's first over, but the Chinaman bowler (essentially spinning his stock ball the same way as Laker into the right-hand batsman, and away from the left-hander) delivered a maiden in his second over. In the third, Hassett tried to emulate Morris's attitude and he was caught and bowled for 17. Yardley did a little jig. England had the breakthrough.

Australia was 1 for 57. Bradman walked out on the ground to another magnificent ovation and guard of honour.

'I'll never forget that reception,' Loxton said. 'It was unbelievable. It was even greater than 100,000 at the MCG could provide. It was a huge tribute.'

It touched Bradman on one level as the finest reception he had received anywhere, including Sydney, Adelaide and Melbourne.

'I know I shall never cherish any memory more than the reception at Leeds,' Bradman said.

On another level it didn't reach him at all. He was not going to be touched emotionally by such a clamour as he had at the beginning of his previous innings. Bradman had a job to do, and a challenge after his failure in the first innings, when he had usually made his runs. In his Test career to that moment, he scored only two centuries in the second innings of a match, and 26 in the first.

Bradman looked at the pavilion clock. It was 1 p.m. There was half an hour until lunch. There were 347 runs to make in four and a half hours – 270 minutes. Simple arithmetic told him that at some point, if Australia were to win, the batsmen would have to surge well ahead of the clock.

As he emerged from the second human tunnel for him and approached the wicket, English commentator H. S. Altham's romantic words were apt:

'In the many pictures I have stored in my mind from the burnt-out Junes of 40 years, there is none more dramatic and compelling than that of Bradman's small, serenely moving figure in the big-peaked, green cap coming out of the pavilion shadows into the sunshine, with the concentration, ardour and apprehension of surrounding thousands centred upon him, and the destiny of a Test match in his hands.'

Concentration, ardour and apprehension summed up the Headingley crowd's reaction to this emperor of the game. They admired him for sure, yet they were concerned that he would produce some of his unmatchable batting magic, so far unseen in the 1948 series, and turn the game against England. It was a love/hate relationship in one sense. They would love to see him cleaned up early, and hate to see him hit his straps.

The crowd's projection had increased the tension in the arena. Laker stood waiting for Bradman as he scratched out his block and surveyed the field. There were three very close short-legs for him. The spinner would be moving the ball across the batsman's body using the same principle as Bedser in attempting to feed that disturbing leg trap. Bradman would avoid it, but be inventive, as few could, in countering the tactic and threat. Laker pitched up, Bradman shuffled to the on-side where the spin was headed, and played not to the on, but the off, against the spin. The ball sped through the vacant mid-off for four. Was it a declaration of intent or the Don being himself? Laker delivered again, this time making it tougher to respond with such unorthodoxy. Bradman hit it back down the wicket to Laker. Then the bowler speared the ball even further to leg. Bradman watched it go harmlessly by. The message was clear. He had worked out tactics to avoid the leg trap and still make runs.

More in response to the spinner challenge than any immediate concerns about beating the clock, these two started to increase the tempo. Compton troubled Bradman with his Chinaman, and one streaky shot was edged past Crapp at slips. Inspired, Yardley tossed the ball to his fellow Yorkshireman Hutton for a bowl of his leg-breaks. The crowd breathed "Utton!' The murmur could be heard round the terraces. He had taken 4 for 44 in a county game in the previous season, and was considered by all as a useful net bowler. But this was a Test. Yardley was gambling, and this was either a touch of desperation or tactical genius, but nothing in between.

Morris frowned. Was he on as a change bowler, or what?

'There were lots of tempting [fielding] spaces in the deep,' Morris noted, 'because Yardley had to take wickets and go for a win.'

Those big gaps were open now to Morris and Bradman, if they were prepared to play their shots. It was a critical moment in the game and the series.

Hutton had Morris pushing carefully at the first three balls. Then three successive full-tosses were dolled up. Morris slammed two to the on and one to off for boundaries. This brought up his 50. There was perfunctory applause. The crowd was stunned.

Compton bowled a second over mainly to Bradman, who was having trouble picking him. Hutton bowled a second over, with Bradman facing. Two more full-tosses were dispatched for fours. Five full-tosses had been belted for five fours in two of Hutton's overs.

These strikes had changed the complexion of the game. Australia was 95 in 90 minutes and for the first time was ahead of the clock.

Hutton's third over was a maiden, which earned him a fourth. Bradman took 10 off it. Hutton had gone for 30 runs in his four overs before lunch, a break which would allow him to be retired from the bowling crease perhaps forever in Tests, but at least while Bradman and Morris were playing. Yardley switched ends for Compton. He delivered an awkward over to Bradman, who edged a difficult chance to Crapp, who did well to touch it, but which he couldn't secure. Yardley took away a short fine-leg and put in a second slip. Bradman then leg-glanced a four through the place from where the new slip had been taken. Next he was beaten again and edged another streaky shot past Crapp. At this moment the Compton experiment looked as if it might work, but the Hutton try had not come off.

Australia went to lunch on 1 for 121. Bradman had 35 runs in half an hour at the crease. Morris had hardly made an error, having been once stranded down the wicket to a ball from Compton that spun so much it even beat the keeper. He was

63 and playing even better than at Lord's and Bristol on a wicket that was turning a long way, and sharply.

The fans did their nervous calculations during the break. Australia needed 283. Assuming that it would face 70 to 80 overs, depending on how much the spinners were used, that still meant four runs an over. By fine batting and the good fortune of the Hutton experiment, Australia was now an outside chance to pull off the near-impossible.

•

At the break, Bradman and Morris discussed tactics. Bradman admitted his trouble with Compton's 'Bosie'.

'I'll take him and knock him out of the attack,' Morris suggested.

It took just two overs after lunch for Morris to achieve his stated objective. He hit Compton for seven fours, and reached the 90s. He secured his century with another four, and had scored 37 out of 40 runs in this burst of mayhem. His hundred had taken 122 minutes. Compton had bowled menacingly before lunch. After the break Morris smacked him off his length and destroyed his confidence. Some critics called Compton's bowling 'woeful,' but they had short or selective memories. Morris had shredded other bowlers this way in earlier games, and was at it again. This act paved the way for a possible Australian victory.

No other bowler would trouble Bradman, so it was a matter of these two outstanding batsmen constructing big innings, which had become a specialty for both. Bradman had a close call after reaching his 50, which had taken an hour, when he viciously cut Cranston past point. Yardley dived forward but failed to grasp a very tough opportunity. Perhaps Harvey was the only fielder likely to take it, and he was not about to substitute for England.

Bradman was circumspect for a few balls after that. He was having trouble picking up the ball without a sightscreen to help. Viewing the pavilion end was 'like looking at a draughts board'.

The red ball might appear in a white square or a black one. If the latter, it could be lost. He pitied the English batsmen facing Lindwall or Miller.

Bradman hooked Cranston hard for a boundary, but the effort strained his rib injury sustained early in the year against India at Melbourne. He doubled up in pain but seemed to recover. Cranston bounced him, and Bradman, his blood running, hooked again. This time, he was in severe pain. Pollard, in a show of remarkable sportsmanship unthinkable in the 21st Century, massaged the troubled area. Bradman recovered slowly and was quiet for a few overs while Morris advanced the score.

Australia reached 202, the half-way point, with 165 minutes to acquire the other 202.

In the dressing room, Lindwall followed a long held superstition about not moving from any chair or position in these tense moments as Australia positioned itself for the chance to pull off a remarkable victory.

'No one is allowed to move,' he said, 'not even to go to the bloody toilet.'

Yardley took the new ball with Australia on 1 for 212. Bradman was still having difficulty, but at 79 took 10 off Bedser, which gave him some pleasure, for his nemesis was no more. Australia was 1 for 243. The 250 came at 4 p.m. with Morris on 133 and in total command of all bowlers, as was Bradman. A few minutes later they had a 200 partnership. At 4.10 p.m. Bradman had his century. It had taken 147 minutes. It was his 29th century in Tests and his 19th against England. At tea, Australia was 1 for 288, with Morris on 150 and Bradman on 108. They had added 167 in the second session (Morris 87, Bradman 73) and now needed just 116 in the final session with nine wickets in hand. That middle period had swung the game Australia's way, and this grand partnership seemed unbreakable, such was their dominance. Assuming 35 to 40 overs would be bowled, Australia's rate had been reduced to around three an over, which would be easy given the heavy hitting line-up to come, should one of these two be dismissed.

After tea, Morris on-drove Pollard for four, bringing up the 300 partnership. Then with the score at 358, and the stand worth 301, Morris was caught by Pollard off Yardley for 182. It had been a great innings. Bradman was on 143, and Australia was 46 short of victory. Bradman took control with cuts and drives, pushing Australia to 396 before Miller (12) missed a straight one from Cranston to be lbw. Harvey came to the wicket and hit the winning boundary, leaving him on 4 not out.

Australia reached 3 for 404 for victory, 15 minutes before the close.

Harvey busied himself trying to souvenir a stump. Bradman ran up the wicket, patted him on the back, and said:

'C'mon son! Let's get out of here!'

They made a dash for the pavilion before the crowds could consume them.

•

Bradman was unconquered on 173, including 29 fours in 255 minutes at the wicket. This innings sat nicely with his 334, 304 and 108 at Leeds in Tests. It proved to be his happiest run chasing arena in the world over an 18-year period. Bradman and Morris had given chances yet their performances under pressure on a turning pitch were of the highest order.

They had hit more than 60 boundaries between them. This pairing, one of the finest ever, displayed concentration and footwork on a difficult wicket, just as they had on a different kind of problem strip at Manchester. Their left–right combination produced the widest range of superb strokes imaginable. Both batsmen had the vital, unseen 'will' to achieve. It was hidden beneath their calm demeanours, which for both was further masked by a quiet, observant sense of humour and acerbic wit. Yet Bradman and Morris had the capacity and heartfelt aggression in their make-ups to destroy any opposition. Their cool assassin's mien characterised their sporting personalities. This Leeds partnership was a link of two intelligent cricketers with perfect temperaments for the game, and a generous understanding of what 'partnership' meant at the wicket.

Australia had achieved the finest-ever come-from-behind success over 30 hours of intense, on many occasions, fantastic cricket to score a memorable victory in front of a record aggregate crowd of 152,000. This clinched the series, now standing at 3:0 to Australia with one draw. Bradman judged the Leeds win as 'the greatest Ashes victory by an Australian team'.

The incredible result was brought about by a combination of factors including skill, stamina, courage and tactics against the odds. Morris, Bradman, Harvey and Miller lifted for the occasion, but each player contributed in a terrific team effort.

Bradman had chalked up two of his aims, the second being to win the rubber outright. He now had his sights firmly on the third prize of making it through the season undefeated.

Such cricket invincibility on the toughest, longest tour for any sporting contest would now become the focus.

21

—

County Capers

KEITH MILLER ONCE said that the three most beautiful things in England were the rolling hills of Derbyshire, the eyes of Princess Margaret and the sweep of Denis Compton. He therefore appreciated the next stop at Derby. But it is doubtful he or any other member of the team would have appreciated the sweep of Denis Compton, the pull of Washbrook, the all-round technique of Hutton, the swing of Bedser or the pace of Pollard the very next day after the Test. Fortunately, none of these stars played for Derbyshire, the next encounter. The Australians would have been fed up with any of them the day after their astounding fight-back at Leeds in a fixture which seemed designed to minimise their chances of going through the season undefeated. Setting aside the train travel, the players would have been forgiven for thinking they were in one continuous never-ending hell of a game.

With no time after the Leeds Test for even a quick beer at the team hotel, the squad had to pack its bags in 45 minutes and head for the train, although it was late and didn't leave Leeds until 9 p.m. The night was hot; the train slow. It arrived at Derby at 11 p.m. No one was in bed before midnight.

Bradman, exhausted and in pain from his recurring rib injury, had to have physiotherapy in the early hours of the next day.

Two of the selectors – Morris and Hassett – were grateful to be rostered off for the game, but Bradman played, as did Barnes, returning after his injury. The Australians presented a strong batting line-up, with sensibly three fresh players – Barnes, Brown and Hamence – in its top six. Two other players who had missed the Test, spinners McCool and Ring, joined the team, along with the energetic Loxton, who was always 'up' to perform. Also selected were Saggers, who was making the most of his replacing injured Tallon, and the workhorse Johnston, who at least had his big feet up on the last day at Leeds after delivering 67 overs there on an unresponsive wicket.

•

More than 17,000 people – a record – attended the first day, 28 July of the game at Derby, which was close to the town's centre and accessible from the Nottingham Road. The tourists were at their zenith in terms of crowd appeal, having just completed an amazing come-from-behind thriller. Spectators were jammed into the pavilion and two small stands. Sardines would have felt claustrophobic, so packed in were the patrons in front of refreshment marquees erected for the occasion between the pavilion and scoreboard.

Bradman and his team had transformed cricket for the summer of 1948. The usual ability to stroll around the many lovely cricket arenas was not possible when they played. The paying public was turning up in unprecedented numbers to glimpse Bradman for the last time, along with the individuals who had legendary status in England, and not just with the sporting public. Television, radio and newspapers had made many of them 'names' within the season itself. Miller with his flowing mane, style, and aggression with bat and ball, was well established as a famous character with a special connection to the UK because of his air force service and efforts in the Victory

Tests. This day at Derby there was a fascination to gain a sight of Harvey after his brilliant century at Leeds a few days earlier, and Loxton, also, in the expectation of some super-hitting once more.

The biggest disappointment for the locals was the absence through injury of fast-medium bowler Bill Copson, and George Pope. Derby without the latter was as empty as Rome without its Pontiff. He was the specialist leg-cutter, who would have challenged the Australians. Pope was said to have a foot injury, but it didn't keep him out of county games before and after the match against the tourists. There was speculation that he had deliberately sidestepped the tour fixture, first to preserve himself for more important county matches; and second because he did not fancy being walloped in the manner that so many bowlers had throughout the summer.

Australia batted first without major discomfort. Brown stayed in his own world, oblivious of heckling or frustration from the crowd. He took over a sheet-anchor role, while his partners in stands – Bradman and Miller – got on with their stroke-making. Brown batted most of the day, collecting 140, including 16 fours, in 290 minutes. Some journalists were critical, but Bradman was supportive, using the hackneyed term (in 1948 England) 'splendid' to describe Brown's performance. Ever vigilant, the captain was concerned that his victorious squad from Leeds would not come up firing at Derby, which was understandable. No one would really have been surprised if the tourists struggled. Brown's performance alleviated concern for Bradman, who himself batted, he said, 'from reflex and memory. I rarely have come up the next day after a big innings. The muscles are fatigued and this slows reaction time. The big thing, however, is the ability to concentrate. Leeds needed a supreme effort on my part. I was worried that I could not possibly do well at Derby the very next morning.'

The captain demonstrated his capacity to push himself beyond the normal limits with a dashing 62, followed by a typical Miller half century of controlled mayhem.

'I was most grateful that Pope and Copson did not play,' Bradman said, 'and with Bill creating the batting backbone, there were no major problems.'

Later Loxton delivered fireworks in his half century, which woke up the spectators in the marquees and had them cheering rather than jeering. Harvey's short innings (32) gave the locals a taste of Australia's future, with his style, confidence and dazzling footwork to the spinners. It was not a common sight in England, where the one stride back and forward drills were thumped into young cricketers by unimaginative coaches.

Australia reached 456. Derbyshire then responded with 240, and there was momentary interest in where Barnes would field. He stayed at mid-wicket and did not even in jest go near his formerly favourite position close to the bat. Nor did he wander around at third man and fine-leg like a lost lamb, as he had under Hassett at Gloucester.

Miller bowled fast, taking three wickets; Johnston served the team as well as he had in the Tests. McCool was disappointing and loose, but it was to be expected after finger trouble, which made him a day-to-day proposition.

The Australians celebrated their Ashes victory on the night of Thursday 29 July – two days after the event. It was a closed-off victory dinner, then a champagne party, which allowed the squad to relax and let loose in a private function room at the team hotel. Bradman had as much bubbly as anyone.

'He smoked a cigar,' Loxton recalled, 'and really enjoyed himself.'

The next morning Bradman and Keith Johnson began to work out the extra expenses with the manager. They did not want this most expensive item of 'champagne' being scrutinised by the Board in Australia. When the manager reached £111, Johnson said:

'That's enough! We'll pay the Lord Nelson, and that's it.'

He and Bradman split the bill between them.

There were a few sore heads that morning, but the Australians were a very happy bunch.

•

Bradman asked Derbyshire to follow on, which was brave given the state of his men. Loxton, despite his 'fatigued' condition, was thrown the ball to open the bowling. Only left-hander Denis Smith, with a defiant 88, provided sustained resistance for 220 minutes, and created a record for the highest score against the Australians by a Derbyshire player. (The previous best was 81 by L. G. Wright in 1896.) McCool performed much better in this innings, flighting the ball well, and collecting 6 for 77 in Derbyshire's second effort of 182. (Loxton took 3 for 16.)

Australia won by an innings and 34. It now had won 18 games and drawn four in 22 matches. The team had come nearly two-thirds the way, but still had 12 games including a Test to negotiate.

•

The gruelling schedule continued to be as much a threat to the Australians as the opposition. Straight after the game, they caught a train from Derby to London and rolled in to the capital at 8 p.m. Bradman stayed in London, while the rest of the squad had to catch another train – at midnight – for the all-night 'flyer' 270 km west to Swansea, arriving before dawn.

•

Subtly now, the selectors made sure that each Australian team chosen had enough muscle to deal with the opposition. On previous tours, Glamorgan at Swansea was not of much concern, with rugby rather than cricket being the more dominant sport in Wales. But this season Glamorgan was a strong chance to win the County Championship and was expected to mount a challenge to the tourists. Several players, including Miller, who had a good double at Derbyshire (57 with the bat and 3 for 31), would have preferred to sunbake on Swansea beach, which was just across from the keyhole-shaped St Helen's ground. But he and Lindwall were chosen to make light work of the county side, along with spinners Johnson and Ring, who would take advantage of the wicket, which had a reputation for crumbling quickly.

Australia's batting line-up was powerful, despite Bradman taking a break and letting Hassett run another show. The top six in the order were Brown, Barnes, Hassett, Miller, Harvey and Hamence.

Miller and the other sunbathers in the Australian squad had no need for swimming trunks as the weather was cold, then wet for most of the Bank Holiday weekend. Amazingly, it did not deter another massive crowd – 50,000 over the two days of the game – turning up. On Saturday 31 July, Glamorgan batted and the openers did well, weathering the first Lindwall/Miller assault until the spinners broke through. Much interest centred on the form of Allan Watkins, the balding, genial 'Friar Tuck' of cricket, whose all-round form for the season had landed him right in front of the England selectors. The left-handed bat did enhance his chances of national selection with several thumping, technically perfect hooks off Miller, which sent his Welsh supporters into paroxysms of delight, and England selectors into cogitating mode. Could they risk putting someone straight into a Test in 12 days time on the basis of his right foot being nicely placed, and the courage to hook Miller? When he reached 19, Lindwall moved a quick delivery enough to beat his bat and trap him lbw. After that only another left-hander, Willie Jones (40) defied the Australians confidently before Glamorgan was all out for 197.

Ten-year-old Tony Lewis, a future county star, England batsman and MCC president, watched the match. He had queued from daybreak to see both days' play. He sat half-way down the rugby stand (on the sea side of the ground), straining without the benefit of binoculars, to see the Australians, and was not let down. Barnes (31) was lbw to Watkins, bowling round the wicket. This caused a unified roar that the conductor of the Welsh National Choir would have found acceptable. Watkins had bowled innocuous fast-medium, but his removal of Australia's aggressive, strong-willed opener may well have convinced England's selectors that they could gamble on the all-rounder. They would wish to forget that Watkins may have received a tad lucky leg before decision delivering left-arm round the wicket.

As Barnes sauntered off, rightly none too happy with the adjudication, there was a second roar from the crowd.

'Down the long run of steps [from the pavilion, opposite the rugby stand] came Keith Miller, flicking back his hair, striding out to the middle,' Lewis recalled. The Welsh related to Miller. Some would have seen him in 1945. Most would have seen him on TV in 1948. Many would have read that he was a lusty, classical music-loving, big-drinking kind of guy, which the Welsh spirit related to, despite his Scottish background and Australian foreground.

'Much to the fans' delight,' Lewis noted, 'the game was transformed as he crashed the ball all over Swansea, playing some strokes from nearer the bowler than the wicket-keeper.'

Miller cannoned five sixes and seven fours in his rapid-fire 84. One of the sixes stunned the crowd and commentators. Miller hammered it high over mid-wicket, ending on one knee with one hand off the bat, and his body in a coiled, corkscrew pose. But Miller every so often played this extraordinary shot, using his balance and the strength in his left arm for control. This one ended up 20 rows back into the crowd. Spectators called, 'Dal ati, Keith y Melinydd!' – 'Keep at it, Keith Miller!'

Torrential rain hit with Australia on 3 for 215 (Hassett 71 not out) and ruined the match. Yet the drenched fans left content after seeing Miller in full flight.

•

The next day, Wednesday 4 August, the caravan now went north about 120 km to Birmingham for the 24th game against Warwickshire at the Edgbaston ground. This spacious, well-placed (away from industry) arena was undergoing positive changes after falling into stagnation between the wars. It had been a first-class ground since 1886. Tests had been played there until 1929. Now it was on the rebound with the Warwickshire committee vowing (in 1946) to build a team to win a championship within five years. (It would succeed in 1951.) After the war the wicket had been lively. For this reason, Bradman sent the county in on a wet track. The Australians expected a big game because of the strong Warwickshire line-up. It had the classy young Indian all-rounder, Abdul Hafeez Kardar, batsmen Tom Dollery and Martin Donnelly, highly regarded leg-spinner Eric Hollies, and New Zealander Tom Pritchard, regarded by many in 1948 as the best fast bowler in the UK.

Bradman opened with Johnston and Loxton, who both managed dangerous lift from the wicket. The latter broke through twice, but it was Lindwall, with a devastating spell, who sealed Warwickshire's fate. He took three wickets in 12 balls to destroy the middle order. Only the diminutive, left-handed New Zealander Donnelly – one of the world's best bats in the immediate post-war era – could withstand this burst in making 28 before Johnston bowled him.

The county clawed its way to just 138.

This meant it was almost certain to lose, but its popular (with a band of local, loud young yobbos) blond, strong, Hollies, aged 36, provided the star turn for the match. His wrong 'un appeared negligible, but the batsmen could not be sure if he were holding it back. Regardless, his deadly accurate top-spinners troubled all the Australians. His impact was seen early in a most unique occurrence when he forced openers Brown and Morris back on their stumps. They were both out hit wicket. Then came the highlight for the locals when he knocked back Bradman's off-stump with what appeared to be a wrong 'un. Bradman, on 31, may have spotted the difference, but too late, judging by his rush to change his shot and play at the ball with his unmatched bat speed. Others thought it was a top-spinner, more or less coming straight on. Such was the mystery surrounding the leg-spinner's art, no one seemed sure, although more than one old leggie in the press area was heard pontificating about its nature with certitude. One thing was certain though. Hollies had wonderful flight. Bradman and the 1938 Australians had been impressed with him then, but the England selectors had studiously ignored him, which had not then made the younger Hollies happy. Momentarily, a decade on, he was pleased, especially with Bradman's wicket, and then that of Harvey (0), who had shown in his Leeds Test century that he was a young master against spin. Hollies broke one back so far to the left-hander that he looked for the umpire's confirmation that the wicket had been hit by the ball, and not by the wicket-keeper.

Hollies had the first five batsmen in the Australian order, a wonderful haul that also included Hassett (68) and Lindwall (45), but not before these two had restored some respectability to Australia's score. It ended up a modest 254.

Hollies in all took 8 for 107 off 43.5 overs with eight maidens. This was by far the best effort against the tourists. His eight included six Australians who would be in the Fifth and final Test. Pritchard failed to take a wicket but he provided danger for the tourists early and supported Hollies well.

Johnston, varying his pace and swing, and McCool, delivering his own high standard of leg-break, took four wickets each in the county's second ordinary effort of 155.

Brown (7, with 33 in the first innings) was Hollies' ninth victim for the match when Australia batted again with just 40 to score for victory. Bradman could have sent in any of eight other batsmen, but he decided to go in himself to have a good look at Hollies as he and Morris knocked off the runs for a nine-wicket win.

Bradman was certain the spinner would be selected for England at the Oval.

22
—

Bad Boy Build-Up

THE AUSTRALIANS KEPT travelling north, this time another
130 km to Manchester again for their second encounter
with the strong, competitive Lancashire, beginning Saturday 7
August. It was to be a benefit match for Cyril Washbrook, and
a useful choice too, because it was sure to draw a full house
and a good return for him. Part of the attraction for many
would be to 'verbal' and boo Lindwall and Miller. No advertising
was needed for the locals to come and see the 'bad boy' opening
bowlers do battle with their heroes. Bradman saw it as a danger
game, especially with Dick Pollard ready to thump in at the
Australians with his flat-footed run and build to considerable
pace. Bradman picked himself and Morris, the in-form batsmen,
along with Barnes who was easing back to his pre-injury touch.

Bradman won the toss and batted on a lively green top. The
superb opening century stand in tough conditions between
Barnes (67) and Morris (49) saw off Pollard and assured Australia
of a fair score, although it slumped steadily after that but for
an impressive effort by Johnson (48). Tallon's score of 33 showed
he could deliver a class act with the bat. His form had slipped
over the last decade from the late 1930s when he was an Adam

Gilchrist of his time. But every so often his batting skill complemented his brilliance behind the stumps.

True to its stoic word, and showing perhaps a lack of imagination or foresight, Lancashire had not chosen Hilton, who had shaken the cricket world, and more importantly the media, when he had dismissed Bradman twice in the previous encounter with the tourists. However, that was 10 weeks and half a season ago, and they had in his place William Roberts, bowling his slow left-armers from around the wicket with delectable, enticing flight. He came on as the sixth change, and troubled everyone, including Bradman, who he had caught for 28. He dismissed the first five Australians for 29 with a long, steady economical spell, and ended with 6 for 73 off 42 overs with 14 maidens. Had Hollies not jumped in with his nine-wicket haul in the previous game, Roberts would have come under consideration for the Fifth Test. His other distinction was in the field, where he excelled.

Australia reached 321, not enough for Bradman to relax against a feisty county that would dearly love to be the first to topple the tourists in this, their 25th encounter of the tour.

When Lancashire batted, Lindwall and Miller flew at Washbrook like falcons hitting a prey and made it a benefit to remember for mixed reasons. The redoubtable opener fell to them in combination – Miller catching him in slips off Lindwall, but not before he had top-scored with 38 from the team score of 130. The strength of the Australian bowling, which only lacked Johnston from its full complement, made this innings exceptional. Sadly, Washbrook paid for it. He was hit several times on the right hand, which left his thumb a mass of bruises and swollen when he returned to the dressing room.

Lindwall especially was delivering at such pace, swing and accuracy, that no batsman could match him.

'He was in stupendous form at this time,' Bradman recalled. 'I have not seen before or since such sustained brilliance from a pace bowler as Ray in the month of August 1948.'

Lancashire was 191 short but Bradman did not enforce the follow-on. His main reason was to make sure the game carried into the third day to increase the 'gate' for Washbrook. He also wanted Lindwall and Miller fit and hungry in the build to the final showdown at the Oval, now just a week away. Better, the captain thought, to bat again and give his bowlers a short, sharp burst at Washbrook (who the crowd would turn up to see) again on the final day of the county game, rather than let him climb on top against his fatigued star bowlers. As it turned out, his injured thumb prevented him from batting a second time.

Bradman said farewell to Old Trafford with a steady 133 not out, his highest score at this ground. It took him 215 minutes and he hit 17 fours. He was in a big partnership with Barnes (90) and declared the innings closed at 3 for 265 at lunch on the third day. This left less than three hours of play to dismiss the county, which, on paper, had 457 to make for victory.

The occasion marked the second time he had played the opposition out of the game (Yorkshire being the other) for reasons to do with bowler preservation, batting form (his own included) and not wanting to give a county any chance whatever of a fluky and glorious victory.

Even in the time allowed, Australian had a strong chance to win, but for an excellent batting effort by Jack Ikin. He reached 99. There were eight minutes left to play and Lancashire was 5 for 199. This would normally indicate that the tourists with two overs to bowl could not win. But Bradman requested the new ball. He asked Miller, who had done little work with just five overs, if he wanted a bowl. He thought Ikin should have been allowed to reach his century, and refused. But Lindwall, who had 2 for 27 in his first spell, happily accepted it. The wind was behind him. He indicated to Tallon that he was going to let loose, signalling that the keeper and the slips should stand well back. The first few deliveries nearly took Tallon with them, and did nothing for his hands and gnarled fingers. The slips eased back even further, and were half-way to the fence.

Bradman at mid-on thought of the speedy Queensland Aborigine Eddie Gilbert knocking the bat out of his hand and Larwood making him duck during the 1932–33 season. This was as quick as a cricket ball gets to be bowled. Observers estimated Lindwall's wind advantage was allowing him to deliver at more than 160 km/h (100 mph).

He uprooted Ikin's stumps and he was on his way for one short of the coveted hundred for the second successive match (having been out for 99 against Essex a week earlier).

Lindwall was not only fast but pinpoint accurate too. Pollard came in, propped at the next ball and was also bowled.

'I didn't see it at all,' a bewildered Pollard said when he returned to the pavilion.

Lancashire was 7 for 199, and on the ropes. Bradman kept the slips back but moved the rest of the field in for the kill and Lindwall's hat-trick. Roberts, who had taken 0 for 64 in Australia's second innings, came in, defended stoutly and denied the tourists victory.

Washbrook walked away with a record benefit of £14,000, but his damaged thumb made him doubtful for the Fifth Test. Those who knew his character said he would have given it all back for a last tilt at Lindwall and Miller at the Oval. But he now seemed an outside chance with the game just four days away. Lindwall may have had an important victim even before the Fifth Test began. Yet Australia had one of its own. Toshack's knee broke down. It was so bad that doctors insisted he have a cartilage operation before he returned to Australia.

•

After the game, Lancashire became the third England county (along with Hampshire and Yorkshire) to make Bradman a life member of the club in 'appreciation of his services to England-Australian cricket'. It was the same kind of citation that went with a knighthood, and at this time, rumours circulated that this would be offered to him. Journalist and friend Arthur Mailey asked him if there were any truth to the rumour.

'It was something in the papers,' Bradman replied, 'but apart from that I know nothing officially or otherwise.'

Mailey then enquired if he would accept the honour if it were offered.

Bradman let the hypothetical delivery go through to the keeper, but then offered a straight bat of sorts.

'It's just like a full-toss. You don't know what you'll do with it until it comes along.'

The persistent story was that he would be offered the knighthood as soon as he retired from the game. There was no question about Bradman accepting it or not. His basic refusal to be drawn was to avoid further distractions in the press. He still considered his main job in England was only a little more than half done.

•

The tourists travelled 200 km north east from Manchester to Sunderland to do battle with minor county Durham in a two-day game. Bradman rested himself, Lindwall, Barnes and Morris, and even let the two keepers, Tallon and Saggers, play in the same side. A crowd of 17,000 felt privileged that the Australians – the biggest team drawcard in modern sport – had taken the trouble to come north a few days before the Oval Test.

Hassett won the toss and batted in damp conditions. Tallon opened with Brown, and was soon on his way for one. Harvey and Loxton followed quickly, leaving Australia 3 for 22. But Brown, who many had criticised for his selection in the tour squad (even wife Barbara – tongue in cheek – said it was because Bradman wanted a player about his own age on tour), proved valuable again for his capacity to remain steady in a crisis. He kept one end going making a solid 49, while McCool (64), and later Miller (55) belted Australia out of trouble. Fortunately, Bradman, in London preparing for the Oval in three days time, did not hear the early scores and was only told that Australia had battled to register 282. He was saved from further heartburn when he learnt that Durham was 5 for 73 at the close. The second day was washed out, giving Australia another draw. It now had 19 wins and seven draws from 26 matches.

The players had a tough rail trip home with some bridges damaged by flooding and their train delayed several hours en route.

•

Bradman's concentration was now 100 per cent on the Oval Test. He had set his mind on this game more than any other since the 1938 experience. He said twice in after-dinner speeches that the 'Oval' owed him something. He was not talking about the two centuries he had scored there against the county. Nor was he thinking necessarily about a big performance himself. His main aim, concentration and energies were focused on demolishing England in a way that would go some way to salving his feelings after the experience a decade earlier. Two other players, Hassett and Barnes, had played in that 'other' game. They sensed Bradman's feelings.

They too were set on revenge.

•

Australia brought back Barnes for the Oval Test and gave Ring his first chance. Out went injured Toshack, and Johnson, dropped to 12th man. These were swaps at the margins. The team's core remained and was highly charged for victory. Every player was in his best, or near best form for the season.

England was forced to replace Washbrook and chose John Dewes, who had been handled so roughly by Miller this season and in 1945. It was not an inspired choice. Crapp had been dropped initially, but when Washbrook was considered unfit for play just before the game, Crapp was popped back into the squad. Hollies, as expected, got his chance at Laker's expense, while Cranston made way for Allan Watkins, the first player from Glamorgan, and probably Wales itself, to represent England against Australia. Jack Young replaced Pollard, who was unlucky after dismissing Bradman at Manchester and Leeds. Reg Simpson was made 12th man again and was considered also unlucky not to be chosen.

England's selection policy seemed to have been based on a combination of musical chairs inside a revolving door, a method that was certain to lead to near-farce. Added to the chaos was the 'anyone-who-dismisses-Bradman-is-in' corollary, and this led to 21 players – almost two teams – being selected for England during the five Tests. This was compared to Australia's use of 15 players (only Hamence and McCool missed a Test), with three players (Barnes, Tallon and Toshack) forced out because of injury. Only two players were dropped – Brown, who played two Tests, and Johnson, who played four. This gave Australia stability.

•

Rain came down hard in the days preceding the Test. This influenced many English pundits to consider the home team had the advantage with two specialist spinners, one right-arm and the other left, who would turn the ball into and away from the Australian batsmen. It would not have been wishful thinking on any other occasion in Ashes history with a dead rubber to play. But this game was very much alive in the Australians' minds as they all began to realise they could be part of something special with a win at the Oval. Bradman's last, and overriding mission was now top of the agenda.

•

The captain's first job on the morning of the match was to let Doug Ring know he was in the side.

'We [the team] had just left the Piccadilly [Hotel] and were preparing to go to the ground,' Ring said, 'when Bradman came up to me and asked me to sit next to him in the cab.'

Ring would never forget that ride from London's West End to Kennington. He had no idea why the captain wanted to chat to him.

'You're in the side today,' Bradman said, enjoying passing on the good news, which was always easier than telling a player he had been dropped.

Ring was stunned. He never thought for a moment that he would be selected for the final Test.

'The pacemen were doing so well and there was the 55-over rule,' Ring said. 'I was resigned to the fact that I'd not get a game [Test].'

In part, this selection was a reward for a player who had given everything in his limited opportunities, without complaint or bitterness. Bradman may not have mixed with the players all the time, but he missed little and forgot nothing. Attitude and team contributions were noted and remembered.

Genial Doug Ring was being given a chance.

23

—

Lindwall Paves the Way

BRADMAN IN OVERCOAT, suit and hat, and Yardley in cricket gear, walked out on the waterlogged Oval to respectful rather than wild applause from the full house on Saturday 14 August. Many people in a crescent of barrack-like flats overlooking the ground were on their balconies to watch the event. Beyond the three gasometers, skies were gloomy, and made darker behind the Vauxhall Stand where black smoke curled from a factory. Passing bus passengers craned their necks, and stationary cranes necked their constructions in the post-war rebuilding close to the ground. Outside the Oval, long lines curled out of sight through Kennington streets. Many fans had slept on the wet streets through the night in order to witness this historic moment when the greatest cricketer ever would play his last Test. Not since Hobbs had bowed out in the corresponding Test of 1930, and Grace had performed there for the last time in 1896, had there been such deference, tension, atmosphere and expectation for the appearance of a cricketer.

The pitch had absorbed incessant London rain over the previous four days. Bradman moved gingerly around the wicket area, testing the surface. It was heavy, and he did not have to

225

examine the outer areas, which would have been weightier. The ball was not going to end up at the boundary often in these conditions. Scoring would be slow.

Bradman came off the field and consulted his team.

'He was in quandary on what to do,' Ring said. A short time later, up went the coin for the ninth time for Bradman as captain in England and he called 'heads' as he always did. It came down tails for the eighth time. He reckoned that by the law of averages it had to come down right for him, but for someone who claimed not to believe in these laws, it was shaky thinking. Bradman should have joined Miller at a roulette table at a casino more often to comprehend that it sometimes took a run of 20 or 30 for those averages to even out. But still the toss did not matter. Yardley did what Bradman wanted: he sent England in to bat.

Half an hour after the scheduled start and right on noon, Bradman, wearing his baggy green and looking confident, stepped down the pavilion steps and onto the Oval. That first jaunty stride onto the ground was captured by a photographer.

Bradman could have had the word 'ready' blazoned across his sweater. He had waited and worried and had bad dreams about 1938. Now he was grateful for the chance, a decade later, to redress a few things.

Grim-looking Hutton marched out with Dewes, who did not need towels stuffed into his gear to appear solid. Facing Miller was going to be an ordeal, and he seemed very nervous. Loxton moved across and shook hands with him as the batsman approached the wicket, a most unusual act before a game began. There was no more willing competitor on the field than Loxton, whose move was spontaneous. He had sensed Dewes' extreme unease and felt sorry for him. Some older observers on the other side of the fence frowned at this. Their attitude was that players should by all means shake hands *after* a game, but not before it.

Dewes jigged around as the field was set for Hutton, who was by contrast, stony-faced and still before facing Lindwall.

Was Dewes resigned to further torment, and even surprised to be selected in such company?

Lindwall bowled a loosening over in the cold conditions, and not one ball was fast or troublesome. Hutton picked a single off his toes. Dewes, a left-hander, did the same. This meant he had to face Miller, who took more time than usual to set his field, with Bradman nodding his head in approval. Miller wheeled in, hair flopping. He bowled a fast, skidding delivery outside the off-stump that Dewes did not have to play. But there was reaction behind the wicket. Tallon took the ball – thwack! – into his gloves. Miller had not bothered to warm up. Yet he was not happy with the slippery run-up. He took more time putting down sawdust. Dewes had to wait, grimacing, or feigning a smile at the other end, for what must have seemed an eternity for the second delivery. Miller bent his cold back and delivered an off cutter, which came in like a flash. The ball skidded past Dewes, propped and groping at the crease, and scattered his stumps. There was a roar from the crowd.

England was one down for two runs. Lindwall kept warming up, over by over at one end. Miller bowled two more overs. Bradman, in an inspired move, replaced him with Johnston after just three overs, and positioned Hassett behind square leg for the catch off new man Edrich. He then had a word to Johnston as he tossed him the ball. Was this bluff or was there a short one coming? Big, lanky Bill, nonchalant as you like, loped in with his giant strides and right on cue dropped one in short. Edrich positioned himself, swivelled and hooked it right down the throat of Hassett, who didn't need a helmet here.

England was 2 for 10.

Compton arrived at the wicket to applause that took a few seconds to warm up. He seemed unfazed by the circumstances, and soon had Lindwall bouncers coming at him. But there was nothing in the wicket, and Lindwall appeared to strain his spine more than normal to get lift. Yet the deliveries were not bouncing over the batsman. They were skidding in at the Adam's apple, which could have been his target, so laser-like was his bowling. Compton received a truly lethal delivery of this variety. The ball knocked the bat out of his hand and flew over slips to third man where Hassett ran around to collect it. Compton didn't know whether to run, go back and pick up the bat and then run, or stay where he was. In the end, Hutton half-solved his dilemma by running through. Compton, like a knight who had dropped his sword, not a cricketer who didn't need his blade, retrieved his wooden weapon and was stranded mid-pitch. Hassett picked up the ball. Instead of spearing it in to effect a near-certain run-out, he smiled and held it up until Compton scrambled into his ground. The batsman acknowledged Hassett's piece of sportsmanship, which not all the Australians on and off the field would have endorsed. O'Reilly for one, rebuked his good friend when he came off the field. But the crowd applauded Hassett's compassion.

Perhaps Compton decided to ride his luck. Bradman set the field meticulously.

'I was fielding fine of the umpire [at square leg],' Morris said, 'and Bradman moved me two yards.'

'I heard him [Bradman] say to Lindwall,' Ring said, '"Bowl it on off-stump, a little short, and make sure he hits it in the air."'

Lindwall delivered another precision bouncer. Compton (4) took it on with a flourish, hooking down with a roll of the wrists, but awkwardly and not down far enough. Morris took a catch on his chest at square leg, and did not have to move. He wandered over to Bradman and asked:

'Why did you move me?'

'I remember him [Compton] playing a similar shot to Ernie McCormick in 1938,' Bradman replied, delighted.

As the series developed, Compton had become the prize wicket. His removal so early for so little was, in the Australians' eyes, an important breakthrough.

England was 3 for 17. The Oval spectators were sadly silent.

Crapp entered the fray, as calm as ever, and seemed at ease to both Lindwall and Johnston, although, like Hutton at the other end, he was intent on defence. Bradman, his antennae working wonderfully, would have none of it this day at the Oval. No one was going to be allowed to settle. He brought back Miller, this time from Lindwall's end, and moved the field in. Until then he had the field set to fit the expected ease with which the batsmen would play. But now, with England reeling, he moved more men into catching positions. Miller managed an edge from Crapp (who had not scored in 20 minutes) to Tallon.

After 90 minutes, England went to lunch at 4 for 29, with Hutton on 17 not out and Yardley on 4 not out. Miller was the pick of the bowlers with 2 for 3 off six overs. Hutton was even more determined to stay at the wicket than a decade ago when he accumulated those 364 runs. Bradman was content, but he would not rest until England was all out or Hutton was on his way.

•

Six runs were added after lunch before Lindwall knocked over skipper Yardley's stumps with a fierce, swinging yorker to reduce England to 5 for 35. Bradman was now aware that regardless of Hutton, his bowlers were going to effect a complete breakthrough, especially the way Lindwall was bowling. His pace was somewhere near the hurricane he had produced at Manchester a few days earlier. The accuracy was there too, and the stumps were his target when he was not softening up the batsman, as had been the case against Lancashire. The bonus was that Miller was looking more menacing than at any time on the tour. Johnston was as good as ever, and Allan Watkins had to face him with the weight of all Wales on his shoulders.

Johnston gave him a bouncer. Watkins played the shot of his life, but missed the ball. Then he was hit on the shoulder by a second bouncer. Two sucker punches from Johnston were followed by a ball well up, which Watkins hit across and was trapped dead in front for a duck.

England was 6 for 42. Bets were being taken around the ground on whether it would reach 50. At this point, Miller, Johnston and Lindwall had two wickets each. Bradman sensed Lindwall's hunger for wickets as he had at Lancashire and kept him on. He proceeded to uproot the stumps of Bedser, Evans and Young in a blistering spell, which Bradman judged as the best and most dangerous he had ever seen in Test cricket. For four wickets in succession, Australia did not need the other 10 fielders, including the keeper, as Lindwall smashed the stumps down every time.

England was cut down to 9 for 47. The only real interest now was in the home side's struggle to avoid the ignominy of being all out in the forties.

Hutton, who had batted magnificently in defence, untroubled by any of the bowlers, sealed the gambling going on around the Oval by smashing Lindwall high and straight for four. The bowler was expected to bounce the gritty Yorkshireman. Instead he let go an in-swinger that pitched middle and travelled to leg. Hutton glanced it perfectly. He turned his head, certain he would see the ball bouncing towards the rope for the second boundary of the innings. Instead, he was incredulous to see Tallon swoop and slide his extended left glove under the ball for a catch, which sent him somersaulting. Tallon came up holding the ball aloft with the minimum of fuss. Many observers, including Bradman, thought that no better catch had ever been taken by a keeper.

England was all out for 52 with not one wicket falling because of any fault in the pitch. It was the lowest score by it at home. All Bradman's planning had culminated in England coming down at this ground from the highest score ever in Tests to this school house tally. The slump of 851 runs was even beyond Bradman's wildest fantasies, which one imagines, would have centred on him helping Australia to a massive score, and then him directing the dismissal of England twice. No one would have been more pleased with this turnaround. He thrived on the knowledge of the numbers and perfection. In less than two sessions on day one, the pain of 1938 had almost been erased.

Bradman nursed (through the drag controversy), advised, counselled (when he attacked Edrich with bouncers), finessed (at Lord's when he ignored the bowler's groin injury), penalised (lightly for being hung-over at Lord's against Middlesex) and inspired Lindwall from the boat trip onwards. The paceman had come through like no other in cricket history, if marked for speed, accuracy, swing and destructive power. The poetry of this bowling brilliance at the Oval in 1948 would bring a wry smile and animation to Bradman's face whenever he was quizzed about it for the rest of his life.

Lindwall took 6 for 20 from 16.1 overs with five maidens. Five of those wickets went down for just eight runs in the post-interval blitz. Miller 2 for 5, and Johnston 2 for 20, backed him up and were just as feverish to remove the opposition. Doug Ring, in his only Test in the series, was not even looked at by Bradman. It was time exclusively for controlled pace.

Hutton had played an innings that would be remembered nearly as much as his dawdle through a few days and a few centuries in 1938. He all but carried his bat, and was dismissed only by arguably the greatest leg-side catching keeper ever at his superlative best. Hutton scored 30 in 130 minutes, and gave not a hint of a chance. Bradman admired Hutton for his faultless technique, but thought he could have done more to counterattack. He was the best equipped to do this, next to Compton, but did not try.

•

After this Lindwall-instigated debacle, Yardley received a letter from a female fan.

'I've been listening to the commentators,' she wrote, 'and they say Lindwall has two short-legs, a square leg and a long leg. What sort of creatures are these Australians?! No wonder we can't win.'

•

Morris and Barnes came to the wicket, and proved it lifeless, and not difficult for batting in polishing off England's score in less than an hour. Allan Watkins, not wanting to miss his big chance in a Test, tried to hide his shoulder injury sustained when batting. But it hindered him and made his appearance at the bowling crease short and unimpressive.

Both batsmen were in masterly touch as they took the score to 117, when Barnes (61) made an error by chasing a wide leg-break from Hollies, which he nicked to Evans.

Then came the moment the crowd had waited for from the first second of the innings. Bradman strolled out slowly, as if he was absorbing the terrific applause. He touched his cap, not feeling pressured to raise it as he had at Leeds when he walked through the human tunnel. As he reached half-way and the cheering kept rising, Yardley gathered his troops.

'We'll give him three cheers,' he said, and then throwing the ball to Hollies added: 'Then you bowl him out, Eric.'

Bradman reached the pitch, and took off his cap. Yardley shook hands with him. The England captain then turned to his players and they responded to the 'hip-hip, hurray!' for the Don. Many scribes, without really knowing, suggested Bradman was teary-eyed after this. But when I asked him about it, he admitted it was a touching moment, but not for a second, he said, was he put off, or did he have a tear in his eye. In other words, there was no excuse for what then transpired. Yet he agreed he was more tense than normal.

'I was anxious,' he said. 'I was naturally keen to do well.'

Hollies rolled in with a leg-break. Bradman pushed forward, connecting with the middle of the bat, although he claimed to not really see it. Hollies then sagely bowled him a wrong 'un, which he had not delivered to Bradman in the second innings of the Warwickshire game 10 days earlier. It was on a perfect length. It curled past his bat, just touched it and hit the off bail, bowling him for a duck. Bradman was propped forward. He looked back at his stumps, straightened up, turned, removed his gloves and walked just as slowly off the arena with the fans now dead silent. This surely was the greatest duck in history, Walt Disney's Donald notwithstanding.

Once back in the dressing room, Bradman removed his pads, and said to Barnes, who was busy with his camera, having snapped the most famous two-ball innings ever:

'Fancy that!'

Hamence came over and commiserated with Bradman.

'One of those things, Ronnie,' he said with a shrug and a grin.

Before this innings, Bradman had scored 6,996 runs from 69 completed innings (out of 79 to that point), and his average stood at 101.35. He had no idea that he needed just 4 to secure a Test average of exactly 100, rather than the 99.94 it ended up because of the duck in his 70th completed knock. For one thing, he would have expected two innings at the Oval, given that he batted twice so far in each of the four previous Tests in the series. For another, a second innings not out of 4 or more would have delivered him that heavenly average of 100.

Alec Bedser said, 'If I'd been bowling, I would have given him a full-toss to get those four runs.'

Australia went to stumps on Saturday night at 2 for 153, with Morris unconquered and travelling marvellously on 77, and Hassett on 10.

•

Despite his duck and the hysteria in the British press on Sunday, Bradman was in the best of spirits attending a concert at the Albert Hall given by Australian pianist Eileen Joyce, whom Percy Grainger described as being 'transcendentally gifted'. Bradman met Joyce backstage and his mood was ebullient. He had joy from experiencing the perfection of others, as he had watching the tennis or playing golf with pros. But his best relaxation came with playing the piano or listening to others more professional than himself. Only outstanding cricket performances, such as Stan McCabe or Lindwall in full flight, meant as much to him. Joyce's recital and her company afterwards lifted him even further after his team's phenomenal start. Australia was 101 ahead with eight wickets in hand. He and his team would not relent on Monday.

Twenty years at the top of cricket told Bradman he could relax on a day off when he and his team were in such a strong position.

24
—

Oval Triumphant

ORRIS, IN COMMAND of himself and the opposition bowlers, continued on Monday at a steady pace while Hassett held up the other end for 100 minutes. Morris took on, and Hassett blunted Bedser, Edrich, Young and Hollies. Along the way, Morris reached his century. He had stayed out of the limelight, which fell on Lindwall, Bradman and then Hollies. The innings was so far underestimated, mainly because while Morris was at the wicket, the bowlers were being controlled, and thus underrated. It seemed that the left-handed opener was so successful during the Tests that everyone was taking his dominance for granted. It wasn't until Young dismissed Hassett (37) lbw, and Hollies had Miller (5) stumped, that attention focused on Morris much more. Miller was out-thought. Hollies noted his desire to come at him. He bowled a faster delivery down leg-side. Evans did the rest, leaving Miller falling forward and doing a push-up on the pitch.

Australia was 4 for 243, and just a fraction wobbly, although the lead was 191. Harvey looked in touch, but Hollies beat him tactically, as he had at Birmingham. This time he noted the batsman's penchant for drives to the off. Harvey loved, and was brilliant at, the one, two, one dance to the spinners. Hollies fed him the shot, then delivered a nicely flighted top-spinner, which dipped on him. Harvey (17) tangoed forward, went through with a drive and sent a catch to Young at mid-off.

Australia was 5 for 265. The lead was 213. If this collapse continued, England would be back in the game, just. Morris, unperturbed by what was happening at the other end, continued to score off all the bowlers, including Hollies, although the leg-spinner had his respect. Morris's asset of marvellous footwork became most apparent now and he had not given the semblance of a chance. Hollies had tried everything in his considerable bag of tricks but they were all worked out by Morris.

The new ball was due. Morris began his innings over again, while Loxton became his 'opening' partner. The latter struggled against the movement from Bedser and Edrich. On 15, Loxton poked at one from Edrich he didn't need to even acknowledge, and Evans accepted the catch.

Australia was 6 for 304.

Lindwall came in without the pressure on him that he experienced at Leeds, and began where he left off there with two big hits for four. At 9, he had a go at one of Young's enticing deliveries and was caught by Edrich diving at cover point.

Australia was 7 for 332, having lost 5 for 179 so far for the day, which meant that England had fought back, only to be thwarted by Morris's now masterly performance as he climbed towards his double century. With the score on 359, Tallon played a ball through slips. Morris called for the run. Simpson, substituting for the injured Watkins, picked up from short third man and in the one action hurled the ball in. Morris was adjudged run out for 196, when he deserved a double hundred.

On reflection, most observers thought this was the *only* way he could have been dismissed, such was his dominance of the England attack.

'I thought he was unlucky to be given run out,' Bradman told me. 'It was a close call.'

'The decision robbed Arthur of a well-deserved double hundred. He had developed steadily through the tour into a young master of the game. That innings [196 at the Oval] and his Leeds knock placed him as the best left-hander in cricket at the time. I regarded him then as the best left-hander I'd ever seen.'

Bradman had not seen Clem Hill, whom author and broadcaster A. G. Moyes rated as good as Morris against slow and medium-pace bowlers, and better at facing speed. Moyes added the caveat that had Morris faced the pacemen that bowled to Hill, he would have handled them 'competently'. And while he appreciated Morris's capability in attacking the bowling, he thought Hill had more power in his shots.

Morris judged his 182 at Leeds as his greatest innings. Bradman thought his Oval knock in this game even better, mainly because he had hardly made a technical error. It was the way they judged such performances. Morris believed his 182 at Leeds was a more important effort. Bradman saw things from the viewpoint of absolute batting perfection in the technical sense, as long as the batsman 'got on with it,' and this was the way he saw the 196. (Bradman also differed with many on what was his own best Test innings. He opted for his 254 at Lord's in 1930. He did not make one shot error and gave no chances; others thought his 334 innings at Leeds in the same series was superior, even though he gave a chance. The England attack was better at Leeds, with Larwood, Tate and Geary all bowling and in good touch.)

Other astute judges also gave this Morris classic rave notices. Maurice Tate, regarded by many observers as the best swing bowler ever, called the 196 knock 'magnificent'. He marvelled at Morris's range of strokes. Cricket and music critic Neville Cardus loved the melody and resonance of this kind of innings. It allowed him to go into overdrive in descriptive terms. He bracketed him with Stan McCabe after his 1938 Ashes 232 at Trent Bridge, which was an odd coupling. McCabe was a right-hander, and had played beyond his, or anyone's means, in that

First Test of 1938. Morris, if anything, had played within his considerable means at the Oval. Cardus explained it further by saying:

'Morris once more was beyond praise – masterful, stylish, imperturbable, sure in defence, quick and handsome in stroke play.'

These words could have been used for McCabe, but the next comment was purely about Morris:

'His batting is true to himself, charming and good-mannered but reliant and thoughtful. Seldom does he spare a ball of suspicious character, yet he is never palpably acquisitive, never brutal. He plunders bowlers tastefully and changes rubbish into cultural art. I never tire of watching him.'

Yardley and his team could not agree with Cardus there. They were thoroughly sick of his domination and happy to see him on his way after never looking like removing him.

Unfortunately for Morris his world-beating innings was overshadowed by Bradman's duck. Few recalled one of the great Ashes innings of all time.

'I'm often asked if I was playing when Don made his duck,' he said with a laugh, 'and I reply, "Yes, I was up the other end." Then the comment is, "Oh really! And how many did you get?" I reply, "196."'

•

But for a sweet cameo from the underestimated Tallon (31), the England team may have been satisfied with its work. But he boosted the Australian score to 389. Yardley and Co. were sobered in the knowledge that the lead was a whopping 337. On this wicket and given the Oval's history of fat scores, it would not seem a major problem for the best England batting line-up. But with Australia's attack – particularly Lindwall, Miller and Johnston – it may as well have been 1,337. There was little confidence in England overcoming it.

•

Hollies returned the best figures for England: 5 for 131 from a marathon 56 overs with 14 maidens. He was both penetrating and economical. It was to be hoped that he framed the scorecard and hung it in his billiards room. His haul of Barnes, Bradman, Miller, Harvey and Tallon was high in the great pantheon of 'Michelles' through history. None of the England team bowled badly. It was more that Morris was so outstanding that Australia's tally was so close to 400.

•

England batted with an hour left for play on day two. Hutton was a rock again, while Dewes wafted at things he should not have, and let balls go that he should have defended. Lindwall soon bowled him for 10 with a quicker one, at which he decided not to play a stroke.

Edrich came to the wicket with England at 1 for 20. He looked sound, and his confidence assisted Hutton in opening up with strokes unseen in the first innings. They took the score to 1 for 54 at stumps, Hutton on 19, and Edrich on 23.

These two had played everyone, including Lindwall and Miller, with such ease that the fans left the Oval feeling that there was some hope for the home team yet. They ignored the 283 deficit and talked of brighter developments on the morrow.

•

Those airy expectations were dented in the first half hour when Lindwall produced his fastest ball of the match so far. It zipped from the off and sent Edrich's middle stump cartwheeling. The speedster has sustained this brilliance for the season, but had peaked by luck, management and planning, and a skipper who understood his finest ever charge in the pace department.

Edrich had departed for 28; England was 2 for 64 and in trouble again. Yet while Hutton remained, there was further hope for England. As in the first innings, he was very sure in defence, even against Lindwall's lightning. One suspects that of the world's batsmen only someone with the technique of Hutton, or the counter-punching attacking skills of Bradman in 1930, could have taken on Lindwall in this form. The Yorkshireman believed in a war of attrition; Bradman was the high priest of do or die. He hated being tied down, and never had been in his 20-year career at the top. Even against Larwood employing Bodyline, he preferred to counter him by unique methods (playing tennis shots), which rationally were the only ones that came near to succeeding over a series.

Compton joined Hutton. They were the last two VC winners in the trench, as the bowlers came at them. Hutton was all follow-through and little penetration. He stroked the ball with style on the off, particularly the covers. But with Loxton and Harvey patrolling, the runs came at just over a trickle. Compton looked awkward, for Compton, and was not his usual ebullient self.

Bradman gave Ring his chance, and he lobbed his slow leg-breaks up for 13 consecutive overs in the pre-lunch session. He was steady and economical, but the feeling at the ground was that Bradman was giving the pacemen a breather for a later onslaught.

The score advanced 67 in 100 minutes to lunch, with England on 2 for 121. Hutton had crawled on 23 to be 42 not out; Compton, even though he was not quite himself, like a mildly sick man with a cold but not the flu, had 37 to his name. England was still 216 short of making Australia bat again. Yet the wicket was innocuous for even good Test bowlers. The sanguine spectators wondered again, and were fortified in knowing that the two best bats in England were still at the wicket.

But as so often is the case, the meal break caused a concentration lapse. Johnston, the unsung hero who let Lindwall and Miller take the limelight, drifted a ball away from the flicking Compton (39) and he edged it to Lindwall, who took a beautiful slips catch. This was galling, if not sickening for England supporters. Compton was close to 40 runs, and for a class batsmen, this would most times lead on somewhere more substantial, especially in the circumstances. But it was not to be. England was 3 for 125. Crapp joined Hutton, and Miller came on to do battle. Seeing Ring's balls turning, Miller tried his beloved fast off-spinners, mixing them in with medium pace, and the odd bumper. One of the latter crashed into Crapp's cranium. He staggered like a stunned boxer, but stayed on his feet, much to the delight of the crowd, who at first were unhappy with yet another strike. Three minutes were lost as he pretended to recover.

Miller kept coming, this time at Hutton (64), and he succumbed, nicking to Tallon standing well back for one of Miller's hair-raising quicker deliveries. It did just enough to defeat England's best performer in this Test.

John Arlott ranked the knock highly:

'[Hutton's innings] must stand with his record score in 1938,' he wrote in *Gone to the Test Match*. 'This innings was full of good strokes and of cool, measured defence under a horrible burden of anxiety and impending defeat.'

Crapp, softened up by Miller, was never the same. He was probably a little concussed and in no shape to carry on. But he was a low-key, taciturn type on or off the pitch, and would not complain, although he reported the next day after arriving at his Cornwall home that he had a nasty headache.

Miller, brought up on the physical, oft times brutal, contact of Aussie Rules football, had no concerns about a dazed opponent. In football, he might deliver another 'shirt front' (the hip and shoulder straight-on bump, which was meant to concuss the opponent) if he could. In cricket there was room for the use of more brain power and subtlety in moments of intimidation and attempts to send a player from the field of battle. Miller let fly another bouncer, which Crapp negotiated from vague memory. Then Miller wheeled in for a quicker one that broke through and bowled him. Crapp (9) didn't see it, couldn't recall it, and didn't worry about it. He was the fifth wicket to fall. England was 164. The innings lights were beginning to flicker, just as the uncertain light at the Oval began to fade. Bradman had Ring on to placate the umpires, and avoid the game being called off for the day. Watkins, with the look of the man without hope and striking out as if he had nothing to lose, belted Ring high towards 'cow corner' between deep mid-wicket and deep mid-on. Hassett ran around, made up a fair amount of ground and took a nice catch. It was his fellow Victorian's first and only Ashes wicket. But as the popular Ring said with his ever genial, fun-loving smile:

'I at least got one more than most people.'

England was on the ropes and waiting for the count. In came Evans. Lindwall knocked over the stumps with one that he didn't see for pace and the blackness behind the bowler's arm.

Yardley, 2 not out, appealed against the gloom and the umpires upheld it.

England was 7 for 178 at stumps. Rain fell soon after the players left the field and was of concern to the Australians who were anxious to speak to the London weather bureau. They still had a 159 lead, and with two days to play the weather that preceded the match would have to return for England to avoid defeat.

•

Bradman reminded Lindwall (who was aware) that Ted McDonald had taken 27 wickets in an Ashes series, which was the record, and the number that Lindwall had secured. Bradman threw him the ball on Wednesday morning, but Johnston stepped in and knocked over the last three wickets to finish with the commendable figures of 4 for 40, giving him 6 for 60 for the match. More pertinently, the victims took his tally also to 27 wickets for the series. Johnston's cost just 23.33 each, as compared to Lindwall's excellent 19.62.

Miller was strong again, with 2 for 27, leaving him with a nice analysis too of 4 for 27 (and 13 at 23.15 for the series). But at the Oval Test of 1948, the best overall bowling award went to Lindwall. He took 3 for 50 off 25 overs in the second innings, giving him 9 for 70 for the match. An amazing seven of his victims were clean-bowled. Lindwall's hallmarks were accuracy, speed, swing and length – always accompanied by a cold sense of intimidation.

Australia won by an innings and 149 runs. The totality of this victory gave Bradman his much-sought-after revenge at the Oval. In my interviews with him, he expressed disappointment about his duck when asked, but it was most apparent that it was insignificant in his mind compared to the size of the win, and what it meant.

Australia won the Ashes 4:0, and so convincingly that many observers began to make comparisons with the greatest teams that had ever played cricket. It would be an argument that would go on forever. It could only ever be a theoretical debate. But the fact that the 1948 team is always mentioned whenever the great teams of all time are considered is testimony to the profundity of its performance and dominance.

•

Taking into account the brilliance of the Australian speed attack, England had three batsman who performed well – Compton (562 runs at 62.44); Washbrook (356 at 50.85) and Hutton (342 at 42.75). Australia also had three top batting performers in all conditions – Morris (696 runs at 87.00); Barnes (329 at 82.25) and Bradman (508 at 72.57). But they were backed up right down the list, especially by Hassett (310 at 44.28); Loxton (144 at 48.00) and Harvey (133 at 66.50).

The bowler of the series award would go to Lindwall, and the batsman of the series award would go to Morris. Compton would take the batting prize for England, and Bedser was its best bowler. My vote for the Compton-Miller Award for the player of the series (retrospectively given) would go to Morris. He and Lindwall were more or less equal in performance in the First, Second, Third and Fifth Tests. But in the Fourth at Leeds, Morris's great innings of 182 would put him just ahead, although Lindwall's all-round effort there (with 4 for 163 and a fine 77 in the first innings) was still strong.

•

A large crowd gathered around the pavilion for the final speeches and presentations. H. D. G. Leveson Gower and Yardley spoke glowingly of Bradman.

'In saying goodbye to Don,' Yardley said graciously, generously and bravely, given that he was in England, 'we are saying goodbye to, without doubt, the greatest cricketer of all time. He is not only a great cricketer but a great sportsman on and off the field. I hope this is not the last time we see Don Bradman in this country.'

Bradman replied: 'It is a very sad occasion for me, but whatever you read to the contrary, this is definitely my last Test match ever. I am sorry my personal contribution has been so small.' Bradman paused momentarily, and that well-known wry smile creased his lips before he added: 'There are two reasons for that. One was the generosity of the reception I received, and, secondly the very fine ball bowled to me.' He paused while the crowd cheered and applauded. 'It has been a great pleasure for me to come on this tour. And I would like you to all know how much I have appreciated it. Our most important matches are over. We have played against a very lovable opposing skipper. He has been kind to us in every way, and it is a great pleasure to have him captain England against us.' He paused once more and added: 'The captain of the losing side has a very difficult job. Norman Yardley had the misfortune to run up against one of the strongest Australian teams ever.' He raised a hand to the crowd, saying: 'It will not be my pleasure to play ever again on the Oval. But I hope it will not be the last time I come to England.'

Bradman shook hands with Yardley and Leveson Gower. The crowd clapped until the little ceremony moved off the balcony; then it dispersed.

•

Bradman's comments were diplomatic and sincere after the 27th match and 20th victory so far. His comment, 'Our important matches are over', was true, but only half the story. There were seven more official fixtures, five of them first-class. He and his team would be keener than ever now not to lose one of them.

They could sense history was in the making.

25

—

End-Games

THE FIFTH TEST'S finish by noon on the final day allowed the Australians their longest break since the gruelling fixture began close to four months earlier at Worcester. It was nearly 72 hours before the chosen squad began its game against Kent on Saturday 21 August at the St Lawrence Ground, Canterbury about 100 km east of London. The weather in this lovely rural setting of six acres was wet and cool. Yet as on almost every occasion on this tour, there was a record crowd (19,000) stuffed into the ground. About 15,000 fans were on various forms of seats, from planks to stone portmanteaus, and in the many tents, which were a distinguishing feature of this arena, along with the tree that stood inside the boundary. They were there to see this all-conquering team and how the local lads fared against it.

The men and women of Kent knew their cricket too. They could lay claim to the county being the true 'cradle of cricket', which was Hambledon's quaint but false selling cry. Many of the ancestors of these Kent fans had played on the local Downs before the Civil War period 1642–51 in which cricket burgeoned when Royalists and courtiers fled London to their country retreats. Cricket's popularity in the region continued to increase through the restoration of the monarchy. By the time of Charles II's death in 1685, the sport was on the way to being the number-one pastime for the gentry and others. It reached this status in the early 1700s, but for more nefarious reasons than historians would sometimes like to remember. The patronage of the nobility either made the game or nearly ruined it, depending on the point of view. The baronets put big bets on games. This increased the focus on the sport, which drew the punting public and the arena bookmakers to take their money. By the mid-1700s this led to match-fixing and throwing of games until cricket was on the nose (in much the same way it was in the late 1990s) and synonymous with corruption.

A judge pronounced in a 1748 lawsuit:

'Cricket is, to be sure, a manly game and not bad in itself, but it is the ill use that is made of it, by betting above ten pounds upon it, that is bad and against the laws.'

After that black period, the game survived, the corrupt betting subsided to a point where it was a novelty rather than the norm, and Kent produced some superb cricketers along the way. They included the dazzling all-rounder Frank Woolley, the slow left-armer Charlie Blythe, and the leading administrator (and early Test player) Lord Harris. In the 1948 team were two more exceptional players: L. E. G. (Les) Ames and Godfrey Evans, both keepers. (Evans, in that betting tradition of the men of Kent, later became an on-ground bookie, complete with grey beard and twirling handlebar moustache. He took the notorious bets from Dennis Lillee and Rod Marsh at 500 to 1 during the 1981 Leeds Test when they bet against their own side winning.) Evans had been Ames' understudy until after the war, when Evans became England's keeper.

The big crowd wanted to see how 33-year-old Arthur Fagg, the county's star opening bat, would fare against Lindwall, who, after the Oval was a drawcard in himself. (Fagg had toured Australia in 1936–37 but returned home with rheumatic fever without a chance to shine.) They were disappointed when

Bradman won the toss and batted. Bill Brown, the backbone of the county games, continued to fulfil his role with a gentle 106, while Morris (43), Bradman (65), Harvey (60) and Hamence (38) played attractive cricket. Brown was slow but still the reliable stalwart at the crease. His head down, cautious approach stiffened his team-mates' performances.

Australia reached 4 for 293 at stumps. Jack Davies' cover fielding was a feature. He cut off many fours in a display rarely matched in the tourists' experience all summer.

•

After play on Saturday, Bradman announced to the team that they had been invited to a party at the home of Kent captain Brian Valentine and his wife, which was to be supported by the 1698-established Kent brewing group, Shepherd Neame. There would not be a shortage of alcohol at the function.

'Hands up those who want to come?' Bradman said.

Only Ian Johnson, Ron Hamence and Sam Loxton responded.

'We'll do that again,' Bradman said and repeated the announcement about the party. Because it was Saturday night, and they were closer to London than for other games, several of the squad had made other arrangements.

Hamence introduced Loxton to Taylor 08 Port at a most convivial party.

'I'd never had it before,' Loxton noted, 'and I didn't think it was alcoholic.'

Bradman, enjoying himself more as the tour progressed, had a turn at the Valentines' piano while imbibing wine. After being introduced to the port, Loxton had an intimate affair with it that night and had to be medicated by Mrs Valentine, who had been a nurse at Dunkirk. Bradman and the others had to assist Loxton back to the hotel.

'Braddles put me in the service lift,' Loxton recalled, but couldn't remember why. 'Perhaps I needed servicing.'

The day off on Sunday was useful for the others, but not Loxton.

'I was playing from memory for the next two weeks,' he said.

•

On the Monday, even more fans – 26,500 – packed into the picturesque setting and spilled onto the arena to see the last six Australians removed for just 68. The tourists' total was, for them, modest at 361.

Out marched Fagg and Leslie Todd to cheering and strong applause. Within minutes the two openers were back in the hatch for ducks, nicely in time for lunch, courtesy of Johnston and Lindwall respectively. At one point they were 5 down for just 16. Les Ames with 11, and Evans 1, could do nothing to stop the rot, which saw the county all out for 51 – one less than England at the Oval. Kent lasted 85 minutes. Lindwall, Johnston, McCool and Loxton (playing very well from memory and taking 3 for 10 off five overs) shared the spoils. Bradman sent the county in again. It was one man short in its second attempt. Opener Todd had been struck on the instep by a very fast swinging Lindwall yorker and was so bruised that he could not put on his boot. He was but one more player battered by Lindwall through the summer. The other notable names on his personal hit-parade were Hutton, Washbrook, Edrich and Middlesex's Jack Robertson. In fact, there were probably few county opening bats who had not felt the sting of Lindwall leather. Miller had also done damage, but he had at times seemed more lethal to spectators with his bat, although he too put many a welt on opposition bodies.

Kent collapsed again to be 5 for 45 before a stand by Tony Pawson (35) and Evans (49 run out) of 71 in 32 minutes livened the crowd, which was let down by the county's showing. It became Australia's 21st victim in 28 encounters when it was all out 124 (Lindwall 4 for 25), beaten by an innings and 186 runs.

•

The early finish gave the Australians a well-appreciated extra day's break to regroup for one of the few designated 'danger' games for the tour – versus the Gentlemen of England at Lord's, beginning 25 August.

Bradman was wary, without being worried, about Walter Robins captaining the Gentlemen. Robins had proved himself a good skipper, leading Middlesex to a championship, and there had been a limited movement for him to lead England. But Bradman was determined to leave Lord's with a big win and a century. He won the toss and came to the wicket at 1 for 40 after Barnes had been dismissed for 19. Bradman's 18th run was up in 25 minutes, and this gave him 2,000 runs for the season. It was the fourth time he had done this on tour in England, an unmatched feat by a tourist. He was also the oldest to do it, after having been the youngest (at 21 in 1930).

Brown was in surprisingly forceful mood, outscoring Bradman. The opener's equilibrium at the wicket was apparent, his technique superb and his capacity to pierce the field inspiring, especially on the on-side and with leg glances. Their partnership was one of the best of the summer, even if the bowling was mediocre, or kept that way by these two master stroke-makers.

English writer E. W. Swanton covered the match.

'His [Bradman's] was mostly a serene, equable piece of batsmanship,' he reported in the London *Telegraph*, 'the runs always accruing quickly, without anything violent except when someone bowled a long hop; then the ball was invariably murdered. As when he was young, he scarcely ever hooks for less than four . . . Bradman today is inevitably slower to judge the length of the ball than in his youth. Thus he was sometimes caught leaning forward, especially to F. R. [Freddie] Brown, where in 1930 he would have been playing back very firmly. But much of his execution shows no sign of age. He played exquisite off-drives and late cuts which could have been taken from his 254 against England here [in 1930], perhaps the most technically perfect innings ever played.'

Brown departed for 120, with 14 fours and a five. It was his eighth century of the tour, and the most attractive. He led the way in the 181-run stand with his skipper. Hassett came to the wicket and played second fiddle to Bradman as he reached his ninth hundred for the tour. It took 150 minutes. After that he slipped into another gear, taking a further 50 in 72 minutes. On 150 (with 19 fours) he threw his wicket away with a wild shot that was caught at mid-on off Brown.

He walked off Lord's for the last time a drained yet contented man. Members in the pavilion and fans around Lord's stood and applauded. Bradman took off his gloves, hung them around his bat handle and raised them high. He then removed his cap and stopped at the gate. He bowed farewell, first to the crowd, then to the members.

Bradman was achieving closure everywhere with a certain satisfaction. He had been aware of the significance of the 'Gentlemen' matches, an arcane but traditional game for amateur cricketers reserved for special occasions, such as the annual match against the Players – the professionals. Bradman always had a quiet pleasure in giving the Gentlemen a not-so-gentle hiding. This had been one of those days.

Australia reached 3 for 478 at stumps. To go on the next day was again overkill in a three-day match but Bradman was happy to indulge in it, especially with Hassett having a chance of hitting a double century.

The next morning, Thursday, Miller on 59, hit at everything, employing his 'corkscrew' shot for four, then six, before being caught deep on the square leg fence. Hassett cruised to 200 (18 fours) in the over before lunch. Bradman declared with Australia on 5 for 610.

Once more he had batted the opposition out of the game, turning the match into an exhibition rather than a contest, simply because he could. This ensured that Australia could not be defeated in this, the 29th fixture. It did not mean that

Australia played for a draw. Miller and Lindwall opened the bowling, which was a fair indication of the Australian attitude to the game. It wanted to win. Reg Simpson, given a belated opportunity, opened for the Gentlemen, and with Edrich (27) began well with a 55-run stand. Simpson's 60 was twice the next batting effort (by Robins, 30) in a steady, but unchallenging, unspectacular performance by the Gentlemen, who were all out for 245. Bradman gave the spinners Johnson (4 for 60) and Ring (3 for 74) most work in this innings and in the follow-on from the Gentlemen.

That evening, Sir Pelham ('Plum') Warner presented Bradman with a big cake in the form of an open book to mark the occasion of him turning 40.

'I see it's not closed,' Bradman said with a big grin when receiving it. 'We still have a few games after this one.'

Friday, 27 August, marked Bradman's actual birthday. When the team moved onto the field, the players gathered around him to sing 'happy birthday,' while the elderly members looked on benignly as they basked in the warm sun. He grinned, having much to be happy about.

The Gentlemen began their second innings and Edrich stole the show. He put on 60 this time with Simpson (27) and moved steadily to 72, then cut loose with seven fours to reach his century in 130 minutes. He went on to 128 in 205 minutes. But it was too little – the Gentlemen could only muster 284 (with no one else except Simpson reaching 20) – and too late. This form would have been better appreciated in the Tests.

Johnson took 4 for 60, giving him 3 for 69 for the match.

Australia won by an innings and 81 runs.

●

Bradman felt comfortable letting Hassett take the train with the squad 250 km west to Taunton in Somerset. The county was weak, and the selectors also were relaxed about leaving out Lindwall and Morris, Australia's two best players in the big games so far. Bradman was looking ahead to two further danger games after Somerset – against the South of England, and Leveson Gower's XI, followed by two second-class matches in Scotland. He intended to play in all four matches to end the tour. He wished to ensure, as far as any skipper/batsman could, that there was no wilting or surprises in the end-games.

•

Australia had a jittery start when Brown was run out on the fourth ball of the match in front of the biggest crowd ever at the Taunton ground of just under 11,000. Later Barnes' injury flared up and he had to retire hurt on 42 (with the score at 69), but Hassett on his 35th birthday (28 August) celebrated with 103 and a second-wicket stand of 187 in 110 minutes with Harvey to right the bulky Australian run-gathering ship. They turned on an exciting exhibition of stroke-play: Hassett all flow and style and Harvey all power and variety. Harvey hit 14 fours, and two sixes in an over from 22-year-old Jim Redman, the Bath medium-pacer who came on as an afterthought with the score at 1 for 247. After taking an early pasting, he managed to dismiss first Hassett, then Harvey and later McCool for 6. Redman finished with a respectable 3 for 78. But the removal of the two centurions did not end the mayhem. Hamence and Johnson then put on 195 for the fifth wicket. Hamence, one of the more popular tourists, and a much underrated batsman, had been the one to receive the least chances to prove himself on tour. He invariably came in after the other heavy scorers had taken up most of the time. Yet here, at last at Somerset, he had a chance for a century. On 99 he became anxious, went for a big hit and was stumped. Everyone was sad for him, but there was a consolation in Johnson (113 not out) scoring his first hundred in first-class cricket.

Miller (37 not out) came in for a little slather and whack at the end of the day, allowing Hassett to declare at stumps on the Saturday at 5 for 560.

Hassett remarked at the end of the day that his batsmen were most grateful for the sightscreens at both ends. They were made of galvanised sheeting, which was painted cream. This reduced both glare and shadows.

'We have never seen sightscreens like them,' the captain said. 'The fact that they were on track rollers caused no delays when they were moved.'

On Monday another bumper crowd turned up to watch the local squad flounder on a two-faced, rather than two-paced, wicket. On Saturday it had been green and fast, just right for Australia's array of shot-makers. Two days later it took spin and began to crumble. Johnston, delivering his left-arm spinners, and McCool with his leg-spinners, took seven of the Somerset wickets and the team was all out after lunch for just 115.

Out came the county again mid-afternoon. Johnston, bowling his quicker stuff with the new ball, then Miller, sent back two batsmen for ducks. After a bit of a flurry from Micky Walford and Bertie Buse (each with 21) took the score into the forties, Johnston reverted to spin again, taking five wickets, and McCool, a further three. The county lost 8 for 25 and fell apart worse than the wicket itself, for 71. Somerset did not even make it to tea on the second day.

Some of the Australians took the chance of an extra day to tour the region, especially nearby Bath. Miller even managed to sneak in a mid-week race meeting before everyone reported for duty in London for the 100 km bus trip south to East Sussex and the seaside town of Hastings.

There, Bradman and his merry men prepared to do battle with the South of England.

They expected just as much success as the Normans in 1066.

•

Hastings carried the cricket season beyond the County Championship into the 60-year-old September Festival. This match against the tourists was the first celebration on the calendar and had a festive flavour for the Wednesday crowd of 20,000. It spilled from the public stands, the deckchair enclosures and the refreshment rooms backing onto the Devonshire Road. At the north end was the packed members' stand and the small pavilion. Long before the first ball of the day, the celebrations began in the club tents and marquees decked out with bunting that fluttered in the gentle breeze.

Bradman found that his toss calling of tails was having much more success outside the Tests. He won and batted in warm, cloudy conditions. As with the previous week at Taunton, the tourists began badly when Barnes (0) edged one behind off Trevor Bailey, back doing combat with the Australians. Bradman, wanting to prove that if not life, then top-class batting could go on at 40, strolled out to tremendous cheering from the assembled multitude. Once more he doffed his cap as if to defray the distraction. He began with a terrific cut for four off Bailey's second ball that sent the crowd scattering near the boundary. Bradman then drove Bailey either side of the wicket for four in his second over and signalled a business-like attitude. He reached 34 with the total score on 46. Brown, stuttering for the first time in the season, was caught for 13 in a fluky manner, when he snicked an away-swinger onto the keeper's boot. The ball rebounded to Edrich at short fine-leg.

This brought the other recent birthday boy Hassett to the wicket. Bradman was in a dictatorial mood, cutting, deflecting and driving his way to 45 in 45 minutes. He put the brakes on for the final 25 minutes before lunch, and meandered in at 64 not out, with Hassett tagging along on 19 not out. Australia was 2 for 99 at the break. Bradman's aggression had never let the opposition sense they could control him. It had been a hallmark of his approach since he was a schoolboy. He would strangle the enemy at birth if given half a chance, and he did not care if he killed the game by sheer dominance in the process.

He had not yet done this at Hastings. But after lunch, the crowd was given an exulted show of vintage Bradman as he kept his foot on the throats of the South's bowlers, never giving them a chance to compete on equal terms.

He and Hassett were in grand form together as at Lord's against the Gentlemen. Captain and vice-captain contrived with skill, excellent placement and lovely strokes to put the game beyond the best the South could muster with a sensational third-wicket partnership of 188. Bradman reached his 50 in an hour and his 10th tour century in just two hours. Hassett, in a season purple patch, headed for his third successive 100, and his seventh for the season. Bradman was going for everything at the end and belted a straight six, always a sign that he had had enough. He lofted Bailey to mid-on and was caught for 143 (17 fours and a six) in 185 minutes. The bowlers were softened up at this stage, and relieved to see the back of the Australian captain, but their horrors were not even half over. Hassett was joined by Harvey, who overshadowed him and even Bradman's efforts with a scintillating century in 90 minutes. They added 175 runs in 110 minutes for the fourth wicket, but were both out early on Monday morning when going for big hits; Harvey for 110, and Hassett for 151. Loxton took his cue from this with a crunching 67 in 71 minutes, and Bradman declared at 7 for 522.

Once more, he was giving the opposition no chance. Observers sensed that the South was out to prove it could match the tourists, beginning with a blistering opening stand by Edrich (52) and Barnett (35) of 78 in 58 minutes. But rain stopped play just after tea and the South's momentum was lost. The final day was interrupted by further heavy showers, yet not enough to stop Compton from a sensational cameo of 82 in 118 minutes. With the game in no doubt, Bradman entered the festival feel of the match for the first time by giving Hassett and Harvey six overs each, and Hamence three. Brown bobbed up with 25 deliveries of his dibbly-dobbly trundling, taking 4 for 16.

The South of England reached 298; the game ended in a draw with Australia in control.

The tourists left Hastings with the same feeling of dominance as the Normans' William, and their captain was now very much Donald the Conqueror.

The record was 23 wins and eight draws in the 31 first-class contests. Bradman was looking forward to the last first-class clash of the season – against Leveson Gower's XI at Yorkshire's delightful seaside holiday resort, Scarborough, which was also caught up in a festival, some 500 km north of Hastings on Yorkshire's east coast. The Australians would now have their biggest break – five days – which was luxury after the continuous blur of matches that ran back to back for the summer. It came at an opportune time for Bradman's older muscles, allowing him to tune up for the final combat of importance and potential danger.

26

Keeping Scarborough Fair

BRADMAN HAD NEVER forgotten or forgiven the selection of a virtual England Sixth Test team for the Scarborough match of 1938. Then he had been recovering from a broken ankle, and did not play. The Australians, led by Stan McCabe, had a below-strength team and were beaten. It was the second defeat for the 1938 season and Bradman was ropable. In the interlude between the 1948 Hastings and Scarborough games, he requested the make-up of the Leveson Gower XI. He discovered that it was, indeed, the strongest team England could put together at the time. It was being treated once more as a Sixth Test match.

Bradman protested, saying that it was misleading and a charade to call it a festival game. He said he thought there would be more of celebratory, relaxed atmosphere if only six of the 11 who had played in the Tests were now picked for Scarborough. Otherwise, why was the game not declared as a Sixth Test for which he, as team captain of the tourists, would have prepared? This of course was a rational and logical request, from the most rational and logical of men, and he just happened to hold considerable sway in the matters of cricket in England at that moment.

His request was acceded to. The 75-year-old Leveson Gower, with almost the perfect establishment cricket pedigree – Winchester, Oxford, Surrey and England – was as cunning as any administrator the UK had ever had. He would do everything to see Bradman's team beaten. His response, in consultation with Robins and the MCC, reflected this. The revised XI was still very strong, and every bit as capable as the five Test teams chosen in the 1948 Ashes. The Test players who remained were Hutton, Edrich, Yardley, Evans, Bedser and Laker.

The first of the other five was Laurie Fishlock, the fine Surrey left-handed opener. He had played two Tests, including one on the 1946–47 tour of Australia. He also happened to have produced the finest opening performances – both for Surrey – against the tourists during the season. He was the best equipped left-handed opening bat in England.

The second choice in the line-up batting at four after Hutton, Fishlock and Edrich, was the dashing little New Zealander Martin Donnelly, who had not performed well against the Australians on tour, but was judged among the top six bats in the world.

Yardley was No. 5 in the line-up, and Robins himself was at six. The latter was the only player – on current form – in the Leveson Gower team not worthy of selection among this elite group. But he was no slouch and had a proven Test record, especially as a leg-spinner. His first-class career (1928–58) saw him take 969 wickets at 23.30, and he scored 13,884 runs at 26.40, including 11 centuries, which made him a pretty fair all-rounder in anyone's language. His Test analysis was about the same. He played 19, scored 612 runs at 26.60, and took 64 wickets at 27.46. At 40 years, he was not the player he was in the 1930s. Yet he still believed he could perform at this level, especially as his hat was nearly in the ring as the 1948 Test captain.

Thirty-seven-year-old Freddie Brown was at No. 7, and was also a Test standard all-rounder, who had toured Australia with Jardine's 1932–33 Ashes team. Evans was at No. 8, Bedser at No. 9, Laker at No. 10. Last man in was Warwickshire's other outstanding New Zealander not qualified to play for England, Tom Pritchard, the fifth of the non-Test players. Many observers in 1948 ranked Pritchard as the best and fastest bowler in England next to Lindwall.

The wily Leveson Gower selections would have made the equally cunning Bradman smile wryly. With the inclusion of Pritchard and Donnelly, England had chosen a very strong side which lacked nothing in comparison to the original line-up.

Bradman's answer to this shrewd ploy, aimed at inflicting at least one defeat on the tourists, was to choose a full-strength team. For no matter what the setting, this was an unofficial 'Test' all but in name and duration – at three days instead of five.

•

The Australians were put up at the Royal Hotel, owned by Tom Laughton, brother of the well-known British actor of the 1930s and 40s, Charles Laughton. It was palatial and was apt for the revelry, gala events and jolly atmosphere.

Bradman did not 'alert' his team to the situation. He simply asked all his players to report for duty and chose the strongest team on the morning of the match – beginning Wednesday 8 September. There was a bit of rumbling from a couple of players, notably Miller, who had yearned for a festival-style game. In private, he told Jim Laker not to think that all the Australians felt like Bradman.

'This is no way to play festival cricket,' Miller said. 'I'm buggered if I am going to support this "heads-down" idea.'

But he did not complain to Bradman. The all-rounder was chosen for the game.

•

The North Marine Road ground at Scarborough was transformed in the first 10 days of September into a spectacular vista of flags, marquees, a bandstand, and a colourful, temporary flower bed. Not even the wet weather could dampen the spirits of the spectators out in force to farewell Bradman in his last match ever in England. But the game was delayed.

He walked out onto the field with Robins to inspect the wicket as a large covering tarpaulin was removed. The strip was a touch green. As ever, Bradman called tails at the toss. He lost and Leveson Gower's team batted.

Lindwall went a long way to settling any anxiety Bradman may have had about the match's outcome when he uprooted Hutton's middle stump with the fourth ball of the match, removing him for a duck. Donnelly joined Fishlock. With Miller doing no more than roll his arm over at one end, these two rotated the strike against Lindwall and were more or less untroubled until the score reached 1 for 69. Rain then interfered and finished the day's play.

In the tradition of this pitch, it spun after the previous day's rain. On day two Johnson was able to make the breakthrough, removing Fishlock (38) and Donnelly (36) early. Bradman then had Lindwall and Johnston in the attack, and that was it for the home team. It lost nine wickets for under 100, courtesy of some sustained brilliance by 26-year-old Lindwall, who was maintaining his absolute career peak. The way he prepared for these games indicated that 'Atomic Ray' was just as intent as anyone to see Australia through without a defeat.

Leveson Gower's multinational 'Test' squad had been put asunder for a mediocre 177, by the second session. Morris and Barnes batted sensibly for an opening stand of 102 before Morris (62) was bowled trying to force the pace against Yardley.

This brought Bradman to the wicket late in the evening for his last ever appearance on English soil. It was apparent from his demeanour and concentration that he intended to remain master of his team's bid for invincibility and even some form of sporting immortality. In typical fashion, he attacked the bowling with more science than force, slicing into the spin attack on a turning wicket with the precision of a master surgeon. He reached 30 not out in the 36 minutes to stumps.

The next morning he continued on with Barnes on a more docile wicket that was spinning less. Bradman applied the brakes, adding just 20 in 54 minutes. He was happy to play a supporting role to Barnes, who moved steadily towards his third big hundred of the season. Bradman then accelerated in the next 46 minutes and reached his century (his 11th for the summer) ahead of Barnes just before lunch in 140 minutes. Australia was well over 100 ahead and with no chance of being beaten. Barnes crashed his way to 151 – four sixes and 15 fours – before hitting the hapless Laker to 'cow corner', where Yardley took a catch on the boundary. Barnes had batted 275 minutes, and, like Morris, had once more performed when his skipper needed him to.

Bradman too went the long handle after lunch, adding 44 to his 109 in 38 minutes before trying to hit Bedser out of the park. He was caught in the covers for 153, the highest score of the game and his third successive century in the last three big games of the season. Bradman gave no chance in the Scarborough match. He did not give any bowler any hope in those last three grand performances until he was done with them and tired of being out in the middle. He netted 153, 143 and 150 – 446 in all – in those final innings, in a continual demonstration of his masterful skills with a blade as a 40-year-old.

There was symmetry about his end in first-class cricket too. In his first ever game for New South Wales, aged 19 in late 1927, and against South Australia with Clarrie Grimmett bowling at his best, he hit a quick-fire 118.

The journey of 338 innings and 117 centuries in first-class cricket was over.

•

Bradman declared the innings closed just after tea at 8 for 489
– a lead of 312. There were two sour notes in the innings:
Loxton swept at a ball from Brown, which slid into, and broke
his nose; less seriously, and not noticed by the press, was Miller's
demotion to No. 7 in the batting order. When he did come
in, he seemed uninterested in proceedings and was caught behind
for just 1 off Bedser.

With little time left, Bradman opened with Johnson (who
dismissed Hutton, 27, and Fishlock, 26) and let the non-bowlers
have a go with the ball. Harvey, Hassett and Morris had a
trundle. Bradman bowled one over of his leg-breaks to finish
the game and his first-class career. For the record, he conceded
two runs, but neither batsman Edrich or Donnelly was prepared
to surrender his wicket to him. This was a pity. The generous
fellow would have gone down as a footnote in sporting history,
or even a Trivial Pursuit question.

For the record, Leveson Gower's team ended with 2 for 75,
and the game was a draw.

Loxton, the casualty, was due to have surgery in Edinburgh
on his battered nose.

'I never swept again after that,' he said. 'When coaching
later [I] disabused young players of playing it. Better to use
your feet to on-drive.'

Australia had now gone through the first-class season of 31
matches – 23 wins and eight draws (the drawn Durham game
was second-class) – without a single defeat.

Bradman had reached his greatest overriding aim. But would
he now have a drink, sit back and relax? Not a bit of it! There
were still two second-class matches, both against Scotland. He
would keep the pressure on himself and the team until those
minor matches too were secure. In fact, he went to the trouble
of playing and leading from the front, so that his main goal –
some would say obsession – of the summer of 1948 would be
gained.

27

—

Last Conqueror of Scotland

N O CIVIL RECEPTION, no bunting or flags, no lord mayor,
no media and no fans scrambling for autographs. There
was a strange atmosphere in the Edinburgh Hotel when the
Australians arrived on the weekend of 11 and 12 September
after the 350 km trip north-west from Scarborough. The tourists
could have been in France for all they knew. This lack of
enthusiasm for the visitors was indicative of the apathy towards
cricket in Scotland, and it was soothing for all of them, except
the captain. Bradman could not even walk the streets of
Edinburgh without being harassed by fans. He would have to
go to Paris, wear a funny hat, false nose and moustache to give
himself a chance of travelling incognito.

There would have been a small eel of apprehension wriggling
in him. He had to hope that in this more relaxed atmosphere
the chosen squad would keep the pressure on and not take the
Scots lightly. They were a second-class team but had a few
players with claims to higher status. It would have given them
enormous delight to cause the upset of the season, if not of all
Ashes tours by defeating the Australians. Especially when no

English or Welsh team had done it, and particularly with Donald George Bradman in his final two games ever in the UK.

The selectors popped into the XI Ring, Saggers, Hamence and McCool and left out Harvey, Loxton (injured), Lindwall and Hassett. In choosing both keepers, the tourists were openly recognising Scotland as a second-class side, as they had Durham. But still there was good batting and bowling strength in the Australian line-up.

A photo of the Australian batting shed early in its innings was revealing. Barnes (5) had already been dismissed. Bradman had sent in Miller at three, and was sitting on a bench padded up, arms folded and, if anything, a grim look on his face. On his right were Johnston and Ring, both in their street clothes, and playing, but obviously not expecting a hit. On Bradman's left were Hamence (batting at 5), who was in his cricket gear, but without his pads; McCool (batting at 6), who was also in his whites, but without pads; and Ian Johnson (batting at 7), who was still in overcoat and hat.

Every one of them was concentrating on play in the middle. No one was playing cards or looking at a Glasgow horseracing form. The picture told the story of how seriously the Australians were taking the game. Moments after this shot was taken, Miller (6) was out, Australia was 2 for very little. The Don was soon marching out, none too happy at having to take charge himself *against Scotland*. At least reliable, brilliant Morris, calm as ever, was in no trouble at all. Bradman defended, played some strokes, stayed around for 38 minutes, and was out 'playing on' for 27. Hamence (6) soon followed him. Australia was in a wee bit of trouble at 4 for 91. But Morris was still in terrific fettle as his innings progressed, and only in need of a partner. McCool rose to the occasion and the two of them put on 109 for the fifth wicket. Morris went on to 112, his eighth hundred for the tour, and his ninth if 115 against Western Australia was included.

Australia, unusually after recent triumphs, scrambled to 236. This was the fourth-lowest total for the tourists for the season, ahead of the collapse on a shocking wicket at Bradford for 101 against the fearsome Yorkies; 117 against Hampshire on a problem pitch; and a 204 on another difficult, wet strip at Manchester versus Lancashire. The score at Edinburgh was on a fair wicket. The Scots played above their means with the team captain, William Laidlaw, spinning his way through half the side for just 51.

The wicket was developing into a turner. Bradman had Johnson (3 for 18) on with Johnston, and the latter was at his sparkling best, taking 6 for 15. Scotland flopped for just 85. Bradman asked the hosts to follow on. The openers, Guy Willatt and Thomas Crosskey began well with 50 in an hour, then 10 wickets fell for a further 61 and the Scots were skittled for 111. The unlikely 'destroyer' was Morris, delivering his innocuous left-arm orthodox floaters, with 5 for 10 off five overs. Ring snared 4 for 20.

Australia won the match 33 by an innings and 40 runs.

•

The game had finished before tea, and Bradman joined Lindwall and Miller for a round of golf. The Australians then had another leisurely two days off mid-week Wednesday and Thursday before travelling on another 220 km north to the final bus stop, at Aberdeen on Scotland's east coast.

The tourists may not have been high on the sporting calendar in the UK's far north, but the pull of Bradman, within days to become the stuff of myth and legend, was still strong. A final record for the tour was established when 10,000 Scots arrived at the local ground to get a glimpse of the most famous individual in the UK in 1948, Winston Churchill included.

Scotland was sent in by Bradman in another two-day game, and Crosskey did well again, this time notching a worthy 49, which helped the home team to a more respectable 178. Morris, Bradman's late season secret weapon, bamboozled the Scots again, taking 3 for 17, and was backed up by Johnson, 3 for 26, and McCool 3 for 31.

Bradman rejigged the batting line-up, opening with McCool and Hamence. But this did not work, and Hamence, Harvey and Lindwall were removed cheaply by the accurate if limited Scots, before McCool and Johnson restored order in a century stand that took the Australians beyond Scotland's score. Johnson went for one big hit too many and was out caught in the deep five short of his century. This brought Bradman to the wicket on day two, still with a job to do, if not some cosmetics to make Australia's score more like the plunderings that had been a summer feature. He laid into the bowling with 17 fours and two sixes – 80 runs in boundaries – in his electrifying 123 not out. In this, his very final knock on this now momentous tour, he made batting looked as simple as counting the 1, 2, 3 that made up his score. Suitably, he remained unconquered as he had in the summary sense for two decades in top cricket.

The Scots liked their cricketers to get on with it. This hard-hitting performance was an apt exhibition of Bradman at his best. He scored quickly, but there was still the control of the architect and master who did not lose his head. He had scored with the exactitude and calculated thought that were characteristic of his game. As Neville Cardus once noted, Bradman batted without vanity, meaning that he never let his murderous destructive capacities go to his head. If he hit two, even three fours in a row, he waited on the next ball and played it on its merits. This was a big factor separating the outstanding Test players of any era, from the good Test players, the first-class players, and the club cricketers right on down to the park batsmen, who could never control their need to 'wallop' for very long at the crease, even if they had a modicum of skill.

Perhaps aptly too, Bill Brown was on a modest, unbeaten 24 and behind Bradman when he walked off the Aberdeen ground that historic day of 18 September 1948. Brown had been a loyal member of the team, who had suffered when dropped, and yet with eight first-class centuries through the summer (second only to Bradman's 11), had done as much as anyone in the squad to guarantee the special epithet that would be given this tour group forever. Despite the focus on the skipper, this was still an extraordinary *team*. Every single one of them performed wonderful cricket acts that contributed to the amazing effort of reaching the end of match 34 without defeat.

•

In that final game, Bradman declared at 6 for 407, giving his team a couple of sessions to make short shrift of Scotland's second innings. To his credit, the other opener, Willatt, hit 52, and bathed himself in glory as the only Scot to reach a half century in the four innings.

Bradman again brought on the dibbly-dobbly bowlers, Brown, Tallon and Harvey, who collectively accounted for half the Scottish wickets to fall in the tally of 142.

Australia's win – by an innings and 87 runs – was its 25th, and carried out with a typical thoroughness and domination that marked most of those victories. There were 18 wins by an innings, 2 by 10 wickets, 1 by nine wickets, and 2 by eight wickets. The Australians scored 350 or more on 24 occasions, and failed to reach 200 only twice. The opposition was dismissed for less than 200 on 37 occasions. Remarkably, the team looked ready to take on another 34 matches, although in actuality, they had all had enough.

•

On Sunday 19 September, the team was taken by car convoy to Balmoral Castle, 80 km from Aberdeen for a meeting with the Royals: King George VI, Queen Elizabeth and their two daughters, Princesses Elizabeth (pregnant) and Margaret, and the Duke of Edinburgh. En route they stopped at the tiny Crathie Church, attended by the Royal family, and then motored on to the palace grounds. When the Royals arrived, the party of cricketers and journalists covering the tour were lined up to meet them. Keith Johnson escorted the King in his kilts, while Bradman escorted the Queen, the Princesses and the Duke.

Later, photographers took shots of the team on this special end to their tour. One shot of Bradman, hands in pockets and walking with the King, captured attention. This broke protocol and the Australian press made much of the captain's easy style. Later Bradman defended himself by saying that no press had been invited in the first place, and added, tongue-in-cheek, 'The King would have done the same thing [put his hands in his pockets] had he not been wearing a kilt.'

But no one could recall the monarch strolling this way.

'Pocket billiards was not a Royal sport,' Lindsay Hassett noted dryly.

The incident was storm in a tea cup that didn't blow over until after the visit.

Undaunted, Bradman was in a jaunty mood at the party for about 60 guests in the afternoon at Balmoral, and perhaps as relaxed as he allowed himself to be with the intrusion of the media. On the terrace outside the Palace, he carried on with the gentle 'mickey-taking' of the Duke, who Bradman noted earlier in the season, had a useful wrist action (when waving to the public) and that he should play for England.

'There you are,' Bradman chided, 'you didn't do what I told you at the Cricket Writers' Dinner. You should have had a practice at the nets and bowled for England as a leg-break bowler. England might have won the Ashes had you taken my advice.'

The journalists present roared laughing at this, and the Duke responded:

'It was thought that my action would give England an unfair advantage.'

•

The tight schedule went on. The next night back in London there was big lunch at the Savoy in honor of Bradman, who was presented with a fabulous silver replica of the Warwick Vase (an ancient vase excavated near Rome in 1770). The money had been raised for this via the British national Sunday *People* newspaper. The funds left over were donated by Bradman for the construction of concrete pitches throughout England's parklands to encourage and assist young cricketers.

The England and Australian teams attended along with many former England players, including seven captains, nine county captains and some of the biggest names who had played against Bradman as far back as the 1928–29 series in Australia. Harold Larwood was one of the 200 in attendance, sitting between Australian team scorer Bill Ferguson and Lindwall. Opposite him was Bill Voce, between Morris and Toshack. Bradman made a point of chatting to the two Bodyline bowlers and this indicated that the hatchet had been buried over Bodyline, nearly. One former captain not present was Douglas Jardine. He had not been invited.

Bradman spent time also with 10 boys who had been selected from the thousands of people who subscribed to the *People*'s fund.

It could not have been a better send-off for Bradman and his all-conquering team, with speeches by Arthur G. Cousins, the chairman of Oldhams Press, who published *People*, and MCC president Lord Gowrie. Bradman responded in his brilliant, accomplished way and, happily, for the last time on the trip.

•

Bradman valued a letter from British Minister of State Philip Noel-Baker for its understanding and appreciation of his and the Australians' efforts. Baker, at age 22, ran for Britain in the Stockholm Olympics of 1912. He competed at the 1920 Antwerp Games (winning a silver medal in the 1,500 metres) where he was a team manager, and finally at the Paris 1924 Olympics, where he again doubled as a competitor and team manager.

This meant that Baker was well qualified to judge the success or otherwise about competing and taking teams abroad at the highest contest level.

The letter reflected this:

'No one in the history of sport has done it [taken a team abroad] with such masterly success as you. I know that it must have meant infinite work and infinite trouble, and that over these months it must have been a great strain. That you should have been able to carry the burden, and to keep your cricket up to your own standard, is almost a miracle.'

Baker added:

'We in the UK owe you a personal debt of gratitude for what you have done; and I know we shall all look back on your magnificent career not only with gratitude, but with pride.'

Baker was highly decorated in both world wars for bravery, and a humanitarian who knew and cared about global issues, being heavily involved in forming the League of Nations. (Later, in 1959 he won the Nobel Peace Prize.) So his next remarks were not platitudinous.

'In these days, it is not easy to know what is of real and lasting value in what we call our civilisation,' he wrote. 'The more I deal in politics, the more convinced I am that our modern games are among the best things in our national life! I agree with every word you said yesterday in your splendid speech at the Savoy. [Bradman had emphasised the value of good sportsmanship and competition between nations, and how sport – particularly cricket – should play a part in national values.] Cricket is indeed a great affair, and its greatness will grow in every country it is played. As that happens, so we shall the more remember what you, the greatest master of the game, have done for it and for us all.'

•

Yardley, Robins and Ronnie Aird (Assistant Secretary at the MCC) all travelled on the boat train to Tilbury to see the

Australians off. There was a short, final broadcast by Bradman on the BBC, a few formalities and then the squad was away on the *Orontes*, homeward bound with a record gate for any tour until then – £64,664. This would be split between the States, with the 'big boys' – New South Wales, Victoria and South Australia receiving 3/13ths each; Queensland 2/13ths; and Western Australia and Tasmania receiving 1/13th each.

The success of Bradman's team would have an immediate positive impact on first-class cricket in Australia.

•

Mission impossible had been accomplished. No team had ever taken on the arduous, exacting tour of England without being defeated at least once. This achievement will remain unique for eternity. After nearly a century of long tours by several nations, shorter seasons by the late 1970s meant that no future team would have the chance to equal such a record. It was an attainment for the ages.

Thirty years afterwards, at a 1978 reunion of the team sponsored by Rothbury Wines, the then New South Wales cricket administrator Bob Radford was the first to dub the 1948 team *The Invincibles*.

The Invincibles: Reflections on Team and Tour

THE FIGURES EMANATING from the 1948 tour were instructive. Bradman dominated the season. He played 23 first-class matches of the 31 played (and 25 of the 34 all up), one more than Hassett, Brown, Loxton, Harvey, Miller, Johnson, and Lindwall, and had two more innings (31) than Morris, and four more than Hassett, Barnes and Harvey. This reflected more than anything the demand for him to play and make appearances. Every single county begged or pushed him to play. He was the biggest drawcard ever seen in cricket, even though at various times Morris, Hassett, Barnes, Harvey and Miller performed faster or better. No one performed more consistently than Bradman. He scored the largest number of runs and had the best average (2,428 at 89.92, with 11 centuries), but only a minority of people came to see his *consistency* or work out his statistics. The majority came to see a master who was as much part of British legend and folklore as he was Australia's. This left even some of his team incredulous. They noted how the crowds would often depart when Bradman was out, even though

Miller or Loxton or even Harvey might replace him and be more exciting.

•

Australia's capacity to build massive scores, usually ranging from 400 to more than 700, was due to its batting depth, which ensured it would not be beaten. Apart from Bradman, there were six other players with averages of 50 or more – Hassett (74.42 with seven centuries); Morris (71.18 with seven centuries); Brown (57.92 with eight centuries); Loxton (57.23 with three centuries); Barnes (56.41 with three centuries), and Harvey (53.76 with four centuries). Miller, who lost interest in proceedings here and there, still managed to be seventh to Bradman in the aggregate with 1,088 runs at 47.30, including two centuries. He also had a strong season with the ball, taking 56 wickets at 17.58, which emphasised his huge value as an all-rounder. He was third in the bowling with Lindwall (86 wickets at 15.68) and Johnston (102 wickets at 16.42). The evenness and depth of the bowling was seen with McCool (57 at 17.82), Johnson (85 at 18.37), Toshack (50 at 21.12), Loxton (32 at 21.71) and Ring (60 at 21.81).

Despite jovial complaints from Ring and McCool that they were underplayed, Ring played in 19 matches, which was only three less than most of the regulars, and he delivered 542.4 overs; McCool's finger injury still saw him play in 17 of the first-class matches, and bowl 399.2 overs. Both spinners suffered from the 55-over rule for the new ball, which killed their opportunities to have impacts in the big games. The pace bowlers were always preferred.

Hamence was the unluckiest of the squad of 17. He was one of two who did not have a chance in the Tests (McCool being the other). He was rarely given a slot at the top of the order, and when he did come in, the tourists had already plundered time and runs that would limit him. Yet he did have 22 innings to return 582 runs at 32.33, which reflected the atmosphere and moment of his innings rather than his capacities.

Australia was very well represented in the field with several players being top-class – including Loxton, Harvey, Morris, Barnes (before he was struck), Miller, Lindwall and Hassett (apart from a lapse in one Test). Saggers took advantage of his opportunities behind the stumps in 17 matches, while Tallon only managed 14 matches. Saggers was always steady and very good, effecting 43 dismissals – 23 catches and 20 stumpings. Tallon also made 43 dismissals – 29 catches and 14 stumpings. He could have his off days, mainly caused by problems with his hands, but when he was on song, he was in a class of his own, with catches, especially down the leg-side that may not have been snaffled by anyone else. Bradman rated him as the finest keeper of all time.

All the depth, variety, skill and brilliance of the squad was complemented by what Bradman called a 'bulldog' courage and determination.

This ranked it as the best cricket team of all until 1948, and possibly of all time.

The Invincibles versus The Rest

The Invincibles of 1948 was the greatest team ever to play cricket until the middle of the 20th Century. Others to challenge it after that have been Peter May's England side in 1956, Ali Bacher's South Africa side in 1969–70, the West Indies under Clive Lloyd, and later Viv Richards, Steve Waugh's Australian side in 2001, and Ricky Ponting's 2006–07 Ashes team.

The first way to make the comparison is to examine each XI, and compare the strengths and weak links. Second, the opposition sides they met must be taken into consideration.

Bradman's 1948 line-up had few weak links. Its batting order for the Fifth Test at the Oval was Barnes, Morris, Bradman, Hassett, Miller, Harvey, Loxton, Lindwall, Tallon, Ring and

Johnston. Neil Harvey said that only one of Steve Waugh's team of 2001 – Shane Warne – would make Bradman's side. He would replace Ring, who was a good first-class leg-spinner, but not in Warne's class. Ponting's form in the 21st Century, if it could be transported back, would also see him make the 1948 team, probably at Hassett's expense.

The other player to come under scrutiny would be Sam Loxton. He was a good all-rounder and terrific field, and had the capacity to lift and play above himself. Bradman liked him because he gave 100 per cent all the time, and was grand for team spirit. The comparison in the modern era would be Ponting's adherence to Andrew Symonds for similar reasons. Loxton and Symonds were both fighters, whose deeds often lifted the entire side. Both captains were strong on psychology and instinct. A Loxton or a Symonds in a team added up to much more than the sum of his parts as a cricketer. Their presence and look put pressure on opposition.

Loxton's Test figures were indicators of his limitations, on paper. He had just 12 Tests scoring 554 runs (with one century) at a good average of 36.93, which placed fairly well in the ranks of all-rounders. But he took only eight wickets at 43.62. His first-class returns show that his batting was more or less consistent. He hit 6,429 runs at 36.97, with 13 centuries, and his bowling at this level reflected the lesser standard of batting opposition, in general, who he bowled to in taking 232 wickets at the very good return of 25.73.

Bradman's team then, had nine top-liners, an all-rounder chosen for his drive as much as his skill, and Ring or Toshack, who were not quite top drawer. The side had a top six that would be hard to improve on. The 7, 8 and 9 – Loxton, Tallon and Lindwall, would again rank with any three batsmen in those positions; the team only had two tail-enders – Ring and Johnston.

The bowling strength was exceptional, giving Bradman plenty of options. The Lindwall/Miller opening combination was one of the best in history, and certainly in the top four combinations in the Australian experience. The other three duets were McDonald and Gregory in 1921, Lillee and Thomson in 1975, and McGrath and Lee in 2001. With Miller doubling as a top six batsman, Bradman had the luxury of being able to choose Johnston (first rate) and Toshack (he was not fit for the Fifth Test but played in the other four in 1948) as third and fourth medium-pacers, and for added variety, they were both left-handers. Johnston also doubled as an effective off-spinner. Loxton was also an option as a more than useful change bowler.

Tallon ranked as one of the great keepers of all time. Most players who teamed with and against him said he was the best. Would Adam Gilchrist replace him? It depends on if you were a selector like Bradman, who would always choose a great keeper first; or if you valued in combination Gilchrist's mighty batting capacities, and 'very good' – but not 'great' – keeping skills.

It is often said that the England team of 1948 was weak and that it was recovering from the war. Often forgotten is the fact that 15 of Australia's side were ex-servicemen. If there were handicaps from this, then the Australians would have suffered equally. In 1947, and right up until the Ashes of 1948, England supporters (including their commentators) were confident of beating Australia, especially after the performances of their batting and bowling line-ups in the previous post-war years. But after being crushed, excuses were found rather than acknowledging the overall strengths of the tourists. Hindsight became a useful tool. After 1948, England took another five years to win back the Ashes. It gained exceptional pace-bowlers, such as Tyson, Statham and Trueman, and spinners (Wardle and Lock in particular) in support of a mature and developed Laker. By 1956, England was noticeably superior to Australia in much the way the 1948 Australians had been over England.

•

England's 1956 Test team under Peter May (that beat Australia 2:1) was outstanding. The Second Test team at Lord's (which was beaten by Ian Johnson's Australians) read: Richardson, Cowdrey, Graveney, May, Watson, Bailey, Evans, Laker, Wardle, Trueman and Statham. The Fifth Test team at the Oval (which Bradman cited as the best and most balanced team of that series) read: Richardson, Cowdrey, Sheppard, May, Compton, Washbrook, Evans, Lock, Laker, Tyson and Statham.

Only two batsmen in the Lord's line-up were absolute top-drawer – Cowdrey and May. The Oval side had a stronger batting six, with Cowdrey, May, Compton and Washbrook who would qualify as warriors in the top rank. Both these sides had an outstanding keeper – Evans – and a strong bowling squad. At Lord's Trueman and Statham provided one of England's best ever opening combinations. The spinners Wardle (left-arm everything) and Laker, who had come a long way since his pasting throughout 1948, were a formidable duo. The Oval side had Statham and Tyson (still then, the quickest bowler in the world), and the spin twins from Surrey on their home pitch – Laker and Lock (left-arm orthodox).

The Oval side was stronger, but two of its top-line batsmen, Compton and Washbrook were past their best. In addition, Sheppard and Richardson were not top-line, which meant that the top six batsmen would cause the team as a whole to rank below most of the others in the 'best ever' list.

•

The South African team of early 1970 led by Ali Bacher against Bill Lawry's Australians (which were beaten 4:0) is also often mentioned as an outstanding team. Its line-up for the Second Test at Durban in which it inflicted the biggest defeat of Australia, read: Richards, Goddard, Bacher, R. G. Pollock, Barlow, Irvine, Lance, Proctor, Gamsy, P. M. Pollock and Traicos.

Three of this side's batsmen – Richards, R. G. (Graeme) Pollock and Barlow – were strong by any era's standard, but Goddard and Bacher were not, whereas Irvine was on the cusp but only played four Tests, all in the 1970 series against Australia. (Then he averaged 50.42 and made 353 with one century.) Proctor and P. M. (Peter) Pollock formed a powerful opening bowling duo, backed up by the medium-pace swing of Barlow. But the rest of this team's bowling line-up were not bracketed with the best of all time. As good as it was against Lawry's accomplished team, it would not have challenged Bradman's side, the West Indies teams of the 1980s, Steve Waugh's Australians of 2001, and Ponting's 2006–07 Ashes team.

•

In the 1980s, possibly the best ever West Indies team was seen in the 1982–83 series against India in the West Indies. It was led by Clive Lloyd. The line-up was Greenidge, Haynes, Richards, Gomes, Logie, Lloyd, Dujon, Marshall, Roberts, Holding and Garner.

Of the top six, there were four top-line batsmen – Greenidge, Hayes, Richards and Lloyd. Gomes (at 4) and Logie (5) were not top drawer, and therefore the West Indies top six were not as strong as Bradman's line-up. Certainly, the 7, 8 and 9 – Marshall, Roberts and Holding – were not as skilled as Australia's. The West Indies' four speedsters, as a combination – Marshall, Roberts, Holding and Garner – were superior to anything in history from the point-of-view of sheer speed. But Australia's line-up of Lindwall, Miller, Johnston and Toshack, had greater variety, with two left-hand bowlers, and two of the four (Miller and Johnston), being able to turn to spin. It is worth noting that in that 1982–83 series against India, the West Indies only won 2:0, and India twice managed more than 400 against the much vaunted attack.

•

Viv Richards' team that toured Australia in 1988–89 was very similar in make-up and strength to Lloyd's. The line-up was

Greenidge, Haynes, Richardson, Hooper, Richards, Logie, Dujon, Marshall, Ambrose, Walsh and Patterson. The top six bats also had two players who were not top-line – Hooper and Logie, while three of the four speed men were top-notch – Marshall, Ambrose and Walsh – but slightly inferior to Lloyd's four.

This team was exposed on a turning wicket in Sydney for the Fourth Test. They dumped Patterson and brought in Harper, and were thrashed by Australia by seven wickets. This demonstrated that the batting order was less than convincing against spin, especially with Allan Border, hardly a top-class spinner, who barely rolled his arm over in club cricket, taking 11 wickets for 96. Leg-spinner Trevor Hohns, another good but not top-class Test bowler, partnered Border. Certainly Bradman's team handled spin far better, and it is hard to imagine Morris, Barnes, Bradman, Hassett, Miller and Harvey having trouble against such a standard of spin on any wicket. Miller was the only one among that sextet who struggled, and then only occasionally, against spin. All the others had brilliant techniques against it.

Harper and Richards were used for spin by the West Indies in that Sydney game, and one can imagine how they would be slaughtered, spin or no spin, by Bradman and his men.

The West Indies won the 1988–89 series 3:1, with one loss (Sydney). In the drawn Fifth Test in Adelaide, Border's men held sway for most of the game. During the match, a humorous, yet instructive incident occurred when Bradman was invited into the West Indies dressing room, accompanied by Dean Jones, Merv Hughes and Mike Whitney, Australia's best performers in the game. (Hughes had managed 72 not out; Jones had made a classic 216 run out in Australia's first-innings score of 515; and Whitney had taken 7 for 89 and 2 for 60.) The West Indians lined up to meet Bradman.

When he was introduced to the giant Patrick Patterson, the West Indian looked down at Bradman, and said:

'Man, you the great Don Bradman? You only a little guy. I'd get you out, no trouble man!'

Bradman looked up at big Patrick, grinned and said:

'How would you get me out? You couldn't even get Merv Hughes out!'

Everyone roared laughing at Bradman's sharp riposte. But he had a point. The 1948 Bradman may have found it tough going facing the West Indian foursomes of the 1980s. But the 1930s Bradman would have been more than a match for any of them. He considered them a fine combination yet without variety, especially with a top-line spinner missing.

•

Steve Waugh's team of 2001 was very strong. Unlike the other outstanding teams in history, it had no weaknesses. Its order read: Hayden, Langer, Ponting, Mark Waugh, Steve Waugh, Martyn, Gilchrist, Lee, Warne, Gillespie and McGrath. The team batted strongly to Gilchrist at 7 (surely the greatest No. 7 ever). Langer had not quite consolidated his position, having taken over from Slater (also a very good opener). But Langer did score a courageous century in this series, and was soon to be heralded by his captain as 'the best player in the world' after a series in New Zealand. The rest of the batsmen were top drawer, including Martyn, who matured in this series. The four bowlers (McGrath, Lee, Gillespie and Warne) rivalled any other four in history as a combination, and provided balance with Warne, the greatest leg-spinner of all time. However, Lee had not yet reached his peak; Gillespie was then on the cusp of being ranked as top-line.

Ricky Ponting's team for the Fifth Test of the 2006–07 Ashes read: Langer, Hayden, Ponting, Hussey, Clarke, Symonds, Gilchrist, Warne, Lee, Clark and McGrath. They proved an outstanding combination, which demoralised England in a 5:0 whitewash. Yet only Ponting, Hayden and Michael Hussey (with Michael Clarke needing to do more to consolidate) would challenge any of the top six in the 1948 team for consistency and ability. The bowling line-up was about on a par with Waugh's 2001 team and the 1948 team.

In this sort of comparative analysis, the longevity of the team comes into the equation. The 1948 team was an extension of Bradman's 1946–47 team and Hassett's team until it went under to England in 1953.

May's England 1956 side was dominant until it hit a brick wall in the form of Benaud's Australians in 1958–59. The West Indies teams captained by Lloyd and Richards were pre-eminent worldwide throughout the 1980s, and were not challenged until Border's 1992–93 Australian side (with Warne winning the Melbourne Test) ran it close. After that, the banner was passed to Mark Taylor's team in the West Indies in 1995. It held sway over the world and developed again under Steve Waugh then Ricky Ponting, who took over as leader from early in 2004.

The West Indies teams 1980–95 were challenged by the Australians 1994 to 2008 for sustained dominance of world cricket.

With all factors considered it is hard to separate Bradman's Invincibles, May's side, Lloyd's team, and the teams of Waugh and Ponting as the best of all time. Each squad was led very well. They all, collectively, had courage, and each of the bowling line-ups was intimidating and brilliant. Only a biased observer would rank one categorically above the other. Bradman's batting line-up was arguably the strongest for three main reasons. First, all the top six were adept at playing pace, swing and spin. Second, the team batted to No. 9, and of them, only Tallon did not score a Test century, and yet he could bat. Third, the 1948 team had Bradman.

However, the bowling line-ups of the May, Lloyd, Waugh and Ponting teams were arguably on a par with, or stronger than the 1948 side; the Lloyd-led West Indies for the sheer class and speed of each of its bowlers; and the 2001 Australians

Sid Barnes is carried off at Manchester in the Third Test after being struck fielding up close by tail-ender Dick Pollard. Barnes often insisted on placing himself close to the lesser batsmen, who were not always concerned about where they hit the ball, as long as they made contact.

Arthur Morris demonstrates his style, which brought him 290 in a game against Somerset; and made him one of the best performing batsmen in the Tests.

Don Tallon – Bradman regarded him as the greatest keeper he ever saw.

Ray Lindwall in action in the Fifth Test.

Leg-spinner Doug Wright finishes his run-up with a jump/skip.
His bowling was often underrated, and the English press and
selectors thought Bradman was bluffing when he praised him.

England's outstanding keeper of the series, Godfrey Evans, with 'Whale' Roberts – a
former Australian Rules footballer – at the Young & Jackson pub in Melbourne.

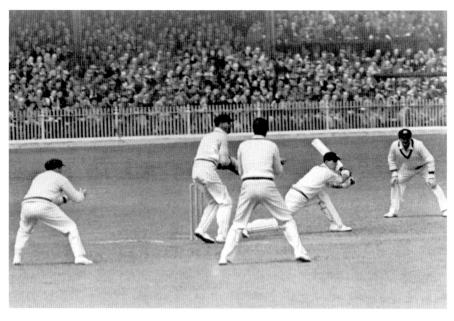

Len Hutton in action against Australia in the second match against Yorkshire.

Bill Edrich cuts wide, leaving Ron Saggers and Doug Ring standing there.

Denis Compton shows his exceptional style and technique. He was the most successful English batsman of the 1948 Ashes series; and his brushes with great mate Keith Miller, who bounced him, were a highlight.

Doug Ring had to sit out four of the Tests – but Bradman surprised him on a taxi ride to the Oval on the morning of the first day of the Fifth Test. 'You're playing,' Bradman told the leg-spinner.

Bradman plays the late cut – the capacity to execute this shot with perfection is a gift of the few. He used it throughout the 1948 season with his usual fluency.

Bradman demonstrates balance, poise, power and timing in executing a textbook off-drive. Approaching the age of 40, he had lost a little of the stroke-play of his younger days. After retiring he put his action into words with the best book ever written about cricket technique – *The Art of Cricket.*

Bradman is caught in the leg trap off Alex Bedser in the Second Test at Lord's. The bowler repeated the feat in the second innings. Bradman scored 38 and 89 – modest scores for the greatest ever batsman at the home of cricket. It was his last appearance there in a Test.

Bradman bowled for a duck in the Fifth Test at the Oval. Before this dismissal he averaged 101.39 – if he had managed to score just 4 in this innings, he would have ended his career with a Test average of exactly 100.00. When he re-entered the dressing room, all he said was 'fancy that', and remained unfazed. His main aim was for the team to win big, and retain the unbeaten record on tour.

Bradman leads his team onto Kennington Oval for
the last time in a Test. Lindsay Hassett follows.

Bradman shakes hands with English skipper Norman Yardley at the
special luncheon held at the Savoy Hotel, London. Looking on are
Ernie Toshack, Ron Saggers and, nearly hidden, Lindsay Hassett.

for a variety of pace, and spin from the number-one leg-spinner of all time; and much the same for the 2006–07 squad.

One thing is certain. Bradman's 1948 squad invites favourable comparison with the best teams of 40 to 60 years on, which speaks volumes in itself for the Invincibles.

The Invincibles

Donald Bradman (Captain)

Don Bradman (1908–2001) has no peer as a cricketer in the history of the game. After 1948 he would be hard to surpass as a captain for his management, strategy, tactics and the capacity to lead from the front. Every team goal was achieved, and one of the main reasons was the unprecedented harmony under his generalship. Bradman didn't play favourites. He liked Ron Hamence and they were the only two South Australians in the side, but the accomplished, compact batsman did not get a chance in the Tests. He wanted to pick McCool, but faced the fact that his splitting finger would not take the strain of five days.

Bradman supported form. He made good friend Sam Loxton prove himself before he was selected. He gave the green light to Bill Johnston for all the Tests after not seriously considering him in the first months of the tour.

Every player in the squad cooperated and pulled his weight throughout the arduous challenge. Everyone interviewed over the decades was in full support, and admiration for Bradman's efforts. They responded to exceptional leadership with exceptional deeds. Even Keith Miller, not a big fan of authority, exploded with his adrenaline rushes with ball and bat in the Tests and county games when they were needed. These efforts went a long way to Australia winning tight matches, and coming back from the dead.

Bradman had the last laugh among many while his detractors looked for every excuse that could bring the 1948 achievement down. The most spurious remark was that England was at its weakest ever. This was a denigration of some good to champion England players, including Hutton, Compton, Washbrook, Edrich, Evans, Laker, Pollard, Bedser, Wright, Young, Hollies and others. They had literally been cricket world beaters until they ran into the Australians who proved to be better. (There is a similarity with England's 2006–07 Ashes squad under Freddie Flintoff. He had a very good, proven squad, which ran into a fired-up Australian team under Ricky Ponting, and cracked under the pressure. Before the series, plenty of UK scribes gave them a fair chance, especially after the 2005 Ashes, and the fact that Australia had an ageing team. After the series, scribes wrote England off as 'woeful'.)

Bradman's strategies worked at every level. Take his advice to Lindwall. By the end of the first game at Worcester, the fast man's dragging of his trailing right foot was not an issue. Tactically and literally he did not put a foot wrong for the rest of the season. Bradman targeted England's top bats, particularly Len Hutton, and stifled any chance of him having a major impact. Laker, with the ball, was also marked down to be attacked and obliterated.

From the moment the *Strathaird* docked at Tilbury, Bradman was centre stage when it was not his natural milieu, although it had become his daily experience. Bradman the person liked being who he was. Bradman the superstar disliked the limelight but bore it in a manner that was hard to fault. He took it as a duty, like royalty. He was not a small-talking champion, but a champion who had to endure small-talk. He was never accomplished at opening his mouth and saying nothing, so he usually used his wry wit, wearing a slightly twisted grin like American comedian George Burns.

Early in his career he was not a natural public speaker. It didn't come easily like hitting balls with bats, racquets or clubs. But instead of stumbling through the endless functions while the UK's brilliant after-dinner speakers had audiences roaring with laughter or applauding the *bon mot*, funny allusion or incisive aphorism, Bradman *made* himself excellent on his feet.

Even his own team was impressed by his capacity to mix it with the best in the UK. (Every Invincible interviewed volunteered this.) It was similar to the way he challenged Walter Lindrum at billiards in 1935. After Lindrum had beaten him, Bradman had a billiards room built to his new home in Kensington Park and after daily practice for a year matched the world champion.

Bradman's addresses had all the timing, with pregnant pauses and inflexions, expected from professionals. He somehow made his piping voice seem mellifluous. There was always the right weight of profundity, humour, 'news', intelligence and philosophy to overcome all shortcomings. He made those speeches memorable, 'important' and relevant enough in the atmosphere of the time to cause even BBC radio to spontaneously hold up the nine o'clock news until he had finished his address. At the time only perhaps the British prime minister or the King could have commanded that.

When Bradman wasn't in the spotlight, he made himself scarce, like a phantom, who you knew was there but few had seen. He would be in his hotel room attending to the endless correspondence. His sense of *noblesse oblige* would not allow anyone else to respond on his behalf. The letters came in at a rate of 600 a day. He answered 'the sensible ones' as he always had. Somehow he contrived to find four hours a day to reply in his pithy, tight style, honed (in 1948) over 20 years since he first became a sporting legend.

When Bradman did venture down a lift to a lobby, he could not move from the foyer to the front desk or out the door to a waiting taxi or bus without being accosted by somebody. More often than not it was *not* a cricket fan, but someone who recognised this individual, who, in 1948, was more popular, better known and better appreciated than anyone in the UK, *including* the prime minister and royalty. Bradman felt an obligation to respond as cheerfully and as courteously as he could when he would always have something else on his mind. Invariably, it would be to do with his team as it criss-crossed England, steamrolling every opposition with hard but fair, brilliant but thorough methods engendered by the captain.

He was elevated above politics and regal ceremony. He had nothing to 'sell' but his sporting genius, which was applauded by all, even those who hated being thrashed by a former far-off dominion. There is a difference between a popular pop or film superstar, and a legend. A person popular for being famous, or on TV or the big screen, might elicit an emotional response when seen in public. This was different than the reaction to Bradman, a verifiable legend, for his feats, his character, his leadership skills and solidity as a great man of Empire. He was a representative of something far more fundamental in society. Cricket was always a metaphor for life in England; even the language expressed this. The exemplar of this in the 19th Century was Dr W. G. Grace. In the 20th Century it was Bradman.

He had a lot to live up to in 1948. UK crowds had an image of the youthful Bradman of the 1930s, who smote big double hundreds and triples at will. He could manage this if he wished, but he would not for two reasons. First, he had done it all before so many times that there were no challenges to stretch the limits any more. He would only pursue a big score beyond

200 if a Test or a series depended on it. In the 1930s, he always had the inclination and desire to score more than anyone else. But also he didn't have a choice if he wished his team to win. Australia was not a strong side, and if Bradman didn't score big, it would lose. In 1948, he had several batsmen in his team who could conjure the big hundred, and he had bowlers who could keep England's scores down. There was not the necessity or the dependence entirely on him for the mammoth performance.

Second, Bradman feared a very long innings might bring on a recurrence of his old ailments, including the fibrositis that enfeebled him during the war, and the rib injury sustained at the end of the 1947–48 season. Consequently, in only four of his 31 innings on tour did he bother scoring 150 or more: against Essex at Southend, he made his top score for the tour of 187, but only because the boundaries and runs came so easily that he batted just 124 minutes – the fastest innings of his entire first-class career; against England at Leeds when it was imperative for an Australian victory, he hit 173 not out; against the Gentlemen of England at Lord's on his last appearance there, he reached 150 and threw his wicket away; and at Scarborough against Leveson Gower's XI, he notched 153 – enough to make certain Australia would not lose its last first-class game on tour.

The Bradman of 1948 was not the Bradman of the 1930s. Yet he was still unsurpassed in range of strokes, in concentration, in pulling off the unorthodox, and in constructing an innings. Gone was the suppleness of youth, the energy for the massive scoring gesture, or indeed the need and desire for it. Yet there remained the same immobility before a ball was delivered, and the same unmatched speed and mobility when the ball was let go at him. Bradman still did the unorthodox things, such as pulling a ball from the off through mid-on to avoid six fielders on the off. He would again shuffle his feet into the *wrong* position to drive the off-spinner's deliveries *against* the spin through the off-side. Just as in the 1930s, he would defy physics in the very late playing of the late cut. As before the war, he relished the short stuff and would dispatch bumpers, with that roll of the wrists, to the boundary. There was a marginal loss of power in his back-foot strokes on both sides of the wicket; yet the ball still shot like a bullet off his bat through the covers. Bradman may have been an older, wiser batsman, but he still attacked any county bowler without pity, no matter if they were young and nervous, at the peak of their form, or old and nearly hobbled. Bradman would put them out of contention for higher cricket calling – the Tests – if he could. In other words, the killer instinct, the desire to win, the fierce competitive edge, not to forget the respect for opposition bowlers and spectators alike, were still all there.

It was tempered here and there to accommodate the needs of the team on the road to invincibility.

·

1948 was not a perfect tour. Bradman made errors. His encouragement to Sid Barnes to field close to Hutton's bat was a dangerous move. It led to Barnes taking up the position on his own volition near less accomplished bats who could not be relied upon to defend or place the ball with precision. Consequently his desire to impress or please 'the boss' caused him to sit under the nose of Dick Pollard – a tail-ender – who had a hoick and collected him in the ribs.

Bradman didn't always handle the press with the respect they felt they deserved. He was said to have insulted Yorkshire and the paying public at Sheffield by not making a game of it. There was no mention in the criticism that Bradman was preserving his bowlers. Allegedly he was just preserving his unbeaten record. There were complaints that he was not giving the opposition a 'fair go' and that Australia was winning by ridiculously big margins. At times he indulged in 'overkill'. But 'winning' was

Bradman's modus operandi. He was the winner's winner, and always went out to crush the opposition by the most direct route possible. There would be no false declarations by this leader that would flatter the other side. He treated the counties with the greatest respect by directing his side to crush them at every turn.

Bradman pointed to the record crowds at every single game and almost every day as vindication for his approach. They came to see greatness. The crowds at all points of the compass right to the final game in Scotland, queued through the night to see the Australians, Bradman argued, because they gave of their best.

The British and Australian press in April started in support of Bradman. But his leadership was too good by mid-tour. There was no bad news. It had to be invented to upset the Australians storming through a season. Lord Tennyson at Lord's (where else?) was a useful vehicle for a press attack. Bradman, the press reported, snubbed the good Lord when he tried to visit him in the dressing room.

Australian reporter Andy Flanagan noted in his book, *On Tour with Bradman*, that Bradman was 'wrong in the manner of his refusal. After all Lord Tennyson is a person of high rank and his position as an ex-captain of the English team should have prompted Bradman at least to have spoken to him personally and perhaps apologised for his inability to entertain him at the moment.'

Flanagan probably did not know it at the time, but Tennyson had been 'entertained' far too much and was inebriated when he knocked on the Australian dressing room door. The reporter may also not have realised that Bradman was advised by Lord's staff *not* to accommodate Tennyson.

In the end, the interference amounted to naught. Don Bradman's quiet obsessions to win the Ashes and drive through a tour undefeated were satisfied, while the team entertained like no side before or after it. The achievement may never be equalled thanks to him and every single member of the tour party from Lindsay Hassett and Arthur Morris to the manager Keith Johnson and the scorer/baggage man Bill Ferguson.

John Arlott in his analysis of Bradman in his book, *Gone to the Test Match*, thought he had missed 'much of the best' of cricket because he was a public figure and a legend. Arlott bemoaned the fact that Bradman could not stroll around a ground 'unmolested' and enter a marquee for a drink. Instead, he had to 'hurry to a car and hide himself from a crowd that pickets his hotel'. In other words, Bradman could never experience the feeling of an ordinary cricketer who played for the love of it in front of fewer spectators than players on the field.

Yet Bradman had experienced relative anonymity at country Bowral until he was 18 years of age. He had been rejected by every club in Sydney at that age before he joined St George. His unmatched capacities needed mass expression and appreciation, so he pursued them, and accepted the adulation that came with it. Not that it didn't touch him. In the first ever letter he wrote to me he said, 'I hate publicity.' I learnt that he meant it. Begrudgingly, though he had to accept the theft of his privacy and private life to a certain degree. It was the trade-off for his success and achievements. Bradman could rarely evade it, even in old age, when he and wife Jessie would take anonymous trips into the country, checking into hotels as 'Mr and Mrs Smith'. Yet it did not mean that he could not gain enjoyment from life. His pleasures had to be less in public view. Nevertheless, I don't know anyone who enjoyed watching cricket more than him. He simply loved experiencing the abilities of others at the ground in person. Bradman was just like any other spectator: he wanted to be entertained by a brilliant bit of fielding, a magnificent stroke, or a formidable ball.

I once asked him if he had his time over again, would he want fame.

'No,' he said, 'I hate it.'

At the time German tennis star Boris Becker was just about the most famous sportsman in the world. Bradman cited his life as most unenviable.

'He couldn't go anywhere in the world without being recognised.'

This to Bradman was the ultimate nightmare.

Later I asked him if he wished to see video footage I had collected from British film archives of his performances, some of which had not been made public.

'No,' he said, and then added surprisingly, 'I am sick of Bradman!'

Not too long after that, in another conversation, I asked him if he regretted his cricket career because of what came with it.

'No,' he replied as succinctly as ever. Bradman would just rather have had his life without all the fuss and attention. But he would have done it all again with glee; especially the 1948 tour of England.

•

For the record, Don Bradman had 338 first-class innings in which he scored 28,067 runs at an average of 95.14. Included were 117 centuries, 69 fifties, 131 catches and a highest score of 452 not out. As stand-in wicket-keeper in the 1937–38 season he effected one stumping. Bradman's leg-spinners were not far off a fair first-class standard, with 36 wickets at 37.97.

In Tests, his batting record stands alone through more than 130 years and among all playing nations. Bradman had 80 Test innings, scoring 6,996 runs at an average of 99.94 – one solitary boundary off a century every innings at the highest level of cricket. His highest score was 334. He scored 13 fifties and 29 Test centuries, including 12 scores of more than 200, and two of more than 300. Bradman held 32 catches, and took two wickets at 36.00.

Lindsay Hassett (Vice-Captain)

Lindsay Hassett (1913–93) played a big part in the 1948 tour success, captaining in eight games and, despite a close call at Bradford against Yorkshire, helping to maintain the team's unbeaten run. He also performed with the bat, scoring seven hundreds, and acted out his duties on and off the field with grace, humour and style. There were contrasting sides to Hassett. He could be the court jester, but when leading the side, he was stricter and more of a disciplinarian than Bradman. The skipper sought his opinion on tactics in every game they played together and he valued this and his knowledge of cricket.

Bradman also admired his batting, especially his sound defence, and drives off his toes in front of square. His fielding as a short-leg specialist was appreciated too. Bradman also liked his demeanour. No situation was too grand for Hassett, whose sharp wit seemed to match every occasion. Fellow tour members began to expect it in all circumstances. In a touring troupe, the good-natured, fun characters made it enjoyable, especially such a long time away from home and loved ones.

•

Observers at times found it comical to watch Hassett waving men twice his size around in the field. But, as with his captain, there was no question about who was in charge. Like Bradman, Hassett also had the verbal skills for any moment – a crisis on the field, giving urgent instructions in the pavilion, or a witty speech at a function.

Both had a quick wit and both liked the odd risqué joke. But they differed in their style and humour. Hassett tended to be a clown, even an up-market larrikin, while never losing the respect of his players. Always lurking was his desire, under any circumstances, to be the impish joker. Hassett never allowed anyone – particularly himself – to be depressed on the team's travels.

•

Arthur Lindsay Hassett, the sixth son of a real-estate agent, was educated at a Victorian private school, Geelong College, where he excelled at cricket, football and tennis. His leadership skills were evident early. He invariably led his Australian Rules and cricket under-age teams right through to the first XI and XVIII. In 1931, at age 17, and in his final year at school, he was Victorian Public Schools Tennis Champion. He was too light to go further in Australian Rules, so he was left with a choice of tennis or cricket for higher accolades. Cricket won when at 17, playing for Victorian Country and while still at school in the 1930–31 season, he made a brilliant 147 against the touring West Indies. After that, tennis was relegated to a fun, social activity. It was widely suggested that he was destined to play Test cricket. Anyone who ever even watched him in the nets had no doubt he would make it. He lacked nothing in courage. His footwork to spinners rivalled even the Don's and he was able to handle Bill O'Reilly, who presented the toughest examination of batsmen in the 1930s. His late cut, always a sign of class, was superb.

Hassett broke into the State side at 19, in 1932–33, the same year as Bill Brown, but couldn't hold his place. It was four years – in 1936–37 – before, at 23, he was a regular for Victoria. In 1937–38 he was chosen in D. G. Bradman's XI against V. Y. Richardson's XI. This game was a testimonial for Clarrie Grimmett and Victor Richardson. It was also a trial for the coming tour of England. Hassett only made 13, before Grimmett, in fine touch for the game, dismissed him. But it didn't matter. A good season for Victoria secured him the second-last batsman's spot in the squad to tour England in 1938.

He was ranked behind Fingleton, Brown, Bradman, McCabe and Badcock, and ahead of young Sid Barnes, then only 21.

The diminutive Hassett was chosen for the first four tour games and scored 43, 146, 220 not out and 57 – enough form to gain a spot in the Test side. He began badly at Trent Bridge with 1 and 2, but lifted for Lord's with 56 and 42. The Third Test was washed out without a ball being bowled. Hassett hit 13, 33, 42 and 10 in the last two Tests for 199 aggregate at 24.88. The 33 at Leeds was a cool final innings knock in a heated moment that did most to bring Australia its only Test win – by five wickets. His complete tour was more impressive. He notched 1,589 runs at 54.79. Just as important was his aid to team morale throughout the long tour. Hassett never lost a chance for a practical joke. After a convivial evening at Grindleford, in the Derbyshire Hills, Hassett waited until room-mates Stan McCabe and Bill O'Reilly were asleep before smuggling a goat into their room. They awoke the next morning to bleating and strange smells.

At 26, in 1940, just when he approached his peak as a batsman, war intervened and he enlisted as a gunner in the 2/2 Anti-Aircraft Regiment. He was sent to Egypt and Palestine in 1941. A year later, while on leave in Australia, he married Tessie Davis, whom he had met earlier working for a Geelong accountant. In 1944 Hassett, 30, like tens of thousands of other Australians, was brought back from the Middle East to defend the country from the invading Japanese, who were coming down through New Guinea. He served at Port Moresby when the enemy was stopped less than 50 km away at Iorabaiwa Ridge.

In 1945, Hassett began to think about playing for Australia again. He was appointed captain of the Australian Services XI and took part in the five Victory Tests against England and other games against India.

Hassett played in the first post-war Test at Wellington under Bill Brown in March 1946 and at 33, was in the Australian side for the resumption of Ashes series in 1946–47. In the opening game at Brisbane, he figured in a 276-run partnership with

Bradman, making 128, his first Test century. He was at an age where most players contemplated retirement. But Hassett, cheated by the war, was determined to play on as long as he could. In that second series, he nearly doubled his average to 47.43 from a 332 aggregate.

Hassett's improvement continued in the next series against India in 1947–48, when from the same aggregate – 332 – he came away with an average of 110.67, second only to Bradman (715 at 178.75). His highest score was 198 not out at Adelaide in the Fourth Test.

His record and experience as a skipper in the Victory Tests in 1945 and as captain of Victoria, made him an ideal vice-captain to Bradman for the 1948 tour of England. He was the life of the party on board ship and in every port.

In England, some of the team were at a reception at a stately home of a wealthy host. Over dinner, the host's well-endowed wife, who was wearing a low-cut dress, asked if Hassett had seen the pyramids. He stood up, leaned across the table and ogled her cleavage.

'I think we may have missed the best of them,' he said.

On another occasion he, Keith Miller, Bill Johnston and Ian Johnson were being chauffeured back to London after a black-tie dinner in Surrey. It was midnight. They had only gone a few kilometres when Hassett asked the driver to call in at the next mansion. The driver obliged, taking them down a long driveway to a grand two-storey abode. Hassett rang the doorbell, waking the household.

A window on the top storey was thrown up. A gentlemen enquired: 'What the hell are you doing?'

'Just thought we'd pop in,' Hassett said.

The man at the window recognised the cheeky intruder.

'Are you Lindsay Hassett?' he asked.

'Indeed I am.'

'Wait there.'

A butler ushered the four revellers in. Port and cigars were offered. The unprepared host, who happened to be a cricket fan, entertained them for two hours. The Australians had an enormous impact on England throughout the summer and most knew them by sight. Hassett heard later that their host dined out on the intrusion for years afterwards.

His love of a good time didn't impact on his 1948 performances. Hassett's tour figures of 1,563 at 74.42 were second to Bradman. Only Ponsford and Bradman ever did better in England.

Wisden made him one of its Five Players of the Year in 1948.

•

Such a glowing report card for a deputy made sure that Hassett was elected Australian captain. He led his country for the first time to South Africa. Hassett began the Tests in style with a century (112) in his first innings as captain, and ended it with 167 in the last Australian innings. His aggregate was 402 and he averaged 67. Harvey's step-up to 660 runs at 132 made sure that Bradman wasn't missed in the batting department. Hassett also demonstrated a shrewdness as captain similar to the Don's. He prolonged South Africa's second innings on a rain-affected pitch at Durban, stretching it out with delaying tactics, defensive fields and instructions to Miller, who was spinning the ball prodigiously, to bowl straight. South Africa scored its last nine runs in more than an hour. Australia began its second innings with a target of 336 to win on a wicket that was drying out, but still dangerous to bat on. In the last 100 minutes of the third day, Australia reached 3 for 80. Harvey (154) batting at five and Sam Loxton (54) at six did most on the final day on a better wicket to give Australia a five-wicket win.

The African tour became traditional for the more adventurous team members attempting off-field conquests. One player was rumoured to have spent the night with three women. Hassett saluted him the next morning at breakfast, saying:

'Congratulations. You're the only man ever to achieve a hat-trick with two balls.'

The happy tourists went home with a 4:0 series win. It was a fine start to the post-Bradman era without the great player/captain's presence after two decades of dominance.

A bigger examination of Hassett's ascension came in 1950–51 when Freddie Brown's England team toured Australia. The Australian team was weaker than the 1948 line-up without Bradman, Sid Barnes, Ernie Toshack and Colin McCool, and with Don Tallon's keeping skills on the decline. Yet England didn't seem any more powerful than in the last Ashes.

Australia was bundled out on a good wicket in the First Test at Brisbane for just 228, then England, not for the first time, was caught on a 'sticky'. Brown declared at 7 for 68, forcing the Australians in on the worst of it. The home side collapsed to be 7 for 32. Instead of hanging on for as many runs as possible, Hassett walked onto the field and waved to the England skipper.

'What's happening, old boy?' a perplexed Brown enquired.

'I'm declaring,' Hassett said.

'Oh, I see,' Brown replied and turning to the wicket added, 'You want us in on *that* again.'

Hassett nodded and said, 'It's your move, old chap.'

England had 70 minutes to bat before stumps and another day to score the modest 193 to win. Instead of playing safe, it attacked and lost 6 for 30 by stumps. The next morning, the wicket had dried out. It looked good. England had 163 runs to make with four wickets in hand. Hassett made great play of pointing out imaginary spots on the pitch. He crowded the batsmen, bluffing them into believing the life that was there previously, remained. Brown placed his two best bats, Denis Compton and Len Hutton at eight and nine. Compton and Godfrey Evans came to the wicket to start the morning. Both soon popped up catches expecting balls to rise when they didn't. Hutton came in, realised it was a good track and batted without fear, reaching 62 not out. But it was too late. England reached 122 and Australia won by 70 runs.

Australia won the series 4:1, the loss being in the last Test at Melbourne. Hassett was one of five batsmen to average in the 40s (40.67 at 366), highlighting starkly for the first time how important Bradman had been in Ashes contests since 1928.

Against the West Indies in Australia the next season, 1951–52, Hassett led another 4:1 series win. Hassett (402 at 57.43) was the only player of both sides to average more than fifty.

In 1952–53, South Africa challenged for a series win for the first time and it ended 2 wins all. Hassett, now 39, maintained his form, hitting 346 at 43.25, but he was leading a team in decline after the heights reached in 1948.

Yet despite Australia beginning to lose its grip on world cricket, Hassett never lost his sense of humour or impish manner, which if anything increased with the pending decline of fortunes of his team. When the captain of a visiting New Zealand women's cricket team asked Hassett if his players (whom she was watching practice) would sign her cricket hat, he obliged and then asked some of his players to sign Ian Johnson's white panama.

'It was brand new too,' Johnson complained, 'but I kept it, as a souvenir.'

•

In 1953, England, relieved at facing an Australia without Bradman for the first time since at home 1926, won the series 1:0. England hadn't won the Ashes since the Bodyline series of 1932–33, 20 years earlier.

Yet Hassett, in public at least, remained himself. At an official function early in the tour he began a speech with:

'Never in my life have I seen so many ugly men –' He then paused for several seconds before adding, 'or so many beautiful women.' That produced as many nervous laughs as genuine ones. But he then added: 'If it were the other way round, I would not be here,' which brought cheering and applause.

In congratulating England skipper Len Hutton at the Oval after the home team had secured the only win of the series,

Hassett was the sporting joker to the end. He had bowled the second-last over of the game, when it was as good as finished.

'England deserved to win,' he said, 'if not from the first ball, at least from the second-last over.'

Away from the microphone, he was congratulated for his speech by several in the winner's camp. Hassett then showed a different face that demonstrated he was just as upset about losing as the next leader.

'Thank you,' he said and then added tartly, 'it [the speech] wasn't bad, considering that Tony Lock chucked half the side out.'

Slow left-arm spinner Lock, who took 5 for 45 in Australia's second innings, had a suspect action, especially with his quicker delivery, which was evident almost every ball in Australia's second innings. Hassett was more than irritated that Lock wasn't 'called' in this game and in earlier encounters. (Lock was later unofficially warned about his action. A few years later he cut out the faster delivery – a throw – altogether.)

Undeterred, Hassett kept his and the team's spirits up. While dining at the Park Royal Hotel with other players, a waiter spilled a Peach Melba dessert on Hassett's jacket. The waiter apologised profusely and asked Hassett if he wished to have his jacket cleaned. Hassett at first declined. The waiter continued to fuss about. Hassett relented and while removing his jacket noticed a spot on his trousers, not related to the tumbling dessert. With the aplomb of a silent movie actor, he pointed to the spot, and motioned for the waiter to wait. Hassett then removed his trousers, folded them and handed them to the astonished waiter. The Australian captain went on eating his meal in his shirt, tie and underpants, much to the mirth of his companions. The waiter returned with the cleaned clothes while the players were finishing their cognacs.

Hassett's 1953 Ashes returns of 365 at 36.50, were again the best for the Australians. He scored 1,236 at 44.14 for the tour.

Hassett realised, at 40, his time had come. Australia needed new blood and was facing a period of transition. His 43 Tests yielded 3,073 runs at 46.56 with 10 centuries. In first-class cricket he scored 16,890 with 59 centuries from 216 matches at an average of 58.24. He captained Australia 24 times for 14 wins, four losses and six draws.

•

Hassett ran a Melbourne sports store for 15 years, and became a cricket commentator with the ABC. He enjoyed supporting the then VFL club Geelong, playing golf (with a handicap of four) and bream fishing. Ernie McCormick, one of his team-mates from the 1938 Ashes tour, was bemused by Hassett's need to have four rods operating at the same time.

'He'd light his pipe and wait,' McCormick recalled, 'like a soldier manning four machine-guns. When two fish would bite simultaneously, he turned into a one-armed paper-hanger, still with the pipe in his mouth.'

The love of bream fishing was an influencing factor in him and wife Tessa retiring to Batehaven, on the New South Wales South Coast, where he could indulge this pastime to his heart's content on the River Clyde. He died there in 1993.

Hassett was one of Australia's finest ambassador captains. His fun-loving, urbane style allowed him to get away with words and pranks that would have been condemned if attempted by others. He was also one of the classiest stroke-makers ever.

Lindsay Hassett's character made him the ideal deputy in Bradman's Invincibles.

Arthur Morris (Co-Selector)

Bradman was fortunate to have Hassett and Arthur Morris, two intelligent, cool heads, and gentlemen, as his co-selectors to support him on and off the field throughout 1948. Morris, like the other two, was not easily ruffled, and with the mental make-up that wins in big sport. He was the most successful batsman of either side when it counted – in the Tests. He possessed a keen wit, and like the other two always looked for a bright spot in a bleak moment. This harmony at the top of the squad was another important factor in the team's unprecedented success. Morris felt the responsibility of being a selector on tour – often a thankless task, especially when players had to be dropped. Yet his own form helped his authority, and like Bradman, he revelled in leading from the front. Attack was always the best form of defence for Morris, except in circumstances where defence was the only way out of a situation, such as at Manchester in the Third Test.

●

Arthur Morris at 15 years was a left-arm slow spinner, who batted down the order for St George's Second XI. The First XI captain, Bill O'Reilly, studied him in the nets and disabused him of a bowling career, suggesting there were plenty ahead of him at the club. O'Reilly calculated in the interests of St George. Morris would be well down the list behind O'Reilly waiting for a bowl, but the club was short of a left-hand opening bat. He thought Morris had a sound technique and ordered him, at 16 in 1938–39, to open. The affable, easygoing Morris had the temperament to take on one of the toughest challenges cricket can offer. Openers are born not made, and the curly-haired teenager of medium height and weight showed all the skills needed to make a strong start to his team's innings.

At 18, in 1940–41, Morris made an impact in his first State game for New South Wales when he hit two attractive innings of 148 and 111 against Queensland. This was the first time a batsman had scored two hundreds in his debut first-class match. The cricket world sat up. Such a display said several things. First, the cricketer most likely had the right mental strength for Test cricket. Second, his powers of concentration were exceptional. Even the most experienced in history rarely came up twice with such force and determination in one match. War stopped him from making a teenage entry into Test cricket in 1940–41 when England would have been due to visit. At 19, instead of opening for his country, he enlisted to fight for it in the 2nd Australian Imperial Force.

Morris was stationed in Australia and New Guinea. He was 23 when the war ended in 1945. He found work with a motor parts distributor that would allow him every chance to resume his rudely interrupted cricket career. Morris began 1946–47 in good touch, scoring 27 run out and 98 versus Queensland at Brisbane. It was enough to achieve selection for his first big trial for an Australian XI against the England touring team at the MCG in early November 1946. Morris was in by default when Bill Brown fell injured. Brown, who had established himself as a Test opener in the 1930s, and Sid Barnes were favoured to open for Australia. It was Morris's big chance. He opened with another prospect, Merv Harvey, from Victoria. Day one was washed out, and by agreement, the game was extended to a fifth day. England, led by Wally Hammond, batted first and made 314. Harvey fell first for 22. Morris, who began cautiously, was joined by Bradman, himself very much on trial. He had batted for South Australia versus the MCC at Adelaide, where he looked frail and a shadow of his former greatness. Should he fail in this match, it was probable that he would resign from cricket. The new partners – it was the first time Morris had met Bradman, who was one of his heroes – were both batting for their cricketing future. Morris was calm and quiet, which was just Bradman's mood at the wicket. They cranked up together. *Wisden* said that Bradman inspired Morris. Bradman saw it another way.

'I have no idea what Arthur was thinking,' he said, 'but he was having no trouble with the bowling when I arrived at the wicket. His defence was excellent, and when he did play shots they were executed with style, placement and power.'

The two built a solid partnership of 196 for the second wicket. Bradman injured a leg muscle, limped up to 106 and then threw his wicket away. Morris pushed on to 115 in 297 minutes. He looked sound – all middle and no edges. The link had wide implications for post-war cricket.

Bradman said he was 'very much impressed' with Morris first up.

Did it help his selection for the First Test at Brisbane?

'Yes,' Bradman told me in a 1998 interview, 'I brought that impression to the selection table.'

Bradman had one more match against Victoria before the Tests, scoring 43 and 119, and declared himself 'available' for selection. Morris faced England again playing for New South Wales and scored 81 not out in a score of 4 for 165 declared in a rain-affected game. Notably, the New South Wales skipper, Sid Barnes, was out for just 1. Morris was doing everything right to gain selection.

•

He made the Test side, and promptly ran into big Alec Bedser. The medium-pacer beat him with an away-swinger and had him caught by Hammond in slips for just 2. In the Second Test at Sydney when on 5 he dragged an ordinary ball from Bill Edrich onto his stumps. These were his only two chances in these games in which Australia amassed 645 and 649. Morris spent long periods in the pavilion watching his team-mates build big scores.

Matters looked even bleaker in the Third Test at Melbourne beginning on 1 January 1947, when he failed for the third successive time, on this occasion lbw to Bedser, who trapped him with an off-cutter. Yet this time Australia batted first, making 365, and when England made 351, Morris was assured of a second chance. He made the most of it, scoring 155 in a solid, 300-minute stay at the wicket. English critic Neville Cardus, ever England's fifth columnist, sowed doubts about Morris by writing that the Australian had a 'loose' technique. Cardus and Fingleton noted that his bat was not straight in defence. Bradman told Morris to ignore the criticism and 'keep doing what he was doing'.

(This criticism came up again in 1948. Morris ignored it and kept on 'doing what he was doing' to brilliant effect.)

Morris was now confident at Test level. He went one better in Adelaide, scoring 122 and 124 not out in the Fourth Test. He now had three successive Test centuries. This entrenched him as Australia's left-handed opener. His double feat at Adelaide put him in a special class. He hit another fine 57 in the Fifth Test and ended his first series with 503 runs at 71.86. He had five starts only against the Indians in 1947–48, but kept up a sound impression by making 209 at 52.25 with a score of 100 not out at the MCG in Australia's second innings, a year after he made his breakthrough 155 against England.

It was enough to ensure Morris a boat trip to England for the 1948 tour. He rated the Ashes that year as the best series for him personally and the most enjoyable of his career.

•

He returned home in 1948–49 and continued on his artful way. One innings among many fine knocks in that season stood out. It was against Queensland, which always seemed to be on the receiving end of Morris adventurism. New South Wales needed 142 to win. Morris smashed 108 not out off 80 balls before lunch, so the story goes, in order to eat with a friend. Bradman was the only other player to have been in such an apparent hurry before lunch. He achieved the same feat four times in State games. Morris kept up the standard that had so impressed his now retired skipper, scoring 1,069 runs at 66.81. This gave him an amazing year of cricket. In 12 months between April 1948 and March 1949, he had 46 first-class innings (3 not outs) and accumulated 2,991 runs at 69.56. He propelled his team to a good start on average every second time he batted. No opener in history could claim such a consistent and brilliant record.

Morris was 27 years old, turning 28 during the 1949–50 tour of South Africa. There seemed nowhere to go but down from such an astonishing height. He was still in form, though not quite as spectacular, as he scored 422 at 52.75 in the Tests. He had trouble with Bedser again in 1950–51. After early failures, the big Surrey man presented Morris with a Lindsay Hassett book on how to play the game. Morris, who always had a determined streak under his gentle exterior, replied to the friendly jibe by hitting 206 out of an Australian innings of 371. It was his seventh Ashes century and a sign that he could still rise to the occasion. But there wasn't quite the will or the inclination to do it as much. This was reflected in his returns of 321 runs at 35.67, and again the next season against the West Indies when he managed just 186 at 23.25. Those wily spinners Sonny Ramadhin and Alf Valentine caused him more trouble than Bedser. Morris lifted his rating against the touring South Africans in a more challenging series for Australia, which was drawn 2-all. He hit 370 at 41.1, with a top score of 99 run out at the MCG in the Fifth Test.

Morris began the 1953 Ashes series campaign with four good innings of 67, 60, 30 and 89, but his form fell away after that as Australia lost its first Ashes since the Bodyline series of 1932–33. Morris's 337 at 33.7 confirmed a permanent fall from the heady days of 1948. He was out of the blocks with 153 in the First Test of the 1954–55 Ashes but only accumulated 223 at 31.86 for the entire series. Despite increasing competition from new young blood such as Colin McDonald from Victoria and Jim Burke from New South Wales, Morris was still chosen for a tour of the West Indies in 1955.

He began with 157 against Jamaica, giving him the record of having scored a century on debut in four countries – England, South Africa, the West Indies and Australia. This effort said much about Morris's will. He could often perform when he was determined. He managed 266 at 44.33, which was close to his career Test average of 46.29 from 3,533 runs in 46 Tests. He hit 12 centuries.

He captained New South Wales at 25, and proved such a capable leader that he was vice-captain of the Test team for several series. He filled in twice as leader in 1951–52 against the West Indies and against England in 1954–55.

Morris had 162 first-class games, in which he accumulated 12,614 runs at 53.67 with 46 hundreds. He put back into the game, which had brought him joy, fame and an exceptional life, as a Trustee of the SCG for 21 years. He was awarded an MBE for his services to cricket and had a successful career as a public relations man for security group Wormald. Morris married twice, first to English performer Valerie Hudson, but she died tragically in 1956. His second wife is Judith Menmuir, and in 2008 they celebrated a 40 year partnership.

Bradman summed up Morris thus:

'His most outstanding quality was plenty of time to play his shots. He could drive, glance, hook and cut. All were executed with the same facility. Arthur was a wonderful player to watch from the beginning of an innings. He often set the tone for a game. He wasn't always straight in defence. But this was merely a sign of genius. He rarely, if ever, got out from this. Arthur had an ideal temperament.'

•

This appreciation from his 1948 captain reflected Arthur Morris's sensational efforts throughout the tour.

Sid Barnes

When Bradman summed up the characteristics of his 1948 team, he mentioned ability, brilliance and bulldog courage, which could have described every player, but particularly Sid Barnes. Arthur Morris reckoned he was best opener he had seen. He and other good judges were firmly of the opinion that Barnes would have developed into one of the best batsmen of all time – perhaps second only to Bradman – had the war not intervened.

He had all the shots, especially the square cut, which no one played better, and no one ever showed more guts fielding close to the wicket. His willingness to risk his life for Australia was symptomatic of an eccentric, one-off character, bound to clash with authority. Some of the types that became cricket administrators without a top sporting background were by nature in the mid-20th Century, conformist, conservative, unimaginative and puritanical. Barnes to them was the anti-Christ. He did things his way. One draconian measure instigated by the Board was that no wives could travel with the players. They were not even allowed to be in England when their husbands were. Barnes defied them; putting his wife up at a hotel in London during the time of 1948 Lord's Test.

The Board paid the players a pittance – around £600 for the eight months they were to be away. On top of that, they would be fined if they attempted to make any extra money on the trip. That left individuals like Barnes, who wanted to make something from the tour, and Miller who wanted to live it up, with little choice but to at least attempt to earn some extra money by gambling. Miller hit the race tracks wherever he could. Barnes bet on his own ability, including him making a century at Lord's. He went one further by stocking up with goods for the trip to England and then selling everything from soap to liquor – door to door at London hotels when he had time off from the cricket. He also bought other goods and returned home with trunk loads of cashmere sweaters, golf shoes, tweed coats, pullovers, cameras, cricket equipment and other odds and sods of which there were shortages in Australia.

Barnes in a way personified the dilemma of the amateur Australian cricketer at the time after the disruption of war. Servicemen felt that they had been 'robbed' of important years, and many felt an urgency about making up for lost time, and potential income. Barnes accentuated this concern and went about 'making hay' while he could. The cliché 'wheeler-dealer' was applied to him, when in reality he was taking advantage of his good fortune to be a touring cricketer. He, as much as the next player, wanted to do well for his country. Yet he saw the sport as a vehicle for greater gain, when there was no hope of regular employment anywhere while he was a top cricketer. Great as the game was, it represented only an interlude from finding ways to survive and support a family.

Barnes also had the perspicacity to take film footage of the 1948 trip, which he had in mind would be of historical value. He even took footage of King George VI and Queen Elizabeth at Lord's during the tourists' match against the MCC. This had been allowed by the Royals. But the distant members of the aptly named Board of Control were horrified that one of its chosen cricketers would have the temerity to film such illustrious personages. Unable to allow for a little Aussie irreverence to the fakeries of the Royal illusion, Barnes' act would later be held against him by the Board; a closed Star Chamber of 13 representatives from all the States. It brought on certain occasions a deal of parochial, petty, vindictive small-mindedness to Board meetings. As one former Board member remarked:

'If some of them were not knifing each other, then they spent a fair time stabbing players from other States. And Barnes presented a juicy torso for heavy incisions. He, and to a lesser extent Miller, were marked down for their individuality after the 1948 tour.'

•

Sid Barnes (1916–73) was born in Mount Isa in north-western Queensland and brought up in Enmore, a Sydney suburb. Every top cricketer has a moment – an epiphany, or a revelation – when they do something extra special as a youngster, which tells them that they might have a future in the game. Barnes' moment came at age 15, when he took seven wickets for one run with his well-flighted leg-breaks. It was in a C-grade match, and the youngster had more interest then in bowling and keeping than batting. But it was enough for him go further. It was 1931.

Don Bradman and Clarrie Grimmett were his heroes after they had demolished England in 1930. Every kid with aspirations in the game had been inspired by that mighty season in England when Bill Woodfull and his team came home unexpectedly with the Ashes.

Like many Aussie kids with outstanding sporting ability, school seemed superfluous. Young Sid couldn't wait to leave at 15 and get a job as a demonstrator of motor cycles, despite not having a licence. He put nothing into his studies and felt the opprobrium of his teachers. But he could not have cared less. He was determined to make a name for himself playing for Australia, and he could see nothing to stop his progress. In 1935, he joined the Petersham club. Barnes copied Bradman's early sharpening-up technique by using a stump to hit a golf ball against a brick wall. (Bradman used the concrete base of a water tank.) He refused to read texts on the game, figuring that the authors had their own style, and he wanted his own. He acquired a mirror and set it up in the bottom of the garden of the family home and worked on his technique.

Stocky, naturally muscular teenager Barnes made the New South Wales State team in 1936–37, first as 12th man against Gubby Allen's touring England team. Just before the Fifth and deciding Test, Barnes could lay claim to having influenced the final selection place, which would go to a paceman, either New South Wales' 'Ginty' Lush, or Victoria's tearaway Laurie Nash. Barnes, batting for Petersham against North Sydney, smashed four sixes and four fours – 40 runs in all – off Lush in one over. (There were eight-ball overs then, and this one included a no ball, making nine deliveries in all.) This spectacular hitting created a Sydney club record. Dudley Seddon, a selector, was batting with Barnes. Word filtered through to Bradman that Lush had taken a pasting from the promising young bladesman. It helped Bradman secure a spot in the Fifth Test team for Nash. (Australia won the Ashes.) Soon after this, Barnes played his first State game against Bradman's South Australia. He was in with the big boys and it was tough and scary. Barnes admitted being fearful of even facing the wily Clarrie Grimmett. Luckily, Test star Stan McCabe shielded him and he made a creditable 31 and 44, both times falling lbw to spinner Frank Ward. (In later encounters, Barnes would boast of 'going in search' of Grimmett for special treatment.)

Barnes knew he was destined for bigger things even then because he found batting at this higher first-class level easier than at club level. For one thing, the wickets were better. For another, the games were played over four days, giving him a chance to develop an innings.

He established himself at first-class level in 1937–38, making 809 at an excellent average of 50, which placed him as the sixth-best batsman in the country. But had his scores against Western Australia of 99 not out and 127 not out been included, his tally of 1,035 would have placed him second only to Bradman for the season. Young Sid was miffed that these figures were not included, but it mattered little. He was chosen at 21 to tour England with Bradman for the 1938 Ashes.

Barnes' first clash with authority came right at the beginning of the tour when the tour manager (and secretary to the Board), W. H. Jeanes, took objection to a 'gaudy' hat he was wearing as the boat left Melbourne for Hobart. In a churlish, bullying act, Jeanes grabbed it and tossed it into the crowd waving the cricketers goodbye. Young Barnes was fuming. The incident was not forgotten by both men. Unfortunately Barnes broke a bone in his hand while training on the boat, and he could not play cricket for 13 weeks. But when he did play his form was strong enough for Test selection. He turned 22 on tour, and broke into the team for the final game of the Ashes at the Oval, making 41 and 33.

War broke out in 1939 and finished first-class cricket for several seasons. Barnes married Alison Edward in 1942, the same year he joined the army, and he did not play Test cricket again until 1946 in the one game early in that year in New Zealand. He resumed top cricket in the 1946–47 Ashes, which meant he missed playing at the top for eight years – from 23 to 30, the absolute peak years of development in a cricketer's life, from which a player of Barnes' skills would have been expected to go on and consolidate a fine career. Instead, he had to start again – at 30.

Barnes had a strong first post-war Ashes, scoring 443 runs at 73.83, and this included his 234 at Sydney when he got himself out on purpose to be on the same score as Bradman, for posterity.

His attitude was that he was on borrowed time trying to balance Test cricket with business. He played three Tests against India, picking up a century and doing enough to secure a trip to England in 1948. It provided a career pinnacle. But then when he could have gone on to establish a terrific record, he opted out of the South African tour in 1949–50, citing the pathetic £450 for the trip as not enough, and that he would be out of pocket after it. This led to two seasons of Test exile. In 1951–52 he was ready to return. He was in good touch (making a fine hundred in December 1951 against Victoria) and the selectors – Bradman, 'Chappie' Dwyer and Jack Ryder – selected him for the Third Test against the West Indies. But a majority of the Board of Control Star Chamber (which included Bradman, who voted *for* Barnes) vetoed the selection.

It was spineless decision, one of the worst in Australian cricket history, even more insidious than the decision not to pick Miller to tour South Africa on the last tour there (which was later corrected). The Board, in the worst tradition of a faceless, facile authority gave no reason for his non-selection, except that it had to be on non-cricketing grounds. A few newspapers, primed by the Board, defended the decision, making out that Barnes had done sinister things that the public should not know about.

English newspapers, perhaps revelling in a split in Australian ranks, were less reticent about the issue. Alan Hoby in the *Sunday Express* claimed that the Board had 'consigned Barnes to the doghouse for daring to be different'. Barnes, the English journalist said, 'was too ebullient, too brutally outspoken and,

ironically enough, far too puckish and cheeky for the graveyard solemnity of international cricket. Is it that pompous officialdom cannot forget the time when Barnes produced a toy bat in the Bradman Testimonial . . . or the occasion when Barnes the comedian picked up a stray dog and offered, with a huge grin, to the umpire, who was not amused? . . . Irritating? Possibly. Teasing? Maybe, Malicious? No. Entertaining? Yes.'

Barnes was a sportsman out of his time, though not out of his depth. Had he played in the 1970s, 80s, and 90s, he would have been seen as another character like Lillee, Marsh, Matthews or Warne. In the staid mid-20th Century, he was too much a personality, an individual, and a likeable character. Every player, from Bradman to Miller, really liked and appreciated Sid Barnes.

The Board said nothing to back their rejection of him, and this caused Barnes a period of intense mental anguish. Everything came to the surface when Barnes sued a letter writer to a Sydney paper in 1952. In courtroom evidence, the Board revealed its petty and vindictive, insubstantial reasons. One was that he had 'insulted Royalty' – King George VI and Queen Elizabeth – when he filmed them at Lord's in the 1948 game against Middlesex. This was not accurate. He had gained permission. Another unforgivable transgression was that Barnes had persuaded Ernie Toshack to have a game of tennis in the courts next to the Northants pavilion while the Australian team was playing. (Barnes had made 11, and the tourists were on the way to more than 500. Toshack was not even in the team.) This was the worst of it, and it was pathetic in the extreme. But then came the shocker. He had forgotten his player's pass one morning when entering the MCG during the Third Test of the 1946–47 Ashes. Barnes jumped the turnstile (he was batting at the time) to get in so he could change and continue his innings. This infuriated the officialdom, noted for their officiousness at this ground. Barnes was also banned for acknowledging, and playing to the gallery. He actually waved and bowed to them!

At least common sense prevailed in the court and Barnes won the defamation case, clearing his name that had been besmirched. But he felt there was no point, at 36, in continuing on in first-class cricket. He retired. In all, with the non-cricketing war years thrown in, Barnes had missed a decade in his prime. Given his performances in the brief time he was on the scene – about five years all up – he could have built a record three times what it was.

•

Sid Barnes was a contradictory human being, always in conflict with someone or something, and finally himself. He took his own life at age 57, in 1973. It was a sad end to a turbulent life from one of the game's most outstanding batsmen, and characters.

•

Barnes played an absurdly low 13 Tests (19 innings) for one so talented, who started so young. He scored 1,072 runs at 63.05, including three centuries, which on pure figures of retired players stands second only to Bradman. (Most comparisons start at 20 Test innings, but Barnes was no tail-ender with copious not outs boosting his average. He could lay claim to having the second-best batting record of all time.) Barnes took 4 wickets (at 54.50) and held 14 catches. His first-class figures (1936–52) better reflected what might have been in a broader Test career. He scored 8,333 runs at 54.11, including 26 centuries. His leg-break bowling received a better run at State level and he took a creditable 57 wickets at 32.21.

•

Sid Barnes always looked back on the 1948 season as his most enjoyable, and he was proud to have been a member of Bradman's all-conquering outfit.

Bill Brown

By any standard, Bill Brown had a successful 1948 tour, with eight centuries (second only to Bradman, 11), a double century against Cambridge, and 1,448 runs at an average of 57.92. This placed him fourth behind Bradman, Hassett and Morris for the first-class season. Brown could not quite complement this form in the Tests, but in fairness to him he was a duck out of water when not opening. The success of Barnes and Morris as an opening combination forced Brown down the list and he was always uncomfortable in this role. He also often came in when the batsmen above him had done the job and there was not much time for him to develop an innings. Consequently he was dropped after two Tests.

His important strength and contribution to the team's eventual invincibility was his preparedness to play the anchor role at the beginning of innings against the counties. This way, he created a backbone between the Tests, which stiffened the Australian performances when otherwise they may have collapsed through lack of concentration or fatigue.

The more thoughtless critics attacked him for his slow progress at times, but Bradman fully appreciated his efforts, and never criticised his performances. The captain knew how he felt himself between the Tests, in having Brown, with his 'perfect' textbook orthodoxy, starting an innings or up the other end with his delicate leg-glancing and range of artistic strokes. Bradman also gave him full marks for his fitness (Brown was 36, and keen on the upkeep of his physical condition), excellent boundary riding, and for being a good team man.

•

Bill Brown (1912–2008), the son of a Toowoomba, Queensland farmer, first played Shield cricket for New South Wales at 20 during the 1932–33 season – marked by the Bodyline controversy. In his only encounter with the MCC tourists he acquitted himself well, scoring 69 and 25. In 1933–34 Brown made 154 versus Queensland in his seventh first-class game. In his 13th match, he made a brilliant 205 versus Victoria. Through the season, Brown opened with Jack Fingleton and at the end of it, there was only a place for one of them to tour England in 1934. They had performed more or less at the same standard. Bradman had batted at No. 3 in the same New South Wales side during the season. The national selectors, naturally, asked Bradman whom he would choose out of the two of them. Bradman chose Brown, suggesting he would bat better on English wickets.

Brown played his first Test at Trent Bridge, scoring 29 and 73. He then made a name for himself with his first Test hundred at Lord's and ended the series with a respectable 300 at 33.33. He followed this with 417 at 59.57, with a top score of 121, in the South African series of 1935–36. Brown had a setback with injury in the home series of 1936–37 against England. He could only manage two games, scoring 95 at 23.75, with a top innings of 42.

Brown moved back to Queensland for the 1937–38 season. He and Fingleton this time were both chosen to tour England in 1938 and they would be opening together in the series.

At Trent Bridge in the first 1938 Ashes Test, Brown compiled 133 in the second innings, and with Bradman (144 not out) saved the Test for Australia. This built Brown's confidence for his return Lord's Test days later.

•

On 25 June, he strode to the wicket in front of a packed Lord's with opening partner Fingleton to begin the chase after England's massive 494. The crowd had seen Wally Hammond mount a magnificent 240 in 367 minutes, and it waited for not Australia's, but Bradman's reply. The purists would love to see a brilliant answering century from the master. But not a double century. That would dent England's chances.

At 69, Fingleton was out. The crowd craned their necks towards the pavilion. Bradman emerged to thunderous applause. Some over the years begrudged Bradman being the centre of attention always, wherever he went or played. But not Brown. He was happy to be playing Test cricket and doing his own thing with the bat, which was exceptional at times and always classy. Besides, he liked his captain and appreciated his genius. If Bradman could top Hammond's effort, which he usually did, Brown would love to be there to contribute to a fighting reply. To his and a big section of the crowd's disappointment, a big Bradman double was not forthcoming. Left-arm spinner Hedley Verity caged then removed him for 18 when he chopped the ball onto his stumps. The biggest scorer in history was out. The responsibility was on Brown and the rest of the line-up to dig a little deeper.

The score was 2 for 101. Stan McCabe came in, batted like a millionaire, 'outside his means' as Bradman would say, and was out for 38 in 30 minutes. It was 3 for 152. Lindsay Hassett then joined Brown, in a partnership of 124 in 100 minutes. Brown was more cautious in his stroke-play than the critics would like to see. But this day, he was not restricting himself to gentle leg deflections and delicate late cuts. Intermingled with his sound defence, Brown was being the 'real' Brown by standing to his full 176 cm and driving with style on both sides of the wicket. He was letting flow the very correct skills that his team-mates knew he had. They had seen this form now and again in Tests, county and Shield games. Somehow, a little of that Bradman aggression had transferred itself to the opener. He was taking the initiative on a huge occasion, which was even bigger than anyone realised. War would ensure it was the last Ashes contest at Lord's for a decade. Brown marked the occasion by moving to his century in 193 minutes. After Hassett was out for 56, Jack Badcock was bowled for a duck. Barnett came in and stayed with Brown (140 not out) until stumps with Australia on 5 for 299.

On day three he carried his bat to 206 not out in 375 minutes from a score of 422. In the end it wasn't far behind Hammond's rate of accumulation. Considering the respective bowling line-ups, Brown's innings was a better one. In fact, it was the finest performance of a distinguished career.

His unconquered 206 put Australia back in the game at Lord's. Brown's 69 at the Oval in the first innings was a fighting knock in Australia's hopeless cause in chasing 903, without Bradman.

Bradman's analysis that Brown was better than Fingleton on English wickets proved correct. Fingleton managed 123 runs at 20.50 during the series. Brown hit 512 in the four Tests played, the highest aggregate of either side, at 73.14.

Australian writer Johnny Moyes put his success in England down partly to lack of harassment from spectators there.

'He could plan his innings [in England],' Moyes noted, 'and pursue that plan to the end without being urged to "have a go". A placid chap was Brown, and he liked to play in peaceful surroundings. When on the job he was as emotionless as a stoic.'

1938 was his best season. He was again second only to Bradman in the averages for the tour, compiling 1,854 at 59.57. This form carried through into Australia's domestic season in 1938–39, where, now as State skipper, he scored 1,057 for Queensland with another carrying of his bat for 174 not out versus South Australia at Adelaide.

In 1940 at 28 he married Barbara Hart, a shipping company receptionist. During the war he was a pilot officer in the RAAF. Brown had the honour of leading Australia against New Zealand in the first post-war Test at Wellington on 29–30 March 1946. In his side was a wealth of leadership talent, proven and potential, in Miller, Hassett, Ian Johnson and Ray Lindwall. New Zealand won the toss and batted on a rain-affected pitch. Brown's toughest task was deciding who should be given the ball to do the destruction. New Zealand made 42 (Bill O'Reilly, in his last Test, 5 for 14; Ernie Toshack, in his first Test, 4 for 12).

Australia replied with 8 for 199 declared. Brown top-scored with 67 and New Zealand was removed for 54 in its second innings. Towards the end of it, Brown resorted to tossing a coin to decide who would bowl between two ex-airmen – Colin McCool and Ian Johnson. Australia won by an innings and 103 runs.

In 1946–47 any further chances of national leadership were thwarted by Bradman's return to Test cricket. An injured thumb kept Brown out of the series versus England. He returned against the Indians in 1947–48, began slowly with 11 and then 18, when he was run out sensationally while backing up too far. Indian left-hand spinner Vinoo Mankad stopped at the wicket and whipped off the bails. It was the second time in a month Mankad had done this to Brown. The verb 'to Mankad' – as in 'he was Mankaded' – became part of the language.

The transgression of not backing up properly and losing his wicket unnecessarily saw Brown dumped for the Third and Fourth Tests. He came back for the Fifth at Melbourne. He was run out for 99, a well-crafted knock that assured him a place in the squad to tour England in 1948. Unfortunately for Brown, two other fine players, Sid Barnes and Arthur Morris, had entrenched themselves as the opening pair. Brown was tried down the order, but the move didn't come off. He had only three innings for a return of 73 runs at 24.33, but there was some satisfaction in having two of them at Lord's where he scored 24 and 32.

Brown's total in 22 Tests was 1,592 at the top-drawer average of 46.82. In first-class cricket, he had 189 matches for a total of 13,838 runs at 51.54. He hit 39 centuries.

There followed a troubling short period as a Test selector where he was abused and harassed for not making sure the national side included Queenslanders.

During the 1999–2000 season, Australian captain Steve Waugh invited Brown, a popular speaker on the cricket circuit, to address his team before the Second Test against Pakistan at Hobart. The players found his words and presence inspiring.

Johnny Moyes summed his batting career as having quality: 'Even when slow, he never wearied, as some do, because his style was cultured and free from jarring faults.'

•

Bill Brown played 22 Tests and captained Australia once in 1946 versus New Zealand. He would rather be remembered for his wonderful 1938 Ashes tour, but his performances on the 1948 tour were important and steady in Bradman's grand scheme for remaining unconquered.

Ron Hamence

Every cricket tour has its unlucky batsman and bowler. Injury, form loss, or even an indiscretion that displeased management, could cause an entire season to be a tough one. In 1948 Ron Hamence was arguably the unluckiest batsman, and for the bowlers, McCool had the most misfortune, through injury. In front of Hamence was a wall of brilliant batsmen. Sam Loxton also confronted this edifice, but he could bowl and got his chance. Hamence only had hope that providence might somehow smile upon him. But it was frustrating. The 'wall' was put up in almost every game outside the Tests as the selectors assessed their likely line-up and strengths. As the tour progressed the top seven – Morris, Barnes, Bradman, Hassett, Harvey, Miller and Brown – were selected more often than not in front of him because the aim was to go through the season undefeated. When he did gain selection he would have to wait to bat. Invariably there was an avalanche of runs on the board, and there was pressure to declare or wind up the innings. These were not conditions conducive to developing a huge innings or two that would make him irresistible to the selectors.

Yet Bradman appreciated the short, compact Hamence and considered him a first-rate batsman with a correct, sound technique and a game based on drives either side of the wicket. The captain also believed Hamence had the temperament for the Tests, based on his consistency against all types of bowling and the way he applied himself in tough situations. Together with this, Bradman was thankful for the way he conducted himself on tour and how he always lifted the side's spirits.

•

Ron Hamence was born at Hindmarsh, Adelaide in 1915, and was playing B-grade games for West Torrens by the time he was 13. He made the State side at 19 in the 1935–36 season, and developed a friendship with Bradman, who was in his first season as South Australian captain. In 1936–37, Hamence managed to score 30s and 40s with his orthodox style, and the State selectors kept picking him. He lifted his rating a fraction in the next season 1937–38, but at 22 he had not quite cemented his place in the State team. However, by 1938–39, he was making the kind of scores batting at No. 5 in a strong side that were now more than promising. His sound technique was making it hard to dislodge him, and he was now a permanent member of the State side.

Hamence was in his mid-20s when all cricket shut down during the war, and this had a detrimental affect on his natural progression as a batsman. His scores and experience were on the up when he had to stop. Hamence returned after the war and had a job in the Government Printing Office. He was allowed leave without pay to play for his State. He turned 30 in the 1945–46 season. Encouraged by Bradman, he continued on, when he could have been forgiven for giving the game away in order to support his wife Nora and daughter.

Like many other players, who had their careers cruelly curtailed by half a decade because of the war, Hamence had something to prove. He slipped into prominence in a big partnership with Bradman against Victoria. They both made centuries. The Australian captain had a front-seat view of

Hamence's beautiful batting skills. This was followed by another hundred against New South Wales. Then in late January 1947, he put in a grand performance against the MCC, making 145 and figuring in a 203 partnership with Phil Ridings (77). This game was an examination of temperament as much as batting skill. He was up against the tourists' big guns, including Voce, Pollard, Wright and Langridge, and after the MCC had racked up 577. It was enough for Bradman and his co-selectors. Hamence was picked for the Fifth Test at Sydney, and acquitted himself with an accomplished 30 not out in the first innings, which was third-top score.

It was sufficient for him to be in contention for the 1947–48 season, and he was selected for the Second Test, again at Sydney. In a rain-ruined draw in mid-December 1947, he managed a top score of 25 in Australia's ignominious score of 107 in its only innings on a difficult pitch.

That effort was enough to get him selected once more in the next Test at Melbourne in early January 1948 when he again managed 25. Hamence was unlucky to be ditched for the final two Tests, but already that line-up of outstanding batsmen was forming for the trip to England.

After that disappointment, he was elated to learn in a memorable moment that he had been selected to tour England in 1948.

He was walking to his home in the Adelaide suburb of The Grange, when the local greengrocer pulled up on his bike.

'Congratulations!' he said pumping his hand.

'For what?' Hamence responded.

'Haven't you heard? You're in the squad for the Ashes tour!'

'How do you know?'

'We heard your name read out on the radio. They listed the 17 players.'

Hamence reached his home and was greeted by Nora at the front door. She had also heard the news.

•

In 1948, Hamence played 19 matches and in 22 innings managed 582 runs at 32.33, including his unfortunate 99 against Somerset at Taunton. Yet he kept up his own and the team's morale through the season. He formed a brilliant tenor duet with Doug Ring lamenting them and McCool being 'ground staff' members of the squad.

Despite his misfortune in 1948, he still had plenty of career highlights. He never played another Test but did make a point with another century for South Australia against the visiting MCC tourists of 1950–51.

In a first-class career spanning 16 years (1935–51), Hamence scored 5,285 runs at 37.75 with 11 centuries. In three Tests he had four innings with an average of 27 from an aggregate of 81.

•

Ron Hamence counted himself fortunate to make the 1948 tour. It turned out to be compensation for the war robbing him of a much bigger Test experience.

Neil Harvey

Neil Harvey was the 'discovery' of the 1948 tour, even though he had played Test cricket against India in the 1947–48 series. The Ashes in England in that era was the supreme test in cricket, and he built on tour and matured enough to force his way into the team. His form by mid-season was irresistible. Often in games against the counties, he would steal the show with a dashing cameo or a brilliant hundred. That he did so well in the Leeds Test when selected was testimony to his tremendous skill and temperament.

•

The dark-haired Harvey, born in 1928, was a cricketing prodigy from a family that produced four brothers who played for

Victoria. One other, opener Mervyn, managed one cap for Australia against England. No other family except for the Gregorys decades before produced so many capable cricketers.

A competitive home environment of long summers of backyard and street cricket equipped the young Harvey with nous and spirit to move well beyond the streets of Fitzroy, an inner Melbourne suburb. His left-handed sparkle and skill surfaced rapidly for the Fitzroy club at just 15 years and Victoria at 18 during the 1946–47 season. Harvey was the first of the post-war players not to have his career interrupted by war. In fact, it was enhanced by it. Selectors in 1945 and 1946 scoured the country searching for young talent to replace the ageing players from the 1930s, a period already being called another 'era'. In the early post-war years, Bradman saw in Harvey a mirror image of himself: short at 171 cm (5 ft 7 in), compact (66.5 kg) and ultra-talented with an aggressive, youthful outlook. Like Bradman, Harvey was nimble footed between the wickets and a brilliant field. When Bradman was first seen in the 1927–28 season playing for New South Wales, commentators dubbed him the best in the country. In the 1940s and 1950s, there was no one swifter or surer than Harvey in the covers. Opposing batsmen, even with the driving capacity of Garry Sobers, Rohan Kanhai, Frank Worrell, Peter May, Tom Graveney and Colin Cowdrey had to be at their best to penetrate an off-side field patrolled by Harvey and the other brilliant cover, Norm O'Neill.

•

Harvey was the third in the line of outstanding Australian left-handers after Clem Hill and Joe Darling. He hit the ball hard like them and inherited their attitude to get on with the game. This is why Bradman smiled upon Harvey and was one selector that wanted him in the Test team as soon as possible. He was just 19 when chosen to play for Australia against India in the Adelaide Fourth Test of the 1947–48 season. He made 13 and thought he would be dumped. But the series against India was already wrapped up by Australia. Bradman was using the Tests as a trial for selection on the 1948 tour of England. Harvey was chosen again for the Fifth Test at Melbourne. In that game Bradman on 57 retired hurt with an attack of fibrositis. Harvey came in at the MCG in front of a partisan home crowd and batted beautifully, compiling a stylish, forthright 153. To many observers, this was a seminal moment in Australian cricket. The young Harvey was expected to carry the baton held since 1928 by Bradman, when as a 20-year-old, he became the mainstay of Australian batting.

A little prematurely, Harvey was being dubbed the left-handed Bradman. His Melbourne performance assured him a boat trip to England for the 1948 tour.

When assessing his charges for that crusade, Bradman said of Harvey:

'He has the brilliance and daring of youth, and the likelihood of rapid improvement.'

That prognosis proved correct.

After his stellar season in England, Harvey came down to earth in the 1948–49 domestic summer scoring 539 runs in first-class cricket at just 33.68. He didn't manage a century and had a top score of 87. But he made amends with a fine tour of South Africa, 1949–50, demonstrating full maturity while turning 21. He plundered bowlers across the Veldt, scoring 1,526 runs at 76.30. He scored eight centuries from 25 innings – at an impressive one every three innings. In the Tests he lifted a notch, scoring 660 at 132. His scores were 34, 178, 23 not out, 2, 151, 56 not out, 100 and 116. Commentators licked their lips at the prospect of another Bradman-like performer in the Australian line-up. He had batted down the list, often at No. 6, but was expected soon to be No. 3, the spot secured for 18 years by Bradman.

But this analogy was pushed aside for a time after the more sobering results of the 1950–51 Ashes series in Australia. Harvey was 'serviceable', scoring 362 at 40.22, and without a century. During the series he lost his No. 3 spot and had to be content with No. 4. Alec Bedser gave him some trouble with his off-cutter (leg-cutter to the right-hander), which swung in hard on Harvey's pads and stumps, and his stock away-swinger outside off-stump. Bedser was the only bowler to remove him – five times – until Freddie Brown bowled him in the second innings of the Fourth Test. Bedser was the *bete noire* of Australia's two great left-handers, Morris and Harvey. The English medium-pacer – the best in the world at the time – also gave Bradman trouble in 1946–47 and 1948.

The following season, 1950–51 – Harvey found more difficulty still in countering the West Indies' spin twins, Alf Valentine and Sonny Ramadhin. Harvey was terrific at using his feet to the spinners, but these two had him in two minds. They too dismissed him five times between them. Harvey was into stride rarely for the second successive series. This time he managed 261 at 26.1 at No. 4. His top score was 74. He relished the next season 1952–53 against South Africa as one to rebuilt his career. Against a similar attack to the one he demolished away in 1949–50, Harvey, now 24, hit a mammoth 834 at 92.67 in nine innings, batting mainly at No. 3. His scores were 109, 52 run out, 11, 60, 190, 84, 116, 205 and 7. This was so very Bradmanesque that he took an aggregate record from him. Bradman had scored 806 at 201.5 from five innings against South Africa in 1931–32.

Harvey kept up this compelling form on the tour of England in 1953 but more in the first-class games than the Tests. In first-class games he scored 2,040 at 65.8 with 10 centuries, which put him up with Victor Trumper and Bradman. Yet in the Tests he was yeoman-like, scoring 346 at 34.6. His top score was a beautifully composed 122 at Manchester.

Australia lost the series. Harvey, who had been in the team in the all-conquering tour of 1948 and the team that held supremacy over England in 1950–51, now had to swallow the bitter pill of defeat in an Ashes series. This was repeated in 1954–55 although Harvey came out of the blocks determined to be part of the team that restored the urn of burnt bails, at least symbolically, to Australia. He smashed 162 at Brisbane and 92 not out at Sydney. After that, he fell victim to the speed of Frank Tyson and the fast off-spin of Bob Appleyard. His aggregate was 354 and he averaged 44.25. Australia lost again. Harvey had experienced the absolute historical highs under Bradman. Now he was feeling what it was like to be in a team battling and well below the best, which was England.

He was in fair touch in the domestic season of 1955–56, scoring 772 at 55.14, with three centuries. This consolidated his position in the squad for the 1956 tour of England, which he and most of his team-mates would prefer to forget. Rotten weather and poor pitches conspired to see him accumulate just 197 at 19.7. His best effort was a fighting 69 in four hours at Headingley. Australia and Harvey were destroyed by Surrey spin twins Jim Laker and Tony Lock. He had now gone through three straight Ashes defeats. The 1956 England team led by Peter May was formidable in both batting and bowling. It looked set for a long reign at the top.

Harvey found touch in 1956 on the way home against India, hitting 253 at 63.25. He had a top score of 140 at Bombay. It boosted his confidence against spin in fair conditions for both bowler and batsman. He was a natural dancer and loved going to the pitch of the ball, which he could do on true wickets.

•

Harvey, 29, was overlooked as captain in 1957–58 in favour of Ian Craig, 22, and for the first time struggled against South Africa, hitting just 131 at 21.83. Nevertheless, Australia won 3:0 against a strong home team. While Craig also failed with the bat, Richie Benaud, the all-rounder, had a fine series, averaging 54.83 with the bat and taking 30 wickets with his leg-spin at 21.93 runs apiece. When Craig was too ill to play in the 1958–59 Ashes it was Benaud with his recent record who took over as skipper against May's all-conquering England team. Harvey, who had further lessened his chances by moving to

Sydney to take up a job offer, was disappointed but pledged his support to Benaud. They both knew that the Australian team had to be at its best and harmonious to overcome the tourists. Personal accolades and positions were nothing as compared to beating England, which Benaud's team did, 4:0. Harvey played his part, scoring 291 at 48.5, which was close to his career average. His grand 167 in the Second Test at Melbourne was the dominant batting performance of the entire series.

On a tour of India and Pakistan in 1959–60, Harvey once more showed his masterful, attacking technique against spin, returning 273 at 54.6 versus Pakistan in three Tests, and 356 at 50.86 against India in five Tests. He hit two centuries, but his finest knock was a brilliant 96 on matting at Dacca against Pakistan.

Harvey was less successful against the talented West Indian line-up in 1960–61 featuring Wes Hall, Frank Worrell, Garry Sobers, Alf Valentine and Lance Gibbs. He struggled in three Tests to score 143 at 17.88 in eight innings and missed the last Test due to injury. Australia scraped in for a 2:1 victory. So far, as deputy to first Craig then Benaud, Harvey had been in six successive series victories. The next, to England in 1961, was most vital to Harvey and Benaud, who had hated the experience of losing the 1953 and 1956 Ashes. Their combined skills and leadership talent ensured a mighty tour for the Australians, who won the Ashes 2:1. Harvey led Australia to victory at Lord's in his one and only chance as skipper when Benaud had an injured shoulder. Harvey began the Tests with a polished 114 at Edgbaston and scored a commendable series aggregate 338 at 42.25. Only Bill Lawry, the best bat of either side for the series, did better. On tour, Harvey hit five centuries in an aggregate of 1,452 at an average of 44.

The Ashes success meant that Harvey had now competed in seven series for four wins and three defeats. He fronted for one more Ashes – in Australia in 1962–63 – and in a dull series drawn 1-all, Harvey was consistent, accumulating 395 at 39.5, including his specialty – one blockbuster innings. He hit 154 at Adelaide in a drawn game.

Harvey, 34, retired after 15 years at the top. He was never dropped from the Australian team and only missed selection through injury. His affable manner endeared him to all who played with and against him. In 79 Tests, Harvey scored 6,149 runs at 48.42, with 21 centuries, and 64 catches. He played in 306 first-class games, amassing 21,699 runs at 50.93 with 67 centuries.

Harvey pulled no punches while a player. In retirement, he gave his opinion when asked and was always direct and quotable. He left the game playing strongly and was most scathing about players who hung on too long. He was not a fan of sledgers. Harvey disliked players who in any way, off or on the field, lowered the game's standards or who did not play according to the spirit of cricket. Harvey could say easily that he was one player who left the game in a better condition than he found it. He expected everyone else to do the same regardless of the professionalism that had taken over cricket since he retired.

In 1998, he toured Australia celebrating 50 years since the Invincibles had their amazing tour of England. In 1999–2000 he was named by a Cricket Australia panel in the best Australian team of the 20th Century.

The crowning accolade for Harvey was to be selected by Bradman, the ultimate peer in the cricket fraternity, to bat next to him in a star-studded Australian 'dream' team chosen from all players since Tests began. It included five other Invincibles: Morris, Bradman, Miller, Lindwall and Tallon.

•

Harvey may have left Test cricket as much as four years too early in an era when players were constantly under pressure to combine their cricket with their working lives. He was just 19 when he set out on the boat to England in 1948. He often said that the experience made him as a cricketer and a man. Harvey went on to successful careers in marketing and promotions with a Sydney brewery, and in Tupperware, kitchen and cosmetics products. While in Johannesburg in 1949–50 he met Iris Greenish. They married four years later in Melbourne and had a son, Robert, and a daughter, Anne. In 1975 at 47, Harvey married his second wife Barbara. They live on Sydney's North Shore, and he still plays golf whenever possible.

Neil Harvey is proud he was fortunate enough to be one of the Invincibles.

Ian Johnson

Ian Johnson pulled his weight on the 1948 tour, making enough runs (543 at 30.16) and taking enough wickets (85 at an excellent 18.37) to justify his selection and claims as a bowling all-rounder. He excelled with his only century on tour at Taunton against Somerset. He loved walloping Laker and the MCC for a power-laden 80 against the MCC at Lord's. His 74 at Southampton against Hampshire (with Brown, 81) won the game when Australia had to come from behind. Johnson's best effort with the ball was against Leicester (7 for 42) and his best match performance was against Gloucester (11 for 100).

This was all at the first-class level. He struggled in the step-up to the Tests and was dropped for the last Ashes game at the Oval. The only consolation was that he took Hutton's wicket thrice, and twice before the England champion could take control of an innings. Nevertheless, from the prospective of the unbeaten record, he contributed in almost every game he played with either bat or ball, doing the donkey work with the ball (second only to Bill Johnston in number of overs). This allowed Lindwall and Miller to be fresh for the Tests.

•

Ian Johnson's career peaked when he was the 25th captain of Australia and had success in the West Indies and India. Unfortunately these outstanding efforts abroad were swamped by two failed Ashes contests at home in 1954–55 and away in 1956. Losses to England in mid-20th Century received more publicity. They are better recalled than the jubilant tours to far-off lands that allowed him to end with two more Test wins than losses. There was no TV or radio coverage of games in Barbados and Bombay. In Georgetown in the Third Test versus West Indies in 1955 Johnson himself took a career best 7 for 44 with his floating off-spinners that won the game. Such a feat in Australia against a powerful batting line-up boasting Clyde Walcott, Everton Weekes, Frank Worrell and Garry Sobers would have seen Johnson feted as a hero. But with no TV and therefore mass eyewitness of his performances as a player and skipper, the memories of the 1954–55 lost Ashes predominated. When Australia was beaten in the Ashes again in 1956, the humiliation of the weak batting performances reflected on the captain no matter how much events were pushed out of his control. Johnson's triumphant 2:0 win in India – never an easy assignment – on the way home from England did little to salvage the image of a beaten side in need of regeneration.

•

Johnson's father Bill, a Melbourne wine and spirit merchant, taught young Ian the fineries of off-spinning when he was in his early teens at Wesley College (the same alma mater as Sam Loxton). One particular ball, spun from the palm rather than the fingers, collected plenty of wickets and earned Johnson praise from Don Bradman. In our correspondence after Johnson died, Bradman said he regarded him as one of the better off-spinners he ever faced, and a 'good' rather than a 'great' player. He also saw him as a 'loyal' friend.

Ian Johnson (1917–98) made the South Melbourne seconds at 15 and the firsts at 16. The famous club was also home for Keith Miller and Lindsay Hassett. The lean, 178 cm Johnson's action – high jumping and looping – was distinctive. He could spin the ball best on Australia's harder pitches. Johnson put 'grunt' into each ball a half-century before Shane Warne's exhalations signalled energy expended. Like Warne, who spun the ball the other way, Johnson used flight as a weapon. He was less inclined than most 'offies' to hurry balls through low for fear of being belted. Johnson would rather gamble on bite and turn once the ball hit the deck from greater elevation. It was successful at home, in South Africa and the West Indies, but less so in England, although Johnson on tour always took wickets.

He made the Victorian side versus Tasmania in 1935–36 at just 18 and remained a State player for the next five seasons without the chance of advance. His spinning was less prodigious that the fine array of leg-spinners around in the 1930s. He was ranked behind Clarrie Grimmett, Bill O'Reilly, 'Chuck' Fleetwood-Smith and Frank Ward and missed the 1938 tour of England. Then war intervened and changed his life. In 1941, aged 23, Johnson joined the RAAF and flew Beaufighters with 22 Squadron. A year later he married Lal Park, the daughter of Dr Roy Park, who played one game for Australia. (Ian and Lal later had two sons, Bill and Bob.) In 1944 he was a flight-lieutenant, seeing action in the south-west Pacific.

After the war, at 28, he was selected for Australia versus New Zealand for the Test match of March 1946. He made 7 not out and didn't bowl for a team that also featured Hassett and Miller. They were with him when he made his Test debut against England in 1946–47 at Brisbane. Johnson made a spirited 47 and felt at home. Not only were two friends in the team. He had known Bradman for more than a decade. Ian's father Bill, who died in 1941, had been a national selector with Bradman. Young Johnson came to know him well.

In four games in 1946–47 he took 10 wickets at 30.60, with a best performance at Sydney in the Second Test when he took 6 for 42, including Len Hutton's wicket. Johnson, who could bat a bit, also collected 106 runs at 21.20. He maintained his bowling form against India in 1947–48 taking 16 wickets at 16.31, including 4 for 59 and 4 for 35 at Melbourne in the Third Test.

Johnson did well on the tour of South Africa in 1949–50 under Hassett where the harder wickets suited him better. His best effort was at Durban in the Third Test where he made 66 in Australia's first innings and took 5 for 34 in South Africa's second innings. Overall he took a creditable 18 wickets at 24.22. He had a mediocre series against England in Australia in 1950–51, taking just 7 at 44.43. His best performance was with the bat – 77 – at Sydney in the Third Test. He had another lean time in the next season at home against the West Indies, taking only 8 at 32.75.

Johnson, 35, was not chosen for the 1953 tour of England. When Hassett returned from that failed campaign he retired. At a dinner after practice at South Melbourne at the commencement of the 1953–54 season, Hassett asked Johnson what his plans were. The spinner had none. He didn't think he would make it back into Test cricket. Hassett told him not 'to die wondering' about a comeback.

'There's no reason why you couldn't be a candidate for the captaincy,' Hassett said. He reminded Johnson that he was 36 when appointed skipper. 'You've got no major injury worries. You could go on until you're 40. But you've got to have the desire. You must be fit and want it.'

Johnson listened without saying anything.

'But of course, if you don't want to be captain –' Hassett said.

'I do want it,' Johnson said with conviction.

After this 'heart to heart', Johnson was inspired to make a supreme effort to get super-fit. He trained hard, especially with sprints and boxing with South Melbourne footballers. He had a good season with Victoria and captained it with distinction. The betting was on recent New South Wales skippers Arthur Morris or Keith Miller to captain Australia against England in 1954–55, especially as they had been on the Ashes tour of 1953. But Miller was not in favour for reasons never fully explained, despite him being a highly regarded leader of his State. (Richie Benaud, for one, said that Miller was the best skipper he played under.)

Johnson was chosen not only to play for Australia, but to lead it. The move seemed inspired when Australia had a runaway victory at Brisbane in the opening Test. Johnson was injured and couldn't play in the Second Test, which England just won. Johnson returned for the Melbourne Test. He was unfortunate to run into a rampant Frank Tyson (7 for 27 in the second innings) on a cracked pitch. He destroyed Australia, which went down by 128 runs. It never recovered. Tyson had the side bluffed and struggling in the Fourth Test at Adelaide, which England won. The Fifth was drawn. Johnson had fair all-round figures, making 116 runs at a flattering average of 58, while taking a steady 12 wickets at 20.25.

The 1:3 series loss might have led to the skipper being sacked, but the following tour to the West Indies in early 1955 needed a diplomat at the helm. England's recent tour had seen riots at Georgetown where bottles had been thrown. It was thought that the English leadership could have handled it better.

Johnson, who had already instigated post-match, on-the-record chats with journalists, did the same in the West Indies.

He won the toss at Sabina Park, Kingston in the First Test. Australia batted attractively, but for some time into the second day. The crowd grew restless. Johnson, himself not out on 18, declared at 9 for 551. As he was walking off, he and his partner Bill Johnston were mobbed by small boys. One insisted on talking to Johnson. Instead of ignoring him, Johnson picked him up and carried him towards the pavilion, engaged in conversation. The crowd cheered. It was a far cry from the more aloof image presented by the English players. This, along with other gestures, endeared the Australians to the West Indians. There was also excellent off-field fraternity, especially with poker games among the players that went well into the night.

After winning the first game, the Australians were on top in the drawn Second Test at Trinidad, where Morris, Harvey and Colin McDonald each scored centuries, and Johnson 66. The Third Test at Georgetown, then British Guiana, was so decisively won by Australia, thanks to Johnson taking 7 for 44, that the locals didn't get a chance to disrupt a close finish, even if they had wished to. The Australians' demeanour, thanks to the tone set by their urbane, ever-gracious skipper, and the evident friendliness on and off the field with their West Indian counterparts, allowed the visit to a potential trouble-spot to go smoothly.

In the Fourth Test at Bridgetown, Barbados there was trouble of a different kind. Australia made a whopping 668 with Miller (137), Lindwall (118) and Archer (98) all in attacking touch. Then the West Indies was reduced to 6 for 147. Miller, on his own volition, dropped his pace about 15 km/h and bowled slow-medium swingers into a cross-wind. In one over he induced a nick behind from Weekes (44) and the dangerous Collie Smith (2).

Two players who Johnson thought would be more suspect to pace, West Indian captain Denis Atkinson and Clairemont Depeiza, were in and handling Miller's medium pace with apparent ease. The always cogitating bowler was working towards an error from one of them. Johnson asked Miller to bowl fast. He kept delivering at a reduced rate. The captain demanded pace.

'Give me some speed, Keith,' he said.

Miller refused. They had a 'chat' at the top of the bowler's mark.

'I'll say who bowls and what they bowl,' Johnson remarked. He took Miller off and put Lindwall on. The speedster was a little fatigued after his batting. He was loose. The batsmen attacked and were on top by stumps. The timing of the switch from Miller to Lindwall seemed wrong.

Miller, who thought he should have been captain for the tour, insulted his skipper in front of team-mates as they filed from the ground.

'You couldn't captain a team of schoolboys,' was one hostile put-down. Johnson waited until most players had left the shed. Then he invited Miller 'outside' to settle the matter in the time-honoured, yet crude manner of a punch-up. Miller, a much bigger man physically, realised his attacks had gone too far. He declined the offer. They continued to argue the issue back at their hotel. It simmered. The next day both men were more subdued as they set about trying to break what had become an unlikely but worrisome partnership. It reached gigantic proportions – 347 and a seventh-wicket Test record. Miller (2 for 113 of 22 overs) was off the boil and dispatched to all corners of the Kensington Oval. Lindwall, also not at his best, took 1 for 96 off 25. Benaud (3 for 73) finally removed Depeiza for 122 and Johnson (3 for 77) had his counterpart Atkinson for 219. The West Indies made 510. Australia scored 249 in its second innings. Johnson top-scored with 57. He perhaps erred again by batting too long and making the chase (408 to win) too difficult. The West Indies was in trouble at 6 for 234 when the game finished in a draw.

In the final Test, the differences between the captain and his brilliant all-rounder appeared settled. Miller was motivated. He turned on his best displays with bat and ball for the tour. Delivering pace and swing as directed this time, he took 6 for 107 in West Indies' first innings. When Australia batted he scored 109, backing up Archer 128 and Harvey 204.

Australia won by an innings and 82 runs, giving it and Johnson a 3:0 triumph against a strong side away. He had his best series, making 191 at 47.75, and taking 14 wickets at 29.00.

It was enough to ensure that, at 38 years of age, he would lead Australia to England for another Ashes battle. But important things had changed by mid-1956. England had developed into a powerful, well-balanced combination with its finest batting line-up in 20 years, and a formidable group of bowlers, including the lethal Surrey spin twins, Jim Laker and Tony Lock. Lindwall broke down on tour and was never fully fit. The wickets prepared were well below Test standard and suited England's spinners far more. This led to Australia's bats, especially its star Neil Harvey, under-performing. He averaged just 19.70, while only one Australian, opener Jim Burke, averaged 30 (30.11) in the worst returns ever for a touring team. No one scored a century in the Tests.

Laker and Lock helped Surrey beat Australia before the Tests. It set a pattern. The tourists seemed in the hunt after drawing the First and winning on a seamer's wicket at Lord's. But the spin twins demolished them in the Third and Fourth Tests at Leeds and Manchester. Laker took a world-record 19 for 90 on an Old Trafford dust bowl. He was more effective with his off-spin pushing the ball through lower and faster than Johnson. (On the figures of their careers, Johnson performed better than the England star on bouncier pitches.)

Australia went down 1:2. Johnson averaged just 7.63 from 61 runs, and took only six wickets at 50.50.

Yet it wasn't quite the end for Johnson, who led the psychologically battered Aussies on the home-coming tour via the subcontinent. Australia was humiliated by Pakistan on matting at Karachi, making just 80 (following the woeful 84 tally at Manchester), which took it nearly a day for the slowest batting in history. It was the first Test between the two countries. Johnson took his unhappy squad on to India for a three-Test contest. The captain, with a top score of 73 in the First Test at Madras, and aided by an in-form Lindwall (7 for 43 in the second innings) did most to secure an innings win. Johnson missed the drawn Second Test at Bombay through injury but was back in charge for the Third at Calcutta. Australia won by 94 runs thanks to Benaud, who took 11 for 105.

The Australians won the series 2:0 and allowed Johnson, approaching 39, to go home on a better note, although the crushing by England a few months earlier predominated in the minds of Australian cricket followers.

Johnson retired after 45 matches, managing the double of 1,000 runs – exactly – at 18.52, and 109 wickets at 29.19. In first-class cricket he played 189 matches, scoring 4,905 runs at 22.92 with two centuries, and taking 619 wickets at 23.30.

Throughout his captaincy, Ian Johnson put a positive spin on events. In down moments in Australian cricket, his diplomatic, mannered style did much for his country's image. Despite the negative public perception – engendered by Ashes losses – of teams he led, the records show that he was a more successful skipper than most.

Johnson was also one of the best off-spinners Australia ever produced. His Test figures would class him as good in any company, and his first-class returns placed him high in the list of Australia spinners (in terms of runs per wicket), ahead of more illustrious performers at the Test level, such as Richie Benaud and Shane Warne. In 45 Tests he captained 17 times, winning seven, losing five, and with five draws.

Ian Johnson was typical of several players on the 1948 tour, such as Brown, Hamence, McCool, Ring and Saggers who were steady contributors to the side's overall success.

Bill Johnston

Bradman was delighted with two surprise packets in 1948 – Neil Harvey with the bat, and Bill Johnston with the ball. The England tour has always been tough, and has accentuated the strengths and weaknesses of players more than at home. The tour, as it was before the 1980s, was always the most challenging season for a visiting team in the world. The games, even against second ranked teams, can be levellers especially if the weather intervenes. So the making of players, who were not necessarily destined for stardom, has always been a cause for celebration in the Australian camp. Bradman had few doubts about Harvey.

He was a gifted teenager with all the equipment, including the mentality, for a mighty career. Even if he had a mediocre 1948, he would have been persevered with. But as Bradman noted, he matured on tour and became one of Australia's finest ever players. That was on the cards, at some stage. Not on the cards were the magnificent performances of Harvey's fellow Victorian, Johnston. Whereas Harvey, with the brashness and confidence of youth, believed he would make it, Johnston older and perhaps wiser at 26, had no such certitude. Yes, he had taken 16 wickets in four Tests against India in 1947–48, at the wonderful, miserly cost per wicket of just 11.38. That happened to be the best return of all the Australian bowlers. But because the opposition was not considered strong, the figures were seen as a guide to capacities, not a confirmation of greatness. Harvey had that much more unnerving commodity 'potential'; Johnston was unknown quantity 'X' on English wickets, which had taken the shape of graveyards for many a promising medium-pacer over the decades. Gangling, loose-limbed big Bill, all 188 cm of him, which was a rare height in the 1940s, knew he had a fight for a Test spot. Miller, Lindwall, Toshack, McCool and Johnson were thought to have the edge on him. He expected to make up the numbers, and enjoy himself as the most popular man in a squad of outstanding characters. Johnston was funny, both verbally and physically. As Bradman noted, he was a most amusing personality 'who saw the lighter side of everything he did.' One of his party tricks was a yoga position of pushing both legs back over his head and around his neck – a pose that would make an Indian exponent of *Banda Pasmasana* green with envy.

He didn't make the team for the first game at Worcester. He did nothing special at Leicester in the second match, but shot to prominence with a match-winning 4 for 22 and 6 for 18 – 10 for 40 against Yorkshire in the third game. What intrigued Bradman was the fact that Johnson, on a wet and turning pitch, could wheel in with his left-arm and deliver spin to devastating effect. It was nothing new to Johnston. He had started as a tweaker as a teenager. Only on national selector Jack Ryder's advice did he turn to medium-pace swing after the war. Yet it demonstrated a huge advantage to the selectors: this player had intelligence, versatility and desire. He was flexible and confident enough to switch styles to suit the wicket. But the selection panel still had not slotted him in after his smashing effort against traditional rivals Yorkshire. As the run-down to the First Test continued, Lindwall, Miller, Toshack, Johnson and McCool were still going to make the side ahead of him.

Bill O'Reilly covering the tour observed that, 'As a bowler he has one failing – he hasn't a temper.' The implication was that if genial Bill hurled a few down with spite, he might be noticed more by the selection panel. But it wasn't Johnston's way. He would make it by skill alone or not at all. In any case, he was fired up after his success at Bradford. He persevered. McCool's injured spinning finger could not be trusted to take the demands of a five-day Test. His misfortune was Johnston's break. He played at Trent Bridge and took 5 for 36 and 4 for 147, a magnificent Ashes debut.

There is always a moment in a person's career – whether fireman or forester, surgeon or sailor – when he or she knows, instinctively that they are in the right job. Johnston knew without a second of doubt that after the first innings, when he sent back half the England bats, he had made it and would continue to do brilliant things at the highest level of the game. Johnston matched it wicket for wicket, performance for performance, with Lindwall, then the finest wicket-taker in the world.

Bradman noted that Johnston constantly removed top batsmen at Lindwall's rate, but that there was more glamour attached to 'Atomic Ray'. This was to be expected. Lindwall was a lethal paceman, who could blast out batsmen and intimidate anyone playing the game. Yet, at the end of the series, they both had 27 wickets, with Lindwall more economical but, over five Tests, not much more effective.

The captain delighted in Johnston's capacity to spin quickly and with a curving flight that was hard to counter. He was most pleased also with his, and Ernie Toshack's response to his batting instructions. They were both ungainly 'rabbits', who swung across the flight and had no impact as run-makers, or players who could stay at the wicket with a batsman to build a score at the end of an innings. Bradman told them to use their height and always push straight. This way they would be more difficult for opposition bowlers to remove. As ever, Bradman saw the heart of a problem and gave the simplest of answers to it: play down the line and stretch to the ball.

It worked in 1948, and so well in fact that in the Ashes in England five years later, Johnston was only dismissed once on the entire 1953 tour while scoring 102 runs from 17 innings with 16 not outs. This left him with the embarrassingly good average of 102, which of course, made a mockery of the importance of the numbers. But it confirmed Bradman's perspicacity.

'He entertained us [in 1953] with his batting and had a marvellous attitude,' Arthur Morris recalled, 'so when he got a few runs early in the tour we all decided he wasn't going to get out.'

Remarking on his century-plus average, Johnston said:

'Class always comes through eventually over an entire tour.'

•

Bill Johnston (1922–2007) was the son of a Victorian Western District dairy farmer. He was born in Beeac and raised in nearby Ondit. He attended Beeac Primary School, then Colac High. Early on, young Bill found he could throw small spheres – tennis, cricket and baseballs – further than any other kid in the region. It was a sweet confidence-builder to be the best at something. Doctors put it down to double-jointedness. This engendered a suppleness that allowed him to unwind and hurl a ball out of sight. In 1939 at 17, he set a world junior record for throwing a baseball 113 metres. At the same age, Johnston moved to Melbourne to play for the Richmond club, and spun his way from the thirds, with 6 for 16 in his first game, to the firsts in the space of a season. Johnston kept up his baseball skills and in 1939 hurled a ball 122 metres. He gained State cricket selection but, as with the majority of Bradman's squad of 1948, his career was curtailed by Hitler's marauding around Europe and Japan's folly in bombing Pearl Harbor in the Pacific. He joined the RAAF, spending four years as a radar technician in Northern Australia. In 1946 on the resumption of cricket, he morphed from adolescent left-arm orthodox spinner to mature medium-fast swinger. This came about when he was bowling to ex-Australian captain Jack Ryder. Johnston slipped in a faster delivery. The experienced ex-Test batsman asked him to deliver a few more. This handful of deliveries so impressed Ryder than he blackmailed young Johnston into delivering pace. His State elevation depended on it.

He was now 24, but still not convinced he should be other than a slow spinner. The matter was settled in the 1946–47 season when Bradman took him aside and said his best chance for Test selection was as a medium-pacer to back up the shock tactics of Lindwall and Miller.

Bradman told him to work on his accuracy and control. Johnston heeded the advice, spending hours on his own, working on his rhythm, length, variations, pace and Bradman's suggestions. At the beginning of the 1947–48 season, Johnston's hard work paid off in the Victoria versus India match. He knocked over the first three wickets in the Indian innings. It gained him selection in the Tests. He took 5 for 48 in the Second Test and 6 for 77 in the Third. These efforts and further success in State games allowed him to book his trip to England in 1948. Johnston followed up that fabulous season with a successful tour of South Africa, returning the best figures in the Tests – 23 wickets at 17.04. He was again dominant in the 1950–51 Ashes, taking 22 wickets at 19.18, and once more in the series against the West Indies (23 wickets at 22.09). Johnston was the workhorse in the 1952–53 series versus South Africa, taking far more wickets than the next bowler – 21 – but at his most expensive since he broke into the Test side: 35.10 runs each. A knee injury slowed him up in the 1953 Ashes, but he was back to his best against England in 1954–55, taking 19 at 22.26 in four Tests. He retired in 1955 after breaking down with that troublesome knee on the West Indies tour.

'There isn't a bowler in the world today who would come within cooee of him,' great Australian left-arm medium-fast bowler Alan Davidson said of his mentor.

'If he was having a good day in the field you'd hear his chuckle, which began like a belly laugh and finished up sounding like a kookaburra. He used to entertain us with all sorts of bird calls. When he bowled someone, he exclaimed, "Fantasmagorical!"'

'In 1948 we thought we were playing with 13 players,' Neil Harvey observed. 'We reckoned Bradman was worth two and Bill Johnston was worth two [because of his ability to bowl pace and spin with equal facility].'

Morris rated his bowling as highly as anyone he played with.

Johnston's first-class career ranged over nearly a decade from 1945–54. He took 554 wickets at 23.35, and made 1,129 runs at 12.68. He played in 40 Tests, taking 160 wickets at 23.91, which placed him among the very best of Australia's Tests bowlers in history. He pushed forward and nudged his way to just 273 runs at a modest 11.70 runs an innings, which may have been far more modest had he not heeded Bradman's instructions. He took 16 catches.

•

Johnston's work after cricket was in sales and marketing of footwear. Later he was a publican and ran a post office. He and wife Judith (who died in 2004) had two sons, Peter, and David, the Chief Executive of the Tasmanian Cricket Association.

'He [Johnston] was pleased to see today's cricketers getting something out of the game,' David commented. 'His generation did it pretty tough, having to take time off work to tour.'

•

Wisden named him as one of its Five Cricketers of the Year of 1948, along with Hassett, Lindwall, Morris and Tallon. (Bradman had been so named for 1930, and Brown for 1938.)

Wisden declared:

'No Australian made a greater personal contribution to the playing success of the 1948 side than wiry William Arras Johnston.'

He was a worthy recipient of this accolade, but such citations were not nearly as important to him as being an Invincible.

'It was a special privilege to have been part of that team,' he said, 'and I enjoyed every second of the experience.'

If talent and popularity were weighted, Bill Johnston came out on top in the 1948 tour group.

Ray Lindwall

Bradman gave Lindwall 10 out of 10 for his magnificent 1948 tour. The captain had set him to destroy England's batting line-up and he carried out those wishes more often than not. Bradman had targeted Hutton, and Lindwall was the man, with fierce support at times from Miller, who put paid to Hutton having a winning influence on the Ashes. In the skipper's eyes, the paceman built on his strengths through the tour until a point where the finest judge of a player – Bradman himself – ranked him in mid-20th Century with Australia's Ted McDonald of a generation earlier.

The captain particularly liked the way Lindwall used his brain. Even though the speedster was capable of intimidation with lethal throat-ball bumpers, he varied his pace to stunning effect, once bowling Hutton with a slower ball on the fourth delivery of the match.

Lindwall was all rhythm, length and control of direction, very much in the Larwood/McDonald moulds, with a lower arm action than those two, which he accentuated on occasions to bounce the batsman, or simply for variety.

In 1948, he was also an asset in the field in several positions, including slips. He took several superb catches, which kept Australia in the game and the pressure on England. He also batted with verve. Bradman believed he may have made Test cricket as a batsman alone had be concentrated on it.

Lindwall, with Morris, Bradman, Barnes and Johnston were the core players who dominated in the 1948 Tests.

•

Ray Lindwall (1921–96) was inspired at age 11 to bowl speed by England's Harold Larwood when he mowed down the Australia's finest with Bodyline bowling in the 1932–33 season. The Marist Brothers at two Catholic schools – Kogarah and Darlinghurst – helped him refine his bowling and outstanding batting. Lindwall was a natural athlete – destined to play Rugby League as well as Test cricket. Later at St George, the uncompromising but astute Bill O'Reilly nudged him further along the road to stardom by ordering him to lengthen his run and let rip with the ball. O'Reilly made him bat last, which affronted the teenager. But the wily old spinner knew what counted most if you wished to play Test cricket. A youth had to make up his mind early to develop one skill above all others. By all means he could grow as an all-rounder. But the best way into the State side and then Test team in the middle of the 20th Century was to shine at one and worry about the secondary skill coming on later.

O'Reilly was thinking first about what was best for St George. It needed a speedster to tear in and put the wind up batsman so that the leg-spinner could come on and remove the shaken batsmen left. This just happened to be the best route forward for Lindwall. His batting was good, but he may not have been assured of making it to the top.

Lindwall was demonic with the ball. But it was controlled, intelligent demonology. His bumper was lethal. His yorker was nigh unplayable. Lindwall concentrated on a magnificent out-swinger for the first decade of his first-class career. After a season in the Lancashire League in the mid-1950s, he came home with a terrific in-swinger. No great batsman of the era knew how to handle him. Bradman only faced him in two innings in a testimonial match at the MCG in December 1948, when he made 123 and 10 and was not dismissed by the paceman. Yet everyone else – all the greats of the 1940s and 1950s including Harvey, Morris, Walcott, Worrell, Weekes, May, Cowdrey, Graveney, Hutton and Compton – were uncomfortable and never felt 'in' against him.

The death of his father, a Water Board employee, caused Lindwall to forgo university and take an office job in 1940. He made the State side at the beginning of the 1941–42 season at age 20, but his career was stopped before it started. War broke out. Lindwall joined the army in the Ack Ack and Fortress Signals unit, which was sent to New Guinea. He was fortunate not to be killed when the Japanese bombed Port Moresby. But he was unfortunate to catch tropical dengue fever and malaria. It didn't stop him being picked for New South Wales in 1945–46 when Shield cricket resumed after the war.

Despite being weakened by those diseases, Lindwall the promising youth before the war was now a war-hardened man. It showed in his bowling. Described as 'poetic' because of his run-up and rhythm, he now had a 'killer' instinct, which was more than a cliché when used to portray his powers with a hard leather ball. With encouragement from O'Reilly, he used the bouncer judiciously and enjoyed softening up or intimidating batsmen. Bradman had a look at him and made sure he was in the Test side against England in 1946–47. The Australian skipper was delighted to have a class speed weapon at his disposal for the first time. Lindwall took 18 wickets at 20.39. He also crashed a terrific even 100 in the Third Test at the MCG, scoring 160 at 32.00 for the series.

He maintained this level of performance against India a year later, taking 18 at 16.88. He and Miller, who was also never shy about delivering bouncers, formed a menacing pace duet – the best for Australia since the brief ascendancy of Jack Gregory and Ted McDonald in the 1920s. On tour in South Africa in 1949–50, Lindwall was ill and injured and did not live up to expectations, taking 12 wickets at 20.66. At 29 years in 1950–51, he fought back for another Ashes encounter and contributed to Australia's fifth successive post-war series success, taking 15 wickets at 22.93. The following year he was in a bumper war with the West Indies. Some considered it the most hostile bowling since Bodyline, although comparisons were odious. Lindwall didn't use eight men on the leg-side. Nevertheless, it heralded an era where all opposing countries would seek pacemen with a bit of devil in them.

Lindwall secured 21 wickets at 23.04 and made 211 runs at 26.37 in the 1951–52 series. He had now been dominant and Australia's best bowler in six series wins in the period 1946–52.

Lindwall took his wife Peggy (whom he married in May 1951) to England where he played a season with Nelson in the Lancashire League. While there, their first child Raymond Robert was born.

Lindwall returned to Australia for the 1952–53 season versus South Africa and kept up his high returns with 19 wickets at 20.16. But at 31, he was finding it tougher to overcome injuries, particularly to the knee and groin, and recurring bouts of the fevers that troubled him after the war. Yet still he lifted for the Ashes contest of 1953, taking 26 wickets at 18.85 to match his fine performances on the last England tour in 1948. It was not Lindwall's fault that Australia was in decline after the series loss 0:1. He maintained his dominance for the eighth successive series.

He ran into inevitable criticism after the next Ashes series in Australia, in 1954–55, which was lost 1:3. Lindwall, now 33, took only 14 wickets at 27.21. Even his old mentor, Bill O'Reilly turned on him and called for his dumping in favour of a younger player. Some were drafted in beside him and his sparring partner Miller, but the old-stagers still produced in the early 1955 series in the West Indies. Both took 20 wickets, Lindwall at 31.85 and Miller at 32.05. This was a terrific performance, considering the mighty batting line-up to which they delivered. Apart from the three Ws – Weekes, Worrell and Walcott – there were the up-and-coming young Garry Sobers and Collie Smith.

Lindwall also scored a dashing 118 at Bridgetown, which boosted his aggregate to 187 and 37.40. (Miller hit 439 at 73.17.) While he was on tour, Peggy gave birth to their second child, Carolyn.

At 34, during the 1956 Ashes in England, injuries and slow spinners' pitches caused Lindwall to hit a wall for the first time in his illustrious career. He took just seven wickets at 34. Things didn't improve for him on the way home at Karachi versus Pakistan on matting. But in India in the three Tests he showed his toughness in trying conditions by being one of the last bowlers standing. On wickets again far more conducive to spin than pace, he took 12 wickets at 16.58, which was second only to leg-spinner Benaud, who took 23 at 16.87.

•

Lindwall took over as captain of Australia at Brabourne Stadium, Bombay under trying conditions. It was the Second Test against India in October 1956. Not only was it exceedingly hot; his was a patchwork team of crocks. The tour skipper Ian Johnson, Keith Miller and Ron Archer were injured and out. Alan Davidson had a stomach upset. Fellow paceman Pat Crawford strained his hip, while spinner John Wilson (after his one and only Test) pulled a muscle. Benaud had a fever and couldn't bowl for part of the game. Only Lindwall himself, and medium-pacer Ken Mackay were happily upright and ready to bowl.

'I was a captain without bowlers,' Lindwall recalled. 'Burke and Harvey made centuries, enabling me to close with seven down and a good lead [of 272]. Over 1,000 runs were scored in the game but the bowlers could not average five wickets a day.'

Somehow, Lindwall's forceful captaincy managed to squeeze efforts out of all his walking wounded. India scored 251 in its first innings. But in the home team's second dig, the Australians could only remove half the side. The game fizzled to a draw. Lindwall, then 35 and the greatest Australian pace bowler of the immediate post-war era, proved an inspiring leader. In another era, he may have been the player chosen to break the convention of not appointing a speed-man as captain. But like his pal Keith Miller, it was not to be. (They had to be content with showing their leadership talents at the State level. Lindwall did that with distinction for Queensland for the last five years of his first-class career.)

•

At 36, he was finally dumped for the 1957–58 series in South Africa. It came as a shock. Lindwall lived for cricket. He considered he was still the best Australian fast bowler. But the selectors, going for youth, thought his time had come. Lindwall followed the South African series with interest. He noted that only Alan Davidson among the speedmen, with 25 wickets at 17, was worthy of selection in front of him. Throughout the long winter of 1958 Lindwall trained like a young boxer, with skipping rope, bike, running and exercises. This gallant effort was rewarded during the series against England in 1958–59. He came back for the last two Tests and broke Clarrie Grimmett's Australian wicket-taking record of 216. Limited opportunities saw him take seven Test wickets at 29.86. Yet the season's figures of 40 wickets at 20.55 demonstrated just what an effort the 37-year-old champion had made.

•

It was enough for his final Test tour – of India and Pakistan. At 38, he lifted his wicket tally in 61 Tests to 228 at 23.03. His run tally was 1,502 at 21.15. This made him the first player ever to score 1,500 runs and take 200 wickets in Tests.

Lindwall played 228 first-class matches, scoring 5,042 runs at 21.82 with five centuries. He took 794 wickets at 21.35.

He and Peggy settled well into a florist business in Brisbane and he put something back into the game by coaching. He died in June 1996, aged 74.

•

Ray Lindwall ranks with Dennis Lillee and Glenn McGrath as one of the best of the Australian pacemen in the history of cricket, and his capacities were seen at their peak in 1948.

Bradman was forever grateful to him for his courage and huge contribution.

Sam Loxton

Energy, courage, drive and determination. These were necessary ingredients to carry through the 1948 eight months tour with hardly an hour to draw breath between engagements for much of the schedule. If there had not been a Sam Loxton to fit into the squad, Bradman would have had to invent one. His selection was criticised by one reporter as 'the worst Australian international cricketer ever to come to England'. Loxton, with the pugilist's look, and a demeanour in any contest to match, proved this wrong from the first practice session to the last game of the tour. He was spurred by this slur before he even bowled or hit a ball. He didn't think he had a chance to play in the Tests, and was especially daunted when he read the Australian line-up for the First Test. In front of him for a batting spot was just about the best top six Australia had ever had in a dressing room together. The bowling line-up was formidable too, and as Loxton, a battling all-rounder, was neither fish nor fowl, not a dominant Test batsman or in the top four bowlers, it was difficult to see how he could squeeze into the side. While Keith Miller, one of the world's most talented all-rounders, was in touch and fit, there was always somebody blocking his run for glory.

But the characteristic that Bradman loved most in Loxton was his fight. Ashes Tests were often won not on brilliance, but belligerence, persistence, desire and chance or luck. Loxton got his chance by the usual permutations that occur in an Ashes series, including loss of form, injury and team balance. Lindwall's tricky groin and Miller's dodgy back triggered Loxton's opportunities. The Australian selectors needed a workhorse to step in if one or both broke down. Loxton was the choice. By the end of the Second Test, Lindwall and Miller were a day-to-day proposition, and Loxton was a 'must' for the Third Test at Manchester. There were bonuses that persuaded Bradman, Hassett and Morris. Loxton could bat. He had shown this from his debut first-class game for Victoria against Queensland, when he scored 232 not out. Only 10 other cricketers had begun at the first-class level with a double century in the history of cricket. That marked him immediately, if not as special, then at least as capable with the blade. The other factor was his brilliant fielding. This would not win him a Test place, but was a bonus for the team once he was in. Loxton lurking in the covers or anywhere was an extra pressure on batsmen, especially as his reputation in the field had preceded him into the Test arena after his efforts against the counties. He ran himself ragged in the field in England's first innings at Manchester, bowled steadily, and was unlucky to miss taking a wicket. His first Ashes innings was 36, a more than commendable effort in a tight, tense game with Australia in trouble. In the Fourth

Test, his whirlwind 93 would rank as a tour highlight, especially as the runs were made when Australia was battling and behind. His 3 for 55 were good figures, and again he could have had more fortune. But Loxton was not one to moan about dropped catches or bad umpiring decisions. He made light of them, forced his own luck, and believed in the adage that it shone on the courageous. He was hardly thrown the ball at the Oval with Lindwall in the form of his life. By the time Loxton batted the tension in the game had gone, along with England's chances for a win.

As well as holding a Test place, Loxton had a fine season overall, running fifth in the batting after 22 matches with 973 runs, including three centuries, at an average of 57.23. He took 32 wickets at 21.71.

Loxton, the character and cricketer, added significantly to the backbone of the tourists, in terms of his steady performances and determination. When Bradman mentioned a strength of his 1948 team being its bulldog courage, he had Sam Loxton in mind.

•

Loxton was born at Albert Park in Melbourne in 1921, and educated at Yarra Park and Armadale State Schools, and four years at Wesley College. His father, an electrical engineer and former Collingwood club cricketer, was the scorer for Prahran Third XI. His mother made afternoon tea for the club for 25 years, and Sam was permanent 12th man. The experience gave him a taste for the game.

As well as being viewed as a future Test cricketer, Loxton was an outstanding schoolboy Australian Rules footballer. In 1938 he played for the Prahran club and the Victorian Colts, the breeding ground for State and Test cricketers. War intervened. Loxton joined the army in the armoured or tank division, and was stationed later in Queensland 'waiting for the Japanese', who never quite made it. During the war years, he played top football for St Kilda alongside Keith Miller. Loxton played 41 games from 1940–46. His best effort at full forward was 8 goals against George Gneil of Geelong. Loxton also liked to relate with a laugh that he also managed an extraordinary 1 goal 13 behinds, 'with four other shots going out-of-bounds'. That game was against Richmond. His full-back opponent was George Smeaton. Richmond's legendary 'Captain Blood' Jack Dyer was playing in that game. Loxton remembers lining up to kick for goal when Dyer ran past and said to Smeaton:

'Good on you, George. He won't kick this one either.'

Loxton made his Test debut at Melbourne against India in the Fifth Test during the 1947–48 series. It was a first rate beginning, in which he made 80 and took 2 for 61 and 1 for 10.

'I would have got a few more,' Loxton joked, 'if bloody Miller had been awake in slips! He dropped a couple of sitters.'

It was enough to secure Loxton a position in the squad to tour England in 1948. He went with the team to South Africa in 1949–50, and did well with the bat, scoring 255 (with a century) and at average of 42.50. He was sixth choice with the ball behind Johnston, Johnson, Miller, Lindwall and McCool, and had few opportunities, taking 2 for 104 from 34 overs. His form did not hold in the 1950–51 Ashes in the three Tests he played, and after that his career at the top of the game was over, although he played another decade for Victoria. He capped off his career by managing the Test team to India and Pakistan in 1959–60, and saddled up for one game on the tour.

Towards the end of his cricket career he was a popular federal Liberal member of parliament, and kept his seat for 24 years. Cricket was not far away, however. He served as a national selector from 1970–81, and began this side-bar career with Bradman and Harvey determining both Ian Chappell's Australian team, and a World team to compete against them in 1971–72. This was the season that Bradman stopped an all-white South African team from touring Australia during the Apartheid era. Bradman's veto meant that a team had to be found or the

1971–72 season would become a huge financial disaster for the Australian Cricket Board. Bradman, Loxton and Harvey chose a multi-racial, international squad, with Garry Sobers as captain. The tour was a success.

Loxton and Harvey are proud of their selections and tell the story of Dennis Lillee's selection. Bradman sent them round Australia in the 1970–71 season in search of a fast bowler to counter England's John Snow. They reported that a young bloke name Lillee was 'quick'. Bradman hadn't heard of him.

'Does he know where they [the balls he delivers] are going?' Bradman asked.

'No,' Loxton replied.

'He doesn't?'

'Look at it this way,' Loxton said, 'if he doesn't know where they are going, the batsman certainly won't.'

Lillee was chosen for the Adelaide Sixth Test of a seven-Test series. He got his first wicket, a tired John Edrich on 130, with score at 1 for 276. Loxton sat with Bradman in the Adelaide members and was waiting for Bradman to say something about the Lillee selection, but he didn't comment. The raw speedster went on to an excellent start taking 5 for 84 in England's score of 470.

At the end of England's innings, Loxton said:

'Not bad, 5 for 84.'

'Yes,' Bradman said, 'and that's the best he will probably do too.'

(Lillee went on to be one of the finest pacemen of all time. Bradman chose him to open the bowling in his world all-time dream team.)

In a first-class career spanning 13 years from 1946–59, Loxton had a first rate record. He made 6,249 runs at 36.97, including 13 centuries; he took 232 wickets at 25.73, and held 83 catches. At the Test level, he had 12 games, keeping up his batting average (36.93) from 554 runs. He took eight wickets at 43.62, and held seven catches.

•

Loxton married his first wife, Gladys, during the war and they were together eight years. He married his second wife Carol in 1952, and they had two boys, Michael and Peter. She made the remark:

'Sam never had affairs, he married them.'

They divorced in 1976, and a year later he married third wife Jo. She died of a heart attack on 13 December 2000, the same tragic day that Loxton's son Michael was taken by a shark in Fiji.

Loxton lives on the Gold Coast in Queensland, and is often called on to speak about his cricket career and the Invincibles.

•

In 1948, Bradman thought Loxton did a 'magnificent' job as a utility player. He liked his physical strength and admired his powerful drive. Bradman judged him the best player of the lofted drive of that era. He would have sent balls into orbit with the bats of the 21st Century. Bradman found him a 'tremendous' fighter. The skipper liked his workhorse capacities, and the fact that he could turn on fast bowling spells that worried the best bats in the opposite camp. Bradman thought highly of his fielding, saying he had the strongest ever throwing arm when off balance.

Sam Loxton was a strong link in the Invincible cricket machine of 1948. And he loved the experience.

Colin McCool

Bradman said leg-spinner Colin McCool was the unluckiest player in the 1948 squad. His split spinning finger allowed him to bowl in short bursts, but would tear open when put through more strenuous sessions. There was no doubt that Bradman favoured him for the Test side. It was obvious from the very first net practice at Lord's in the wet, cold days of mid-April. Bradman spent time showing him how to bat on slow England wickets. The instruction went on for a few minutes only; the captain's time was precious. If he singled out a player so early in the tour for comment, assistance or a strategy, a lot of thought was behind it. McCool was being groomed for a big 1948 Ashes. He would be Bradman's number-one spinner; he would bat as high as No. 7, and be followed in by Tallon and Lindwall, making it the most brilliant batting line-up Australia ever assembled.

Bradman was gambling on a repeat of McCool's fine form in the 1946–47 Ashes, when he returned a fine double: 18 wickets at 27.28, and 272 runs at 54.40, including scores of 104 not out and 95. If he could repeat anything like that he would be a success. But that bad third finger on his right hand put paid to that possibility.

Instead McCool was forced into a more than useful secondary role along with Hamence, Ring, Saggers and Brown, who between them had just four Tests. Yet still, he performed excellently on tour when his injury allowed, taking 57 wickets at 17.82. But his batting let him down. He scored just 306, with a top score of 76 at an average of 20.40. Bradman concluded that the UK's slower wickets, which needed more back-foot play than the harder Australian pitches, were not ideal for McCool's style.

•

Colin McCool (1916–86) was born at Paddington, Sydney and attended Crown Street Primary, which had also been Victor Trumper's first school, then Moore Park, a traditional cricket nursery close to the Sydney Cricket Ground. McCool followed further in Trumper's footsteps by playing for the Paddington club, captained by Alan McGilvray, a friend of Bradman who first alerted him to the young all-rounder's skills and temperament.

McCool had a near-perfect leg-spinner's delivery, which was often more round-arm than over-arm, and allowed him more leverage and biting turn. He was selected for Bill O'Reilly's Invitation XI, which toured northern New South Wales (and included Sid Barnes and Ron Saggers). The experience under O'Reilly was a tough one. He found 'Tiger' the most bad-tempered of all cricketers, and the hardest man he met on a cricket field. Off the field, it was different. The great man was opinionated but more accommodating.

McCool progressed to the State Second XI and Colts, and made his debut at 23 with the State firsts in the 1939–40 season.

The game that stuck in his mind forever was the last first-class match of that season when New South Wales played 'Rest of Australia' captained by Bradman. With the outstanding line-up of bowlers – including Lush, Cheetham, and two excellent leg-spinners in Pepper and O'Reilly, McCool was lucky to bowl. But when he did in the second innings, he was expensive, taking 1 for 51. Yet he took five catches, four in slips. One of them was Bradman. McCool could hardly believe it. He worshipped Bradman, and could remember a decade earlier crawling under the fence at Sydney to watch his heroes – Bradman, Archie Jackson and Stan McCabe – play.

'To see the back of the Don,' he said, 'and being a part of it, was a surreal experience.'

War intervened and McCool joined the RAAF, flying transporters to New Guinea and the Pacific. The break made him think about cutting his losses in cricket. He thought that if he stayed in New South Wales, with Pepper and O'Reilly at least in front of him for selection, he would have no chance of making the national side. McCool decided to move to Queensland for the truncated 1945–46 season. He played in the historic State game versus South Australia at Adelaide over Christmas. This was Bradman's first game for several years, and he was said to be a shadow of his former self. If he failed in this game, he might not return to cricket.

Every Queensland bowler wished to be the one to dismiss the Don early and so make a name for himself. But Bradman did just enough, scoring 68 and 52 not out to suggest he could make a comeback. Despite this, McCool stole the show with one of the best all-round performances ever in Australian first-class cricket. He took 7 for 106, including Bradman's wicket caught by Tallon, in South Australia's first innings. (It was 1 for 110 in its second innings.) McCool next proceeded to smash 172, which *Wisden* observed, 'scattered the field . . . with a wide variety of strokes'.

McCool's wonderful understanding with keeper Tallon (who caught four and stumped one of the leg-spinner's victims) was the beginning of one of the most compelling spinner/keeper relationships in Australian cricket history.

McCool may have felt a moment of despair when he realised that O'Reilly (retired after the New Zealand Test) and Pepper (playing in the Lancashire League) would not block his path in New South Wales. But this would have been quickly overcome when he experienced the rapport with the country's finest ever keeper.

That magnificent double effort in front of Bradman was just about the perfect audition for the 1946–47 Ashes, in which McCool excelled.

After the disappointment of 1948, he toured South Africa, and although restricted by his finger problem, still managed to play in the five Tests in a strong all-round effort. He made 134 from 6 innings with a top score of 49 not out and an average of 33.50. He took 13 wickets at 20.62. Had it not been for the amazing intervention of spinner Jack Iverson, he would have played in the 1950–51 Ashes. He also missed out against the West Indies in the following season and South Africa in 1952–53.

In 1953, aged 36 and with a family, he decided to quit Australia, and try his hand as a professional cricketer in the Lancashire League (playing for East Lancashire) for three seasons. In 1956 he was lured back into first-class cricket, playing for Somerset. The West Country side recruited widely in a successful attempt to rise up the championship table after being on the bottom for four years. McCool was a success – with the bat, scoring the largest number of runs – 1,644 (including two hundreds) at the second-best average: 34.25. His injured finger would not allow him more than bursts of leg-spin, but he still secured 45 wickets at 31.40. McCool returned similar figures in 1957, '58, '59, and '60, with a peak in 1959 when he scored 1,599 runs at 39.97 and collected 49 wickets at 28.63. With the help of Australian Bill Alley, McCool was a key figure in the wet summer of 1958 when Somerset rose to third on the championship table in its best season since 1892.

•

McCool retired after the 1960 season in England at age 43, completing a grand career spanning 21 years. He scored 12,420 runs at 32.85, including 19 centuries and snared 602 wickets at 27.48, which were among the best returns ever for an all-rounder. In another era he would have played many more Tests than his 14. Yet his Test figures were consistent with his first-class returns – 459 runs at 35.30, and 36 wickets at 26.61, and 14 catches.

Colin McCool returned to Australia and retired to Umina on the Central Coast of New South Wales. His entire career demonstrates that nothing like the best of this outstanding cricketer was seen in 1948 when he was an unsung hero. Despite this, there were few more worthy players among the Invincibles.

Keith Miller

Keith Miller sacrificed his chance to attain the heights in the UK in 1948 with the bat by opening the bowling with Lindwall. This was not a new situation. He had been a front-line bowler for four years since the middle of the Victory Tests in England in 1945, when he began, more or less, to take his speed seriously. Nothing much was planned or trained for by Miller. He was whimsical, instinctive and emotional by nature. He was also incredibly gifted at all aspects of cricket (and Aussie Rules). He had *wanted* to be a batsman, just as Lindwall had early in his career. But by bowling in 1948 and with so many other top bats – Morris, Barnes, Bradman, Harvey and Hassett–performing well, there was not that much for Miller to do. He showed his mettle at Leeds in the Fourth Test with 58 when a kick-start to the innings was needed. He lifted at Lord's, the ground he loved most in the world. In his first return there since the Victory Tests, he compiled a dashing 163 in May against the MCC. Again at Lord's in the second innings of the Test he demonstrated his batting prowess with 74. Then there was that unconquered double century against Leicester in the second game of the tour. There were also the odd cameos – hard-hitting bursts – to belt Australia out of trouble, such as his 34 at Bradford early in May.

But in general in the Tests he fell well below his capacities with just 184 in seven Tests at a disappointing 26.28, about half what would have been expected of him. When his back was not playing up, he gave strong support to Lindwall, especially in attempts to shake up the England bats, particularly its champions Hutton, Compton and Washbrook. Yet it was Johnston that was called upon more to support Lindwall as both an attacking bowler and a workhorse. Miller only had any impact in the First and Fifth Tests. Even then he was not as effective as the other two bowlers.

But still he did enough to be a factor in Australia's supremacy, in slips as much as anything else. His ability to take the near-impossible catch at critical times was team-lifting. In terms of the tourists' eventual record he was vital on occasions when Australia looked in trouble. And his figures for the tour as a whole with 1,088 runs and 56 wickets cheaply added to his impact.

Miller's alleged difficulties with Bradman in 1948, blown to unreal proportions by some journalists who knew the facts, and some who did not, was symptomatic of something deeper with Miller, who was trouble for future Australia captains Hassett and Johnson at times. Miller hated authority figures of any kind, mainly because of clashes he had in the armed services.

1948 did not see the best of Miller, who over time would become Australia's best all-rounder ever. No one (with the exception of Adam Gilchrist – another kind of 'all-rounder') has come near him for his effectiveness in two facets of the game (and that's not including Miller's luminescence in the field).

Bradman's appreciation of Miller as expressed in his book *Farewell to Cricket* was diplomatic yet coded. He called him 'volatile', which was a euphemism for difficult and unfocused. Bradman referred to the all-rounder's attempts to hits sixes with 'abandon', which was code for him being undisciplined. He praised his bowling as 'dangerous' and judged him the best slips fieldsman in the world that year. Bradman compared him to the 'crowd-pleasing personality' of Jack Gregory (a paceman of the 1920s) and noted his limitations due to his incapacity to stay focused. This lack of concentration was not altogether an uncommon fault for all-rounders. At some point, one aspect of their game would suffer through fatigue.

•

The 1948 Ashes tour was Miller's worst Test series and an anomaly in an outstanding career. He was a hero and role model to a generation of cricketers and spectators after the war. He matched his film star looks and an athlete's physique with skills good enough to win Tests with bat or ball, or even simply as an extraordinary fielder. Miller was admired too by opposition on the field. Batsmen feared him, especially when he decided to bounce them. And bowlers were worried if he was in the mood with the bat to bounce them – over the fence. But there was more to Miller than cricketing heroics. He was a flamboyant individual; a one-off, who played the game in a spirit that mixed up the ages. He never bent the rules to his advantage, and played cricket with a brilliance that caused observers like Neville Cardus, who saw cricket's Golden Age early in the 20th Century, to compare him with Victor Trumper.

Yet Miller had the devil in him more in keeping with the most intimidating bowlers of the late 20th Century, such as Dennis Lillee and Malcolm Marshall. With his theatrical flick of his ample black hair, he could move in from any length run-up and deliver ferocious bouncers. They reminded observers of Bodyline deliveries aimed at the batsman that could bruise or intimidate. Once, at Nottingham in 1948, he was booed from the ground for his aggression with the ball. Another time, in 1951–52 against the West Indies, he was attacked even by friendly commentators for his overuse of the bouncer in tandem with his speed partner Ray Lindwall. Yet Miller took it all with an apparent nonchalance that brought him legendary status during the war.

Contrary to myth, Miller's wartime achievements did not come from his capacities as a night fighter pilot. He only served on two bombing missions in the very last days of the war in Europe in May 1945. The legend was built around his amazing fortune in surviving crashes, bombs clinging to his plane, overshot runways, and disabled planes. He was also lucky not to be in places where bombs were dropped in England.

The phrase, 'Miller's Luck' was coined because of these many incidents in which the odds were against his survival.

The upshot of those experiences meant that he was hardly going to be upset by a mindless mob or a commentator while playing sport after the war. Miller was also left with a nervous disposition, which on occasions translated into an adrenaline rush with bat or ball which would have an impact on any game he was in.

•

Keith Ross Miller (1919–2004) was named after two famous Australian aviators, Sir Ross and Sir Keith Smith, and this 'branding' seemed to destine him. He was always adventurous. Brought up in Sunshine then Elsternwick in Melbourne, Miller, the son of an engineer and teacher, was an outstanding sport at his school, Melbourne High. As a young teenager he was known as a talented, aggressive performer on cricket and Australian Rules football fields. He made up for his lack of height with vigour, courage and skill. At 16 he was just under 5 ft (150 cm). His ambition was to be a jockey and win the Melbourne Cup. A year later, that dream was in tatters as he reached more than 6 ft (183 cm) and grew an amazing 30 cm (13 in) in 13 months. The nearest he came to racing horses after that was as a punter and a mate of the great Australian jockey Scobie Breasley and many others.

Miller joined South Melbourne Cricket Club at 16. At 18 in February 1938, he made his first-class debut for Victoria against Tasmania (not yet in the Sheffield Shield competition) and scored 181. In the following season 1938–39, he was on tour for Victoria against Tasmania and Western Australia, the other State not yet with Sheffield Shield status. He scored 125 at an average of 25 with a top score of 55 against Western Australia. Remarkably, the bowling columns under Miller's name remained blank. He and selectors saw him as a batsman only.

In the following season, 1939–40, Miller had his initial taste of first-class Sheffield Shield cricket against Bradman's South Australian side. Miller was caught in slips for 4, and was bowled playing back to Clarrie Grimmett in the second innings for 7. Miller's big moment in a lean start came when he ran out Bradman for 76.

In the return match against South Australia at the MCG a month later, he played easily his best innings for the season, scoring 108. Yet the rest of his season was ordinary. He had trouble with Bill O'Reilly's spin versus New South Wales and scored 298 runs at 29.80 for the season. At that point Miller was a player with potential, but the 20-year-old's aspirations to go further were thwarted by war. First-class cricket was shut down after the 1939–40 season. The VFL Australian Rules competition continued and Miller played for the St Kilda club for the 1940, '41 and '42 seasons.

•

Early in 1942, Miller enlisted as a trainee pilot. Just short of his 23rd birthday in November, he was awarded his pilot's Flying Badge. Early in 1943 he was shipped to New England in the US. While waiting in Boston for the boat to England for active service he met American Peggy Wagner whom he married after the war. (They had four sons.) He was in training in England on various aircraft throughout most of his 30 months on active duty and ended up a Mosquito pilot with the RAF's 169 Squadron. The stories about 'Miller's Luck' began in 1943 when he had some narrow escapes; he once walked away from a plane he crash-landed, quipping to those who rushed to his aid:

'Nearly stumps drawn that time, gents.'

In 1944, Miller hurt his back in a wrestling match. This injury interfered with his cricket at various times and plagued him from then on.

He kept his hand in with cricket during 1943 and 1944 for the RAAF, and began bowling. There was no one around quite as good as him, so he kept delivering. Opposition players such as England's star batsman Denis Compton found him particularly quick. In July 1944 he collared a century at Lord's while German 'flying bombs' (early missiles) were dropping near the ground. Two months later he made a dashing 85 at Lord's playing for 'Australia' against 'England'. In 1945, after Germany had surrendered on 8 May, Miller played in five 'Victory matches' between England and the Australian servicemen in the country. He discovered a new-found aggression and impact with a cricket ball. It pleased him. He delivered bouncers, making the batsmen duck, flinch and hurt. Miller had developed into a carefree showman, who liked to assert his physical presence with the bat, and now the ball.

Miller headed the batting with 443 runs at 63.29 in the Victory Tests. He took 10 wickets at 27.00. The series was drawn 2-all.

He demonstrated his glittering skills when England played 'the Dominions,' also at Lord's, in August 1945. This composite side was made up of mainly Australian cricketers and led by the outstanding, volatile West Indian all-rounder Learie Constantine. Miller played the most dynamic innings of the entire summer. He was 61 not out at the end of day two. Those who turned up for the morning of day three witnessed an exceptional exhibition of graceful strokes and controlled power hitting that was unprecedented at Lord's. Miller smote seven sixes en route to 185. One landed on the top tier of the pavilion. Another crashed into Block Q to the right of the pavilion. A third landed in a shrapnel dent in the roof of the broadcasting box above the England players' dressing room. A fourth mighty blow to the Nursery End nearly saw the ball lost.

None of his shots in the evening before or on that explosive morning seemed unplanned. English commentators were at once agog and in love with Miller's display of aristocratic destruction. They reached for superlatives and compared him with Trumper for his dash, and Hammond for his class and strength. His technique based on front-foot play – especially his cover-drive – had something more English about it, it was reckoned, than Australian.

English experts and current players viewed him as a brilliant all-rounder who would be a force in post-war cricket.

•

Miller made Australian cricket sit up on returning home with a superb innings of 105 in the 1945–46 season against a New South Wales team that included the other new 'find' – speedster Ray Lindwall, and wily Bill O'Reilly. It was an important occasion for Australian cricket. Miller made the acquaintance of Lindwall for the first time. They became mates, forming one of the finest opening bowling combinations ever.

The next step was a tour of New Zealand in March and April 1946 by the best Australian team available. Only Hassett and Miller from the Services team made the side, which was led by Bill Brown. (Bradman was still months away from attempting a comeback after illness.)

Miller played his first Test – the only one on tour – at Wellington and acquitted himself well (30 and 2 for 6, before his back gave him trouble) in damp conditions. Australia's post-war cricket was off to a fine start with a big innings win. In the Australian winter of 1946, Miller, 26, made a comeback for St Kilda football club and was selected to play for Victoria.

In September 1946, Miller took a boat to the US to marry Peggy Wagner. They returned to Australia in October. Miller, as expected, was picked to play for Australia. He made an immediate impact in the First Test of the 1946–47 series with a driving 79 before falling lbw to fast leg-break bowler Doug Wright. Australia reached 645. Rain produced a 'sticky'. Miller, bowling off-breaks, took 7 for 60. Unlucky England made 145 and 172 in its second innings. Miller took 2 for 17. Australia won by an innings and 332. Miller's all-round performance made him the star of the match. He joined with Lindwall in bumping Australia's main target, Len Hutton. Miller removed him twice cheaply and established an early psychological hold on the England champion. All the tourists' bats were uncomfortable against the sustained attack from two ruthless yet fair competitors. English commentators murmured the word 'Bodyline'. While it technically – in field placing and the bowler's line – was not the same as the method used by Douglas Jardine in 1932–33 to attack Bradman, the tactic of using the short ball frequently did intimidate the batsmen. In that way the aims and result were the same.

This plus the rivalry between the two captains – Bradman and Hammond – created a tense atmosphere between the two teams. Miller bowled steadily for the rest of the series and ended with 16 wickets at 20.88. His batting was consistent with scores of 79, 40, 33 and 34, 141 not out, 23 and 34 not out. His 141 at Adelaide was one of his finest ever innings. Bradman spoke of the 'sheer artistry, the classical style and power' of the innings. Miller hit hard and often, but with the polish that had so excited spectators at Lord's.

Miller's series average was 76.80 from an aggregate of 384. This put him second in both bowling and batting averages (to Lindwall and Bradman) for the series. He had established himself as world-class all-rounder in his first Test series, which Australia won 3:0.

Yet it seemed for a while Miller might be lost to Australian cricket. Now married and with plans for a family, he needed income security, a problem common to Australian cricketers (until the 1990s). He was offered a contract to play with Rawtenstall in the Lancashire League, but ended taking a job with a Sydney alcoholic drinks distributor, a position that did not last long. Miller enjoyed the product too much himself and saw the dangers of indulging an already strong drinking habit further. But he had made the move to Sydney. There was no turning back. He would be playing cricket for New South Wales, but he first represented its Australian Rules team as vice-captain at a football carnival in Hobart during the 1947 winter. He then saddled up for his new State in 1947–48 and played for Australia against India in a five-Test series. He had a less effective second series – scoring 185 at 37.00 with a top score of 67, and taking nine wickets at 24.78. Yet these figures were still more than respectable for a Test all-rounder. He was also a regular partner for the lethal Lindwall.

•

Miller's lethargy, or career dip in the 1948 tour, spilled over into the 1948–49 season back in Australia, when he put in his least impressive all-round first-class season (there were no Tests) of his career to that point, scoring just 400 runs at 33.33 from 13 innings. Back problems allowed him to take only 11 wickets, but still at the very good rate of 24.09. Despite the figures there were two top performances with the bat – 109 in the opening game against Queensland and 99 in a hard-fought match versus Victoria.

Late in the season, Miller bowled in a testimonial match at Sydney for Alan Kippax and Bert Oldfield, which was Bradman's second-last first-class match. Bradman, now 40, had not played cricket for nearly three months, but still delivered a superb innings, scoring 53 in 65 minutes. Miller sent down several bouncers. Bradman mistimed a hook off one of them and was caught. The Sydney crowd booed Miller for his petulance. They felt robbed of a final century from the Don.

Through the season, Miller declared he wanted to be considered as a batsman, rather than an all-rounder. The selectors – Bradman, 'Chappie' Dwyer and Jack Ryder – perhaps taking him at his word, dumped him from the squad to tour South Africa in the 1949–50 season. This plus his poor season may have seen Miller as a fringe selection tipped out by the usual trade-offs between the States. Yet it was an ill-considered non-selection. While Miller's returns had not been good in 1948–49, he was still the best all-rounder in Australia, if not the world at that time, however he viewed himself then or in the future. The omission stunned the cricket world. Critics attacked the selectors. They searched for a reason for the dumping. It was even rumoured that Bradman had not wanted Miller because he had bowled bumpers at him in the Kippax–Oldfield testimonial.

When the tour of South Africa began in November 1949, it wasn't long before a thin excuse – a minor car accident involving fast bowler Bill Johnston – was used to invite Miller to join the Australians.

His batting in South Africa was strong and consistent. He made 246 at 41.00 in the Tests, which ranked him sixth behind Harvey, Hassett, Morris, Jack Moroney and Sam Loxton. But he was placed second behind Johnston with the ball taking 17 wickets at 22.94, which was important for the tourists. His partner Lindwall lost form during the series and was dropped after four Tests. Whether Miller liked it or not, he was being forced to perform as an all-rounder. His country needed him.

•

England provided the best opposition in that era, and when it returned to fight for the Ashes in 1950–51, Miller lifted his rating perceptibly around the country in preparation for the Tests. In the opener against Queensland he smashed 201 with five sixes. Another double hundred – 214 against the tourists, followed this soon after. He was in superb touch with the bat and in six innings ran up 616 runs at 154. It was nigh impossible to keep up such a rate and there were predictable lapses, which carried into the Tests. But by the time he reached Sydney for the Third, he found that pre-series touch and made a two stage innings to reach 145. In stage one, he made a slow 96 not out before stumps one day and then clipped another 49 the next morning. He was also in form in the field, taking a brilliant one-hand catch at second slip to get rid of Cyril Washbrook (34) off Johnston in England's first innings. Then in a devastating spell with the old ball he mopped up Hutton, Compton and Reg Simpson for five runs inside four overs. Miller finished with 4 for 37 off 15.7 overs.

Spinner Jack Iverson upstaged him with the ball but his overall effort at catching, bowling and batting would have ranked him as player of the match. The story was similar in the Fourth Test at Adelaide. There were other fine individual performances. Morris hit 206, Hutton managed to carry his bat with 156 not out, and Bill Johnston took 4 for 73 in England's second innings. But Miller chimed in with 44 and 99, and took 3 for 27, also in England's second innings. Those three wickets came for just three runs to close out the match in Australia's favour. It had four wins to nil, but England won the last.

Miller's series figures were 350 runs at 43.75 and 17 wickets at 17.71. He was the most decisive player in the series. The Ashes, and a wish to do well against England, drew out the best in him.

Miller was similarly dominant during the 1951–52 season's five Tests versus the West Indies. He was hardly out of any game, making an impact with either bat or ball or both. Miller and Lindwall were at different times in the series again wrongly accused of delivering a variation of Bodyline. But there was a surfeit of bouncers and again they were intimidatory. The West Indies, led by its three champion bats – Clyde Walcott, Frank Worrell and Everton Weekes – was never comfortable against them. Miller took 20 wickets 19.90, Lindwall 21 at 23.05. Bill Johnston's medium-pace left-armers (23 at 22.09) completed a trio of speed that left the West Indies with little relief.

Miller was once more consistent with the bat, collecting 362 at 40.22, with a best effort of 129 at Sydney in the Second Test.

•

Miller, 32 going on 33, was surprised to be named as New South Wales captain from the beginning of the 1952–53 season, replacing Arthur Morris. He was also named vice-captain of the Australian team, and most observers thought he would be the natural successor to Lindsay Hassett. Miller led New South Wales to three Shield wins in four years. He had a poor series with the bat against South Africa in a 2-all contest, scoring just 153 runs at 25.50. He had problems with off-spinner Hugh Tayfield, who removed him five times in six knocks. Yet his impact with the ball (13 wickets at 18.54) was up to the standard of previous seasons. He injured his back in the Fourth Test and this put him out of action for the Fifth Test. Lindwall was also out injured. Their loss saw South Africa win by six wickets and draw the series.

Miller was replaced by Morris as vice-captain on the tour of England in 1953, which created the unusual situation of the

New South Wales State captain being subordinate to the national vice-captain. Miller seemed to have not pleased the authorities with incidents through his career that were deemed unacceptable. He had a maverick streak off the field. But on it, he was proving a strong leader of his State. Players such as Richie Benaud, Alan Davidson, Bob Simpson and Ian Craig looked up to 'Nugget,' as he was nicknamed. He could deliver telling performances – with runs or an important wicket – at critical moments. Yet Miller was overlooked. He didn't help his cause by the ill-timed comments in a book, *Bumper*, released in April 1953 and coincident with the beginning of the 1953 Ashes tour.

He criticised Hassett's captaincy, saying he was too cautious and 'no lover of criticism'. On the way he had a more careful swipe at Bradman. This was all public at a time when the Australian team would have wished to appear united. Excuses were made that it was more the words of his writer/collaborator Richard Whitington. Yet the book was under Miller's name. It was not an intelligent move, especially when England sniffed a chance to beat Australia for the first time in England since 1926.

Hassett would pay Miller back later by not supporting him for the captaincy. For now, the skipper was pleased that the star all-rounder seemed to have assumed the role of an unofficial leader of a young, inexperienced side with a responsible, attacking 220 not out at Worcester in the opening match. This set a pattern for the first-class season and Miller produced excellent all-round figures. In 31 innings he accumulated 1,433 with a dazzling 262 not out highest score against the Combined Services that included a fiery young Freddie Trueman, who was clobbered. Miller's tour average was 51.7. He took 45 wickets at 22.51. Yet in the tighter, more competitive war of attrition in the Tests he appeared limited. He did manage 55 in the first innings of the First Test at Trent Bridge. Miller lifted for 109 in the second innings at his spiritual home Lord's in the Second Test. But apart from those innings his efforts were negligible and he was left with 223 runs at 24.78. It was much the same with the ball.

Miller took just 10 wickets at 30.30, and turned in only one top display in England's second innings of the Fourth Test at Headingley (4 for 63). Overall it wasn't enough to force victory for Australia, which went down 0:1 in the 1953 Ashes.

After the Ashes loss – the first in 20 years – the critics hoed into the Australians. Jack Fingleton remarked that 'Miller should be allowed to die an honourable death as a bowler' – in other words, not bowl at all.

Hassett retired and left the Australian captaincy vacant. There were three candidates: Morris, Ian Johnson, who had been left out of the 1953 tour, and Miller, who was popular with the press and the public. Miller would have been a surprise selection given that he had been demoted for the 1953 Ashes tour. The 13 members of the Australian Board – each with a vote – decided on Ian Johnson, which meant that as ever a certain amount of horse-trading between the States had gone on.

Miller was not surprised that he was ignored. He later wrote that he never seriously entertained election, saying he was 'impulsive' and that he hadn't ever been Bradman's 'pin-up'. The Don, he said, rated high when it came to policy matters.

Had Miller overstated Bradman's influence? The Don had just one vote out of 13 and was not chairman of the Board when it came to the vote for captain. Furthermore, he was South Australia's representative on the Board, and even if he were lobbying against Miller, the inevitable trade-off between the States would have further diluted his influence. When there was not one outstanding candidate in the eyes of the electors, a compromise candidate who nobody disliked – Ian Johnson – received the collective nod.

In 1953–54, Miller turned his mind towards New South Wales attempting to win another Shield. In 12 innings, he scored 710 at 71.10, but his bowling figures (16 wickets at 33.75) seemed to echo Fingleton's observation.

Yet Miller, who again grumbled about being seen as an all-rounder, could still perform brilliantly with the ball, although in shorter spells. He showed this in the First Test at Brisbane in the 1954–55 Ashes. He only took one wicket in each innings, but each was an opener – Reg Simpson and Hutton – back in the pavilion cheaply.

Miller was now 35, and with a knee injury to add to his chronic back problem. He missed the Second Test, but came back for the Third at the MCG. In that and the Fourth at Adelaide he produced short, penetrative spells that rocked England. He took 3 for 14 off 11 overs with eight maidens in England's first innings at Melbourne, which reduced it to 4 for 41. In Adelaide, he cut England down to 3 for 18 and 4 for 49 when it was chasing just 97 for victory.

Miller ended the series with 10 wickets at 24.30, and indicated he was not quite ready for the post-bowling pastures recommended by Fingleton. His batting however, disappointed. He made just 167 at 23.86. Hutton's team won the Ashes 3:1, thanks mainly to speedsters Tyson (28 wickets at 20.82) and Statham (18 wickets at 27.72). England went home ecstatic. It had unearthed bowlers to more than match Australia's ageing trio of Miller, Lindwall and Bill Johnston (19 wickets at 22.26).

•

In March 1955, soon after the thrashing from England, Miller was vice-captain of the Australian team in the Caribbean and faced with new challenges, particularly as a bowler. He and Lindwall would have to take on the strong West Indian batting line-up featuring Worrell, Weekes and Walcott, along with John Holt, Cammie Smith and Denis Atkinson. It was to be a big scoring series and Miller turned it on with the bat, hitting 147, 137 and 109 in an aggregate of 439 at 73.17.

Miller took charge as acting captain in Kingston's First Test on day two when Johnson's foot was injured. It was an easy time to take over. Australia had notched 9 for 515 (Miller 147, Harvey 133) and the West Indies could only manage 259 and 275. Australia won by nine wickets. Miller took 2 for 36 and

3 for 62. It was his one time as acting skipper and it turned out to be very much his match.

He did little in the drawn Second Test at Port of Spain but knocked over three openers at Georgetown in the Third, won by Australia. At Bridgetown in the Fourth Test, he made 137 as Australia compiled 668. The West Indies replied with 510, made notable by young Garry Sobers belting Miller for several fours in a bright opening of 43. Denis Atkinson (219) figured in a record 347 seventh-wicket partnership with Clairmonte Depeiza. Miller was in dispute with his captain on how he should bowl during this stand. Miller wanted to deliver his off-breaks. Johnson wanted speed. It became a little nasty in the dressing room with Johnson offering to settle the matter 'outside'. It was patched up, but it did highlight a frustration in Miller. He wasn't the leader, but wanted to do things his way. He considered himself a better skipper than Johnson and didn't always control the urge to express it.

After the drawn Fourth Test, the teams returned to Kingston where Miller dominated again. This time he made 109 and took 6 for 107 and 2 for 58. Australia won by an innings and 82 runs, giving it a great 3:0 victory. Miller took 20 wickets at 32.05 and Lindwall 20 at 31.85. On paper, these figures looked expensive, but considering the batting line-up, they were outstanding. Walcott, for instance, scored 827 at 82.7 with a record four centuries. Weekes notched 469 at 58.63.

It was the last combined effort by Lindwall and Miller that won a series for Australia. Lindwall, struggling against injury in England in 1956, could only take seven Test wickets. Miller, however, showed all the doubters on his last tour that at 36 he could still turn it on with the ball. He saved his best performance for Lord's – something he had done for more than a decade – where he took 5 for 72 and 5 for 80. Australia won by 185 runs. It was his best return in a Test, which was a most satisfying way for him to bow out at the historic arena.

Miller took 21 wickets at 22.24 for the series – the best figures by an Australian. His batting on poorly prepared wickets suffered at the hands of off-spinner Jim Laker (who snared him six times in 10 innings), as did all the Australians.

Despite the gloom for the tourists, Miller accompanied Johnson to Buckingham Palace where they received their MBEs. He also mixed with the movers and shakers in British society who had invited him to join them whenever he was in England.

The press now attacked the Australian line-up and called for the sackings of the older players, including Miller. He didn't need to be told and jumped before he was pushed after playing one more Test against Pakistan in Karachi in October 1956. Despite his injuries, he was still athletic enough to carry on for a season or two more, but he'd had enough.

Miller played 55 Tests making 2,958 runs at 36.98. He scored seven centuries and 13 fifties, and took 38 catches. He captured 170 wickets at 22.98 with seven five-wicket hauls and one 10-wicket match – at Lord's in his last game there in 1956. In first-class cricket he played in 226 matches in which he scored 14,183, including 41 hundreds and 63 fifties. His average was 48.90. Miller took 497 wickets at 22.30.

Miller's name was on several cricket books with Whitington from 1950–69, and he continued to represent the *Daily Express* until 1974, when he took a public relations job with Vernons Pools in Australia.

Miller never lost his love of horse racing and music. He will be remembered for his exceptional cricket ability, positive approach and fine sportsmanship, which went a long way towards him being one of the most popular men to play the game and Australia's greatest ever all-rounder. He died in October 2004.

•

Despite Miller's lack of interest in the lopsided competitions of 1948, the all-rounder strained his hardest when his team was in trouble. He may well have bemoaned the massive scores and the crushing of all opposition, but when the crunch came, he as much as Bradman or anyone else, did not wish to be beaten.

It was just the way his captain went about it that Miller disagreed with.

Yet in the end these two excellent Australian sportsmen had their nation's interests at heart.

Doug Ring

Doug Ring often joked that he was one of 'ground staff' bowlers during the 1948 tour. He and Colin McCool had one Test between them, although both bowled well during the long season. Ring had a workhorse and support role in his 19 games, but he managed to capture 60 wickets at 21.81. This underpinned the team's overall strength. He was the seventh choice on the bowling list to make the Tests, but on form would have probably acquitted himself in all five contests, especially with sticky and turning wickets being encountered throughout the Ashes.

Bradman liked Ring's character and the fact that he would attack the bowling when batting and stalk batsmen when bowling. Bradman's only criticism was that Ring may have tried to bowl too fast on England's spin-friendly pitches, which tended to be slower than Australia's harder strips. But this was a matter of opinion. Bradman himself bowled leg-spinners, and knew a bit about the art. He wished Ring had enticed batsmen more by giving the ball more air, but even if he had done this, it is doubtful that his tour figures would have been better, or that he would have been given more chances in the Tests. The influence of all the spinners was doomed before a ball was delivered at Worcester because of the 55-over rule. A new ball was available so quickly that any captain would opt for speed against spin. Spinners were also condemned, in the skipper's eyes, by history. His previous (1938) Ashes tour had been dominated by spin when there was a dearth of quality pace in the side. Never again would he lead a side that capitulated to a powerful England batting line-up.

To Ring's credit, he kept his head high. He remained in good spirits when men of lesser character would have been grumbling in bars and hotel rooms. His selection for the Fifth Test at the Oval was as much recognition for his consistently good efforts and demeanour through the tour as any specific performance that caught the selectors' eyes.

•

Doug Ring (1918–2003) was born in Hobart, and educated at Melbourne High School. He had a sniff of club cricket for Prahran at the end of the 1935–36 season, playing the last two games in the firsts. But he was brushed aside the next season and had to spend two years playing second-grade cricket (and topping the bowling averages) before Richmond gave him a second chance. This led him to being selected to play for Victoria against New South Wales in the 1938–39 season. He replaced a slow, left-arm bowler, Ern Bromley. Tall, well-built Ring's welcome to the State side was instructive concerning how new selections were often treated. Keith Rigg, his Victorian captain, met him and they discussed how he (Ring) set his field.

'That's unusual for a left-hander,' Rigg said with a frown.

'I'm not a left-hander,' Ring replied, surprised that his new leader was so misinformed, 'I'm a right-handed leg-break bowler.'

'Good God!' Rigg responded. 'I'll have to revise my thinking.'

Ring wondered if this meant his selection in the team might also be 'revised'. But it wasn't. He began his first-class career against New South Wales. One of his proudest moments was when he bowled Bradman (for 64) that season on the Adelaide Oval playing against South Australia.

'How could I forget that moment?' he said on Victorian TV show *World of Sport* in 1960. 'Bradman in full flight was an amazing experience. The balls would be flying [off his bat] everywhere, like bullets. He had twice as many shots as the rest of us and a fantastic ability to concentrate . . . Bradman was the hardest batsman to bowl to.'

Bradman didn't forget Ring either. He hated being deceived by a spinner at any time, and especially when he was 'set'. He was always stunned to be dismissed when in full flight, as if something had gone wrong with a perfect computer – his cricket brain – and his capacity for lightning responses to every bowler and every ball.

Ring had to wait until after the war for his chance in a Test. But Bradman had always been impressed with him and it came at the end of 1947–48 when Ring was picked for the Fifth Test on his 'home' wicket at the MCG. He was 29. He had waited a decade for his opportunity at the highest level.

Familiarity with a pitch bred contentment. He took 3 for 103 and 3 for 17, and it was that latter effort that showed Ring could utilise a spinning wicket. The performance saw him pack his bags for England.

Ring missed the tour to South Africa in 1949–50, and the freak spinning ability of Jack Iverson kept him out of the 1950–51 Ashes. He was back in favour for the 1951–52 series against the West Indies when he played all five Tests. He returned his best figures with the ball, and the bat, in a good all-round performance. Ring's best returns came in Brisbane, where he took 6 for 80 in the second innings, giving him 8 for 132 for the game.

The most memorable moment came in the Fourth Test of the series, in Melbourne. Australia was nine wickets down in its second innings with 38 to make to win. Ring was batting with Richmond club-mate Bill Johnston. Johnston dropped anchor in the manner he had been taught during the 1948 Ashes and pushed forward at everything from the spinners and the pacemen. This left Ring to go for the runs, which he did with aplomb, scoring 32 not out and securing a win for Australia. The cheerful attitude of these two in the clinches was testimony to their characters. They made the tensest of moments, with a huge audience listening on radio, look like fun. They may have surprised themselves that they pulled it off, but both men remained unflustered under extreme pressure.

Ring played again in all five Tests of the 1952–53 season against South Africa, and shone with the bat twice with hard-hitting scores of 53 and 58. He was picked again for England in 1953, where the 1948 pattern of events were repeated. He once more used his lovely tenor voice to sing the 'ground staff' song, and played in just one Test – at Lord's – where he didn't do enough in a drawn game to have the selectors smile benignly on him again. He had to sit out the rest of the series. It was particularly galling for him and Richie Benaud to be left out of the final Test at the Oval. Benaud had had a poor series – with just two wickets at 87 from three Tests (and with the bat, 15 runs from five completed innings). But many observers, some with the benefit of hindsight, thought that either Ring or Benaud should have played on a turner at the Oval. As it was, England's Tony Lock, with his mix of left-arm spinners and suspect faster balls (throws), won it for England on his home pitch, taking 5 for 45 in Australia's second innings.

Ring did exceptionally well on tour, taking 69 wickets to bolster the team against the counties. But at 34, and with a family (wife Lesley and three children), he decided to retire from first-class cricket after a career spanning 15 years from 1938–53. He scored 3,184 runs (with one century) at a respectable 22.25, and took 451 wickets at 28.48, confirming he was a good bowling all-rounder. In 13 Tests he hit 426 runs at 22.42, and took 35 wickets at 37.28, with five catches.

•

Ring had another life in gentle limelight after cricket as a TV commentator on the game. His banter with Lou Richards, a former captain of Collingwood Football Club, was a regular part of *World of Sport* on Channel 7.

•

Doug Ring proved to be an ideal selection for the 1948 tour. Apart from his capacities as a good leg-break and wrong 'un bowler, he fielded well, and showed on occasions that he could do more than hold up an end in a crisis. On top of that, he was forever joyful, and while not triumphant as much as he would have liked, his hearty cooperation with the rest of the squad was a distinct asset.

Ron Saggers

There had to be one quiet one in the class of 1948. It was Ron Saggers, one of the better looking, more dapper gents of the group. Aptly too, he was Don Tallon's understudy – the number-two keeper in the side. It suited his demeanour: not too obtrusive, selfless, a good team man ready for an emergency. Saggers said little; one reason being that he nearly always had a cigarette in his mouth. Team-mates swore he would smoke on the field if he could. This addiction to nicotine did not diminish his skills behind the stumps when he got his chance in the 1948 Leeds Test after Tallon was injured. Saggers chose his moment well. Leeds was one of the most sensational Tests of all time, with the most remarkable come-from-behind victory of all.

The debonair, always well-dressed Saggers may not have said much in his career, or at any time, but he was most appreciative of that game. When asked by a reporter how he felt about his first dismissal (Compton caught off Lindwall) in his first Test, he responded:

'Hmm. "Compton caught Saggers bowled Lindwall." I am in exalted company there . . .'

He snared two other victims (caught) in the game. Bradman, in a typically blunt assessment of his performance, gave him the highest praise saying that Australia was no worse off because Saggers performed so well. Bradman conceded that Saggers was not as quick or agile as Tallon; yet he was reliable and would always perform strongly. There was something refined and quietly assured about his efforts. He also drew praise from the captain for his batting. Bradman cited his century against Essex as demonstrating he was better equipped than most keepers with the bat.

•

Ron Saggers (1917–87) was born in inner-city Sydney at Sydenham, and played cricket for Marrickville with Ernie Toshack. A big break came in the late 1930s when Saggers was invited to tour northern New South Wales in a team made up of experienced first-class players and young club performers showing promise. The team was captained by Bill O'Reilly, and keeping to him was an education in itself. The fact that O'Reilly was impressed with his skills behind the stumps was an important accolade. He was the best spinner in the world and a perfectionist not given to platitudinous praise. Also in that team were Sid Barnes and Colin McCool.

When Saggers first made the New South Wales team in 1939, he was considered good enough to make the side as a batsman alone. But as so often happens with an all-rounder – a player who has at least two major strings to his bow – one of his contributions was bound to suffer. He concentrated on his keeping and his batting declined. In the 1940–41 season he caught a record 7 playing for New South Wales against a Combined XI in Brisbane. Any thoughts of him concentrating on his batting evaporated. Saggers would attempt to make his mark as a keeper. In 1941, he married Margaret. Soon afterwards, he joined the RAAF and did not resume his cricket until the 1945–46 season.

In his 11-year first-class career (1939–50) he made 1,888 runs at 23.89, including that one century against Essex in 1948, and 221 dismissals – 147 catches and a high number of stumpings – 74, which reflected his effective work with spinners.

Saggers played five Tests on the South African tour in 1949–50, snaring 13 catches and 8 stumpings. This bettered his unusually high ratio of about two catches to every stumping, which was due to keeping a lot to McCool and Johnson. He only had six Tests in all, scoring 30 runs at 10, and effecting 24 dismissals – 16 catches and 8 stumpings. He captained New South Wales for several seasons.

After the South African tour Saggers retired from Test cricket, going as quietly as he came. He and Margaret (with two daughters and a son) moved from southern Sydney to Harbord on the Northern Beaches. He died at 69 in 1987.

Ron Saggers was a neat and industrious keeper who reminded observers of Bert Oldfield in the 1930s. He was another popular member of the Invincibles. His skills and manner contributed to the success of 1948.

Don Tallon

Don Bradman wanted Don Tallon as the 1948 team's principal wicket-keeper simply because he was the best stumpsman he ever saw. Tallon's batting, which had its glittering moments in the 1930s, did not enter Bradman's thinking. He always thought it better to have someone of Tallon's brilliance behind the stumps, regardless of his batting credentials. His amazing catching, especially down the leg-side, and lightning stumping presented an extra dimension for wicket-taking by a fielding side. Often the wicket taken was credited to the bowler. In fairness, it should have gone to Tallon. He created a wicket when there wasn't one there. His anticipation, leap and agility made him outstanding whether keeping to pace or spin.

Tallon perfected a leg-side movement copied by Wally Grout and Godfrey Evans whereby he positioned himself to take the fine leg-glance in his right glove, while still keeping the slim option of catching a thick glance with his left glove.

Australian Test bowler Alan Davidson judged Tallon as far ahead of all other keepers as Bradman was ahead of other batsmen. Even his keeper peers acknowledged it. England's Godfrey Evans, who entered the Test scene at about the same time as Tallon, saw him as an inspiration and the most accomplished gloveman of all time. Lindsay Hassett, who captained him near the end of Tallon's career, said he had the fastest reflexes of all keepers.

'No Wild West gunman was quicker on the draw,' Hassett said, 'when it came to a stumping. But Don personified "quick". He was tall for a keeper and lithe and had the mobility to move into position with speed. I don't recall his feet in my mind's eye, but they must have been dainty. His movements were always swift. He used to skip to keep fit and I'm told he was good on the dance floor.'

●

If there was a standout prodigy in cricket it was Don Tallon (1916–84). At 12 he volunteered to keep wickets in a match in Bundaberg, a country town in Queensland, so he could get into the game. He rarely had the gloves off over the next quarter century. It helped that Don had three brothers (older brother Bill went on to play for Queensland) and games in the backyard on rough pitches. They went on summer after summer until he was playing grade cricket. His father Les, a boilermaker by trade, and a one-time cricket ground curator, often joined in and offered coaching advice. He was authoritarian, but not too rigid in his observations to ignore Don's skills. Les stopped him playing Rugby League so that Don would concentrate on cricket. He captained a Queensland schoolboy team at 13. About this time his batting began to attract attention too. He was a forceful driver, who could play all the key attacking shots.

Tallon became Bundaberg's regular keeper after taking part in a match against a touring New South Wales State team in April 1931 led by Alan Kippax. Bradman, 22, was in the team but injured for the Bundaberg match.

'I was in hospital [with an injured foot] and did not see Don play,' Bradman said, 'but I heard very good reports about his ability from Kippax. He was clearly, at 15, a player of enormous potential.'

Later during the 1931–32 season, Queensland selectors were so impressed with Tallon that they trialled him at the Gabba against State bowlers, including the Aboriginal speedster Eddie Gilbert, who was then regarded as the quickest bowler in Australia.

Tallon had just turned 17 in February 1933, when he played against the touring England team at Toowoomba. The teenager had the honour of being bowled for 2 by Harold Larwood, who had just won the Bodyline Ashes for his team. He showed his skill with the gloves by stumping England's Herbert Sutcliffe off a leg-spinner. The batsman's back foot slid out of the crease for a fraction of a second. Tallon whipped off a bail.

In 1933–34, he made the State team while still aged 17 and a year later toured the southern States. At 19 in 1935–36, while playing against a touring MCC side, Tallon took six wickets in an innings and demonstrated a facility for keeping to leg-spinners when he stumped four victims. His keeping was gaining in confidence with every game, as was his batting.

More important for his career was his performance in a State game against South Australia at Adelaide played over Christmas 1935. South Australia amassed 8 for 642 declared. Bradman, back after his near-death experience in England when ill with peritonitis, showed the cricket world that he was still a force by smashing the Queensland attack for 233 in 175 minutes. Tallon could not recall anything going through to him when Bradman faced. Bradman praised his keeping effort, in which he conceded just 7 byes.

Queensland replied with 127 and 289, and in its second innings Tallon batted with style and force to score 88, thus displaying his all-round talent to the most influential person in Australian cricket.

Suddenly at the end of the 1935–36 season, it all gelled for him. He smashed a magnificent 193 in 187 minutes against Victoria at the Gabba. In a formidable all-round effort, he also took five Victorian wickets in an innings.

His efforts against South Australia and Victoria played a big part in his selection in a Test trial at the beginning of the next season, 1936–37, between the team captained by Victor Richardson that had been successful in South Africa, and a side led by Bradman. Significantly, Bradman chose Tallon to bat at No. 5 behind Leo O'Brien, Jack Badcock, himself, and Ray Robinson (the cricketer not the journalist). It was an early indication of Bradman's thoughts about Tallon's batting prowess. But the keeper missed a golden opportunity when bowled for 3 after batting for a short time with Bradman, who was alight in a glorious knock of 212. Bert Oldfield was still the keeper of choice for the national team, but Tallon was now in contention for Test selection.

He hit 100 at the Gabba against New South Wales in the first State game of the season a few weeks later, in a game notable for the exceptional keeping of Oldfield, who did not concede a bye in either innings. Tallon was challenging with the bat, but he was never going to succeed Oldfield while he was keeping so proficiently. Yet in November 1936 Tallon was chosen to play under Bradman in an Australian XI against an MCC XI. Tallon kept efficiently and made a creditable 31 in an Australian score of 8 for 544 declared. Again, it wasn't quite enough for him to force the issue with Oldfield, who was never going to bat as well as his young rival. Tallon missed selection and Oldfield kept throughout the Tests. Nevertheless, the youthful Tallon, still only 20, continued to impress around the country with his keeping and batting. He hit three centuries for the season and nearly made it four when he was removed for 96 against Victoria at the Gabba in mid-January 1937. A month later, the Queenslander had one more chance to impress Bradman that season, in a State game at Brisbane. Tallon made just one dismissal, but the right one – Bradman stumped for 123. Tallon batted well again in front of the Don in a cameo knock of 48 in an hour.

Unfortunately in the following season 1937–38, he could not repeat his batting form. This told against him in the selection of the two keepers to go to England in 1938. Had he batted with the same force as in the 1936–37 season there is little doubt he would have toured. Oldfield, at 43, was considered too old. That left Tallon, Ben Barnett of Victoria and Charlie Walker from South Australia. Not for the last time, Bradman was outvoted at the selection table. He opted for Tallon and Walker but horse-trading between the States saw a compromise selection of Barnett and Walker.

The omission brought greater determination into Tallon's play the following season, 1938–39, when he began it in November with impact by taking six wickets – three stumpings – in an innings versus New South Wales. In December in Sydney he proved how great he could be by taking six wickets in *each* NSW innings, giving him 12 for the match. This equalled a world record held by Surrey keeper Edward Poole, which had stood since 1869. Tallon caught nine and stumped three.

In February 1939, he snared seven in an innings (four stumpings) against Victoria at the Gabba, equalling another world record set by Fred Price of Middlesex against Yorkshire at Lord's in 1937. These mighty performances, along with the occasional explosive batting effort, placed him ahead of all other keepers in Australia. In six matches he made 34 dismissals – 21 catches and 13 stumpings; all at eye-blink speed. Tallon's movement began before he took the ball, his gloves heading towards the stumps in one swift operation. His eye was so good that often just one bail would go flying. Yet he was too quick for scorers. On several occasions in 1938–39 they had to ask umpires the mode of dismissal – stumped or bowled to medium-pacer Geoff Cook.

Tallon, 23, was a near certainty to play for Australia in the next scheduled Ashes series in Australia in 1940–41. War intervened. Tallon joined the army and he was robbed of his greatest years. He was rarely to rise to quite the dizzying heights of the pre-war days with either bat or gloves. Yet he was still ahead of the rest of the world's keepers and an attacking bat as he demonstrated in Melbourne during the Third Ashes Test of 1946–47. Then he dashed off 92 in 105 minutes. He and Lindwall (100) thumped 154 in 87 minutes in a sustained burst of power hitting rarely seen in Test cricket.

Stomach ulcers hampered Tallon. In 1943, he suffered from a life-threatening ruptured duodenal ulcer. He was discharged from the army and had to wait another two years before resuming Test cricket. He toured New Zealand with Bill Brown's team in March–April 1946. Tallon made a stumping, took a catch and made 5. It wasn't sensational on paper, but newspaper reports suggested he performed admirably.

After a long wait he was on his way as a Test player. England toured Australia in 1946 and he had his first encounter with it while captaining Queensland at the Gabba. The year was a good one for him. He married a Queenslander, Marjorie Beattie, which settled him down. On the field he built a first-rate cricketing relationship with leg-spinner Colin McCool. Keeper and bowler ambushed Hammond's men at the Gabba. McCool took nine wickets. Tallon helped in six of them – four stumpings and two catches. He was, from that moment, a psychological force in the Ashes. The England players had heard much about him. Now they had experienced his genius behind the stumps. It was daunting. They were not just facing the bowler but a keeper with an aggressive demeanour. He appealed loudly and patrolled the stumps like a hungry panther at close quarters.

'It did feel like Don was literally breathing down my neck,' Denis Compton remarked, 'especially with McCool bowling. You had to block it out of your mind or it would affect your stroke-play.'

Tallon further demonstrated his freak skills in the Second Test at Sydney. During the lunch break on day one, Tallon told Bradman he thought he could remove Len Hutton – 39 not out – caught down leg-side. McCool's stock leg-break broke to the off so he was less likely to induce a nick. Bradman brought on off-spinner Ian Johnson, with the instruction to push for a catch down leg-side, which meant the precision placement of a ball on middle stump, breaking slightly to leg. Johnson obliged.

Hutton played back and glanced, expecting to look round and see the ball on its way to the boundary. Instead he saw Tallon running towards square leg, appealing. He had snaffled the catch.

'I was positioned to see the ball slide off the bat,' Tallon said, making the toughest of dismissals sound routine, 'and I caught it.'

The second outstanding dismissal came when standing up to McCool. Compton went to drive a leg-break outside off but misjudged it and edged it to Ian Johnson at slips. The ball slapped him in the chest and headed towards the grass. Tallon threw himself backwards and just managed to slide a glove under the ball to take one of the great Test catches of all time. Witnesses doubted that anyone else but Tallon could have moved with such alacrity and precision.

Despite his ulcers, which upset him on some days, Tallon, 30, was a success in his first Test series, making 20 dismissals, then an Australian record. It would never make up for the lost years, but Tallon was at least satisfied he had performed at the highest level with exceptional credit. Yet he was hungry for more. There were few laurels to rest on. Although a man of few words – team-mates called him 'mumbles' – Tallon made it clear that he wanted to be around at the top for as long as possible.

He was unassailable in 1947–48 in all five Tests against India but his batting fell away.

'He lost confidence in his ability to drive forward of the wicket,' Bradman recalled, 'and this diminished his opportunities to score. But it still remains that he was a very good bat indeed before the war.'

Tallon's keeping in 1948 went a long way towards the Australian team's invincibility. On three occasions he took sensational catches that influenced the course of the Tests.

He made some errors – a couple of dropped catches he should have taken – but it didn't amount to much. *Wisden* selected him as one of its Five Cricketers the Year of 1948. It was a peak period in his career.

Tallon showed his prowess with the bat was not far away in a Bradman Testimonial at the MCG in December 1948, Bradman's XI versus Hassett's XI. On the fourth day, Bradman's XI was 7 for 210, still 192 runs short of victory. Tallon let loose and smashed his way to 55 in no time. With one hour to go in the game and 101 needed for victory, Tallon proceeded to play what Bradman described as his best ever innings. He crunched his way to 91 out of 100 and was left on 146 not out when play ceased. The match was a tie.

•

Tallon played Test cricket for another five years but by 1953 had trouble holding his place in the Test side. Apart from his ulcers, he had some trouble with deafness, and earned the harsh new nickname 'Deafie'.

Still, there were flashes of genius with both gloves and bat. He hit a thrilling 77 at Sydney in the Third Test of the 1950–51 Ashes.

Tallon played 21 Tests. He kept in 41 innings and made 58 dismissals, taking 50 catches and making eight stumpings. He batted 26 times, scoring 394 runs at an average of 17.13.

Tallon's capacity to pull off the breathtaking dismissal, especially of a top player such as Hutton, made him worth selection above all others.

This was especially so in 1948 when Tallon took catches that perhaps only he could take, and helped swing games Australia's way. John Arlott summed him up best after viewing him through the Invincibles triumphs.

'The surname tells everything,' he said. 'Instinctively prehensile, naturally predatory.'

Ernie Toshack

Ernie Toshack was another success on the 1948 tour until he broke down at the Leeds Test with an injured knee that would soon end his career. The 33-year-old's joint had been suspect for some time and he had to prove himself in a rigorous test before he was invited to pack his bags for England. He and the selectors were pleased he made it. He took 10 wickets in the first three Tests and bowled Jack Crapp in the Fourth before his knee gave way. He had been a steady backup to Lindwall and Miller in the first two Tests. They were both injured in these games, and it was vital for Bradman to have a versatile bowler to be thrown into the front-line to support them and Johnston, who was destined to bowl more than any other player. With Miller unable to bowl because of a lingering back injury, and Lindwall needing relief for a troublesome groin, Toshack took up the slack brilliantly in England's second innings at Lord's, taking 5 for 40.

From Bradman's point of view, Lindwall, Johnston and Toshack had all lifted their ratings under pressure and when it was vital. No wonder the captain was delighted with his pacemen.

Bradman regarded left-armer Toshack as a one-off. He had never known another bowler to concentrate on cutting the ball from the right-hander's off-stump to his leg-stump. That was his stock ball, and set up a unique field of four on the off (including a slip), and five on the leg. He would often have a leg slip and a short-leg. But Bradman, who faced him in the nets and in State games, was aware also of Toshack's clever variations, which included an orthodox left-hand spinner that moved from the leg-stump to the off, a faster delivery that zipped straight through, and the capacity to flight a ball that would drift either to leg or off.

Toshack was tricky for all England's top bats, and would have been far more effective with stronger results but for his injury, which he had to nurse through the early part of the tour. It eventually needed an operation (after Leeds) in England. As it was, he took 50 wickets for the tour at 21.12.

Bradman was pleased that Toshack took his advice and played straight with the bat. It brought a surprising result. He averaged 51 in collecting an aggregate of 51 runs for once out. It placed him fifth in the batting list, something that would give him bragging rights for the rest of his life.

•

Toshack was born at outback Cobar, in western New South Wales, the son of a country railway stationmaster. When Ernie was six, the family moved to Lyndhurst, near Cowra, in New South Wales. At 25, in 1939, the lean youth with the dark, film star looks married Kathleen, a local Cowra girl. At 27 in 1942, Toshack was judged as unfit for war service, partly because of sporting injuries, including his knees, which were never strong. He did his bit for the war effort by joining a manufacturer of hand guns in Lithgow. In 1945, he and his wife moved to Petersham in Sydney's inner-west, but like Bradman 19 years earlier, he was rejected by the local club. Petersham regretted both. Bradman began with St George, and Toshack played for Marrickville, to which he remained loyal.

He made an immediate impact in the big smoke of Sydney club cricket, so big in fact that he slipped quickly into the New South Wales State side and then was selected to tour New Zealand early in 1946, in Bill Brown's team. He was picked for the solitary Test at Wellington, and must have thought the game at the highest level was well within his capacities. He took 4 for 12, and 2 for 6.

Those troublesome knees played up again, but he gained selection for the 1946–47 Test series against England, and started his Ashes career with a bang – 9 for 99 over two innings in the First Test at the Gabba. He played in all games and took 17 wickets at 25.71. This gained him further chances against India in 1947–48, and he was a sensation, again at the Gabba, taking five wickets for 2 in 19 balls in India's first innings, and 6 for 29 in the second. Toshack's rise without trace seemed complete, but for those wretched joints in his legs. He managed one more Test in that series, and after proving his fitness was selected for the 1948 tour.

Toshack played 12 Tests, taking 47 wickets at 21.04. He took four catches and made 73 runs at 14.60. His first-class record was also good. He took 195 wickets at 20.37, but not even Bradman's dictum about playing straight could save him from a batting average of 5.78 from an aggregate of 185.

Ernie Toshack's career was short – just four years – but it was that experience under Bradman in England that forever would be the highlight of his sporting life.

Keith Johnson (Manager)

On the way home on HMS *Orontes*, the team presented manager Keith Johnson with a solid silver Georgian salver, for his unstinting service to the team. Each player's signature was engraved on it, which expressed the feeling they had collectively for an exceptional job done. (Little did they know that the 1948 team would be so long remembered. One wonders how much that gift would be worth in the memorabilia market in the 21st Century.) Johnson kept the cogs of the Invincibles team turning. Nothing was too much for him. Bradman marvelled at his efforts and energy and worried about his health mid-tour. But Johnson's quiet determination carried him through, in keeping with the team on the field. He attempted to out-Bradman Bradman in handling the team correspondence, and never stopped answering the phone. Johnson thought of the little things that kept the team happy even before players asked for them. For instance, he would arrange tickets for Wimbledon even during the Lord's Test for the players left out of the team.

Johnson was a highly organised, thoughtful back-room type: the perfect backup to Bradman and Hassett.

Reporter Andy Flanagan described Johnson as 'conscientious, reserved, dignified, extraordinarily industrious, and scrupulously trustworthy'.

Johnson brought home approaching £65,000 profit for the Board of Control, who knew in advance that the tour would generate enormous revenue. But it allowed him just £75 expenses to cover contingencies for a touring party of 20 men over eight months.

Keith Johnson may not have been able to create miracles with loaves and fish, but his incredible juggling of the 1948 tour was a small miracle in itself.

Bill Ferguson (Scorer and Baggage Man)

Bill 'Fergie' Ferguson won the admiration of the captain and the team for efforts in not losing a single bag on the entire tour. He also organised the laundry, and did the innumerable errands for the management and players. And on top of that he made not one single error on the scoresheets of 34 matches. He often had to correct scoreboards that had fallen behind or help scorers who were lost with the Australians' prolific scoring.

This very organised planner fitted well with the skipper and the manager, who were like-minded. Bradman and Johnson marvelled at how he conjured porters, lorries, railway carriages, cabs, buses and other transport out of thin air, and never with a fanfare or fuss. The team was on time for every single one of the 200 functions attended. It turned out looking neat and clean for every single day of competition, thanks to the popular 'evergreen' Fergie.

Arthur James (Masseur)

Another important individual in the limited support staff was masseur Arthur James. He attended to the injuries of all but a couple of the team for eight long months. Towards the end of the tour, the niggles, the tears, the strains and the bruises mounted until James could well have been called 'the Octopus'. He needed eight arms to keep the hundreds of muscles under his squeeze in order. James also assisted Bradman and Johnson with the little things such as posting the letters and organising autographs at every ground.

Only two players had to be omitted from the Test team for injuries: Barnes with his bruised ribs and Tallon with his finger and hand problems. James looked after Bradman's side, Miller's back and Lindwall's groin with equal facility and success during the Tests, and helped maintain their performances.

Profiles of England's players in the 1948 Ashes Series

Norman Yardley (Captain)

Bradman's compliments at the Oval about his opposite number in the Tests, Norman Yardley, reflected the cricket world's appreciation of a gentleman of the game.

'We have played against a very lovable opposing skipper,' Bradman remarked. 'He has been kind to us in every way, and it is a great pleasure to have him captain England against us.'

The Australian skipper would never have said that about Yardley's predecessor Wally Hammond. He and Bradman just didn't get on. But everyone got on with unflappable Norman, a kindly, genial character, who was not dealt the best possible hand by the selectors, who seemed to make at times less than logical choices. Perhaps the worst decision was to go into the Leeds Test with just one full-time spinner. Someone like Eric Hollies could have made a difference on the final day when Bradman and Morris ran rampant.

•

Norman Yardley (1915–89) was born in Royston, Yorkshire. At St Peter's School, York, he demonstrated a tremendous aptitude for sport and he followed through at Cambridge University winning Blues at cricket, squash, rugby fives and hockey. He was North of England squash champion six times. Yardley made his cricket debut for Yorkshire at age 21 in 1936 as a right-hand batsman and medium-pace bowler. He toured India in Lord Tennyson's team in 1937–38, and led Cambridge in 1938. In 1938–39, he toured South Africa under Hammond, making his Test debut at Johannesburg, scoring 7 and not getting a bowl.

That was it for Yardley pre-war. After serving in the army (in the Green Howards) in the Middle East and Italy, and being wounded in the Western Desert, he was fit enough to return to Test cricket after the war. At 31, he was vice-captain to Hammond on the 1946–47 Ashes tour of Australia. Yardley's figures were fair to good. He scored 252 at 31.50, and took 10 wickets at 37.20. But he made a modest name for himself by dismissing Bradman three times: once at Sydney when Bradman had scored 234, and twice in Melbourne for 79 and 49 (caught and bowled both times). In that game, Yardley became the first England player to score two half centuries (61 and 53 not out) and take five wickets in Test.

It all looked impressive on the CV, and it was no surprise that he was chosen to lead England in the post-Hammond era (after having done this once, in the final Test at Adelaide in 1946–47, when a disgruntled, depressed Hammond opted out of the game).

In the 4:0 loss to the Australians in 1948, he failed with the bat, scoring just 150 runs in nine innings at 16.66, but returned the best bowling figures, taking nine wickets at 22.66. In 1950 he led England again in three Tests against the West Indies in his last series.

Business and injury restricted him in his last decade of cricket, but he battled on in first-class until he was 40, having been chairman of selectors in 1951 and 1952. He was on the selection panel again from 1953–54. After cricket, Norman Yardley joined the media, writing and broadcasting on BBC radio.

•

In first-class cricket he scored 18,173 runs at 31.17, with 27 centuries. His best effort was 183 not out against Hampshire at Headingley in 1951. Yardley took 279 wickets at 30.49, with his best-ever bowling haul 6 for 29 playing for the MCC against Cambridge at Lord's in 1946. He topped 1,000 runs in a season on eight occasions. He was president of Yorkshire County from 1981–84.

Yardley had 20 Tests, scoring 812 runs at 25.37, and taking 21 wickets at 33.66, and 14 catches.

•

Norman Yardley's approach to the 1948 Ashes restored a degree of goodwill in the Ashes competition after the bitterness engendered by the Bodyline series, and the bitter battles that followed it in the 1930s when cricket was closer to war than sport.

Len Hutton (Vice-Captain)

Bradman succeeded in curtailing Len Hutton in 1948 by a mix of muscle and mind using speed and spin. The Lindwall–Miller combination was the fastest pairing Hutton ever encountered. He had come through it showing courage and skill, but with not enough big scores to make England more competitive. Each bowler snared him three times, and Johnson slipped in with his off-spin to remove him twice, probably because his guard was down. Hutton only failed three times – once at Trent Bridge when Miller bowled him for 3, and twice at Lord's (20 and 13). In his other five innings he scored 74, 81, 57, 30 and 64, demonstrating that he fought well, but with no support at the Oval.

Hutton's experience in 1948 was similar to Bradman's in the Bodyline series of 1932–33. The reaction from captains Jardine and Bradman to a big-scoring opposition batsman in the previous Ashes series (Bradman in 1930, and Hutton in 1938) was the same.

Jardine was hell-bent on limiting, if not destroying Bradman with pace (primarily Larwood and Voce) and with spin (Verity) used on occasions for the *coup de grâce*. Bradman did not use Bodyline tactics in 1948 but his bowlers were just as intimidatory as Larwood and Voce, and the intent was the same. The No. 1 batsmen had to be targeted, softened up and then dismissed wherever possible. The residual impact on other batsmen was huge when they saw their key leading run-maker reduced in effectiveness.

●

Leonard Hutton (1916–90), the son of a builder and youngest of five children, was raised in Fulneck, mid-way between Bradford and Leeds. He first came to notice as a promising cricketer while playing for Pudsey St Lawrence's first XI in 1933, when he turned 17 mid-season. The quiet, modest yet determined young Hutton did well enough to gain the attention of the county club and was placed in the Second XI. His elegant, correct, left elbow-up style caught the eye of those who knew the game. His score of 86 not out against a weak Derbyshire team was noted. There was early criticism for his tardiness and lack of aggression. But his footwork and range of strokes caused most critics to forgive him or at least rate him worth a second and third look. Attacking strokes could come at any time, it was felt. The display of such class in one so young would carry him forward. The critics, for once, were uniformly correct as they watched him develop. A highlight of that year was a confrontation with the great Sydney Barnes, then 60, who was playing for Staffordshire. Bradman had selected this medium-fast purveyor of swing, cut and spin in his best-ever England XI. The combat between one of England's finest bowlers, whose skills peaked in the 19th Century, with one of the country's finest batsmen of the 20th Century, was a special moment in time. According to the *Leeds Mercury*, which covered the match, Barnes' bowling, despite his years, was 'a little short of miraculous in conception'. Hutton stood up to it 'with a confidence and correctness which could hardly have been surpassed by Sutcliffe himself'. He was 69 not out in two hours at the crease before rain ended the match.

In all games with the Yorkshire Second XI in 1933 he notched 699 at 69.90. It was an outstanding beginning. The club nursed him along in 1934. He made the firsts permanently in 1935, scoring a century as an opener with Sutcliffe.

The *Yorkshire Post*'s correspondent in 1935 showed a remarkable prescience with the comment: 'In this 18-year-old batsman Yorkshire have surely found a future Colossus of the game. He may be safely entrusted with the task of regaining for England records which Bradman has made his own.'

In 1936, not long after his 20th birthday, Hutton was 'capped' as a professional by the county. It placed him among the elite of the working class, and would allow a certain mobility in England's economically and socially layered society.

In the last game of the season against the MCC, Hutton took 8 for 77 and made 58, but it was too late and too little for him to be considered for the 1936–37 Ashes tour to Australia in the team led by Gubby Allen.

•

Hutton played his first Test at Lord's against New Zealand three days after his 21st birthday. He took half an hour making 0 and 1 in a drawn game. In the Second Test at Old Trafford, Hutton cracked a 'professional' century in 210 minutes in the first innings and 14 in the second. England won by 130 runs.

The Third Test saw him score 12 in another drawn game. It was a mixed start, but he was on his way at the highest level. *Wisden* named him as the only 'new' player in its Five Cricketers of the Year.

1938 heralded the arrival of Bradman's Australians in England and rumblings in Europe that promised war. Hutton hit the ground running with three superb centuries in games against counties. This confirmed his sure-footed maturity against all types of bowlers and on every variety of wicket. He carried this form into the First Test at Trent Bridge and scored an even 100, which was ranked seventh out of seven by observers. Yet it was his second hundred in four Test innings. His 4 and 5 at Lord's was further disappointment in a Test at the home of cricket. A broken finger kept him from the crease until the final Ashes game at the Oval.

Hutton knew that if ever he was going to make a big score the conditions there were tailor-made for it. The weather was fine; the pitch perfect for batting thanks to groundsman 'Bosser' Martin; the game was timeless, and therefore dictating big scores; and Australia had a very weak bowling attack. Yes, there was O'Reilly delivering his fast leg-breaks but after him there was only left-hand 'Chinaman' bowler Chuck Fleetwood-Smith. The team's sole fast bowler, Ernie McCormick, was out injured. Captain Bradman could then only turn to his part-timers, Mervyn Waite, the medium-pacer, and Stan McCabe, also a medium-trundler at the best of times.

Hutton played his role at the Oval to perfection, scoring 364 in 13 hours and 20 minutes (800 minutes), the longest innings in Test history. He eclipsed Bradman's 334 at Leeds in 1930, an innings that inspired a 14-year-old Hutton who witnessed it. His mighty effort was a formidable performance in terms of concentration, determination and stamina. Every stroke was executed in fluent textbook style. Only brilliance and aggression were lacking.

Hammond was able to close at 7 for 903, allowing England to win by an innings and 579 runs, the biggest victory in Test history. Australia held the Ashes yet England was satisfied to have achieved parity with the old enemy.

•

England took the boat to South Africa for five Tests in 1938–39, and Hutton hit form early with two hundreds and big opening stands with Bill Edrich. But his advance towards the Tests was cut short by a bouncer from Transvaal's express bowler, Eric Davies. It knocked Hutton unconscious and out of the First Test. His confidence was dented when he came back for 17 and 31 in the next two Tests, but he mastered tough bowling on a damp wicket in the Fourth Test at Johannesburg, scoring 92 in 210 minutes. The Fifth Test at Durban was set up as a decider with England leading 1:0 in the series. The wicket provided a run feast but Hutton missed the chance for another huge score when run out for 38 in the first innings. In the second he reached 55 and was bowled playing over a looping delivery from spinner Bruce Mitchell. The 'timeless' Test went on for 10 playing days – the longest in history – but was declared a draw when the England team had to make a two-day 'dash' for Cape Town to catch a boat home. With war clouds gathering over Europe, no one wanted to be far from home, a Test without end not withstanding.

Hutton gave himself a 23rd birthday present at Lord's in the 1939 summer against the West Indies with 196, but again paled a little in comparison with the dashing Compton (120), who outscored him in a blistering fourth-wicket stand of 248 in 122 minutes. They were both upstaged by the fight and brilliance of George Headley who scored a century in each Test innings; the second time it had been done by him and the first time by anyone at cricket headquarters. England's superior all-round skills gave it the game by eight wickets.

Hutton this time failed at Old Trafford but came back at the Oval, the scene of his triumph over the Australians a year earlier, with scores of 73 and 165 not out. He and Hammond

(138) flayed the bowling for a then world-record third-wicket stand of 264 in just 181 minutes. Even though he was not as aggressive as his partners, Hutton was prepared to step up a notch in Tests if the occasion was right.

County cricket ceased in 1940 because of the war, but the Leagues continued and thrived. Hutton played for Pudsey St Lawrence again in the Bradford League and topped the averages. He had joined the Army Physical Training Corps and was made a sergeant-instructor. He trained to be a commando. This would have led him to combat on the continent but a gymnasium accident damaged his left forearm and wrist. Three operations later his left arm was a few centimetres shorter than the right. It was thought that his career was in jeopardy, He could not play cricket at all in 1942 – the year wife Dorothy gave birth to a son, Richard. After rehabilitation, Hutton played again in 1943. In 1944 and 1945 he maintained form with games for Pudsey and in international matches against Australian services teams that included Lindsay Hassett and Keith Miller, whom he found a formidable foe on the field. The five Victory Tests versus the Australians were at times played with the intensity of real Tests and Hutton was the better for them. In the third – at Lord's – he made 104 and 69. Hutton had just turned 29 and he looked like the young star that dominated Australia at the Oval in 1938.

•

Hutton lived up to expectations in 1946 as crowds flocked to see the three Tests against the visiting Indians. He made 183 not out against them for Yorkshire and it was almost as if the year was 1940. It was typically correct big Hutton knock. He eschewed the desire to take the attack apart, yet still compiled his runs at a comfortable rate and with a wide range of shots. Only one, the hook, was made difficult by his injured arm.

In the Tests versus India he had only one reasonable score – 67 – at Old Trafford, and averaged just 30.75. Still, his form in other first-class cricket demonstrated he was in a class shared by few in the world. The end of the 1946 season was soon followed by the boat trip to Australia, which Hutton regarded as a main achievement. The Australians took to him with ease. Not only was he a batsman of elegance and enormous skill. His laconic, naturally friendly manner and humility engaged cricketers and fans alike. Like Bradman, he was vanity-free. Australians appreciated this in their heroes above all else. Hutton responded with fine performances in the build-up to the Tests, including centuries at Adelaide and Melbourne. Before the international contests most cricket fans Down Under now had a feel for Hutton's superiority. They looked forward to the contests against Australia's untested new bowling line-up led by Lindwall and Miller. The latter was regarded by Hutton and most of the tourists as a tough opponent.

Miller jumped him in Brisbane, sending him back bowled for 7 and caught for a duck. Both the Australian speedmen did not spare him short-pitched deliveries. England suffered from the weather. It was twice forced to bat after violent storms and lost by a wide margin.

The Second Test saw Hutton combat the pacemen on a friendlier, slower wicket with lugubrious defence but then fell to Ian Johnson's off-spinning. Hutton nicked Johnson's third ball in Test cricket to keeper Tallon. His 39 took 122 minutes. In the second innings, England faced an impossible situation after Australia had amassed 8 for 659. Hutton responded with one of the finest of cameos. Playing every shot, he slammed 37 in 24 minutes.

'Then he hit his wicket [bowled Miller],' A. G. Moyes wrote in his *Century of Cricketers*, 'and the sun was hidden by clouds. It was a glorious piece of batting, a choice miniature that I will carry with me always. The Hutton who scintillated that day was one of the masters, a man who removed the dungarees he wore at the Oval [in making 364] and had arrayed himself again in flannels.'

In the Third Test at Melbourne, Lindwall dismissed him for 2. When he struggled beyond the menacing speedsters in the second, the more docile medium pace of Ernie Toshack saw him caught by Bradman for 40. The match was drawn.

By the Fourth Test, Hutton was looking like the Hutton England knew and Australia had seen in the games against the States. He fell to the spinners, McCool for 90, and Johnson for 76. The second dig was brilliant as he counterattacked the speedsters. Yet Compton and Arthur Morris, who both scored centuries in each innings, out-performed him. The game was a draw once more; the Ashes and the series were lost. With the pressure off, Hutton hit his first century in Australia – 122 retired ill – but it was not a knock to remember, being laborious and taking a day to compile. A day later Hutton had a sore throat and fell ill with tonsillitis. He missed the only Test in New Zealand, yet was well enough to fly home, a novelty in 1947.

He hit his straps at Headingley in the Fourth Test versus South Africa in 1947 with 100 run out and 32 not out, followed by 83 and 36 at the Oval. Those last four innings in the series won 3:0 by England silenced his critics who were suggesting other openers. Hutton seemed stronger by the end of the season. He ended it with more running than he began it, scoring 270 not out against Hampshire in the final game.

Hutton, Edrich, Compton and Bedser (England's four best performers) were stood down for a tour of the Caribbean in an early version of the current 'rotation' system in modern one-day cricket. England's selectors wanted this group to be fit and ready for Bradman's Australians set to tour England in 1948. However, Hutton received an SOS from the tourists after injuries in the first two Tests in January and February 1948. The West Indies in the Caribbean in 1947–48 proved a much stronger opposition than in previous decades with players such as the brilliant batsmen Everton Weekes and Frank Worrell dominant. Hutton had little impact on the 2:0 result in favour of the West Indies from four Tests. His scores were 31, 24, 56 and 60. It was a warning to the cricket world that the calypso cricketers were no longer easy-beats.

Hutton carried Yorkshire in 1948, scoring eight centuries and averaging 92.05, which indicated that despite the Tests, he was in good touch overall. He was more comfortable against South Africa away in 1948–49, where he played a dominant part in its narrow 2:0 win from five Tests. The home team was always competitive. Hutton notched three centuries before the First Test at Durban where he scored 83 and 5 in a tight game, which the tourists won by just two wickets. He handled the express pace of Cuan McCarthy well and commented at the end of the series: 'It's never easy, but after the summer [in England] against Lindwall and Miller, I was well prepared.'

He and Washbrook set a world-record opening stand of 359 in 310 minutes (Washbrook 195, Hutton 158) in the Second Test at Johannesburg. But in compiling 608, England didn't leave enough time to dismiss South Africa twice. The game was drawn.

Hutton followed with 41 (run out) and what *The Times* called a 'masterful cameo' of 87 in the Cape Town Test. In the Fourth Test at Johannesburg, his second innings 123 held England together and warded off defeat. He contributed 46 and 32 in the Final Test at Port Elizabeth, which England won by three wickets.

•

Hutton led from the front in the 1949 Tests in England versus New Zealand with scores of 101, 0, 23, 66, 73 and 206. In this double hundred, his third fifty took just 35 minutes showing his frustrated critics like A. G. Moyes, Neville Cardus, Bradman and others that he could deliver if he wished.

•

Amateur Norman Yardley was appointed to lead England at home against the touring West Indies in 1950 and was thrashed

3:1. It wasn't just the Australians who were tough to beat at the beginning of the second half of the 20th Century. Hutton struggled to combat the spin twins Valentine and Ramadhin, notching 39, 45, 35, 10, and a magnificent 202 not out at the Oval – surely his favourite ground outside Yorkshire – in carrying his bat in the final Test. Freddie Brown replaced Yardley in that game, only to perform with about the same impact.

England stumbled down to Australia for the 1950–51 Ashes under Brown once more and was given a 4:1 hiding. Hutton was dropped down the order for the First Test at Brisbane and in the second innings made 62 not out from 122 on a rain-affected pitch. *Wisden* did not understate by calling the innings 'one of the most remarkable in Test cricket'. Some observers argued it was Hutton's best effort ever. He played with dead bat and soft hands, the ball often ending close to his feet. England went down by 70 runs, and then lost by just 28 at the Second Test at Melbourne. Hutton, still down the order, made 12 and 40. He was restored to opening at Sydney where he made 62 and 9, while England went down by an innings and 13 runs. Jack Iverson's variety of spinners tantalised and bamboozled the tourists, allowing him to take 6 for 27 in England's second innings. At Adelaide, Hutton with 156 (run out) and 45, was the only tourist to consistently defy the powerful bowling line-up of Lindwall, Miller, Johnson, Iverson and Bill Johnston. In the Fifth Test at Melbourne, which England won well by eight wickets, Hutton again led from the front with 79. When the game had to be won in a small chase of 95 in the final innings, he made an 'in-control' 60 not out.

This victory made the England team members ecstatic. They had beaten Australia in a Test for the first time since the Oval in 1938 – a break of nearly 13 years. It may have been a dead rubber, but it didn't matter to England. The psychological boost to the team's morale as it headed for two Tests in New Zealand (won 1:0 by England) was huge.

In the 1951 home series against South Africa, Hutton was less inspired than in Australia, scoring one century. In his last innings of the series, he was out in a most unusual way: *obstructing the field*. In defending his wicket from a ball he had hit, which may have deflected onto the stumps, he accidentally prevented the keeper from taking a catch.

England's 3:1 series win saw Brown bow out as somewhat a hero. Hutton and other top players did not tour India, Pakistan and Ceylon in 1951–52. Amateurs Nigel Howard (four Tests) and Donald Carr (one Test) led the side. But when it came to the home season of 1952, the selectors, Norman Yardley, Freddie Brown, Bob Wyatt (all amateurs who led England) and Leslie Ames, the former champion keeper/batsman, chose Hutton to lead his country for the first time, against India. He would turn 36 during the season.

The decision was six years late, but better than never.

•

Hutton had no choice, or desire, but to stay a professional, an act that would change the attitude to leadership in England forever and for the better. No longer would a captain have to have the right pedigree, and come from the South of England and Oxbridge. Nor would he need to be from the MCC, which barred professionals. Class as a performer, not in the social structure, would be the key determinant in selecting an England skipper. It was the first big step in the quest to win back the Ashes.

Hutton scored only 10 and 10 in his first Test as leader – at Headingley in 1952 versus India – but had at his command an impressive looking team. Fred Trueman, the son of a Yorkshire miner, on debut took 3 for 89 and 4 for 27, and put fear into the Indians with his quick bowling. Jim Laker, the off-spinner, was now a world-class performer. Alec Bedser could still deliver. The batting line-up of Hutton, Reg Simpson, Peter May, Denis Compton, Tom Graveney and Allan Watkins was strong and of high calibre. Evans was by now the world's best keeper, ahead of Tallon, whose skills were fluctuating.

It took Hutton that one Test to adjust to the captaincy. In the next three Tests of a series of four, he scored 150, 39 not out at Lord's, 104 at Old Trafford and 86 at the Oval. England won the series comfortably 3:0. The country was now brimming with confidence that the new look, classy line-up would rock the Australians in 1953. Certainly Hutton was now king of English cricket.

There was no away tour in the winter of 1952–53, which was the perfect preparation for the coming tough Ashes battle in 1953. The series was marred by poor weather, which helped, along with unenterprising leadership by both Hutton and his counterpart Lindsay Hassett, four games to end in draws. Nevertheless, the crowds – a record 549,650 – flocked to the grim matches. In the Fourth Test at Headingley, all-rounder Trevor Bailey became a hero of sorts by batting 262 minutes for 38 runs in England's second innings. This knock shortened the time for Australia to win. Bailey then bowled leg-theory under Hutton's direction, on or outside leg-stump to a packed leg-side field. This slowed Australia to such an extent that a draw was forced with the tourists 30 short, with six wickets in hand. The competition drew out the Yorkshireman in Hutton. He made it tougher for himself by losing the toss in all five Tests.

After the wars of attrition of the first four games, Hutton knew he had to win to retain the leadership. A loss would surely see a reversion to the old England system of choosing a rank amateur, even if highly ranked. There was terrific pressure coming into the match. World War II was now eight years away and the nation was yearning for a big victory over the Australians, especially in the year of the Queen's coronation. A loss would simply not do. England had the best looking attack in decades – Trueman, Bedser, Laker and left-arm spinner Tony Lock (like Laker also from Surrey). Trueman was back in the squad after his national service, and Hutton hoped he would wreak havoc. It was retribution time for the Australians after their years of intimidation by Miller and Lindwall. Trueman

played his part, taking the figures with 4 for 86 in Australia's first innings of 275. Only Hassett (53) at the top of the order, and Lindwall (62) near the bottom of it, reached fifty.

England replied with 306 (Hutton top-scored with 82) – these scores typical of the tight series. The lead was just 31. There was TV coverage of the game as the wonderful day three for England unfolded with Laker and Lock taking nine wickets. Australia was dismissed for 162. England had 132 to get to win, which it did easily, losing just two wickets. Hutton was run out for 17.

'The nation was riveted by the series and by this game in particular,' Bradman said. 'A kind of fever gripped England. Then with victory, delirium followed.'

Hutton, immortalised for his 364 in 1938, had risen among the gods of English cricket once more at the Oval, this time with an Ashes win after a long break. He had performed well and dourly to suit the mood of the contest, scoring 43, 60 not out, 145 (his only century – at Lord's – and hampered by an attack of fibrositis), 5, 66, 0, 25, 82 and 17 run out. This gave him 443 at 55.38, easily the highest aggregate and best average – the only one of more than fifty – in the series.

•

Even with a strong team, England went down in the First Test of the 1953–54 series against the West Indies at Sabina Park by 140 runs. Hutton warmed up with 24 and 56, but he and the other bats struggled with the spin of Ramadhin and Valentine, who had troubled them in 1950 (taking 59 out of 77 wickets to fall in the Tests). The game was notable for two incidents. Tony Lock became the second player after Australia's Ernie Jones to be called for throwing. And when umpire Perry Burke gave local player John Holt out lbw six short of his century, the umpire's wife and child were physically assaulted. Riots were always a potential problem.

Hutton stepped up a notch in the Second Test at Bridgetown, scoring a fine double, 72 and 77, but England went down again, this time by 181 runs. He led a fight-back in the Third Test at Georgetown, making a fine, fighting 169 in 480 minutes in England's nine-wicket win. Hutton showed his cool in a real crisis in this game, when, after a clear run-out of West Indian Clifford McWatt, the crowd rioted and threw bottles and other missiles onto the field. The main problem was not so much the rum consumed, but the bets placed on McWatt making a century stand with John Holt for the eighth wicket. Hutton would not leave the pitch, despite officials pleading with him to do so.

'I want a couple of wickets before the close of play tonight,' were his immortal words in the face of danger.

The game went on. Hutton got his wickets and eventual victory. He drew high praise for his classic batting and the courageous way he faced the ugly situation. The game did much to enhance him as a leader. The players were more than ever united behind him.

In the Fourth Test at Port-of-Spain high scores were assured on a jute matting pitch. Hutton managed a modest 44 and 30 not out, while the West Indies big guns – Worrell (167), Weekes (206) and Walcott (124) all got going. The game was drawn, leaving the need for a face-saving effort by the tourists in the final Test at Sabina Park. Hutton led the way, making 205 and becoming the first England captain to score a double century in an overseas Test. England won by nine wickets again, thus levelling the series at 2-all. Hutton sailed away from the Caribbean with an aggregate of 677 and an average of 96.7. Just as important to him was the prestige of a much heralded revival by England after the 1953 Ashes triumph. It was still intact.

Hutton was mentally and physically exhausted on return to England and, on the advice of his doctor, opted out of the second and third of four Tests against Pakistan. In his place the selectors chose the Rev. David Sheppard, another amateur who captained Cambridge and Sussex. Hutton's health brought media speculation that Sheppard should be chosen to lead England Down Under in 1954–55. The spectre of 'amateurs first' emerged again. After much back-room caballing, the MCC chose Hutton for the Australian tour and defence of the Ashes.

•

Hutton had a strong squad, but his 'team within a team' of Frank Tyson and Brian Statham, was his strongest asset. He erred in Brisbane in the First Test by putting Australia in when he won the toss. The response was 601 with Neil Harvey and Arthur Morris scoring big hundreds. Hutton's old foes Lindwall and Miller had him cheaply in both innings, and England went under by an innings and 154.

Hutton scored 30 and 28 in the Second Test at Sydney, with only Peter May (104) in the second innings putting up strong resistance as England recorded 154 and 296. Tyson made up for the batting failures by taking 4 for 45 and then in a devastating spell, 6 for 85. Hutton put down Tyson's fire to the fact that Lindwall had knocked him out with a bouncer. England won in a tight game by 38 runs.

The blow apparently still riled Tyson less than two weeks later in Melbourne in the Third Test, when he took 7 for 27. Most observers thought that he bowled as fast as anyone had ever done in a Test. It was enough to give England another win, by 128 runs. Hutton struggled with 6 and 42, the latter innings taking 146 minutes. Despite its tardiness incurring the wrath of the Melbourne crowd, the knock was invaluable. Hutton proved to be unperturbed by this and continual criticism of his slow over-rate. England was delivering at the miserable rate of 11.5 overs an hour (69 overs a day – 21 overs less than desirable in the 21st Century) compared with Australia's 14. Hutton had a habit of changing the field when the bowler was at the top of his mark. He admitted it was a tactic particularly directed at Harvey, who liked to get on with the game.

England now led 2:1 with two Tests to play. Australia had to win both to retrieve the Ashes. In Adelaide, Hutton struck better form with a top score of 80 in the first innings, which gave England a narrow 18-run lead. Then Tyson, Statham and Bob Appleyard (bowling medium-pace off-spinners) each took three wickets and reduced Australia to 111. England had 94 to make for victory. It lost five wickets doing it. The win gave England the Ashes. (The final game at Sydney was hampered by rain and drawn.)

Hutton, at 38 years, had triumphed. He had done what no other Englishman had done by being on the field for every Test in two winning series against Australia. He skippered on for two Tests in New Zealand and made 53 in his last Test innings – not far short of his Test average 56.67. He made 6,971 runs in 79 Tests and included 19 centuries.

He seemed set to go on for a series at home against South Africa, but illness (severe lumbago) and a lack of enthusiasm for the demands of another season as skipper saw him retire. Hutton was just short of his 39th birthday. He continued on in the 1955 season spasmodically for Yorkshire and ended his first-class career with 40,140 runs at 55.51, including 129 centuries. Hutton's bowling returns of 173 wickets at 29.51 suggested he may have been under-bowled through his long career.

Hutton wrote for the London *Evening News* until 1963. In 1960 he began a 25-year career at J.H. Fenner and Co, a power transmission engineering group.

In many ways, Hutton's career paralleled Bradman's. They both held the world record score and were their country's leading batsman over two decades. Both men proved successful captains and led their teams to convincing Ashes victories before retiring.

Len Hutton was knighted for his services to cricket in 1956.

Alec Bedser

Alec Bedser was by far England's most effective bowler in the 1948 Ashes, sending down nearly twice as many overs as the next bowler Laker, and taking twice as many wickets (18) as the next on England's list: Yardley and Laker (nine each). Only Bill Johnston's stint of 309.2 overs was greater than Bedser's efforts (274.3 overs). Bedser was both strike and stock bowler; workhorse and breakthrough striker. His efforts take on another dimension when the Australian batting line-up is taken into consideration.

Bradman regarded Bedser as the most difficult bowler he ever faced in conditions conducive to swing and cut. The bowler troubled him during the Ashes of 1948 with deliveries that dipped late in from the off and caused him to be caught three times at backward short-leg.

'After I had dismissed Don in Australia [during the 1946–47 Ashes] with a leg-cutter [fast leg-break],' Bedser said, 'it was clear that if I was to get a delivery [in-swinger] in the right spot, he would be committed to play it in case it was the leg-cutter again.'

Bedser dismissed Bradman six times in all, and remarkably in five successive innings. Bradman's scores in those five knocks were 63, 138, 0, 38 and 89. His only real failure was a second-ball duck at Adelaide during the 1946–47 Ashes in Australia. He regarded this Bedser delivery as the best ball that ever dismissed him. It headed a list of 547 dismissals in his entire career from country to club, through first-class and Test level.

According to Bradman, this golden delivery swung and dipped to leg late, hit the deck outside leg stump and cut past the bat to crash into the off-stump.

'It was a fast leg-break,' Sir Alec told me in a September 2001 interview at his Woking home near London. 'I very nearly got him with the same kind of delivery before he had scored in the second innings [of that Adelaide Test]. It missed the off-stump by a whisker.'

During the 1950–51 Ashes, Bedser took 30 wickets at just 16.06, and this in a losing team beaten 4:1. Ten of these wickets were secured in the final Test at Melbourne in England's breakthrough Test win – the first since 1938. Bedser was easily player of the match. *Wisden* acknowledged his dominance too. It was a momentous time for him. He had at last been in a team that had beaten Australia in a Test. Bedser's influence made it all the more worth savouring.

He followed this up with a performance in South Africa with 30 wickets claimed at a miserly 17.23. Then he collected 20 wickets at 13.95 at home against India in 1952. In England in the 1953 Ashes, Bedser had his most triumphant series. He was the decisive bowler in an Ashes victory; the first time England had achieved this since the Bodyline series in Australia in 1932–33. Bedser had reached performance nirvana. He took 39 wickets at 17.48 and broke Maurice Tate's record. The highlight was Bedser's 14 for 99 at Trent Bridge in the First Test.

'This effort must surely be bracketed in the top few bowling performances of all time,' Bradman noted. 'It was certainly in the top two or three I ever saw against Australia.'

Bedser had an enormous capacity for hard work in the field, and demonstrated a never-say-die spirit, and determination, even when carrying an injury. He was never forced from the field through a breakdown. About as close as he came to the fence was at Adelaide when he succumbed to the fierce heat and vomited near the boundary. Yet he was back in the middle bowling minutes later.

'I bowled more than 3,200 overs between April 1950 and August 1951,' he noted. This was many times the number of overs sent down over a similar stretch of time by England's modern fast bowlers, who are now not required to play for their counties during seasons when contracted to play international games.

Bedser was sceptical about modern fitness methods and athletic training. He reckoned that solid work on the field was the only true way to be fit for cricket. He was always the tireless operator. His captains, Wally Hammond, Len Hutton, Peter May (England and Surrey) and others, could rely on him day in, day out. He and his identical twin Eric put their strength and capacity for labour down to the physical work they did from the age of 10. They both made Pythonesque declarations about their early years digging ditches, working in gardens, chopping wood and so on. Yet their records of endurance on the cricket field, which would not be countenanced today by professionals, were testimony to their decades of genuine toil.

They were ground staff bowlers at the Oval in their late teenage years. The Bedsers joined the RAF in 1939 at 21, when the war began and were 27 in 1946 on returning to civilian life. They missed prime years but claimed that the war experience toughened them mentally and physically.

'They talk about tension today in cricket,' Bedser remarked, 'but after experiencing the war years, tension on the cricket field was nothing.'

By the standards of the 1940s and 1950s, Bedser was regarded as a fitness fanatic and his inspiration came in part from his wartime RAF physical training. A big-framed man of 6 ft 3 in (191 cm), Bedser would be seen stretching, doing knee bends, sit-ups, side bends and running on the spot in the dressing room before taking the field. The aim was to be loose and ready to let rip in his first over. Bedser would curl his large right hand over the ball for the in-swinger, the away-swinger or his specialty, the leg-cutter.

Bedser demonstrated his leg-break grip by placing his paw across the seam. Only someone with such a hand, and strong fingers, could exact the 'cut' or 'spin' he managed.

He was nowhere near the speed of his contemporaries: Statham, Trueman, Lindwall and Miller. The keeper, Godfrey Evans for the most part, would stand up to the wicket. It took nerve and skill for bowler and keeper to succeed in such a difficult double act. The bowler had to be dead accurate. Nothing could stray down leg-side. Bedser could make the ball rear from his relatively short 10-pace run-up. He had one of the most deceptive in-swingers of all time. His delivery action suggested an away-swinger. If not bamboozled by that, a right-hand bat might well have trouble with the very late swing. The sight of a batsman squared up and jamming down far too late was a common experience across England from 1946–60 whenever Bedser bowled for Surrey and England. It didn't matter if the batsman was waiting for this delivery. It fooled most first-class batsmen at least once in their careers. The same applied to the leg-cutter, which was usually employed on poor pitches. It was far tougher to perfect. But when it worked, it was unplayable, even for the finest batsmen. Hassett joked of swatting at the ball three times and missing each – once as it swung in the air, a second time when it hit the deck and a third occasion when it whipped past the bat.

•

Born in 1918, Alec Bedser was similar to two other 'giants' of English cricket, S. F. Barnes and Maurice Tate. They bowled with laser-like accuracy, employing swing, seam and pace. Bedser's strength allowed him to bowl for long periods without sacrificing line and length. In his prime, batsmen never felt 'in' against him. They had their temperament and concentration tested by him.

Big Alec had a lot of fun bowling to left-handers. Bedser dismissed Australia's Arthur Morris 18 times in 21 Tests. Admittedly, Morris's average was outstanding – more than 60 – throughout these contests. Yet Bedser would claim him, if not as his bunny, then a brilliant bat he could break through more often than not at some time in an innings. Bedser also checked the aggressive Neil Harvey, who was capable of taking a game by force. Bedser thought all left-handers were vulnerable to the ball that moved in quickly to them from their off. He would bowl his in-swinger or the off-cutter (the fast leg-break) to trouble lefties.

•

Alec was born at Reading, Berkshire, within minutes of his identical twin brother Eric, who was a talented county bowling all-rounder. They were raised in Woking. Their father was a bricklayer and they helped him build their Woking home in 1953 where they lived as inseparable twins. The fates of the Bedser twins, perhaps, were sealed when they tossed a coin to see who would bowl pace or spin. Alec won the toss and chose pace. Eric was one of the finest off-spinners not to play Test cricket. They both began in the city as clerks in lawyers' offices, but they only ever dreamed of playing cricket, and for Surrey. They both attained their dreams. Their skills as professionals played a huge part in the county's golden years of seven successive championships from 1952–58. In each of the first six years of this amazing run, Alec took more than 80 wickets at less than 19 runs per wicket. It was a sustained stretch of brilliance rarely matched in the history of first-class cricket.

Alec's Test career began in an illustrious manner in 1946 when he collected 11 Indian scalps in each of his first two Tests. To his surprise, it was enough to ensure a trip to Australia under Wally Hammond in 1946–47. It wasn't an entirely happy time, with Hammond an aloof, unhelpful leader, who travelled separately from the team. Bedser got no advice from him and found England's premier bat of the 1920s and 1930s uninspiring. It didn't help that the tourists failed to win a Test or even challenge the Australians. Bedser returned home with unflattering figures and a sense that he had been fortunate to start against the weak Indian line-up of 1946. This was confirmed in 1948 against the Invincibles, yet his figures were this time relatively good, considering the batsmen to whom he had to bowl.

The wheel turned in 1950–51, when he starred Down Under and established himself as one of the game's best-ever bowlers. He became a key to England winning the Ashes in 1953 under Hutton, an achievement that paved the way for its world dominance for the next years.

Bedser was vice-captain to Peter May at Surrey in 1957 when the county won the sixth of their straight titles, and again in 1958, '59 and '60. It was at a time when a professional could not captain Surrey. Had this arcane rule not been in vogue, Bedser, one of the most acute thinkers on the game, would certainly have led his county.

Bedser passed Clarrie Grimmett's world record and ended his career with 236 wickets from 51 Tests at an average of 24.89 (while scoring 714 runs at 12.75 and holding 26 catches). This was a laudable effort considering his late start at 27 years of age. His Test career ended without fanfare in 1954–55 in Australia. Hutton preferred the tearaway speed of Frank Tyson, and the steady Brian Statham. Injury in the form of debilitating shingles lessened Bedser's powers early in the tour and allowed the others to make their marks. He played just one more Test in 1955 against South Africa, replacing the injured Statham.

His first-class career went on until 1960. In 485 matches he took 1,924 wickets at 20.41, held 289 catches, and made 5,735 runs at 14.51.

•

Bedser put an enormous amount back into the game for little or no reward financially. He was an England selector for a record 23 years, starting as a member of the MCC committee in 1962, and being chairman for 13 years between 1969 and 1981. In that time England played seven Ashes series and lost just two of them. This record and his own playing performances have given more than usual credence to the cliché, 'in my day', when uttered by Bedser.

He was a popular assistant manager to the Duke of Norfolk during the MCC tour of Australia in 1962–63. England, led by Ted Dexter, forced a 1-all series against Richie Benaud's Australians. Bedser managed the MCC tours of Australia led by Mike Denness in 1974–75, and by Mike Brearley in 1979–80.

The Bedser twins invested proceeds from their days at Surrey and ran a successful office equipment company. Alec was awarded an OBE in 1964 and a CBE in 1982 for his services to cricket and was president of Surrey in 1987, an honour that meant much to him. He served on both Surrey and MCC committees. On 1 January 1997, Bedser became only the second bowler – after Sir Richard Hadlee – to be knighted.

Denis Compton

Denis Compton's performances in 1948 rank high in the history of the Ashes, especially as he was playing in a losing side facing a formidable attack. He was easily England's best bat in the series, scoring 562, with two centuries at an average of 62.44. Not only did he bat exceptionally well and consistently (except at the Oval), he sustained some brutal knocks and came back from them to show that he was not just a master batsman; he had exceptional courage to go with his status.

At times Australia had no counter to him. Lindwall and Miller resorted to attempts at blasting him out, still to little avail.

•

Denis Compton (1918–97) was the mid-20th Century's cavalier of UK sport, who although professional at both soccer and cricket, always gave the impression of being carefree. Sport seemed to be fun to him. This does not mean he didn't play it hard. He was one of England's finest competitors, especially against Australia, which drew the best from him. It was just that Compton competed with finesse and good humour.

The son of a lorry driver, Denis was brought up in Hendon, Middlesex, near Lord's, which was to become his other 'home'. He had a poor but happy childhood in the 1920s, when boys swarmed in the street outside his home playing cricket. School matches were competitive events played in the evening and watched by hundreds from the neighbourhood. Such a cauldron, missing now in suburban England, was bound to produce talent. Compton excelled at games, particularly cricket and soccer, and at 12, in 1930, he played in his father Harry's team, Stamford Hill. At 14, in 1932, he played for Elementary Schools against the Public Schools and was the most successful player in the game, scoring a stylish 114 and taking two wickets for five runs. It won him a cricket bat from the *Star* newspaper and a little publicity. It was the first recognition on a national level for a sporting prodigy. More important still was the impression made on Sir Pelham ('Plum') Warner, the former England and Middlesex player. Young Compton had just finished school. Warner, who was an excellent judge of a cricketer, asked him to join the ground staff at Lord's. That took care of employment for half the year. A few months later, Compton was picked to play soccer for England schoolboys against Wales. His brilliant play was reported to Arsenal and led to him being offered work with the ground staff at Arsenal's Highbury North London home. Now the teenager had income all year round in a fairy tale beginning to a career that would span another generation. It was a case of exceptional skill spotted early and rewarded.

This progress fitted well with Compton's demeanour. He always looked the part, right down to his neat attire and parted hair, and played his roles with flair and dash. Here was a sporting hero in the making.

Compton's individual style was not tampered with, but he was shown a few things. He had been a left-arm purveyor of orthodox off-spin, but was introduced by Jack Walsh, the Leicester spinner, to wrist spinning. Compton liked the trickery he could indulge in with his 'Chinaman'. It suited the more adventurous side of his character.

In batting, he was a natural at all the strokes, but the one he loved most and developed in this early period was the sweep. It became a Compton signature. His trick was not to brush the ball square. Instead he used timing to help it along behind square or fine. It became an enormous source of runs for him. So did his cover-drive and cut. He was a fearless hooker and liked to pull. Perhaps only the true straight drive eluded him. But Compton didn't consider it as productive as his other drives.

He was 16 in 1934 when Woodfull's Australian tourists were fighting to take back the Ashes after they had been so rudely removed from the Southern Hemisphere by Douglas Jardine. Compton blossomed in his limited chances for the MCC, scoring 222 at 44.40. A year later, he managed 16 matches, scoring 690 at 46. At 18, in 1936, he came in last for Middlesex led by Walter Robins (and including Gubby Allen). He batted well enough in scoring 20 to suggest he should have been at least five places up the order. Compton's next match was against Nottinghamshire and the combination of Harold Larwood and Bill Voce – the most feared duo in cricket. Compton drove Larwood for four in the first innings. Larwood responded with his trademark accurate bouncer, which was hooked for four. Scores of 26 and 14 appear modest, but his attitude in handling pace said much more about his potential. This was demonstrated further in the next game against Northamptonshire, when he made 87.

The Times' cricket writer noted:

'He has style, he has discretion, and he has the strokes.'

Progress continued and in the return match against Northants he hit his initial first-class century – an even 100 not out.

Wisden said: 'By perfect timing, Compton drove, pulled and cut with remarkable power, and took out his bat, with 14 fours as his best strokes, in one and three-quarter hours . . .'

It wasn't just the batting that impressed. He showed fight with the tail, a pugnacity that England could well do with on its coming tour to Australia for the 1936–37 Ashes contest. There was criticism. It had to do with his unorthodoxy, born of a free spirit and attitude. But Compton was a superior talent *because of* his natural flamboyance, which dictated his capacity to take to bowlers and win the battle.

Compton's development, now acknowledged at first hand by Warner, Robins, Allen, *The Times*, *Wisden*, and all the other scribes that saw him, was a fraction late to be included on tour. His first-class season ended with an aggregate of 1,004 runs at 34.62, with just that one hundred against Northants and eight fifties. It was not enough to cause selectors to take a punt with such precocious talent.

This non-selection left Compton with the wonderful option of playing on the wing for Arsenal. The confidence gained from first-class cricket was transferred to the football pitch. His first game was against Glasgow Rangers, who were so impressed they offered to poach him for £2,000. Compton rejected the offer. Arsenal had nurtured him. The young man had his loyalties. Besides, his natural environment was North London, not Glasgow, which would have been a world away from his comfort zone.

Compton was rewarded straightaway by selection in Arsenal's next home game played in front of 68,000. In turn, he paid back the club with the first goal after a sprint down the wing, a pass, a receive and a cool guide into the net in front of ecstatic fans.

He developed into a fine soccer player – an outside left – with an outstanding temperament. One fault was a tendency to hold on to the ball too long. Compton loved to dribble and baulk around an opponent. It wasn't because he was a showman. It was just that this was a one-on-one aspect of combat that he had performed in the streets of Hendon since he was very young.

With this breakthrough football season behind him, Compton turned up at Lord's in April 1937 with renewed zest for a big cricket season, which it proved to be. His 1,980 runs was nearly double his 1936 aggregate. He scored three centuries, with a top of 177 at Lord's against Gloucestershire, and averaged 47.14. Compton was aided by mentor Patsy Hendren, then 48 and in his last season. Hendren's Irish background ensured he played for enjoyment and he imparted this to the 19-year-old up and comer. Hendren's attitude of always letting the opposition think you were relaxed and on top of things fitted with Compton's natural demeanour. England selectors noted this, acknowledged he had runs on the board, and picked him for the Third Test of a three-match series versus New Zealand. He was then the youngest player ever selected for England; an enormous act of faith and contrary to a cricketing tradition known more for bringing back veterans than blooding youth. Len Hutton had made his debut in this series too. But his typically serious Northern mien and capabilities made him appear like someone much older than his 21 years. Compton's selection at just 19 was an inspired choice in favour of potential brilliance. He didn't let anyone down with his 65 run out in his only innings in the Oval Test. Compton already had a poor reputation as a caller for a run. His cry of 'Yes', it was joked, was merely an opening bid. But in his first Test knock, the ball was deflected onto the stumps after the other batsman had hit it straight back. Denis was left out of his ground. The innings itself was praised for his judgement of which deliveries to hit hard.

His 1938 first-class figures remained similar to the previous season, except that he hit five hundreds, and showed that the territory beyond a century was now common ground for him. One of those hundreds came in the opening Test against Bradman's Australian team at Trent Bridge. His 102 made him the youngest centurion – at 20 years and 19 days – for England in an Ashes competition. He hit 15 fours and figured in a record fifth-wicket stand with Eddie Paynter (216 not out) of 206 in just 138 minutes, including 141 in the last 90 minutes of the first day's play. This innings was the first where Compton was seen as 'cavalier'. *The Times* reporter liked his range of shots, particularly his cuts and drives. His on-side play was 'aggressive'.

Nevertheless, he was admonished by his grim skipper Wally Hammond for not going on to a double, especially against the Australians. *Wisden*, however, was kinder, naming him as one of its Five Cricketers of the Year of 1938.

Compton managed 76 not out at Lord's in the second innings of the Test. It was another brilliant knock of a different variety on a rain-affected wicket. In the Fifth Test at the Oval, he grew restless waiting for Len Hutton to wade his way towards a triple century. When Compton finally came in at 4 for 547, he was bowled for just 1. It was not a situation to inspire a fighting innings. His 1938 series aggregate was 214 at an average of 42.80.

Compton was chosen to tour South Africa for the 1938–39 season, but he remained loyal to his winter sport, and played for Arsenal. Yet he could not find a regular spot in the team. Nevertheless, he was now an early pick for England's cricket XI, and he showed why in the first of three Tests versus the West Indies during the 1939 season. Compton cracked a stylish 120. A slashing 181 against Essex even surpassed this innings. The last 131 came in just 100 minutes. His dominance just failed to give Middlesex the County Championship. It finished second to Yorkshire for the third year in succession through no fault of Compton, who had a fine season scoring 2,468 runs, including eight centuries, at 56.09.

•

He was 21 and reaching a peak just when war hit and suspended cricket for six years. Compton was called up into an anti-aircraft regiment of the Royal Artillery not far from London. He next moved to Aldershot in Hampshire where he did a Physical Training Instructors' Course. By all accounts, Sergeant-Major Compton was not well suited to his rank and army work. He had always been averse to rigorous exercise, except in competition on the pitch.

Compton was able to keep up his soccer, playing 127 games (many with brother Leslie) for Arsenal and scoring 72 goals. He also played for England against Scotland and Wales in a team that was considered not far below the best that could be produced in peacetime.

Compton surfaced again in pads here and there until 1945 and the Victory Tests. He encountered Australians Keith Miller and Lindsay Hassett in these contests. They were later rivals in Ashes combat and became lifelong friends.

County cricket revived in 1946. Compton, now 28, began in a horror stretch that continued until he was bowled first ball at Lord's in the first of three Tests against India. It took him until the end of June to find form when he hit 122 versus Warwickshire at Lord's. Inside two months, he was back to his 1939 best. He ended the season with figures that were similar to that final pre-war effort. Compton scored 2,403, with 10 centuries, at 61.61. His four Test innings against India registered 0, 51, 71 not out and 24 not out.

Compton could have played with Arsenal again in 1946–47, but this time he answered the MCC's call to join the England team for the Ashes in Australia. It was not a happy tour on the field. Hammond's leadership was uninspired as opposed to Bradman's, which always was. England didn't win a Test. Compton's series began slowly with scores of 17, 15 and 5. But in the second innings of the Second Test at Sydney he fought well for 54.

During the Melbourne Test and after Compton had failed with a score of 11 in the first innings, Bradman invited him to dine at the Windsor Hotel. Bradman spoke of the importance of confidence, no matter what the circumstances. It had resonance for Compton, who had suffered at the beginning of the 1946 season and was in trouble again at that moment. Bradman was reassuring, saying that once self-reliance returned, Compton would get runs. The two had a rapport, and Compton was relieved that off the field Bradman was congenial company.

His on-field intensity often made opposing players feel he was a cold and distant character.

Compton was run out for 14 in the second innings at Melbourne, but his confidence returned in Adelaide and he scored 147 in the first innings. In the second innings, Compton again played well. He was intent on keeping England in the middle long enough to ensure a draw, and even give the tourists a semblance of a chance with Australia having to bat last. He figured in a bizarre but effective stand with keeper Evans, where Compton hogged the strike and refused to take singles offered by Bradman's field placings. Bradman, ever-conscious of the paying public as this tedious stand developed, complained that this was not the way cricket should be played. Compton suggested he bring his fielders in to normal positions. Bradman obliged. Compton promptly belted a four. A peeved Bradman put his fielders out again and the farce resumed. The atmosphere of their convivial dinner in Melbourne had evaporated. Compton went on to 103 not out, and the usually rare double in a Test. Australia's Arthur Morris did the same in this game, making it an exceptional batting event.

The game fizzled to a draw. Compton made 17 and a strong 76 in the final Test at Melbourne and so went home with the good series figures of 459 runs at 51.00.

Compton returned to England a more rounded and hardened cricketer, his sense of competitive spirit up a few notches after taking on the Australians and succeeding. The touring South Africans were a far less daunting task and he played a big part in the 3:0 thrashing handed out in the five-Test series. Compton hit 65, 163, 208, 115, 6 (hit wicket), 30, 53 and 113 for an aggregate of 750 runs at 93.75.

His 163 in 286 minutes at Trent Bridge was out of a team score of 291 in a chanceless effort, which was more defensive, as the situation demanded. His 208 came at Lord's in a 370 third wicket with Bill Edrich (189). It was then a world record.

By the end of the series, Compton had bowled far more than normal, and this, coupled with his huge run production, put enormous strain on an injured knee sustained in a soccer game. If stress was to come, it had to be in 1947. Compton had 50 innings for 8 not outs. He scored a record 3,816 runs, including a record 18 centuries (taking Hobbs' 1925 tally of 16 hundreds), with a highest score of 246 in the last innings of the season for Middlesex, the champion county, against the Rest of England. His 1947 season average was 90.85. He bowled 635.4 overs and took 73 wickets at a cost of 28.12. His batting was the most dominant since Bradman rocked England in 1930 for figures of 2,960 runs at 98.66.

Like Bradman, Compton's intent was always to entertain. If there were a chance to be adventurous he would take it. His uncanny eye and placement were seen at their best in that glorious summer of 1947.

On paper it seemed that Compton never reached such dizzy heights again, but his 1948 season returns and the opposition he faced tell a different story. In first-class cricket he tallied 2,451 runs in 47 innings at 61.27, with 10 centuries. These figures were remarkably similar to those of the 1946 season.

•

In late 1948, Compton became one of the first ever sports stars to use an agent, Bagenal Harvey, who did a deal with Brylcreem. From then on, Compton was known as 'the Brylcreem boy', featuring in advertisements for the hair product. It fitted his image as a dasher, which was enhanced by the fastest recorded first-class triple century. It was belted against North-Eastern Transvaal at the town of Benoni on the England tour of South Africa in 1948–49. The first hundred took 66 minutes, the second 78 minutes and the third a whirlwind 37 minutes, adding up to a minute over three hours of controlled mayhem.

His Test series versus South Africa was less spectacular but he still managed strong contributions in four of the five Tests. Compton was the key player in the First at Durban. His bowling for England's thin attack was important. In South Africa's second innings he sent down 16 overs for 11 maidens and took 1 for 11. This restricted the opposition, and helped Alec Bedser and leg-spinner Doug Wright to take wickets. Compton hit a second-top score of 72 in the first innings and a top score of 28 in the second innings, which saw England scrape home by two wickets on the last ball of the match. He was dismissed before the winning bye was scored, and could not bear to watch. Instead, he locked himself in a toilet, unable to avoid the unfolding drama. No one appeared to have more nerve and verve than Denis Compton. He conveyed a sense that he was enjoying himself. Batting seemed pleasurable, not a graft or a chore. Bowling, too, when he got the chance, was something to enthuse about. Slip fielding was a joy. But off the field, as a spectator, he was a nervous wreck.

Yet he recovered by the Second Test at Johannesburg, where he hit 114 in England's massive 608 in a drawn match. At Cape Town, he contributed 51 in England's second innings and also took 5 for 70 off 25.2 overs with three maidens – his only five-wicket haul in his 78 Tests. At Port Elizabeth in the Fifth and final Test he made 49 in the first innings. His top score of 42 in the second innings was the highest contribution in England's second narrow win in the series, this time by three wickets.

England won the close series 2:0, with Compton playing a big part. His magnificent form of 1947 and 1948 on England's green fields flowed on across the browner pastures of South Africa through to February 1949. He cracked eight centuries in an aggregate of 1,781 runs at an average of 84.80. He took 30 wickets at more than 30, but was more than useful in the Tests with the ball.

Off the field too, Compton was having a momentous time. He met his second wife, Valerie. (His first marriage during the war to Doris had failed.) They had two sons, but this marriage too did not last long. Denis, the cavalier on the field, seemed to have a similar attitude to matrimony. In those heady days when he was a household name in England, good times with the lads took precedence over domestic bliss.

1949 was Compton's benefit year (it netted him £12,200), and there was a dropping off of the incredible two-year run as a player in the very top bracket of world batsmen. Yet he still managed impressive Test centuries against a battling New Zealand team at Headingley and Lord's. For the entire 1949 season, he scored 2,530 at 48.65, with another fine collection of nine centuries. At 31, and with nagging soccer injuries, especially his right knee, he had peaked. There would be many more triumphs but Compton had 'been there' before. On occasions now, he gave the impression of being a bit jaded. His football career was even more in jeopardy because of his wonky knee. The wing dash didn't have quite the same acceleration seen in his 14 capped games during the war. He spoke about retirement. But in a last spark he performed well in early 1950 for Arsenal. It scraped into the FA Cup final against Liverpool and won 4:1. Compton scored a goal and admitted to being pepped up in the second half after being given a liberal shot of brandy. He was a very lucky footballer, who finished on the highest note possible with a cup-winner's medal. But that was it for Compton and soccer. His injuries had made a crock of him, and he retired before he was pushed.

From the 1950 summer on, cricket was his only professional sport.

Injury and poor form kept him out of the England team until the Fourth and final Test versus West Indies at the Oval in 1950, where he was run out for 44 and hit just 11 in the second innings. The West Indies, with Frank Worrell, Everton Weekes and Clyde Walcott dominant with the bat, and its spin twins Sonny Ramadhin and Alf Valentine in control, crushed England 3:1. Compton's form in Australia in 1950–51 was again dismal. He failed to get going in any of eight innings, returning a paltry 53 at 7.57. It was depressing for fans to see Compton struggle because of his damaged knee. He couldn't move with alacrity to spinners or swivel against the quicks. Courage, it seemed to Australian fans, was all he was left with. Yet it was far from the end.

Compton battled on, making a better fist of easier attacks in the domestic England summer of 1951, where he scored 909 in May, his best effort yet in that first full month of cricket. Despite his handicap, he made 2,193 at 64.50. His appointment as joint captain of Middlesex with Bill Edrich was another achievement, and he began the Test series against South Africa with a century at Trent Bridge. England lost the game by 71 runs.

At Lord's Compton made 79 in a Test won by England by 10 wickets. An infected toe kept him out of the Third Test. He returned for scores of 25, 73 and 18 in the final two Tests. His series figures of 312 at 52.00 were strong.

After a luxurious first-ever winter off from 'work', he found it difficult to get enthusiastic for the 1952 cricket season. He was 34 and appeared stale. It reflected in his figures – just 1,880 runs at 39.16. He did worse in the Tests against the Indian tourists, scoring 59 runs at 29.50 in four innings. Feeling out of sorts, he dropped out of the last two Tests.

Compton fired up for the next season – 1953 – against the Australians and was part of England's 1:0 series win and the return of the Ashes for the first time in two decades. But there was no century contribution from this great player of yesteryear. Scores of 0, 57, 33, 45, 0, 61, 16 and 22 not out produced a yeoman-like 234 at 33.43. His most brilliant and aggressive foe, Lindwall, had him four times out of the seven he was dismissed. It was not the performance of the 1948 vintage Compton.

Yet still he was always an early pick for England and he was taken on tour to the West Indies.

•

England ran into wild crowds in the Caribbean and two Test losses in succession at Jamaica, where there were riots, and Bridgetown. Compton checked a run of outs with a fighting top score of 93 in England's second innings in the Second Test, but his team was thrashed by 181 runs. In the first innings of the Third Test at Georgetown, he continued his return to form with a 64. He followed this at Port-of-Spain with 133 in a high-scoring draw. Hutton used him as a bowler and he took 2 for 40 in the West Indies' first innings. Compton and the other England players thought it should have been three when a slips catch was adjudged not out. It was a bump ball, the umpire said. Compton remonstrated with the decision and made a sarcastic remark about rule interpretation being different in the West Indies. The umpire made a formal complaint.

The game was drawn. In the final Test at Sabina Park, he was out hit wicket for 31 in England's heroic win, which levelled the series at 2-all under Len Hutton's leadership. Compton's figures of 348 at 49.71 were strong enough to suggest that he could still mix it with the best.

•

The next home season, 1954, brought abundant proof of this. Compton managed 453 at 90.60 in England against Pakistan. The series was dominated by his highest Test innings of 278 at Trent Bridge in the Second Test. His 200 took just 245 minutes and his innings in all took just 290 minutes, making it one of the fastest big Test performances ever recorded. He showed remarkable stamina and fought the knee pain.

Wisden observed the innings as '...a torrent of strokes, orthodox and improvised, crashing and delicate...'

Compton had two further fine innings in the series: a top score of 93 at Old Trafford, and a gutsy 53 at the Oval.

He felt in good form for the tour to Australia for the 1954–55 series, and despite a delayed start because of his injury, ended as an important player in the series won by England 3:1. He scored 191 at 38.20, which was third in the averages for England behind younger stars Tom Graveney and Peter May.

At home, he had a good Test series against South Africa, notching 492 at 54.66, with a top score of 158 at Old Trafford in the Third Test. No one else reached 50 against the pace of

Peter Heine and Neil Adcock. He followed that up with 71 in the second innings, an even more polished knock, but still England lost by three wickets. The thrilling series went to England 3:2.

A few months after the season in November 1955, Compton had his right kneecap removed. It was placed in a biscuit tin at Lord's for posterity. Compton rehabilitated himself in quick time and turned out for Middlesex against Australia well into the season. He scored a sparkling 61 in 106 minutes. It was enough, along with some other useful county form, for selectors to bring him back for the final Test of the Ashes at the Oval. He struggled against the fire of Miller and spin of Benaud, but went on to play a beautiful innings of 94 with all his favourite strokes – the sweep, the late cut and the cover-drive. In the second innings there was more of the same with 35 not out. It gave him enormous satisfaction to withstand and come out on top against Lindwall and Miller, one last time. Compton toured for the final time to South Africa and managed 242 from 10 innings at an average of 24.20 with a top score of 64.

His Test career figures were 5,807 runs with 17 hundreds, at an average of 50.06. Compton's full-time first-class career finished after the 1957 season. His aggregate was 38,942 runs, with 123 centuries, at 51.85. As a bowler, he took 622 wickets at 32.27. He took 416 catches, mainly at slips.

Compton married for the third time in 1972 to Christine and they had two daughters. Compton's work after cricket involved public relations consultancy. He also did some BBC commentary and was a long-term correspondent for the UK *Sunday Express*. He worked for his beloved Middlesex, putting in a five-year stint as president in the 1990s.

He remained a close friend of Keith Miller and kept up good relations with Bradman, even turning up in Australia for his 85th birthday party in 1993.

Denis Compton was one of the finest artists and characters cricket has known. His warm-hearted, carefree approach made him an unusual champion.

Bill Edrich

Bill Edrich was the fourth of England's top four bats, and like Hutton and Washbrook, it took him three Tests to warm up to something like his best form. In his sixth innings he scored a fifty (53 run out). He followed this up with a century and another fifty at Leeds. He too, stumbled early against the variety and skill of, and intimidation by, Australia's bowlers.

Shortish, stocky Edrich had been expected to do well after his fabulous 1947 domestic season for Middlesex when he hit 3,539 runs at an average of 80.43 with 12 centuries. He also took 67 wickets at 22.58 in one of the most remarkable 'doubles' in the history of first-class cricket. Bradman's team brought a brutal reality check to all that. Edrich's batting figures in the Tests were a more modest 319 runs at 31.90, while the limitations of his bowling were exposed when delivering to a world-class batting line-up. He took just three wickets at 79.33.

•

William John 'Bill' Edrich (1916–86) was born in Norfolk. His three brothers Brian, Eric and Geoff and his cousin John all played first-class cricket. In the 1920s in Lingwood, the Edrich clan could always present a full XI if required for a local park game.

He made the Norfolk side in the minor counties soon after his 16th birthday in 1932, and also played soccer as an amateur for Norwich City and Tottenham Hotspur for several years. In 1937, Edrich qualified to play for Middlesex, and was an instant hit, scoring more than 2,000 runs in his first season. A year later, he reached 1,000 runs in May and was rewarded with his first Test – against the Australians – in 1938 but failed in his first four innings. However, in the next series in South Africa, he finally gave an exhibition of his patience and skills in scoring 219 not out in the final timeless Test at Durban.

Edrich's 'reward' for his tardy start in returning a big score was to be dumped for the entire series against the West Indies in England in 1939 (although *Wisden* still named him as one of its 'Cricketers of the Year' for that year). For the next six years, his cricket was reduced to whatever he could find between flying missions while a member of the RAF stationed at Great Massingham in Norfolk (where Keith Miller also spent time later in the war).

One mission in 1941, when he was in a squadron of seven Blenheim bombers, exemplified his good fortune in surviving the war. The aim was to bomb an island off Germany but they found it surrounded by German shipping that fired at the British planes. Three Blenheims were shot down. Then four German Messerschmitts came up to engage the remaining four Blenheims. A dog-fight ensued for 20 minutes, which seemed like an eternity, or as Edrich said, 'like two or three lifetimes in one.'

All but one of the combatants was out of ammunition. Edrich saw the one remaining armed Messerschmitt coming after him. It was within 25 metres when Edrich could see the attacking pilot attempting to fire at him. But his guns jammed. The German flew off in frustration. Edrich had been spared.

He became a squadron leader and was awarded the DFC (Distinguished Flying Cross). Because of such life-and-death incidents, Edrich had a different attitude to games and life after the war. Life was for living every day as if it were his last. He knew from those combat experiences that there was a fair chance that there would be no 'tomorrows,' as there were not for many of his friends.

Edrich's change of attitude showed after the war. He ditched his professional status before the conflict and turned amateur. The uncertainty of his game had gone. He was a far more confident performer. It showed in the 1946–47 Ashes in Australia when he scored 462 runs at 46.20, and followed up with that bumper 1947 season. It included six double-hundred partnerships with Denis Compton, including two in the Tests against South

Africa, in which Edrich scored 532 runs at 106.40 from five completed innings.

He struggled against the spin of the West Indies' Sonny Ramadhin and Alf Valentine in 1950, and was an intermittent Test performer after that. His Test career was over by 1954 after 39 games, in which he scored 2,440 runs at 40.00 including six centuries. He took 41 wickets at 41.29, and held 39 catches. He jointly captained Middlesex with Compton in 1951 and 1952, and was the county's sole skipper from 1953–57.

Edrich's first-class career spanned nearly a quarter of a century, from 1934–58. He scored 36,985 runs, including 86 centuries with a highest score of 267 not out, at an average of 42.39. He took 479 wickets at 33.31 and managed 529 catches and one stumping.

After retiring from Middlesex, he returned to his roots and played again for Norfolk for another 13 years until 1972, aged 56.

Bill Edrich had nearly as many wives (five) as he did Test centuries. The MCC named the twin stands at his Middlesex home ground (Lord's) after him and Denis Compton.

Godfrey Evans

Godfrey Evans had a productive 1948 Ashes with both the bat (fifth on England's batting table with 188 runs at 26.85) and the gloves (effecting eight catches and three stumpings). His indefatigable spirit and skill behind the stumps were his contributions to English cricket, especially in the golden years of the 1950s, when the Test team was the best in the world. No matter whether the opposition was 8 for 80, or 2 for 400, Evans' enthusiasm and drive lifted English spirits like no other. It was his personality as much as his diving for miraculous leg-side catches or brilliant stumpings that made him such an important part of a winning team. Spectators loved him too. His theatrics, smiles and boundless energy made him worth watching. Evans loved his cricket and it loved him. His batting too had a certain attraction. He was never dull except for the odd occasion when he had to shut up shop for the team.

Keepers have always been characters, but most like to go about their work unobtrusively. Evans was too fun loving and extrovert not to be noticed at every chance. And there were plenty of opportunities in his position on the field. If he kept to the menacing spin of Jim Laker and Tony Lock, his very presence was intimidating to batsmen, who knew that the merest slip forward of the crease would invite a swift dismissal. Evans would effect an exaggerated twist of broad shoulders and upper body towards the square leg umpire. The gloves would be swept and the pose, like a discus thrower, held until the umpire either agreed with the appeal or turned it down. He was daring too, quite often keeping up to medium-pacers, which took both lightning reflexes and courage. The stocky and muscular Evans loved being up at the stumps, not the least reason being his ability to dive forward of the wicket for a catch or to stop a run. Yet he was equally adept at standing back to Frank Tyson when he bowled faster than anyone ever did in Australia in 1954–55. Then Evans was seen diving like a soccer goalie leg-side, off-side and high.

•

Godfrey Evans (1920–99) was brought up in Kent at Lords, Sheldwich near Faversham, the 100-acre farm home of his once rich stockbroker grandfather. Evans' mother died when he was three. His father, an electrical engineer, was often abroad. Evans boarded at Kent College from age 8 to 16. At 14 he made a quick-fire 101 not out for his school in an evening match against Choir School Canterbury. It was his good fortune to be watched by a member of the Kent County staff at the St Lawrence Ground, Canterbury. It led to his own staff appointment at Kent at the beginning of the 1937 season, where he decided to become a keeper like his hero, Les Ames, who was also at

Kent, along with another former Test champion all-rounder, Frank Woolley. The ground became Evans' cricket headquarters for the next 22 years.

That first season saw him working the scoreboard at Dover when Kent scored 219 in 71 minutes and managed a memorable victory against Gloucestershire. His efforts that day, he said later, were more a test of agility – and mathematics – than coping with Alec Bedser's late swingers.

In his second year – 1938 – he was assigned to pavilion duties, which included whitening the boots of the visitors, Bradman's Australians.

'I didn't miss a ball,' Evans recalled. 'All the Australians batted well. Bradman hit a fifty in no time. Les Ames made a century in our second innings and Frank Woolley belted 80 in an hour.'

Kent was beaten by 10 wickets, but the game was an early inspiration for Evans to play Test cricket. Over the winter of 1937–38, he took up boxing to earn extra money – 30 shillings a fight – and knocked out two opponents in three fights. But Kent was not happy with his off-season activity. He was advised that eye injuries could cause his cricket some problems. He gave away boxing, taking up hockey and squash to keep fit in the winter.

Ames blocked his way as a keeper for Kent and Evans was initially chosen in July 1939 as a batsman. He appeared in another four games, in which Ames stepped aside and fielded at first slip while Evans, now 18, kept. The youth was most grateful to the older man for his advice and encouragement even though Ames knew Evans was being groomed to take his place.

Ames told him not worry about missed chances. Everyone had them.

•

War intervened. Evans joined the army. He married Jean at Maidstone, Kent in January 1941 (and had one son, Howard Leslie, after Howard Levett and Leslie Ames, both Kent keepers, and mentors). While stationed at Aldershot he was seen keeping in 1943 by former Test skipper Arthur Gilligan. Within weeks he was playing for an England XI against the Dominions at Lord's. Evans by now had adopted his style of acrobatics behind the stumps, which included much diving and confident appealing.

He admitted in his autobiography, *The Gloves are Off*, that this was all calculated to get noticed first for Kent and later, England. It worked. His stance was different from the conventional approach of sitting back on the heels. Evans rocked forward on his toes, allowing him to press his knuckles into the ground, exposing the red underside of his gloves, another factor that made him stand out.

Soon after the war he was back playing for Kent as its number-one keeper.

•

In 1946, in the first post-war Test series, versus India in England, he was chosen at 25 to guard wickets for England in the Third Test at the Oval. It was a forgettable start. The game was almost washed out, with India making 331 and England 3 for 95 in reply. Evans didn't make a dismissal or have a bat. The game fizzled to a draw.

Evans was chosen to tour Australia for the 1946–47 series, but was kept out of the First Test at the Gabba. He blamed his omission on captain Wally Hammond's great rivalry with Bradman. Bradman played for South Australia against England early in the season. Evans dropped a tough chance at the wicket when Bradman was 2, then again when he was 50. Had Bradman been dismissed for 2, he may not have battled on after his severe fibrositis illness during the war. As it was, he scored 76 and his confidence was restored. Evans felt that Hammond left him out of the First Test at Brisbane for those two lapses against

Bradman. Cambridge University and Yorkshire amateur Paul Gibb was chosen instead.

Evans was a better keeper. Gibb was not as efficient at handling the spin of Doug Wright, Evans' Kent team-mate. This influenced Evans' recall for the Second Test at Sydney in mid-December 1946 and he set a standard that future keepers would find hard to emulate. During the game, Bradman made a point of telling Evans that he had kept magnificently and that the Australians were most pleased with his form. According to Evans in his autobiography, Bradman added:

'You gave the English boys all the encouragement possible by the way you kept wicket. Carry on doing it.'

Bradman played hard and shrewdly, Evans noted, but this sort of remark showed his dedication to good sportsmanship and what was best for the game and competition.

Australia amassed 695 in that Sydney Test. Evans did not concede a bye. He took part in his first Test dismissal, catching Keith Miller (40) off leg-break bowler Peter Smith. It was still a lean experience for Evans with the bat. In his first Test innings, he was bowled for 5 by Ian Johnson. In the second, he was stumped by Don Tallon off Colin McCool for 9.

'He was on his toes throughout our long innings and never lost his zest or good humour,' Bradman noted. 'He kept his fielders at it under trying conditions. He was an outstanding keeper.'

Evans didn't concede a bye in Australia's first innings of the drawn Third Test at Melbourne. It wasn't until well into the second innings of that Test that he let some through, but not before 1,054 runs, including those in the Australian Second Test innings, had been scored. Yet there were blemishes. Like all keepers, he had his off days, and for Evans they were extreme. In this Test he missed four catches, including one off Arthur Morris on the first ball of an innings and later, Bradman.

In the Fourth Test at Adelaide, he was noteworthy again, this time for failing to score until he had been at the wicket for 97 minutes. This was a world record in first-class cricket.

Evans was an attacking bat, but he went defensive to help England avoid defeat. His defiance (he remained 10 not out in 133 minutes) with Denis Compton (103 not out) didn't allow Australia enough time for victory. In these Tests, Evans amazed onlookers by standing up to medium-pacer Alec Bedser, which added to the bowler's menace. It proved effective. Evans hardly let anything through, relying on his eye, balance, quick footwork and fitness. It prompted Bill O'Reilly to compare Evans favourably with Don Tallon. Evans was delighted. He regarded Tallon as the best keeper he had ever seen.

The tour ended with four matches in New Zealand. In the only Test, Evans took two catches at the wicket off Bedser and demonstrated that his standing up was not just for show or to pressure batsmen. He finished the long Antipodean tour with 33 dismissals (28 catches and five stumpings). Evans' success convinced him that standing up to pace if possible was the best way. He claimed that by standing back a keeper missed chances that fell short. This, he felt, compensated for those he might miss by being so close. Evans also pointed out that by standing up there were chances for stumpings too. He had amazed onlookers in a match against Victoria when he stumped Ken Meuleman off a quick ball down the leg-side from Dick Pollard.

Evans' worth with the bat was further in evidence at home in 1947 when he scored 74 against South Africa in the First Test at Trent Bridge. In the Fifth Test he made 45 run out and 39 not out. He scored more than 1,000 runs for the season and made 95 dismissals. It was the nearest he was ever to come to the 'double' of 1,000 runs and 100 wickets in a first-class season.

Evans toured the West Indies in 1947–48 and then played in the 1948 Ashes series in England. He had some lapses yet bounced back in the next series versus South Africa in 1948–49, taking three fine catches in the first innings of the First Test at Durban. In the only completed South African innings of the Second Test he made another three dismissals. Evans' form continued in the Third Test at Cape Town when he pulled off three stumpings and a catch. In the following series against

New Zealand in 1949, his batting was unimpressive, but his displays behind the stumps ensured his place. He capped off the series in the Fourth and final Test at the Oval with four catches and a stumping, his best effort yet.

•

Evans had no peer in England by 1950 when he reached a peak at age 29 and played in the shock series against the touring West Indians, who won 3:1. He and England began poorly at Old Trafford in the First Test against the fine left-arm spin of Alf Valentine. Evans came to the wicket at 5 for 88 and turned the match around by unleashing a flurry of cuts and front-foot drives. He belted 104 in 140 minutes, which included 17 fours. His innings was the only century of the game. It was his maiden first-class and Test hundred. He swung, hit and occasionally missed but still gave no chance. It was one of those days that went right for a batsman whose hit-and-miss style often saw him dismissed early.

Evans also effected three stumpings, took a catch and let through only four byes in two innings. He was easily player of the match in England's 202-run win. Despite performing at this level again in the next two Tests, England was beaten in both games. He made four dismissals (two stumpings and two catches) in one innings of the Second Test at Lord's and scored 32 and 63, favouring attack again against the spin twins Valentine and Sonny Ramadhin at Trent Bridge. An injured thumb kept him out of the final Test, won again by the West Indies, and the rest of the season.

Evans toured Australia for the second time in 1950–51 and judged the Second Test at Melbourne as his best ever behind the stumps. He took two catches in each innings and revelled in the hot, humid conditions over Christmas. Just like a batsman in form he saw the ball as big as a pumpkin as it sailed cleanly into the gloves. He also made 49, second-top score over England's two innings in a low-scoring thriller.

After losing the First Test by 70 runs, England fell just 28 short in this one. Evans felt the Australians were not the 'Invincibles' of 1946–47 and 1948. He was thrilled, although not surprised that England won the last Test. He was pleased with his form and fitness, especially standing up to Bedser. He had successfully copied Tallon's method of taking down the leg-side on the right side of his body. His powers of concentration, alertness and agility had peaked on the 1950–51 tour. Evans returned to England for the 1951 season full of confidence, but had not allowed for mental fatigue. His enthusiasm for the game waned. He lost form and was dropped after the Third Test at home against South Africa and replaced by Yorkshire's Don Brennan.

Evans, now 30, had to rekindle his passion for playing. He decided against an invitation to tour India with the MCC team during England's winter of 1951–52, and was again in good touch when India came to England for the 1952 season. His batting against the battling Indians was also outstanding. He hit a second-top score of 66 in the First Test at Leeds. It earned him a bottle of champagne, promised by his skipper Len Hutton if he managed a fifty.

Evans followed this up in the Second Test at Lord's with a blistering 98 before lunch on day three. No Englishman had ever hit a century before lunch in a Test and with two minutes to go before the break he had every chance to join the magnificent company of Bradman, Charlie Macartney and Victor Trumper, who had all managed the feat. But the Indian skipper, Vijay Hazare, took his time setting the field. Umpire Frank Chester, in an uncharitable act, called lunch. Evans trailed off the ground disappointed. He did, however, get his century after lunch before being caught and bowled by Ghulam Ahmed for 104.

In was Evans' match. He claimed his 100th victim – Sadu Shinde stumped Evans bowled Allan Watkins – and then signalled the dressing room to break open the champagne. The keeper was now legendary for his exploits off the field as much as on it. It was the way he played cricket and lived.

He surprised even himself by finishing third in the batting averages with 60.5, behind Hutton and David Sheppard, but was not carried away. India fielded a weak side.

For the entire 1952 first-class season, Evans scored more than 1,600 runs and collected 70 victims. He had come back to form with character and flair at just the right moment. The Australians were due in 1953, and Evans kept fit over the winter by playing hockey and squash. He needed to be in shape.

The Ashes series was hard-fought and tense and Evans performed at his best. In the drawn Third Test at Old Trafford, he hit third-top score of 44 not out and made six dismissals, but personally didn't rank his effort highly after dropping a tough chance from Neil Harvey early in his innings. Harvey went on to 122. The Fourth Test was drawn, but England won the last by eight wickets to give it the Ashes for the first time in more than 20 years.

Evans and England celebrated long and hard. It was his benefit year and £5,000 was raised for him after a game against the Australians that ended on 1 September.

•

In 1954 at home in the final Test of a series against Pakistan, Evans caught Fazal Mahmood off new fast man Peter Loader, the keeper's 131st victim. This broke the record set by Australia's Bert Oldfield in the 1930s. Evans signalled the dressing room. It was a good excuse to break open the champagne yet again.

Evans was impressed with first-gamer Loader, yet even more pleased with the debut in this game of Northamptonshire speedman, Frank Tyson, who played for the first time in the final Test at the Oval. He took 4 for 35 and 1 for 22. Tyson was the fastest bowler to whom Evans ever kept. The keeper rubbed his gloves together with glee at the thought of what

Tyson would do on the next tour Down Under for the 1954–55 Ashes contest.

Neil Harvey was England's prime target. In the vital Third Test at Melbourne, when the series was 1-all, Evans took one of the best ever leg-side diving catches to dismiss the Australian champion left-hander off Tyson. Evans took five catches in all off Tyson and the accurate speedsters Brian Statham, and three in the Second Test. Tyson proved the difference. England won the series. Len Hutton retired after the success of the 1954–55 Ashes and the more serious Peter May took over. Evans, who enjoyed his cricket and knew how to relax on and off the field, found himself a tad inhibited. He didn't feel inclined to whistle between overs or joke as he had under the less strict Len Hutton.

May inherited a fine squad and at home led England against South Africa. And he had Tyson, the most exciting cricketer in the world after his devastation of Australia. Wherever he turned up, the grounds were packed with spectators, which brought back memories of the glory days of Nottingham's Harold Larwood and Bill Voce in the 1920s and 1930s. Evans loved keeping to him, not the least reason being the fear he instilled in batsmen, which led to edged strokes. There was no keeping up to Tyson. Evans found himself looking for a new position further back from the stumps than ever before.

Tyson took eight wickets and was again the decisive player again in the First Test at Trent Bridge that England won easily. But injury plagued him and he played only one more Test in the series. Evans and England were fortunate to have replacements such as Fred Trueman and Loader to partner Brian Statham, who was a permanent fixture in the side.

At Lord's in the Second Test, Evans had the unusual distinction of taking a catch off the first ball by Statham. Tyson was back for the Third Test at Manchester, and Evans became a victim of his express pace when he chipped a bone in a finger and missed the last two Tests. England scraped in with a 3:2 series win after winning the first two Tests.

During the off season 1955–56, Evans worked hard on his finger with specific exercises, hockey and squash. At 35, he wanted to be extra-fit for the coming 1956 season against Ian Johnson's Australians. Evans, who liked a bet and a drink, mixed well with the visitors, particularly Keith Miller. They bet on the outcome of the Lord's Second Test, which happened to be the only one Australia won. At Leeds in the Third Test, Evans backed up May (101) and Cyril Washbrook (98) with a bright 40, which he put down to Johnson's mistake of using the spinners against him. Lindwall bowled him soon after coming on.

Something similar happened at Leeds in the Fourth Test. After Peter Richardson (101) and David Sheppard (113) had set England up for a big score, Evans came in and belted 47 in 29 balls, and just missed scoring the then fastest fifty in Test cricket. England made 459.

Oddly, Evans was involved in just one dismissal in Jim Laker's off-spinning rampage when he stumped Ron Archer in Australia's first innings. Most of Laker's 19 wickets for the match fell to catches close to the wicket as the Australians fumbled and stumbled. He kept the ball up and spinning in, forcing the batsmen to play. Evans regarded it as the most brilliant, sustained display of spin bowling he ever saw. England won by an innings and 170, and retained the Ashes. It was on top in the drawn Fifth Test, giving England a 2:1 victory, its third successive Ashes win.

Evans next toured South Africa for a five-Test series over 1956–57. He began well with the bat, scoring 20 and 30 and making four dismissals in a win at Johannesburg, then followed this up with a smashing 62 in 50 minutes at Cape Town. He also effected five dismissals and England won again. Evans finished well in the final Test at Port Elizabeth, making six dismissals. England lost the game despite a fine eight-wicket haul by Tyson, and in a slight dent to its sense of world superiority could only manage a 2-all drawn series. Evans' form, however, at 36, was as good as ever. *Wisden* made special note of his keeping on an atrocious pitch that made batting and keeping difficult. Despite the *Wisden* scorecard showing 13 byes, its reporter noted:

'He allowed only one bye, an extraordinary performance by an extraordinary man.'

With such praise, Evans' place as King of Keepers in England was assured. He continued on during the home season of 1957 against the West Indies. Even his batting was more reliable with scores of 14, 29 not out, 26 not out, 10, 40 and 82 at Lord's, a happy hunting ground for him. It was made in a stand of 174 with Colin Cowdrey, a seventh wicket record versus the West Indies. Evans' runs came in 115 minutes. It was a smack, bang, wallop innings in which he was dropped five times. Yet as he said himself, 'It was not elegant but it was effective.' It was the true Evans method with the bat. The ball was there to be hit hard and as often as possible. If he connected it usually reached the boundary. Given England's batting power above him, including Peter Richardson, Tom Graveney, May, Cowdrey and Sheppard, he was a useful man to come in at No. 7.

In the Fourth Test at Leeds, Evans became the first keeper to take 200 Test wickets when he caught Collie Smith. As soon as the catch was taken, Evans outlined the shape of a champagne bottle to the dressing room.

England won 3:0, and maintained its top of the world table ranking. It was far too strong in 1958 at home for New Zealand, winning the first four Tests – three of them by an innings. Then came the unexpected shock of a 4:0 loss to Australia in 1958–59. Evans' form with the bat fell away and a finger injury caused him to miss half the series behind the stumps. The team was unsettled before the series began by the prospect of facing several Australian pace bowlers suspected of throwing. But this aside, Benaud's Australians outplayed England. The wheel had turned after five years of England dominance. Heads were sure to roll.

Evans felt he had kept his standards up at Trent Bridge in the First Test of the 1959 series against India. He also made a handy 73. But rumours abounded that at 38 he was 'tired' after batting and that this affected his keeping. It was something that Evans scoffed at. He was his ebullient self on and off the field.

At Lord's in the Second Test, the rumours were given substance for those wanting to dump him when he missed four stumpings off leg-spinner Tommy Greenhough inside a session. He was dropped after 91 Tests. He had been dumped before. Yet there was finality about this non-selection that shook him. Evans was disappointed. His form in general had been good for Kent in 1959, but selectors, it was said, were 'looking for younger players'. Those supporting Evans' inclusion argued that the best players of the moment should be chosen for 'now'. He would have carried on longer. He loved the game and playing for his country. His Test omission dispirited him and caused him to retire from first-class cricket at the end of 1959.

•

Evans scored 2,439 runs at 20.49, and hit two Test centuries. He held 173 catches and made 46 stumpings. In first-class cricket he scored 14,882 runs from 1939–59 at 21.22 and made seven centuries. He took 816 catches and stumped 250.

Evans, who received a CBE in 1960, tried many areas of work after retirement. He was twice a publican and ran a jewellery business. He attempted running battery hens and a sportsman's club. He invested in a leisure complex, a dice game and a pitch drier. When cricket tours became popular in the 1980s, he ran overseas package tours. Evans put his love for a bet to good use for 20 years by advising the Ladbrokes agency on what odds to lay at big cricket matches. His later appearance featured greying mutton chop whiskers, which seemed to copy the look of his stockbroker grandfather, who influenced his early life so much.

Godfrey Evans married three times and had another child, a daughter, by his third wife Angela. His exceptional ability as a keeper was matched by his character, which was in keeping with the true spirit of cricket.

Jim Laker

Bradman's Invincibles gave tall, well-built Jim Laker a fearful battering throughout 1948. In the three Tests he played it was bad enough: 9 wickets at 52.44. Outside the Ashes in games against the tourists for Surrey and Leveson Gower's XI, he took an even more fearful hammering, with 5 more wickets at 71.80.

Laker had been targeted by the Australians. They recognised his record as the best bowler in the previous Test series against the West Indies, and regarded him as a threat. Consequently some of the biggest hitters ever in Test cricket sought to smash him and destroy his confidence as a Test cricketer. They belted him in front of the members at Lord's, and his county supporters at Surrey. They slaughtered him at Trent Bridge, and pushed him out of the Tests after two games. When he came back at Leeds for more punishment, they buried him in front of Yorkshire spectators, who prevaricated about claiming this Bradford-born 26-year-old as one of their own. And in the final humiliation at Scarborough, Barnes on 151 gave his wicket away to Laker, in an act of sympathy; but not before the Australians had taken 95 runs off him.

That 1948 experience left its mark, more on Test selectors than 'Big Jim' himself. But in many ways it was the making of him. Before the Invincibles dealt with him, he disliked batsmen. After 1948, he hated them, and it showed in a 1950 Test trial at Bradford on a wet wicket. He took eight wickets for two runs in 14 overs, of which 12 were maidens, playing for England versus the Rest. When he sniffed uncertainty now against his biting off-spin, he went for the jugular without being jocular. The genial character demonstrated a hitherto unseen fierceness, but it didn't earn him a boat trip to Australia in 1950–51. More often than not, he was left out of the Test side for the next six years. He did, however, return the match figures of 10 for 119 to win the final Test against South Africa in 1951. This along with more than 100 wickets for Surrey caused *Wisden* to call him one of Five Cricketers of the Year. After that he built his confidence and restored his reputation year after year with the Surrey side from 1952 as it dominated the County Championship (winning seven successive times from 1952–58). Laker played a support role to Tony Lock at the Oval in the winning Ashes Fifth Test of 1953, taking 1 for 34, and 4 for 74. It was a sliver of revenge against the Australians, but not nearly enough for those scars from 1948.

Yet once more in 1954–55, the selectors were nervous about taking Laker to Australia. They went for Frank Tyson and speed instead, with spin backup from Wardle and Appleyard.

Then came 1956. Ian Johnson led an Australian team that carried several members of the 1948 side – himself, Lindwall, Miller and Harvey. Not quite enough for Laker's liking, but enough, and anyway, he just wanted revenge, pure and simple against *any* Australian team. It began so very sweetly for Surrey at the Oval. Once a ground of embarrassment when crucified by Barnes, Morris, Bradman and Hassett in May 1948, it was now a heavenly cloud for him to float on as he collected a sensational 10 for 88 in one innings. As a nice by-product, Surrey beat Australia and became the first county to do so since 1912.

Laker began less emphatically but still well with 4 for 58 and 2 for 29 at the First 1956 Ashes Test at Nottingham. How sweet it was to remove Miller twice, Johnson (with memories of being brutalised by them at Lord's) and Lindwall. Next came Lord's, in which Miller excelled, taking 10 wickets and winning the match, while Laker returned more modest figures of 3 for 47 and 0 for 17.

Headingley, Leeds and the Third Test was next. He cleaned up brilliantly taking 11 for 113. Captain Peter May hit a grand hundred, and Washbrook, at 42, may have fulfilled every mature-age fantasy by making a comeback and missing his century by just 2. But Laker stole the show and would have been given Player of the Match, had there been one. He had a large slice back from those awful days under the last Bradman steamroller.

This was followed by the Old Trafford Test. The wicket was substandard, perhaps the worst ever prepared for a 20th Century Test. It became a dustbowl within hours; perfect for the bite and turn of a fast off-break bowler who could deliver six variations of delivery in one over. Laker began with a monumental effort in Australia's first innings, taking 9 for 37. He followed that with the unthinkable, taking another 10-wicket haul, giving 19 for 90 for the match. This had never been done before in a first-class match, let alone a Test. No one, in fact, had ever snared more than 17 wickets. It was as much a fluke as it was a sensational performance. First, there had to be a strip that would allow it. Second, he had to have enormous luck, especially with the brilliant Lock bowling at the other end, and delivering just as well. The big difference was that Lock, a left-armer, was sending down balls that spun into the right-handed Australians from the leg, which they had plenty of experience of with right-arm leg-break bowlers at home. Laker was bowling fast off-breaks, which were a novelty. He ended the 1956 series with a phenomenal 46 wickets at 9.61. In seven games in all against Johnson's team he captured 63 wickets for less than 10 runs each, compared to 14 at approaching 60 in 1948. How the wheel had turned, and how 'Big Jim' revelled in it. But even then there were scores to settle with some detractors at the MCC, a few enemies at Surrey, and the odd twit in the press who had written him off as a loser after 1948. The best way to gain further revenge was to keep taking big hauls of wickets, and especially against the Australians. Now all he needed was to succeed Down Under. He had a let-down in South Africa with just 12 wickets at 26.16. This was followed by his long overdue first tour to Australia in 1958–59 with 15 wickets at 21.20. Laker was outshone by Richie Benaud (31 at 18.84) on wickets more conducive to leg-spin. Yet still Laker was England's best bowler.

Laker was having trouble with an arthritic spinning finger. He decided against the New Zealand part of the 1958–59 tour. In the England summer of 1959, he still took 74 at 26.61 but the finger worsened. Laker was never happy at the thought of a shellacking from the opposition again, not after his unmatched triumphs of 1956. And he had been to the mountain top of Test cricket. There was little left to achieve. So he retired from Surrey at the end of the 1959 season.

It was not quite the end. His mate Trevor Bailey persuaded him to make 30 appearances for Essex, sporadically, through 1962, '63 and '64.

•

Jim Laker (1922–86) was born at Frizinghall, near Bradford. Cardus might have said he 'looked like a Yorkie, was built like a Yorkie and played like one.' But after being schooled in the county, he was too young at 17 to play for it before war broke out. He served in the army in the Middle East, and after the war emerged as a promising off-spinner after having only bowled fast, and batted with some skill, in his teen years in the 1930s. Before being demobilised in 1945, he was stationed at Catford, and played for its cricket club. A patron of Surrey players, Andrew Kempton, spotted his talents and recommended him to the county. They tried him twice against the Combined Services side in 1946. On the strength of his showings in those games, he was offered a job on the Oval's ground staff. Laker topped the county's bowling averages in 1947. Playing under Gubby Allen in the West Indies in 1947, he took 7 for 103 and 2 for 95 in the First Test at Bridgetown, Barbados. It led to him topping the Test averages and he looked to be on his way.

But then in 1948 he ran into that powerful phalanx of Australian batting. It was back to square one for a short period before he emerged in the mid-1950s as, if not *the* greatest off-spinner of all time, then one of the top three or four in history.

•

In all first-class cricket, from 1946–64, Laker took 1,994 wickets at 18.44, made 7,304 runs at 16.60 and held 270 catches. He played in 46 Tests, taking 193 wickets at 21.24, making 676 runs at 14.08 and holding 12 catches. His Ashes bowling figures were telling. He played in 15 matches and took 79 wickets at 18.28.

Jim Laker became a familiar, dry and laconic cricket commentator on BBC TV, and wrote several books. One – *Over to Me* – was a forthright autobiography, which slapped around some individuals at the MCC and Surrey. But after getting some justified grievances off his chest, Laker was forgiven and lauded as one of the giants of the game.

Cyril Washbrook

Cyril Washbrook struggled in the first two 1948 Tests. He had little experience on English wickets facing true fast bowlers who could feed him the away-swinger. Consequently he suffered from flicking outside the off-stump when looking for runs through gully and point that had always been profitable for him. Washbrook could not go back to county games between the Tests and face similar bowlers. There was none. He had to work out how to counter such bowling, 'on the job' in the Tests themselves. His skill and professionalism came through in the sixth innings of the series, scoring 85 not out. It was not an innings too soon. Had he failed at his home ground of Old Trafford in the Third Test, there is little doubt he would have been dropped for the Leeds Fourth Test.

He continued on to grand style at Leeds with 143 and 65, at last overcoming Lindwall, Miller, Johnston and Toshack. But in the county game against the tourists after Leeds, Washbrook ran into a rampant Lindwall, who hit him on the hands several times, and put him out of the Fifth Test. Nevertheless, his fifty-plus average told a true story of his fighting qualities and batsmanship against the hardest bowling force he ever faced.

•

Cyril Washbrook (1914–99) was born in Barrow, near Clitheroe and he made his first-ever 50-run innings for the local school. A whip-around by spectators collected 12 shillings and 8 pence for him, which he proudly showed his parents. He realised at just 11 years that he wanted to make a career as a professional cricketer. Soon after that first 'benefit' match, his family moved to Shropshire, and he attended Bridgnorth Grammar School. He made his debut for Lancashire in 1933 aged 18, and hit 152 in just his second match.

Neville Cardus wrote in the *Manchester Guardian*:

'He looks like a cricketer, has a cricketer's face and wears his flannels like a cricketer.'

It was a broad hint that the commentator thought the teenager might have a future in the game, especially under Lancashire's astute coach, Harry Makepeace. There were setbacks. He didn't establish himself in the county firsts until his third season (in 1935), when he collected 1,724 runs and came fifth in the national averages. In 1937 he made his England debut along with Denis Compton at the Oval against New Zealand. His scores of 9 and 8 not out were not enough for him to hold his place for the 1938 Ashes.

Washbrook was 24 when war was declared on Germany. He became a fitness instructor in the RAF and did not resume his cricket career in earnest until 1945 when he played in the Victory Tests against Australian servicemen. In those Tests he had his first bruising encounter of many with Miller.

There were more encounters in Australia in the 1946–47 Ashes when Washbrook made 363 runs (with one century – a six hour battle at Melbourne) at 36.30. He had three century partnerships with Hutton.

Washbrook had established himself against the toughest opposition. He captured the English imagination because he displayed the sort of grit that could stand up to, and counterattack, the Australians. Cardus loved him:

'. . . the chin, always strong and thrust out a little,' he wrote in rapt description of a Lancashire warrior, 'the square shoulders, the pouting chest, the cock of cricket cap, his easy loose movement . . . [he displayed] every sign of determined awareness, every sign of combined attack and defence, his mind ready to signal swiftly either to infantry, cavalry, or for cover behind the sand bags.'

It was a relief for him and Hutton a few months after the 1948 Ashes to face South Africa. On the first day of the First Test ever at Ellis Park, Johannesburg, they opened with an England record of 359 runs in 310 minutes. Washbrook managed 195, his highest Test score, and Hutton made 158.

Back in England against New Zealand in 1949, he hit 103 not out at Leeds. He followed this in 1950 with two centuries against the West Indies. In 1950–51 he returned Down Under to do battle with the old enemy and had his worst Test series, scoring just 173 runs at 17.30. He struggled against Lindwall, Johnston and the tricky spin from Jack Iverson. He fell out of favour after that at Test level, but became Lancashire's first professional captain. In 1956, he emerged as a Test selector. He was involved in a sensational incident when he expressed a desire to make a Test comeback after Australia had won at Lord's, giving it a 1:0 lead. It was a gamble. Washbrook was 42, and not fully fit. The other selectors asked him to leave the room so they could discuss his selection. They chose him for Leeds at the Third Test of 1956. There were many jittery observers as he marched jauntily out to bat with England at 3 for 17. He survived a confident lbw appeal on 4 and went on to make 98 in a 187 partnership with Peter May (101) that paved the way for an England win. However, he could not sustain his form, and in the next two Tests managed just 6 and 0. That was it. There would be no more comebacks.

In all, Washbrook played 37 Tests, scoring 2,569 runs at 42.81, with six centuries. In first-class cricket, he hit 34,101 runs at 42.68, with 76 centuries.

•

Cyril Washbrook loved the battle with Australia and performed admirably in three out of four Ashes contests.

The Rest of England's Vincibles

Cornishman *Jack Crapp* (1912–81) of Gloucestershire never lived up to his name, but never quite fulfilled his promise either. His splendid century against the tourists in 1948 demonstrated an impressive power of concentration. And in the tradition of many solid, defensive batsmen, he did not waste words. According to John Arlott, keeper Evans recalled Crapp speaking to him once from Crapp's speciality of slip in the three 1948 Tests he played.

'Jack's silence can melt into a dry wit and gentle manner,' Arlott wrote in *Gone to the Test Match*. 'He is kindly as well as solid and a good man to know.'

In the 1948 Ashes he had six innings for a modest aggregate of 88 at an average of 17.60. In his seven Tests overall he scored 319 at 29.00. His first-class career covered 20 years from 1936–56 and he scored 23,615 runs at 35.03.

•

By contrast, left-arm spinner *Jack Young* (1912–93) of Middlesex did fulfil his promise in the three Tests against the Australians, and cheerfully counted himself lucky to have made the England side. He took only five wickets at 58.40. These figures look woeful on paper but he was inexpensive, sending down 156 overs with 64 maidens. He did his job of mild containment with the air of a player just happy to be out there representing his country. This is in the light of being low on the cricket totem pole at 33 just after the war, when he was a ground staff bowler at Lord's. In the next three years he played against South Africa and Australia. Small, dapper Jack delivered an immaculate length, which was his saving virtue.

In eight Tests for England he took 17 wickets at 44.52. In a career spanning 23 years from 1933–56 for Middlesex mainly, and England, he collected 1,361 wickets at 19.68.

•

Lancashire's 36-year-old *Dick Pollard* (1912–85), who played two Tests in 1948, at Manchester and Leeds, was ranked highly by the Australians, who were glad to see him dropped from the Fifth Test at the Oval. He was classed as medium-fast, but, with his long, padding run-up, could generate real pace. He could swing both ways. His 3 for 53 at Manchester included Bradman (whom he dismissed cheaply also at Leeds), Miller and Loxton, a nice little bag. His best effort in Tests was against India in 1946 when he took 5 for 24 from 27 overs. He played one Test against New Zealand in March 1947 after touring Australia, and took 3 for 73.

In his four Tests, Pollard took 15 wickets at 25.20. In first-class games for Lancashire from 1933–50 he took 1,122 wickets at 22.56.

•

The only other player with more than one Test in 1948 was Warwickshire's *Tom Dollery* (1914–87). He had three innings and managed 38 runs at 12.66, and a further handful of games against South Africa and the West Indies. In four Tests he managed just 72 runs at 10.28. Dollery was well into his thirties when his Test 'career' began. His peak was in the 1930s when he was Warwickshire's top batsman. He topped 1,000 runs in a season 15 times, and from 1933–55 made 24,413 runs at 37.50.

•

Another nine players had one Test each in the 1948 series.

Charlie Barnett (1910–93) of Gloucester hit just 8 and 6 at Trent Bridge, but was well past his prime, having peaked in the 1930s with two centuries against Australia – one at Adelaide in 1936–37, and another at Trent Bridge in 1938. He had 20 Tests in all, scoring 1,098 runs at 35.41, including those two centuries. He hit 48 first-class centuries in all, in a career covering 1927–53, in which he scored 25,389 runs at 32.71. He was a fast-medium change bowler who took 394 wickets at 30.98.

•

Fast-medium bowling form for Yorkshire's *Alex Coxon* (1916–2006) earned him his one shot at glory at Lord's in 1948. In his only Test he took 2 for 90 and 1 for 82. He at least had bragging rights that he had dismissed Australia's three openers – Barnes (0), Morris (105) and Brown (32) – in the game. He scored 19 and 0. He peaked at age 34 in 1950, taking 131 wickets at 18.60 and joined Durham as a professional from 1951–54.

From 1945–50 for Yorkshire, he scored 2,814 runs at 18.15, and took 473 wickets at 20.91.

•

All-rounder *Ken Cranston* (1917–2007) of Lancashire had an all-too-short first-class and Test career from 1947–50, making 10 and 0 in his only Test in 1948 at Leeds. He took 1 for 79, but it was Miller, lbw for 12, and one that friends would mention for decades afterwards. Cranston could not afford the time for cricket with his profession as a dentist. He played in eight Tests and scored 209 runs at 14.92. He took 18 wickets with his fast-medium deliveries at 25.61. In first-class cricket, Cranston hit 3,099 runs (with three centuries) at 34.82, and took 178 wickets at 28.00.

•

John Dewes (1926–) suffered in 1948 from a chequered past against bruising speed from Miller and Lindwall. In 1945, Miller roughed him up in the Lord's Victory Test, and three years later made him nervous again in the tour game against

Cambridge University (although he made a competent 40 in the second innings). At the Oval in the Fifth Test, Dewes, on debut aged 22, was on his way twice before being settled, bowled by Miller for 1, and Lindwall for 10. He had a wonderful 1950 season, scoring 2,432 at an average of 59.31, with nine centuries. It was enough to force his way into the Test team again against the West Indies in the Third Test at Trent Bridge, where he managed a duck and a fine 67 in his second innings. It kept him in the team for the Fourth Test but he failed twice again. However, the bumper season saw him as one of the last picked for the tour of Australia in 1950–51, where he kept his place for the First Test at Brisbane. Two more failures there against Miller saw him on his last chance at Melbourne in the Second Test, where Johnston and Iverson picked him up cheaply. This finished his Test aspirations.

In five Tests he made 121 at 12.10. In first-class cricket from 1945–57, he scored 8,564 at 41.78, including 18 centuries.

•

George Emmett (1912–76) of Gloucester was picked for the Manchester Third Test to replace Hutton, but the move did not work. Lindwall removed him twice for 10 and 0. It was the short, slightly built 36-year-old Emmett's only Test. Between 1936 and 1959 he scored 25,602 runs at 31.41, including 37 centuries. His slow left-armers picked up 60 wickets at 44.01, and he held 296 catches. He scored more than 1,000 in a season 14 times and captained Gloucester from 1955–58. Emmett coached the team.

•

'Young Joe' Hardstaff (1911–90) was perhaps the best of the players to be selected only once in 1948 – at his home ground, Nottingham, in the First Test. He made 0 and 43, the latter innings showing some of his 1930s capabilities. In 1938 at the Oval he figured in a 215 partnership with Hutton, and went

on to 169 unconquered. He toured Australia three times: once with the MCC in 1935–36, when he was aged 24, and twice on Ashes campaigns in 1936–37 and 1946–47. In nine Ashes Tests he scored 559 runs at 37.26 (which was not far off the record of his father – Joe Sr – who played in five Ashes Tests and scored 311 runs at 31.10). In all his 23 Tests, Joe Jr scored 1,636 runs at 46.74, including four centuries. In first-class cricket from 1930–55, Hardstaff scored 31,847 runs at 44.35, including 83 centuries.

•

Leg-spinner *Eric Hollies* (1912–81) was the best of the bowlers who only played one Test in 1948, and should have been given more chances before the Oval. He took five wickets for 131, from 56 overs with 14 maidens, which fairly represented his penetration and economy. His 8 for 107 in one Australian innings for Warwickshire in early August in the tour game was a further instance of his abilities as a leg-spinner. It was by far the best effort with the ball against the Australians in the 34 matches played. He may have had a lukewarm wrong 'un, but his top-spinner was brilliant, and he certainly gave all the key Australian batsmen trouble, or at least a lot to think about.

He took 1 for 150 in his first ever county game in 1932, a return reminiscent of another solid, blond leg-spinner (Shane Warne) in a Test (versus India) for Australia nearly 60 years later.

Hollies took more than 100 wickets in a season 14 times. His best bowling return was 10 for 49 in an innings against Nottingham in 1946. Although he preferred to talk about his (appalling) batting, Eric Hollies will forever be remembered as the bowler who deprived the greatest cricketer of all time of an average of 100 in Tests.

In 13 Tests, Hollies took 44 wickets at 30.27, and made 37 runs at 5.28, which was marginally better than his first-class record with the bat (5.01 from 1,673 runs). In a career spanning

25 years from 1932–57, he took 2,323 wickets at the excellent return of 20.94. It is a travesty that such a talent did not have many more Tests.

•

Allan Watkins (1922–) was one of the 'younger' players at age 26 in the 1948 Tests, making his debut at the Oval. He had a rough start, scoring a duck and 2, and injuring his shoulder in a way that impaired his bowling. Watkins had a strong 1947 as a promising left-handed bat, and developed his left-arm medium-pace swingers only in 1948. He ranked highly as a close to the wicket (short-leg) fielder with the courage of Sid Barnes and the reflexes of Garry Sobers. This facet of his cricket would have tipped him into the England team.

Watkins topped 1,000 runs 13 times. His Test career peaked in 1951–52 in India when he was the highest scoring bat of either side with 451 runs at 64.42.

He played 15 Tests, scoring 810 runs at 40.50, including two centuries, and took 11 wickets at 50.36, while holding 17 catches. In first-class cricket from 1939–63, Watkins hit 20,361 runs at 30.57, including 32 centuries and took 833 wickets at 24.48. He held 462 catches.

•

Leg-spinner *Doug Wright* (1914–98) was another fine cricketer who turned in a poor performance against Bradman's Invincibles. He could not get going in the 1948 Lord's Test, taking only one wicket in each innings. Yet there was no question about his class. He took more than 100 wickets 10 times in a season, and in 1947 was another England player who encouraged the UK to believe Australia would be beaten. He took a terrific 177 wickets at 21.12.

Wright also took more wickets than anyone in the 1946–47 Ashes in Australia – 23 – but he was expensive. Each wicket cost 43.04 runs. In the Tests against South Africa, he took 19 at 25.47 in four Tests. Wright's Lord's effort in 1947 when he took 10 for 175, gave selectors confidence in choosing him against Australia.

In 34 Tests Doug Wright took 108 wickets at 39.11. In first-class cricket for Kent and England he took 2,056 wickets at 23.98.

Bibliography

Arlott, John, *Gone to the Test Match*, Longmans, Green and Co, London, 1949.
Barnes, Sid, *It Isn't Cricket*, Collins, Sydney, 1953.
Bedser, Alec and Eric, *Following On*, Evans Brothers Ltd, London, 1954.
Bradman, Don, *Farewell to Cricket*, Hodder and Stoughton, London, 1950.
Bromby, Robin, Ed., *A Century of Ashes*, Resolution Press, Sydney, 1982.
Fingleton, Jack, *Brightly Fades the Don*, Collins, London, 1949.
Harvey, Neil, *My World of Cricket*, Hodder and Stoughton, London, 1963.
Heald, Tim, *Denis Compton*, Pavilion, London, 1994.
Howat, Gerald, *Len Hutton*, Heinemann Kingswood, London, 1988.
Lindwall, Ray, *Flying Stumps*, Stanley Paul and Co, London, 1954.
McHarg, Jack, *Arthur Morris, An Elegant Genius*, ABC Books, Sydney, 1995.
O'Reilly, W. J. *Cricket Conquest*, Werner Laurie, London, 1949.
Perry, Roland, *The Don*, Macmillan, Sydney, 1994.
Perry, Roland, *Miller's Luck*, Random House Australia, Sydney, 2005.
Preston, Hubert, Ed. *Wisden Cricketers' Almanack, 1949*, London, 1949.
Rippon, Anton, *Classic Moments of the Ashes*, J.M. Dent, Melbourne, 1982.
Yardley, N. W. D. and Kilburn, J. M. *Homes of Sport*, Peter Garnett, 1952.

Photos

Index

Index